INHERITANCE ACT CLAIMS

INHERITANCE ACT CLAIMS

Second edition

Nasreen Pearce

Wildy, Simmonds & Hill Publishing

Copyright © 2011 Nasreen Pearce
Contains public sector information licensed under the Open Government
Licence v1.0

Inheritance Act Claims, 2nd edition

British Library Cataloguing in Publication Data
A catalogue record for this book is available from the British Library

ISBN 978-0854900-787

Typeset in Times New Roman and Optima LT by Cornubia Press Ltd
Printed and bound in the United Kingdom by Antony Rowe Ltd, Chippenham,
Wiltshire

The right of Nasreen Pearce to be identified as the Author of this Work has
been asserted by her in accordance with Copyright, Designs and Patents Act
1988, sections 77 and 78.

Second edition published in 2011 by
Wildy, Simmonds & Hill Publishing
58 Carey Street
London WC2A 2JF
England

MIX
Paper from
responsible sources
FSC FSC® C013604
www.fsc.org

Contents

Table of Cases

Table of Statutes

Table of Statutory Instruments

References are to page numbers

Table of International Materials

Chapter 1

Introduction

1.1 BACKGROUND

It has long been a characteristic of English law that, provided a person has testamentary capacity and complies with the formalities relating to the making of a valid will, he/she may in his/her will make provision for the disposal of his/her entire estate on his/her death as he/she chooses, and his/her estate will devolve in accordance with the terms of the will. If a person dies without having made a will, or if he/she leaves a will which in law is not valid, the law relating to intestacy operates and the estate will devolve in accordance with that law. If the provisions made in the will do not dispose of the entirety of the estate, then the property will devolve in part in accordance with the terms of the will, and the remainder will pass under the law of intestacy.

Statutes have, however, made inroads into this freedom. The first statutory provision to do so was the Inheritance (Family Provision) Act 1938 (I(FP)A 1938). It applied to the estates of persons dying after 13 July 1939 who were domiciled in England and Wales. It introduced into English law the concept of reasonable testamentary provision and provided for the maintenance of dependants out of the deceased's estate. The Intestates' Estates Act 1952 amended the I(FP)A 1938. The most important change was the extension of the I(FP)A 1938 to cases where the deceased was intestate. It also permitted the court to award to a surviving spouse the whole of the income of the net estate; increased the amount of the lump sum order which could be made; provided for the extension of the 6-month time limit within which claims had to be brought in certain circumstances; and made provisions for the protection of personal representatives.

Matrimonial Causes Act 1965, ss 26–28 made provisions for a former spouse to apply for an order for maintenance from the deceased's estate on the ground that the deceased had not made reasonable provision for the survivor's maintenance after the deceased's death. The Family Provision Act 1966 further amended the I(FP)A 1938, most importantly by extending the court's jurisdiction to hear such claims to the county courts where the value of the net estate did not exceed £5,000.

The Inheritance (Provision for Family and Dependants) Act 1975 (I(PFD)A 1975), which came into force on 1 April 1976, repealed the previous enactments and made comprehensive provisions for those who claim that the disposition of an estate (whether effected by will or the intestacy rules or the combination of the two) has failed to make reasonable financial provision for them and for the court to make orders out of the estate of a deceased in favour of the class of dependants of the deceased identified in s 1(1) of that Act. Section 15 was extended by the Matrimonial and Family Proceedings Act 1984 (MFPA 1984) to give the court power, when dealing with a claim under the MFPA 1984 for financial relief after an overseas divorce, annulment of marriage or legal separation order, to make an order disentitling one or both of the parties from making any claims for an order under the I(PFD)A 1975.

The Law Reform (Succession) Act 1995 amended the I(PFD)A 1975 by extending the class of persons who can apply for financial provision, to include any person (not the spouse or a former spouse of the deceased) who, during the 2 years immediately preceding the death of the deceased, had been living with the deceased in the same household as the deceased as the husband or wife of the deceased.

The Civil Partnership Act 2004 (CPA 2004) led to further amendments to the I(PFD)A 1975. The CPA 2004 makes provision to enable same sex couples to make a formal commitment to each other by registering their civil partnership. This is done by both individuals signing a civil partnership document in the presence of each other, the registrar and two witnesses. The civil partnership document must then also be signed by the registrar and the witnesses. Once the partnership has been registered the couples' relationship is treated in the same way as a marriage. In order to take account of this the I(PFD)A 1975 has been further amended by CPA 2004, Sch 4, paras 15–27, to give same sex couples, who have entered into a civil partnership, the same rights as those enjoyed by married heterosexual couples, and give the court the same powers upon an application by a surviving civil partner as it has for claims made by a surviving spouse. With effect from 5 December 2005, a surviving civil partner of the deceased has the right to apply for financial provision on the same basis as a surviving spouse. Where the same sex couple have not entered into a civil partnership, on the death of one of them, the survivor may claim as a cohabitant of the deceased provided the conditions set out in CPA 2004, s 1(B) are met.

The I(PFD)A 1975, as amended, governs claims by specified dependants of a deceased person, against the estate of the deceased who died domiciled in England and Wales, on the ground that the disposition of the deceased's estate effected by his/her will or the law of intestacy, or the combination of his/her will and that law, is not such as to make reasonable financial provision for the claimant (see Chapter 4). Thus a claim arises only if it can be established that:

(1) the deceased died domiciled in England and Wales;
(2) the claimant is one of the restricted classes of person, set out in s 1(1), as amended, who has a right to make a claim (see Chapter 4); and
(3) the deceased failed to make reasonable financial provision for the claimant.

A claim for an order for financial provision under I(PFD)A 1975, s 2 must be made within 6 months from the date on which representation with respect to the estate of the deceased is first taken out. A general discretion, however, is conferred by s 4 on the court to extend that time limit (see Chapter 3).

In the definition of 'financial provision', the I(PFD)A 1975 makes a distinction between a surviving spouse and civil partner of the deceased and other claimants. In the case of a surviving spouse/surviving civil partner, it means such financial provision as it would be reasonable in all the circumstances of the case for the surviving spouse/surviving civil partner to receive, whether or not that provision is required for his/her maintenance. In respect of all other claimants, it means such financial provision as it would be reasonable for the claimant to receive for his/her maintenance (s 1(2)). It is thus for the claimant to establish whether the deceased's disposition considered objectively makes or fails to make reasonable provision for the claimant in all the circumstances of the case.

If the court finds that the deceased has not made reasonable financial provision for the claimant, then, in determining whether and in what manner the court should exercise its powers under the I(PFD)A 1975, there is a mandatory duty on the court to have regard to each of the matters set out in s 3, as amended (see Chapter 7).

The orders which the court may make are set out in I(PFD)A 1975, s 2. The court also has powers to vary, discharge or suspend orders made for periodical payments under s 2(1)(a) and a limited power to vary a lump sum order. Secured periodical payments orders made under the Matrimonial Causes Act 1973 and maintenance agreements may also be varied or discharged (see Chapter 8, para 8.12).

The orders made by the court under the I(PFD)A 1975 may be met only out of the net estate of the deceased as defined by s 25(1). Sections 8 and 9 make further provisions for property disposed of by way of a gift in contemplation of death but not to take effect until death, provision made to a nominated person and property held on a joint tenancy to be regarded as part of the net estate of the deceased. Where the claimant intends to apply under s 9 for the deceased's severable share of property held on a joint tenancy to be included as part of the net estate, the application must be made within 6 months from the date on which representation with respect to the deceased's estate was first taken out; the time limit cannot be extended (see Chapter 9).

The court also has powers under I(PFD)A 1975, ss 10 and 11 in relation to transactions entered into by the deceased with the intention of defeating a claim for financial provision under the Act where it would facilitate the making of financial provision for the claimant (see Chapter 10).

Finally, a claim under the I(PFD)A 1975 is personal to the claimant, so that if the claimant dies during the course of the proceedings the claim comes to an end and is not enforceable by the personal representatives of the claimant. Only where an order has been made upon a claim is there an enforceable cause of action, which can continue to subsist for the benefit of one estate against the other (see *Whyte v Ticehurst* [1986] Fam 64 and *Re R* (1986) 14 Fam Law 58).

1.2   PROPOSALS FOR LAW REFORM

In 1980, the Law Commission considered that the intestacy laws should be re-examined and that the I(PFD)A 1975 should also be reviewed. In 2005, the Ministry of Justice (the Department of Constitutional Affairs as it then was) carried out a consultation on the statutory legacy paid to a surviving spouse and asked the Law Commission to review the law. In May 2006, the Law Commission in its Consultation Paper, *Cohabitation: The Financial Consequences of Relationship Breakdown* (Consultation Paper No 179), suggested reform of the Act to entitle a cohabitant of the deceased the right to claim for financial provision under the Act, but the Ministry of Justice preferred some more research to be undertaken before considering any amendments to the Act.

On 29 October 2009, the Law Commission published a Consultation Paper, *Intestacy and Family Provision: Claims on Death* (Consultation Paper No 191), in which it reviewed the current law and highlighted areas for potential reform in relation to intestacy and claims brought under the I(PFD)A 1975.

With regard to claims under the I(PFD)A 1975, the Law Commission has proposed reform in the following areas:

- *Domicil* – the Law Commission's provisional proposal is that the precondition to an application under the Act which requires that the deceased should be domiciled in England and Wales at the time of death should not apply. The Law Commission has asked consultees to consider whether the precondition should be habitual residence in England and Wales or whether an application should be possible in any case where there is property in the estate that is governed by English succession law. The Law Commission has also invited views on whether there should be any other requirement limiting the circumstances in which an application may be made for financial provision.
- *Applications before grant of representation* – the Law Commission has invited views on whether the claimant should be able to make an application under the Act in the absence of a grant of representation.
- *Cohabitants* – the Law Commission proposes that if the surviving cohabitant and the deceased are by law together the parents of a child, there should be no minimum duration requirement for the survivor to be entitled to apply under the Act, provided that the cohabitation was continuing at the date of death. The Law Commission also proposes that in all cases, in order to qualify for an award under the Act as a cohabitant the applicant must have been living as a couple in a joint household with the deceased immediately before the death. The Law Commission has also invited views on whether, where the couple had not had a child together, the current 2-year qualifying period for the survivor to be entitled to apply should be retained.
- *Financial provision for cohabitants* – the Law Commission proposes that the Act should be amended to define 'reasonable financial provision' for cohabitants to mean 'such financial provision as it would be reasonable in all the circumstances of the case for the applicant to receive, whether or not that provision is required for the applicant's maintenance'.
- *Children* – views are sought on whether an adult child should be given a greater chance of success in an application under the Act and if so on what basis.
- *Other dependants and relatives* – the Law Commission proposes that a person who was treated by the deceased as his/her child should be able to apply under the Act irrespective of whether or not that treatment was referable to any other relationship to which the deceased was a party. In relation to the requirement that the deceased must have assumed responsibility before an applicant can qualify as a dependant under the

Act, it is proposed that this requirement should not apply but should be one of the factors which should be taken account of with other factors. It is also proposed that the requirement in a claim brought by a dependant under the Act that the deceased must have contributed substantially more to the parties' relationship than did the claimant should no longer apply. Views are also sought on whether the categories of applicant for family provision should be further widened to include relatives such as parents, descendants other than children, siblings, nephews and nieces and so on.

- *Section 9 and the 6-month time limit* – views are sought on whether the court should have discretion in an appropriate case to extend the time limit.
- *Value of the net estate for the purposes of ss 8 and 9* – the Law Commission proposes that the value of the assets for the purposes of these two sections of the Act should be their value at the date of the application and not at the date of death.

The consultation process ended on 28 February 2010. It is likely therefore that the I(PFD)A 1975 will be further amended after this book is published. The contents of this book should be read subject to any subsequent changes in the law.

Chapter 2

Domicile

2.1 INTRODUCTION

An application for financial provision may only be brought against the estate of a deceased person who was domiciled in England and Wales at the time of his/her death (I(PFD)A 1975, s 1(1)). Domicile of the deceased is thus the first pre-condition which a claimant must establish when applying for financial provision under the Act and it is also an issue which may be taken as a preliminary issue by a defendant who intends to resist the claimant's application. If the deceased died domiciled elsewhere than in England and Wales, a claim under the Act cannot be entertained by the court. The Act does not extend to Scotland and Northern Ireland (s 27(2)).

Domicile is a legal concept of law which is not easily defined. It is based on where a person has his/her permanent home and is relevant in many situations where it is necessary to establish which legal system should be applied, particularly relating to issues of personal status. It is not the same as a person's ordinary residence or habitual residence.

Domicile as a pre-condition to any claim under the I(PFD)A 1975 has been the subject of criticism particularly given the social and political changes which have occurred since the commencement of the Act. As a result of the European Union, globalisation and the ability and freedom to move freely between countries, people now live, work and have homes and businesses in countries other than the country of their nationality. It is therefore not surprising that there are many who take the view that 'habitual residence' of the deceased immediately before his/her death should be the basis on which a claim should be brought against the estate of the deceased.

In *Cyganik v Agulian* [2006] EWCA Civ 129, [2006] 1 FCR 406, Longmore LJ observed at para [58] that:

I find it rather surprising that the somewhat antiquated notion of domicile should govern the question whether the estate of a person who was, on any view, habitually resident in England should make provision for his dependants. Now that many family matters are decided by reference to habitual residence there may, perhaps, be something to be said for reconsidering the terms of s1 of the Inheritance (Provision for Family and Dependants) Act 1975. As Dr JHC Morris observed of the concept of domicile in the last (3rd) edition of his *Conflict of Laws* (1984), which he wrote before he died,

> 'Originally it was good idea; but the once simple concept has been so overloaded by a multitude of cases that it has been transmuted into something further and further removed from the practicalities of life.'

This observation has not been preserved by subsequent editors (6th edition (2005)) but it deserves to be (see para 2.7).

There are three types of domicile, namely domicile of origin, domicile of choice and domicile of dependency.

2.2 DOMICILE OF ORIGIN

A person acquires a domicile of origin at birth from his/her parents and retains that domicile until it is changed by choice. The place where a child is born is immaterial (see *Re Flynn, Flynn v Flynn* [1968] 1 All ER 49, 52). A domicile of origin is capable of persisting during the lifetime of a person.

The domicile of origin of a legitimate child born during the lifetime of his/her father is that of the child's father. If the father dies before the child's birth the child acquires the domicile of his/her mother (see *Urquhart v Butterfield* [1887] 37 Ch 357, 377).

An illegitimate child acquires the domicile of his/her mother at birth (see Dicey and Morris, *The Conflict of Laws* (Sweet & Maxwell, 14th edn, 4th Supplement, 2010).

A child's domicile thereafter will change if and when the parent(s) change their domicile.

Once a child attains the age of 16 he/she is able to acquire a domicile of choice independently of his/her parents.

A foundling's domicile of origin is that of the country where he/she is found.

The domicile of an adopted child will be that of his/her adopters because once an adoption order is made the adopted child is regarded in law as if he/she had been born to the adopters (Adoption and Children Act 2002, s 67(1)). As from the date of the adoption the adopted child is treated as the legitimate child of his/her adopter(s) if adopted by a couple or by one of a couple (s 51(2)).

The domicile of origin of a child who has been the subject of a parental order will be that of the applicants in whose favour the parental order was made because, as in the case of adoption, the effect of a parental order is that the child is treated in law as the child of the applicants (Human Fertilisation and Embryology Act 2008 (HFEA 2008), ss 54(1) and 55).

2.3   DOMICILE OF DEPENDENCY

A child under 16 or a person who lacks mental capacity has a domicile of dependency, which is that of his/her parents. Where the parents are married and living together the domicile is that of the father. Where the parents are separated, the child's domicile or the domicile of the person lacking capacity is that of the parent with whom he/she has his/her home to the exclusion of the other; for example, if the child lives with his/her mother he/she takes his/her mother's domicile (Domicile and Matrimonial Proceedings Act 1973, s 4). Once a child attains the age of 16 he/she is able to acquire a domicile of choice independently of his/her parents but until then his/her domicile will remain that which he/she acquired from his/her parents.

2.4   DOMICILE OF CHOICE

A domicile of choice is acquired when a person leaves his/her domicile of origin and lives in a country of his/her choice with the intention of permanently or indefinitely living there. There are therefore two elements which must both be satisfied before a domicile of choice is acquired, ie (1) actual residence in the country of choice; and (2) the intention to live there permanently. The circumstances which led the person to leave his/her original domicile is immaterial. The test is whether the person intended to make his/her home in the new country until the end of his/her days and until something happens to change his/her mind (see *IRC v Bullock* [1976] 1 WLR 1178):

> Domicile of choice is a conclusion or inference which the law derives from the fact of a man fixing voluntarily his sole or chief residence in a particular place with the intention of continuing to reside there for an unlimited time. This is a

description of the circumstances which create or constitute a domicil and not a definition of the term. There must be a residence freely chosen, and not prescribed or dictated by any external necessity, such as the duties of office, the demands of creditors, or the relief from illness; and it must be residence fixed not for a limited period or particular purpose, but general and indefinite in its future contemplation. It is true that residence originally temporary, or intended for a limited period, may afterwards become general and unlimited, and in such a case so soon as the change of purpose, or *animus manendi*, can be inferred the fact of domicil is established (per Lord Westbury in *Udny v Udny* (1869) 1 LR Sc & Div 441)

If that person subsequently abandons that domicile and fails to acquire another domicile of choice he/she reverts to his/her domicile of origin.

2.4.1   Residence

It is essential for the person who intends to change his/her domicile of origin to live in the country of his/her choice. The duration of the residence or the motive for so doing is immaterial provided that it is accompanied by the necessary intention to live in that country permanently or indefinitely.

A domicile of choice may be acquired by living in a country unlawfully in breach of immigration law. In *Mark v Mark* [2005] UKHL 42, [2005] 2 FLR 1193, HL, a Nigerian woman established a home in England and obtained leave to remain in England until a specific date. Thereafter she did not apply for an extension of her stay and she remained in England in breach of immigration law as an overstayer. In due course she petitioned for divorce and applied for ancillary relief relying on her habitual residence. She also claimed that she had acquired a domicile of choice in England. Her husband opposed the proceedings on the ground that the English courts did not have jurisdiction because the wife's stay in England was unlawful. She succeeded in her claim both at first instance and before the Court of Appeal. The husband appealed to the House of Lords. Baroness Hale in her judgment ruled that residence for the purpose of Domicile and Matrimonial Proceedings Act 1973, s 5(2) need not be lawful residence. The question of whether the residence is habitual is a factual one which should be answered by applying the test derived from tax cases. Her Ladyship said:

> It is possible that the legality of a person's residence here might be relevant to the factual question of whether that residence is 'habitual'. A person who was on the run after a deportation order or removal directions might find it hard to establish a habitual residence here. But such cases will be rare compared with the large numbers of people who have remained here leading perfectly ordinary lives here for long periods, despite having no permission to do so. There will, however, be

other statutory provisions, in particular those conferring entitlement to some benefit from the state, where it would be proper to imply a requirement that the residence be lawful.

In relation to whether an unlawful presence in England will prevent a person acquiring a domicile of choice, Her Ladyship said that there is no reason in principle why a person whose presence here is unlawful cannot acquire a domicile of choice in this country because although the person's presence may amount to the commission of a criminal offence, it could not be said with any certainty that the person would be required to leave the country if he/she was discovered. If the person has chosen to make his/her home in a new country for an indefinite period, it would be appropriate that the person should be connected to the system of law for purposes where domicile was relevant. The legality of a person's presence in a country may be relevant to establish the required intention. The issue is one of fact and dependent on the court scrutinising the evidence produced to establish the necessary intention that the person intended to live in the country of choice permanently despite the unlawfulness. It is not a question of law nor is it a matter on which the court has discretion. It is for the court to decide on the facts whether or not a person unlawfully in the country has acquired a domicile of choice. If on the facts the person has acquired a domicile of choice in this country, the person cannot be denied it because the court considers the person's case to be unmeritorious or tainted with 'moral or legal turpitude'. If the evidence does not establish the acquisition of domicile of choice by the person the court does not have the power to grant it because it considers the person's case a deserving one. (Note that the decision in *Mark v Mark* overruled many of the decisions referred to in the judgment of Baroness Hale that had been cited previously as indicating that the person's presence in a country unlawfully would prevent that person acquiring a domicile of choice in that country, and differed from the proposition of law that had hitherto been stated by Dicey and Morris.)

If it can be established that a domicile of choice was acquired although the presence in England was unlawful, it will be unaffected by a subsequent deportation order (see *Cruh v Cruh* [1945] 2 All ER 545).

In the case of those who are refugees or seeking asylum from persecution or by reason of other forced circumstances, a change of domicile will not occur unless there is strong evidence which indicates that a domicile of choice has been acquired (see *Re Lloyd Evans, National Provincial Bank v Evans* [1947] Ch 695).

Where a person takes up residence in a country for reasons of health, the residence alone will not suffice to lead to a change of domicile. The issue of whether a domicile of choice has been acquired in such circumstances will depend on the person's state of mind.

2.4.2   Intention

In addition to living in the country of choice, it must be established that the deceased had the intention of making England his/her permanent home. An intention to live in England for a fixed period or until the occurrence of a specific event, for example until the person's health improves, or for the purposes of employment (see *Irvin v Irvin* [2001] 1 FLR 178), or if his/her country becomes independent (see *Pletinka v Pletinka (Boucher cited)* (1964) 109 Sol Jo 72) will not suffice.

2.4.3   Burden of proof

It will be observed, therefore, that the presumption is against a change of domicile by an individual. Where the question of whether or not the deceased died domiciled in England is in issue or is likely to be raised, it is for the applicant to establish the deceased's domicile on clear and credible evidence based on all the circumstances relating to the deceased's life.

2.4.4   Standard of proof

It is for the applicant to establish that the deceased was domiciled in England and Wales on the civil standard of proof, ie on the balance of probabilities, but since it is a serious issue, the court is unlikely to infer it from slight indications or casual words. The claimant will have to provide convincing evidence of that fact. The evidence must be clear, cogent and convincing (see *Re Fuld's Estate (No 3), Hartley v Fuld* [1968] P 675).

2.4.5   Evidence

It is for the claimant to establish that the deceased died domiciled in England and Wales. The burden of proof remains throughout on the claimant.

Where there is or may be any doubt of the deceased's domicile, the evidence on which it is intended to rely to establish domicile should be stated in the sworn statement in support of the claim. Application for a grant of probate will require a sworn statement confirming where the deceased died. This will provide *prima facie* evidence of the deceased's domicile at the time of his/her death but it is not conclusive proof and may be challenged. If a claim under the I(PFD)A 1975 is made, the issue of domicile may become pertinent particularly where the evidence filed raises doubts.

If the statement on the grant states that the deceased had a domicile in a country other than England and Wales, the claimant will need to disprove that statement. Where there is or may be any doubt about the deceased's domicile, the evidence upon which it is intended to rely to establish domicile should be stated in the sworn statement in support of the claim.

In determining the issue of a change of domicile, particularly a change of domicile of origin, the court has to consider all the circumstances and factors from which the deceased's intention to change his/her domicile of origin can be ascertained. This will include looking back at the whole of the deceased's life, at what he/she had done with his/her life, at what life had done to him/her and what were his/her inferred intentions in order to determine whether he/she had acquired a domicile of choice in England by the date of his/her death. The deceased's age, religion, language, family and business ties and commitments, ownership of property, length of time the deceased remained in a country, his/her nationality, whether or not he/she changed that nationality or citizenship, whether he/she has made a will and if so the form and content of that will, the degree of his/her assimilation in the new country, will all be relevant factors.

There is no end to the evidence that may be adduced; the whole of a person's life and all that he/she has said and done, however trivial, may be prayed upon in aid in determining what his/her intention was at any given moment of time (see *Re Flynn* [1968] 1 WLR 103).

Statements or declarations made on the application for a grant of representation or by the deceased during his/her lifetime are not conclusive. Nor does any one factor override other relevant factors. The following examples of cases demonstrate the scrutiny with which the court will consider the issue of domicile.

In *Re Evans (Deceased), National Provincial Bank v Evans* [1947] 1 Ch 695, the deceased had been born in Wales. He eventually settled in Belgium, but in 1940, during the war, he moved to the south of France and wrote a statement in which he confirmed that he was domiciled in Belgium. The document was accepted as providing evidence that the deceased had not abandoned his domicile of choice in Belgium.

In *Re Liddell-Grainger's Will Trusts* [1936] 3 All ER 173, an English man had moved to Scotland. He lived there for almost four decades before his death. In his will he asserted that he had not abandoned his domicile of origin. It was, however, contended that the statement in the will had been made to avoid the effect of the law in Scotland, which restricted a testator's right to dispose of property. The court held that the deceased's actions during his life and his continued residence in Scotland were strong evidence of his having acquired a domicile of choice in Scotland.

In *Mastaka v Midland Bank Executors and Trustees Co Ltd* [1941] Ch 192, the deceased testatrix had married a Russian in England. As the law then stood the testatrix, on marriage, acquired the domicile of her husband. His whereabouts at the time of the deceased's death were not known. There was no direct evidence either that he was dead or that he had acquired a domicile of choice in England. In the absence of evidence to the contrary, the deceased was held not to be domiciled in England and Wales.

In *Bheekhun v Williams* [1999] 2 FLR 229, a couple from Mauritius set up home in England. They retained their British nationality when Mauritius became independent. The husband had business interests and property in both England and Mauritius. The couple separated and the wife obtained a decree nisi, but before decree absolute and the resolution of her claim for financial relief the husband died leaving his entire estate to his niece. It was contended by the personal representatives that the deceased had retained his domicile of origin and had not acquired a domicile of choice in England. It was held that evidence of the deceased's actions during his lifetime, and taking into consideration his British nationality, the length of his residency in England, and statements that he had made during the divorce proceedings, clearly indicated that the deceased had considered England his domicile of choice.

Cyganik v Agulian [2006] EWCA Civ 129, [2006] 1 FCR 406 is a recent example of the nature of the evidence which will be required to establish a change of domicile of origin and the careful scrutiny required of the events in the whole of the deceased's life and not merely of one factor or event in his/her life. Although at first instance the claimant had succeeded in her claim, on appeal it was found that the deceased had not acquired a domicile of choice in England and that he had retained his Cypriot domicile of origin.

The deceased in *Cyganik* had been born in Cyprus, where he had lived until 1958. His domicile of origin was Cyprus. In 1993 he formed a relationship with the claimant and became engaged to her in 1999. He executed a will in 1995. In a claim brought under the I(PFD)A 1975 it was maintained by the claimant that the deceased had died domiciled in England. The court at first instance found on the facts that the deceased had not had the intention before 1995 of living permanently in England although he had resided here for

34 years and had established a substantial business. However, the court, relying on the development of the relationship between the deceased and the claimant, found that between 1995 when he made his will including the claimant as a beneficiary, and 1999 when he became engaged to her, the deceased acquired a domicile of choice in England. On appeal, the Court of Appeal ruled that the inference made by the trial judge of the deceased's change of intention was wrong. The court held that although it was appropriate and helpful to trace the deceased's life events, special care had to be taken in the analysis of the evidence about isolating individual factors from all the other factors present over time and treating a particular factor as decisive. On the facts it was clear that apart from the commencement of the relationship with the claimant and his engagement to her and his expressed intention to marry her, nothing else in his life had altered and therefore the fact of his relationship with the claimant had to be examined carefully. On the facts the court held that:

(1)   the adhesiveness of the domicile of origin, the incidence of the burden of proof and the level of the standard of proof all require the person contending for a domicile of choice to establish a clear case that the deceased intended to live permanently or indefinitely in England;

(2)   the matrimonial factor, although relevant was not determinative or conclusive in establishing the necessary intention;

(3)   in order to determine the issue of 'intention' of a change of domicile of origin it is necessary for the court to consider the whole of the deceased's life in retrospect to see whether an inference could be made that he intended to make his home permanently or indefinitely in England; the evidence has to be sufficiently 'cogent and convincing' to establish a change and the cumulative effect of the preponderance of the factors must 'clearly and unequivocally' point to an intention to change the domicile of origin. The evidence in this case had not been so clear. On the contrary the evidence had 're-inforced the enduring character of the deceased's domicile of origin'.

(See also *Morgan v Cilento & others; Re Shaffer* [2004] EWHC 188 (Ch), where the claimant who was the deceased's lover sought to prove that the deceased had not lost his English domicile when he left to live in Australia and, alternatively, that he reacquired it when he left Australia and returned to England.)

In *Dellar v Zivy* [2007] EWHC 2266 (Ch), a case which did not directly concern the deceased's domicile, the issue was whether English or French law applied to the interpretation of the deceased's will. In deciding that English law applied, the court had regard to the fact that the will had been made in England, written in English by English solicitors, who were appointed executors of the will, and by his will he had created a trust for sale. The will also expressly declared that the deceased was domiciled in England.

In *Kearly v Kearly* [2009] EWHC 1876 (Fam), [2010] 1 FLR 619, the issue of domicile arose in divorce proceedings to establish the court's jurisdiction to hear the petition for divorce. The wife was Australian and living in Australia. The husband was English but currently living in France where he worked. The wife issued divorce proceedings in England relying on the husband's English domicile of origin to establish jurisdiction. The husband belatedly sought to challenge the court's jurisdiction contending that he was domiciled in Australia. The evidence established that the husband's address for tax purposes was that of his parents in England. He had not declared himself domiciled in Australia on Australian family application forms but had claimed to be simply resident there. He had not taken up Australian citizenship despite having had the opportunity to do so on two occasions. He had sought to liquidate his Australian assets. In dismissing the husband's case on the facts, and referring to the evidence necessary to displace domicile of origin, Ryder J said, 'The hurdle is relatively high. Domicile of choice has to be established on clear, cogent evidence. A mere assertion as to being Australian is hardly sufficient'.

In *Holliday v Musa* [2010] EWCA Civ 335, [2010] 2 FLR 702, the deceased was of Turkish Cypriot origin and was born in Cyprus. He had emigrated to England in 1958 with his wife and children. He owned properties in Cyprus and England and visited Cyprus regularly with his family. In 1980, he and his wife separated and in 1998 he commenced a relationship and had a child. For tax purposes he claimed non-domiciled status. He died in Cyprus but his body was brought to England for burial. In a claim made by his partner under the I(PFD)A 1975, the deceased's adult children contested the claim on the basis that the deceased had not lost his domicile of origin and therefore the court had no jurisdiction to hear the claim brought under the Act. In dismissing their appeal against the decision at first instance, the Court of Appeal followed the case of *Cyganik v Agulian* and the principles laid down in *Re Fuld Estate (No 3), Re Harley v Fuld* [1965] 3 All ER 776. The court took account as its starting point the fact that the deceased had been resident in England and that it was the home of his family and balanced it against all the evidence relating to his connection with Cyprus. It also took account of the fact that the deceased had not chosen to retire to Cyprus despite expressing an intention to do so. On the evidence the court concluded that the deceased had continued to have his permanent home in England where he wished to spend the rest of his life and be buried in England.

2.4.6 Summary

Hence, unless satisfactory evidence is produced to show that a domicile of choice was acquired by the deceased and had been retained by him/her until his/her death, the presumption that the domicile of origin subsisted will prevail.

Residence by itself, even if it is for a long period, without evidence of the necessary intent to abandon the domicile of origin and to remain in the country of choice, does not lead to the acquisition of a domicile of choice. Reference should be made to works on the conflict of laws for the law relating to domicile and on the distinction between habitual residence and domicile. Case law under the Child Abduction and Custody Act 1985, where the issue of habitual residence is frequently raised, may also assist in distinguishing between habitual residence and domicile.

In order to establish a domicile of choice the evidence must establish that the deceased's intention to change his/her domicile was not influenced by external pressures; that he/she intended to live permanently and indefinitely in England and Wales; and that the circumstances in his/her life and up to his/her death do not disclose any suggestion of any indecision on his/her part or anything which would suggest that he/she had not made up his/her mind.

Before challenging the issue of domicile, consideration should be given to the effect this might have on the estate both in terms of the possible reduction in the value of the estate if inheritance tax becomes payable and the costs of litigation.

2.5 THE LAW COMMISSION'S CONSULTATION PAPER, 26 OCTOBER 2009

The Law Commission in its Consultation Paper, *Intestacy and Family Provision Claims on Death*, reviewed the current law and highlighted the various approaches and options for basing a claim under the I(PFD)A 1975 and acknowledged that there was force in all these arguments but went on to make the following provisional proposals and observations in paras 7.53–7.55:

> We provisionally propose that it should not be a precondition to an application under the Inheritance (Provision for Family and Dependants) Act 1975 that the deceased died domiciled in England and Wales. We ask consultees whether it should be a precondition to an application under the Inheritance (Provision for Family and Dependants) Act 1975 that the deceased died habitually resident in England and Wales, or whether an application for family provision should be possible in any case where there is property comprised in the estate that is governed by English succession law. We also invite views on whether there

should be any other requirement limiting the circumstances in which an application for family provision may be made. We note that this would enable the court to consider the deceased's entire estate, whether or not governed by English succession law, although in practice orders would not be made in circumstances where they could not be enforced.

If the prerequisite to bringing a claim under the I(PFD)A 1975 is altered to that of the deceased's habitual residence at the time of death, it is submitted that it would not simplify matters because each case would depend on its particular facts. Hence it would be difficult for legal practitioners to advise with any certainty what the outcome may be and this in turn would lead to more cases being litigated. One has only to study the jurisprudence that has developed over the years in child abduction cases over this issue to see that, invariably, it leads to the opposing party raising it as a mechanism to avoid the consequences of the statutory provisions.

Although it is accepted that reform of the I(PFD)A 1975 is needed, the discussion is still ongoing and it may be dependent on the outcome of the European proposals for reform on the issue of succession (see Commission of the European Communities, Green Paper, *Succession and Wills*, COM (2005) 65 final), which propose that succession to estates (whatever property they comprise) should be governed by the laws of the Member State in which the deceased was habitually resident at the time of his/her death (or in some cases, of his/her nationality), and the Law Commission's consultation process dated 21 October 2009.

Chapter 3

Time Limits

3.1 INTRODUCTION

Time limits have always applied to claims for financial provision from a deceased's estate, ever since the right to make such claims was introduced by the I(FP)A 1938. The Act limited the time within which an application could be made to 6 months from the issue of a grant of representation, with a provision for time to be extended with leave of the court. The Intestates' Estates Act 1952 introduced a provision for the court to extend the time limit of 6 months in specified circumstances.

The Family Provision Act 1966 repealed the earlier provisions and gave the court a general discretion to extend the limitation period. This provision is now incorporated in the I(PFD)A 1975, s 4, which provides that:

> an application for an order under section 2 of the Act shall not, except with the permission of the court, be made after the end of the period of six months from the date on which representation with respect to the estate of the deceased is first taken out.

It is thus essential that a claim for an order under I(PFD)A 1975, s 2 is issued within the prescribed time limit.

3.2 COMMENCEMENT OF THE PERIOD OF 6 MONTHS

I(PFD)A 1975, s 23 provides that, in considering when representation with respect to the estate of a deceased person was taken out, a grant limited to settled land or trust property is to be left out of account; and a grant limited to real estate or to personal estate is to be left out of account unless a grant limited to the remainder of the estate has previously been made or is made at the same time. The Act makes no other provision for determining the date for the commencement of the 6-month limitation period, nor does it make any reference to grants which are limited for a particular purpose. Thus, the effects of these grants for the purposes of the time limit under the Act are unclear. They are dealt with briefly below.

3.2.1   Grant *ad colligenda bona*

A grant of letters of administration *ad colligenda bona* is applied for when it is necessary to prevent loss to the estate because there is no one authorised to administer it. The grant is limited to the purposes of collecting and getting in and receiving the deceased's estate and doing such acts as may be necessary to preserve the estate, until further representation is granted. The grant ceases when the object for which it was granted has been achieved or a full grant has been issued.

It is submitted that, by reason of its limited nature, a grant *ad colligenda bona* does not operate to start time running in respect of claims under the I(PFD)A 1975.

3.2.2   Grant pending determination of claim

Under Senior Courts Act 1981, s 117, a limited grant of letters of administration pending determination of a probate claim commenced in the Chancery Division may be issued as a matter of urgency when there is a dispute which gives rise to a probate claim, for example, to determine the validity of a testator's will. In such cases the administrator has all the rights and duties of a general administrator except that he/she is subject to the immediate control of the court and must act under its direction. The object of this grant is to enable the administrator to collect and safeguard assets pending the outcome of the claim. Once the claim has been determined, the grant terminates and the person entitled as a result of the probate claim may take out a grant of probate or administration.

In this case too it is unlikely that time will begin to run in respect of any claim under the I(PFD)A 1975, but it would be prudent, if it is intended to make a claim under the Act, to notify the executors and the beneficiaries of that intention. In some cases it may be desirable to have all issues relating to the deceased's will and estate to be determined by the same tribunal. If a probate claim is pending, the court's direction should be sought (see, also, para 3.3 on claims made before a grant is issued).

3.2.3 Grant *ad litem*

A grant *ad litem* enables proceedings to be begun or continued on behalf of the deceased's estate or against it. It is limited to bringing or defending a claim, or otherwise being a party to a claim. Once the proceedings are over, application may be made for a general grant, and on the issue of a general grant the limited grant terminates.

In *Re Johnson (Paul Anthony) (Deceased)* [1987] CLY 3882, a grant limited to solicitors for the purposes of issuing a claim for negligence in respect of the deceased's estate was held not to be the first taking out of representation in respect of the estate of the deceased. On the basis of the decision in *Re Johnson*, a general proposition is often made that a grant *ad litem* does not start time running in respect of claims under the I(PFD)A 1975. It is, however, submitted that the decision is not unequivocal, because such a grant may be issued to commence or defend proceedings brought under the Act itself, and in such circumstances the limitation period should start running as soon as the grant is issued.

On the other hand, such a grant does not allow the administrator to distribute the estate. The administrator may not have full knowledge of the extent and nature of the estate or the identity of the beneficiaries entitled, and therefore time ought not to run. It is submitted that in such cases the practitioner will need to consider the nature of the proceedings in respect of which the grant was issued, and make a decision whether time may begin to run.

If the circumstances are unclear, it may be wise to err on the side of caution; it is suggested that, to avoid any risk, proceedings under the I(PFD)A 1975 should be commenced to protect the client and, if necessary, adjourned generally or stayed until the outcome of any pending proceedings.

3.2.4 Grant in common form

Where a grant in common form is followed by a grant in solemn form in respect of the same will, time begins to run from the date on which the grant in common form was granted (see *Re Miller, Miller v De Courcey* [1969] 1 WLR 583).

3.2.5 Successive grants

Where letters of administration are replaced by a grant of probate, for example, because a will is subsequently found, time begins to run from the grant of probate (see *Re Bidie, Bidie v General Accident Fire and Life Assurance Corporation* [1949] Ch 121). In *Re Bidie*, the deceased made a will on 10 February 1937. He died on 16 January 1945. The will was not found. On 13 April 1945, letters of administration were issued to his widow and one of their children. The will was later found and probate was granted on 7 September 1946. On 8 January 1947, the widow applied for financial provision under the I(FP)A 1938. Her claim was allowed to proceed as it had been made within 6 months of the grant of probate.

Similarly, where the grant of probate is revoked and replaced by letters of administration, time begins to run from the grant of letters of administration, because, for the purposes of I(PFD)A 1975, s 4, time begins to run from the date on which 'effective' or 'valid' representation was 'first taken out' (see *Re Freeman, Weston v Freeman* [1984] 1 WLR 1419, for the absurd situation which would have prevailed if the court had taken a different view).

3.2.6   *De bonis non* grant

A grant of letters of administration *de bonis non* is made following the death of the sole or last personal representative who obtained a grant in relation to the estate of the deceased but died before completing its administration. The grant relates only to the estate remaining unadministered. It is a second effective and valid grant, but it does not relate to the whole estate. Time therefore runs from the date of the original grant (see, also, *cessate* grant, para 3.2.7).

3.2.7   *Cessate* grant

A *cessate* grant issues when the first grant was conditional or limited and the condition or limitation has been fulfilled, or the grantee dies without fulfilling the purpose for which the grant was made. Unlike a *de bonis non* grant, a *cessate* grant operates in respect of the whole estate. In this case, time begins to run from the original grant, because the second grant is a re-grant.

3.2.8   Standing search for grant

To ensure that a claimant is notified of the issue of a grant of representation, facilities are available for a standing search to be made for an office copy of every grant of representation which tallies with the particulars given on the application, and which either was issued in the 12 months before receipt of the application or is issued within 6 months thereafter.

The application is made by completing Form 2 (see Appendix A1.1) and sending it to, or lodging it at, any probate registry or sub-registry. The appropriate fee must accompany the application. Where the applicant wishes to extend the period of search, a written application for an extension should be lodged or sent by post to the registry at which the standing search was entered. A standing search which has been extended may be further extended by filing a further application for extension. See Non-Contentious Probate Rules 1987 (SI 1987/2024), r 43, as amended.

It should also be noted that *Practice Direction (Names of Deceased: Death Certificates)*, 12 January 1999 [1999] 1 WLR 259 directs that in all instances where the deceased died in the United Kingdom and the death has been recorded in the Register of Deaths:

(1)   the names and dates of birth and death of the deceased as recorded in the register must be included in the oath lodged in support of an application made through a solicitor or probate practitioner for a grant of representation;

(2)   the names and date of death of the deceased as recorded in the register must be included in the notice for a standing search or caveat;

(3)   in any case where the name of the deceased or by which the deceased was known differs from that recorded in the register, the name must also be included in the oath or the notice, as the case may be.

Pursuant to the *President's Direction: Probate Records: Grants of Representation*, 3 November 1998 [1999] 1 FLR 102, as from November 1998, records of all grants of representation made in the Principal Registry of the Family Division and in district probate registries after that date, kept pursuant to Senior Courts Act 1981, s 111, are maintained in the form of computer records. Records from 1980 to 1988 are maintained on microfilm. The annual calendar books continue to be maintained for the years prior to 1980. The information comprises:

(1)   the full names of the deceased and any alias names;

(2)   the last address of the deceased;

(3)   the date of death and domicile of the deceased;

(4)   the name(s) and address(es) of the executor(s) or administrator(s);

(5)   the type of grant;

(6)   the gross and net values of the estate or, in the case of an exempted estate, the limits within which the estate falls;

(7)   the name and address of the extracting solicitor (if any) or the
       fact that the grant was obtained by way of personal application;
(8)   the date of the grant and the issuing registry.

3.3   CLAIM MADE BEFORE GRANT

There are two conflicting authorities on whether a claim for an order under
I(PFD)A 1975, s 2 can be issued before the grant of representation has been
taken out.

In cases under the I(FP)A 1938, it has been held that a claim which is made
before the time on which representation was taken out is not invalid (see
Searle, Searle v Siems [1949] Ch 73). In *Re Searle, Searle v Siems*, the
originating summons was issued before probate was granted. A grant of
representation was obtained before the final hearing. It was argued that an
application made before the grant had been taken out was a nullity. Roxburgh
J rejected this submission because it would have been contrary to natural
justice to prevent the applicant from making the claim. He also considered that
the objection raised was one of procedure and could be dispensed with,
particularly as it had not been made at any stage prior to the final hearing.

It has been argued that the decision in *Re Searle, Searle v Siems* does not
apply to applications under the I(PFD)A 1975 by reason of the provisions of
s 4 and the Civil Procedure Rules 1998 (SI 1998/3132) (CPR) which now
apply to such applications.

I(PFD)A 1975, s 4 provides:

> An application for an order under section 2 of the Act shall not, except with the
> permission of the court, be made after the end of the period of six months from
> the date on which representation with respect to the estate of the deceased is
> first taken out.

The practice and procedure for claims under the I(PFD)A 1975 are now
governed by CPR Part 57 and the Pre-Action Protocol.

CPR r 57.16(3) provides that:

> The written evidence filed and served by the claimant with the clam form must
> have exhibited to it an official copy of–
>
> (a)   the grant of probate or letters of administration in respect of the
>   deceased's estate; and

(b)   every testamentary document in respect of which probate or letters of administration were granted.

Both the provision of I(PFD)A 1975, s 4 and the rules are mandatory and therefore no application should be issued unless some grant or representation in the estate has been granted.

In addition, in *Re McBroom Deceased* [1992] 2 FLR 49 it was held that it was essential for a grant of probate or letters of representation to have been obtained before an application under I(PFD)A 1975, s 2 could be issued. In *Re McBroom*, the applicant issued proceedings before a grant of representation had been issued, seeking orders under s 9 against the deceased's severable share in property jointly owned. No attempt had been made to obtain a grant before the final hearing, nor was there any indication whether or not a grant of representation would be obtained before the final hearing. Eastham J struck out the claim on the basis that it was premature.

It is arguable, however, that the right to make a claim arises, as a result of the provisions of I(PFD)A 1975, s 1. Section 1(1) provides that where a person dies domiciled in England and Wales and is survived by any of the persons referred to in the section, such a person may apply to the court for an order under s 2 on the grounds set out in the section. The right to make a claim therefore accrues against the estate on the death of the testator, not on the grant of representation.

In setting the time limit within which such a claim may be made, I(PFD)A 1975, s 4 provides that the claim cannot, except with the permission of the court, be made after the end of 6 months from the date on which representation with respect to the estate of the deceased is first taken out. It therefore fixes the moment from which time begins to run, not the point at which the right to make a claim accrues. There is no provision in the Act which prohibits the making of a claim until a grant of representation has been issued. Furthermore, if a claim for financial provision under the Act could not be made until a grant of representation has been taken out, the court would be deprived of its power to preserve property pending trial.

If it were the case that the claim does not accrue until the first effective grant of representation is issued, the consequence would be that, if the will is contested, the claim for financial provision could not be commenced until the probate claim has been concluded. The resultant delay in pursuing the claim for financial provision would lead to injustice and possibly more expense. There may be situations where the person contesting the will could also have a claim under the I(PFD)A 1975. The two matters could be conveniently and expeditiously dealt with by the same court simultaneously if the claim under the Act does not have to await the result of the probate claim. If the decision in *Re McBroom* is to be followed, then where there is a contested probate claim which fails, it is inevitable that the claim for financial provision under the Act will be out of time because it is not until the probate claim has been determined that it will become clear whether the grant of representation issued, if any, is effective. It is inevitable that this claim will take longer than 6 months. If the challenge fails and the grant is found to be effective, then the claimant will be out of time. It is therefore submitted that, in the absence of any specific provision in the Act preventing the issue of proceedings until after the grant of representation has been issued, a claimant under the Act should be able to proceed as soon as practicable after the deceased's death.

Where there is no person willing or able to take out a grant of representation, application should be made to the court to appoint an appropriate person to act, or for the Official Solicitor to represent the estate of the deceased.

In cases where there is, or is likely to be a dispute over who is to take a grant, it is possible for a claimant to apply for a grant to a nominated person under the Senior Courts Act 1981, on the grounds that there are special circumstances that make it necessary and expedient for the court to appoint a person other than the person entitled to the grant. This procedure, if adopted, is particularly useful where the claim includes an application for interim relief and has the benefit of avoiding delay.

However, as soon as it becomes apparent that a claim under the I(PFD)A 1975 may be made, whether this is before or after the grant of representation has been obtained, it is incumbent on the applicant to comply with the General Pre-Action Protocol. Failure to comply with the Protocol may lead to costs implications, and delay in issuing the application within the time limit without good reason could also result in any application for leave to issue out of time being refused. It will have the added benefit of supporting a case for an extension of the 6-month period if the need arises to do so.

It is thus essential for practitioners to ensure that the pre-action letter is sent as soon as it appears their client may have a claim under the I(PFD)A 1975 and to identify two specific issues:

(1)   whether and when the grant of representation has been taken out; and

(2)   the date from which the commencement of the 6 months is calculated and, if that time limit has expired, whether or not there are good reasons for the delay to justify an application for an extension of the 6-month period.

It also has the advantage of identifying the nature and extent of the claimant's case and for negotiations for a compromise to be reached at an early stage.

In the alternative an application may be made for a grant *ad litem* (see para 3.2.3).

3.4 APPLICATIONS IN RESPECT OF JOINT PROPERTY – I(PFD)A 1975, SECTION 9

An application under I(PFD)A 1975, s 9, to treat the deceased's severable share of a joint tenancy as part of the net estate of the deceased (see para 9.8), must be made within the period of 6 months from the date on which representation with respect to the deceased's estate was first taken out. The court does not have the power to extend the time limit imposed by statute in cases under s 9.

3.5 EXTENSION OF TIME

3.5.1 Powers of the court

In addition to setting the time limit for bringing a claim under the I(PFD)A 1975, s 4 confers on the court a general discretion to extend the time limit. The Act does not, however, set out any criteria or principle which the court should apply when considering an application for an extension of time, nor does it in any way restrict the court's power. The court thus has unfettered discretion, and the circumstances in which the court may be asked to exercise its discretion are limitless.

In dealing with an application for an extension of time, guidance is often sought from case law following the I(FP)A 1938 under which the time limit of 6 months was first imposed. Regard should, however, be had to the fact that, as respects the estates of persons dying after 1952 and before 1967, when the Family Provision Act 1966 came into force, the court's discretion to extend the 6-month period was limited by the Intestates' Estates Act 1952. That Act provided that the period could be extended only in limited specified circumstances, and then only if it could be shown to the satisfaction of the court that the time limit would operate 'unfairly'. The pre-1966 case law may be said to be of limited value to an application under I(PFD)A 1975, s 4, particularly as social conditions and attitudes have changed significantly and continue to do so.

However, the cases may be of relevance in so far as CPR r 1.1 requires the court when dealing with any case to apply the 'overriding objective' with a view to dealing with the case justly and fairly and ensuring that the parties are on an equal footing.

Additionally, the court is now obliged in determining any issue to have regard to the provisions of the European Convention for the Protection of Human Rights and Fundamental Freedoms 1950 (Human Rights Convention). In an application under I(PFD)A 1975, s 4 for an extension of time, the provisions of Art 6 of the Convention, which entitles every person to a fair and public hearing, will be a significant factor in the determination of the application. It should also be borne in mind that social conditions and attitudes have changed significantly and continue to do so.

In exercising its discretion the court will take account of all the circumstances of the case and carry out a balancing exercise between the merits of each party's case, and exercise its discretion on the basis of what is just and fair and give reasons for its decision (see *Fielden and Graham v Cunliffe* [2005] EWCA Civ 1508, [2006] 1 FLR 745). Case law provides some guidance on the principles which have been considered as relevant to such applications.

3.5.2   The relevant criteria to be applied in an application for extension of time

Case law provides guidance on the factors which will be relevant in an application to bring a claim out of time. The leading case which gives such guidance and which has been consistently followed is *Re Salmon (Deceased), Coard v National Westminster Bank* [1981] Ch 167.

The principles formulated by Megarry VC in his judgment in *Re Salmon (Deceased), Coard v National Westminster Bank*, are generally relied on by courts when exercising the discretion under I(PFD)A 1975, s 4. These principles are:

(1)   The discretion is unfettered and one that is exercised judicially in accordance with what is just and proper.

(2)   The onus lies on the applicant to establish sufficient grounds for taking the case out of the general rule and depriving those who are protected by it of its benefits. Furthermore, the time limit prescribed is a substantive provision laid down in the I(PFD)A 1975 itself, and is not merely a procedural time limit imposed by rules of court which may be treated with indulgence appropriate to procedural rules. The burden on the applicant is thus not a

triviality. The applicant must make out a substantial case for it being just and proper for the court to exercise its statutory discretion to extend the time.

(3) The court must consider how promptly and in what circumstances the applicant is seeking an extension of time. The whole of the circumstances must be looked at, including the reasons for the delay and how promptly the applicant gave a warning to the defendant of the proposed application.

(4) It is material whether or not negotiations have been commenced within the time limit; if they have, and time has run out while they are proceeding, this is likely to encourage the court to extend the time. Negotiations commenced after the time limit has expired might also aid the applicant, at any rate, if the defendants have not taken the point that time has expired.

(5) It is relevant to consider whether the estate had been distributed before the claim was notified.

(6) The court should also consider whether refusal to extend time would leave the applicant without redress against anybody.

In *Re Dennis (Deceased), Dennis v Lloyds Bank* [1981] 2 All ER 140, Browne-Wilkinson J, while applying the principles stated by Megarry VC, formulated two further factors which should be adopted when exercising the court's discretion. These are:

(7) The applicant must show that 'he has an arguable case, a case fit to go to trial and that in approaching that matter the court's approach is rather the same as it adopts when considering proceedings for summary judgment' (see CPR Part 24).

(8) Where, after a full understanding of the nature of the claim and the prospect of success, the applicant makes a conscious decision not to make a claim and then later changes his/her mind, the court ought not to permit the claim to be made irrespective of the length of time which has elapsed, save only that no distribution has taken place (see *Escritt v Escritt* (1982) 3 FLR 280).

In *Re Dennis (Deceased)*, the applicant was the son of the deceased. He had received £90,000 by way of a gift, with other sums, during the deceased's lifetime. The deceased had left him a legacy, free of duty, of £10,000, and £30,000 in trust. Probate was granted on 17 January 1978. On 19 February 1980 the son applied for financial provision and for an extension of time. His claim was limited to such sums as would enable him to discharge the capital transfer tax on the £90,000 received during the deceased's lifetime. The court found the application totally unmeritorious.

The principles set out in the above two cases are 'guidelines' and should assist the practitioner in advising whether the case merits an application being made under the I(PFD)A 1975 and for permission to apply for the application out of time and the nature of the evidence which will be required for the application for permission to apply out of time to succeed.

The application of each of the above eight factors to the facts of individual cases, and the consideration of them by the courts, are reviewed below.

3.5.3   Merits of the claim

In *Re Salmon (Deceased), Coard v National Westminster Bank*, it was held that the applicant must show a substantial case for it being just and proper for the court to exercise its statutory discretion to extend the time. It would seem from the authorities, however, that, to take the case out of the general rule, the applicant must not only establish sufficient reason for the delay in making the application, but must also show a good prospect of succeeding in the claim. The following cases further illustrate the court's approach to an application for leave to extend time.

In *Re Stone* (1969) 114 SJ 36, the Court of Appeal stated that the applicant must establish that there is a triable issue, and satisfy the court that in all the circumstances of the case the court ought to exercise its discretion.

In *Re Dennis (Deceased), Dennis v Lloyds Bank* (above), it was held that, in exercising its discretion, a factor to which the court was required to have regard, in addition to other matters, was whether the applicant was able to satisfy the court that he had an arguable case that he was entitled to reasonable financial provision out of the estate. The criterion to be applied in deciding whether the applicant had an arguable case was the same as that applied by the court in deciding whether a defendant should have leave to defend (see CPR Part 24), but note also that under this rule the test appears to be whether there is a 'real prospect' of success, or 'compelling' reasons. In *Re Dymott, Spooner v Carroll*, CAT, 15 December 1980, the principle applied was whether there was any merit in the application, rather than whether the applicant had an arguable case.

In *Smith v Loosley*, CAT, 18 June 1986, the issue was decided on the basis of whether the applicant had an arguable case. The applicant was 7 weeks out of time. She did not understand what a life interest meant and she had been involved in a dispute with one of the members of the extended family. The delay was not regarded as excessive. In addition, a warning letter had been sent by her solicitors to the executors a day before the time expired.

In *Polackova v Sobiewski*, CAT, 28 October 1985, there had been inactivity for 6 months after the solicitors and the applicant discovered that probate had been granted, and the application was made 3 months out of time. No satisfactory explanation for the delay was given, but leave was granted on the basis that, at the date of the hearing, the applicant had an arguable case. It is difficult to reconcile this decision with the principles set out by Megarry VC in *Re Dennis (Deceased)* and the other authorities. It can be explained only on the basis that the court took the view that as the applicant was the former spouse of the deceased, the case must have some merit.

These authorities seem to suggest that the onus on the applicant has gradually shifted from having to 'make a substantial case'; to having to show an 'arguable case' or a 'triable issue' (*Re Dennis (Deceased)*); to showing that the applicant's case has merit (*Re Dymott*); and, if *Polackova v Sobiewski* is to be regarded as good law, to a 'triviality' and an inquiry which is superficial. It is submitted that *Polackova v Sobiewski* should not be regarded as setting a new standard, but as a case which turned on its own facts; and that the correct approach is to show that the applicant has a good arguable case on the merits which ought to be tried, or that the applicant has a 'real prospect of success'.

In *Re C (Deceased)* [1995] 2 FLR 24, leave was granted although there had been a delay of 2 years before the mother of the deceased's child sought to make a claim. The delay was not properly explained. There had not been any distribution of the estate. If leave was refused the child would have suffered as a result of her mother's default. The court considered the merits of the application and the prospects of success if the child's claim was allowed to be made. It was inevitable that there would be a substantial provision out of the estate in favour of the child for the child's ordinary maintenance requirements. Wilson J (as he then was) stated that in none of the reported cases to which he had been referred had the prospects of substantial success been so clear as in this case, and 'in the end the task is to determine whether the net weight of the relevant factors is such as to justify permission outside the normal period'.

In *Budd v Fowler* [1999] CLY 4635, the widower of the deceased having accepted a lump sum of £700 in full and final settlement of all claims against the estate of the deceased including all claims under the I(PFD)A 1975, applied to make a claim out of time. In determining the application the court, *inter alia*, applied the test of whether the claimant had reasonable grounds for making a claim and whether there was a real and substantial question to be tried. On the facts, the application for permission to bring a claim under the Act was refused because the applicant had agreed to settle all claims including those under the Act and the applicant's case lacked merit.

In *McNulty v McNulty* [2002] EWHC 123 (Ch), [2002] WTLR 737, the applicant succeeded in her application for permission to issue her claim against the estate of the deceased although she was in excess of 3 years out of time. The court found on the facts that her case had merit; the estate had not been distributed and there would be no prejudice to any of the beneficiaries if permission was granted (see further under claims by those with disability).

3.5.4   Delay in bringing the claim

In considering an application for an extension of time, the court looks not only at the length of time that has elapsed, but at the whole of the circumstances. In *Re Salmon (Deceased), Coard v National Westminster Bank* (at paras 3.5.2 and 3.5.3), the reasons for the delay, as well as the promptness with which the applicant gave warning to the defendants of the proposed claim, were regarded as important considerations. In *Re Ruttie (Deceased) Ruttie v Saul* [1970] 1 WLR 89, the court considered the hardship to the applicant if an extension was not granted, the fact that the estate had not yet been distributed and the fact that the application was just 6 weeks out of time against the fact that there would be no prejudice whatsoever to the defendants except what was inevitably involved in any extension of time, that is, the loss of the advantage of a rigid time limit. The delay in making the application earlier was explained on three grounds, namely:

(1)   there had been lengthy negotiations with a view to reaching a compromise, during which arose the question whether the doctrine of community of property under Polish law would be applicable;

(2)   the applicant had been ill;

(3)   in concentrating on the issue of community of property the solicitors had overlooked the time limit.

In *Re Gonin (Deceased), Gonin v Garmeson* [1979] Ch 16, where the delay was of 2 years, the court refused the application because the applicant had been in control throughout and the delay had occurred as a result of the negligence of the applicant's solicitors and the advice they gave her. The applicant had a good case against her solicitors and the injustice to her could therefore be remedied by an action against them.

In *Re Bone (Deceased), Bone v Midland Bank* [1955] 1 WLR 703, an issue had arisen as to the construction of the deceased's will. The widow's solicitors were informed that an application would be issued for the question to be determined by the court. The application was not made, so the widow issued an application under the I(FP)A 1938. The application was 2 days out of time and leave was sought to extend time. Leave was granted because the executor's solicitors had led the widow to suppose that proceedings would be commenced; the delay was short; and refusal would have caused hardship.

In *Re Trott, Trott v Miles* [1958] 1 WLR 604, the deceased had died on 8 October 1954. Probate was granted on 17 November 1954. The widow applied for financial provision for herself. On 13 April 1955 the widow gave birth to the deceased's daughter. The application on behalf of the daughter was not issued until 11 July 1955, almost 2 months out of time. Leave was granted, as it was plain that on the birth of the child another circumstance affecting the administration or distribution of the estate arose. No time had been wasted between the date of the child's birth and the date of the application; an application for the child to be represented by means of public funds had also been in progress.

In *Re McNare, McNare v McNare* [1964] 1 WLR 1255, the deceased died in 1961. Probate was granted to his son on 8 May 1962. The deceased had left nothing to his widow, who was blind, crippled and 71 years of age, and who had not discovered the deceased's death until the end of October 1962. She had no information regarding the deceased's assets. Her sister, on her behalf, sought legal advice and as a result the son was contacted, but he refused to give any information. Solicitors were instructed on the widow's behalf and there then followed preliminary negotiations between them and the son's solicitors. There was deadlock. The widow then issued the application for financial provision and sought an extension of time. Leave was granted because:

(1)   the applicant had not had any information about the deceased's estate;

(2)   there were negotiations between solicitors;

(3)   refusal to extend the time would have caused hardship and would have operated unfairly against the applicant.

In *Re Longley (Deceased), Longley and Longley v Longley* [1981] CLY 2885, the application for an extension of time was refused because there had been a delay of about 14 months before making the application; distribution of the estate had taken place; there had been no negotiations for a settlement; and the applicant had a good case for negligence against her solicitors.

In *Re Adams, Adams and Adams v Schofield and Adams*, CAT, 22 July 1981, an appeal succeeded because the judge had placed too great an emphasis on the fact that the delay was wholly due to the negligence of the solicitors and that the applicant would have had a good claim against them; and had failed to give due weight to the other factors in favour of the applicant.

In *Escritt v Escritt* (1982) 3 FLR 280, despite the fact that the applicant had been properly advised, she had delayed for 3 years in bringing her claim, to avoid differences within the family. Leave to apply out of time was refused.

Where there are related proceedings with regard to the construction or validity of the deceased's will the issue of a possible claim under the I(PFD)A 1975 can be easily overlooked as occurred in *Anthony v Donges* [1998] 2 FLR 775. In such cases it is advisable to issue a claim under the Act to protect the claim from being out of time and then either to apply for a stay of the proceedings or for the matter to be consolidated with the probate action.

3.5.5   Negotiations

Where delay has occurred because the parties have been attempting to negotiate a settlement, the court will consider an application for permission to bring a claim out of time favourably. The basis of the application will obviously include the fact that the executors and any beneficiaries were made aware of the claim and therefore there would be no prejudice to them. If assurances were given whilst negotiations were being undertaken that the issue of the time limit under I(PFD)A 1975, s 4 would not be relied on against the claimant if negotiations failed, the application for permission will be granted. Now that under the CPR the emphasis is on mediation and attempting a settlement before issuing any claim and following the Pre-Action Protocol, if delay has occurred in pursuit of effecting a settlement the court is likely to treat an application under s 4 sympathetically. However, so as to protect the claimant in such cases, it is desirable that the pre-action letter includes a request for confirmation that the 'time' factor will not be raised against the claimant, to enable negotiations to be undertaken and to avoid the costs of issuing a claim and then applying for a stay.

Cases where this principle is demonstrated include *Re McNare, McNare v McNare* (above). See also *Re Ruttie* (above) where the negotiations with a view to compromising the claim had commenced before the grant of probate and had continued for the whole of the period of 6 months.

In *Re John, John v John* (1966) 111 SJ 115, the application was made by the widow of the deceased 3 years after probate was taken out because she had relied on promises made to her by the legatees which never materialised. Her application was granted.

3.5.6 Distribution of the estate

I(PFD)A 1975, s 20(1) stipulates that the provisions of the Act do not render the personal representative of the deceased person liable for having distributed any part of the estate of the deceased, after the end of the period of 6 months from the date on which representation with respect to the estate of the deceased is first taken out, on the ground that he ought to have taken into account the possibility that the court might permit the making of an application after the end of 6 months, or might exercise its powers under s 6 (see, further, para 8.11). The section goes on to provide that this does not prejudice any power to recover, by reason of the making of an order under the Act, any part of the estate distributed. If, therefore, distribution has taken place, the prejudice to the beneficiaries will be that much greater by reason of the conversion of hope and expectation to reality when they received their shares:

> For most people, there is a real difference between the bird in the hand and the bird in the bush. In addition, of course, the beneficiaries are more likely to have changed their position in reliance on the benefaction if they have actually received it than if it lies merely in prospect. If it is always prejudicial to claimants not to receive money that they are entitled to receive at the earliest moment, it is likely to be even more prejudicial to have taken away from them money that they have actually received and have begun to enjoy. The point is strengthened if they have changed their position in reliance on what they have received, as by making a purchase or gifts they would otherwise not have made. (per Megarry VC in *Re Salmon (Deceased)* (above))

Although Megarry VC referred to the fact that the court could go behind the fact of distribution, it is submitted that the applicant for an extension of time would be required to establish compelling reasons and exceptional circumstances to succeed. There have been no reported cases of leave being granted after distribution has taken place. In *Re Longley (Deceased), Longley and Longley v Longley* [1981] CLY 2885, distribution had taken place when the application was made. It was a factor which the court took into account when refusing leave.

Compelling and exceptional circumstances may for instance include a situation where the distribution has occurred very recently, or where the assets distributed are still in the hands of the beneficiary, or can be traced with little or no prejudice to the beneficiary who has received the asset. It could also arise where negotiations have led to an agreement which has not yet been put into effect or where the defendant reneged on the agreement and distributed the estate without any prior warning to the claimant.

3.5.7   Claimant's possible claim against third parties or solicitors

In *Re Salmon (Deceased), Coard v National Westminster Bank* [1981] Ch 167, Megarry VC stated that a relevant factor in exercising the court's discretion when dealing with an application for permission to bring a claim under the I(PFD)A 1975 was the fact that the applicant had a possible claim against a third party. Subsequent cases, however, have not considered this factor as tipping the balance against the applicant, but only one of many factors which the court will take into account when assessing all the circumstances of the individual case. The decision in *Re Adams, Adams and Adams v Schofield and Adams*, CAT, 22 July 1981, supports this view because on appeal it was held that the trial judge had placed too great an emphasis on the fact that the claimant had a possible claim against his legal advisers and had failed to give sufficient weight to the other factors which supported the claimant's case. In *Re Longley (Deceased), Longley and Longley v Longley* [1981] CLY 2885, the claimant's remedy against her lawyers was one amongst other relevant factors considered by the court in exercising its discretion and refusing permission. In that case, the deceased had made a will appointing his mistress executor, and bequeathed to her his house, in which she was then living with her daughter. The remainder of his estate devolved on his widow on a partial intestacy. The mistress wished to make a claim against the estate under the Act. She renounced probate in the widow's favour. Thereafter, although her solicitors were involved, the matter did not result in any settlement. The solicitors took no further action to pursue the claim on behalf of the mistress or her child. The mistress took further advice, but when she issued proceedings the claim was 14 months out of time and the estate had been distributed. Her application for an extension of time was refused because of the delay; the fact that distribution had taken place and that she had a claim against her former solicitors. In exercising its discretion and carrying out the balancing exercise the court had regard to all the important issues involved. It seems therefore that where the application for an extension of time is opposed on the basis that the applicant has a possible claim against a third party, the success or otherwise of the application will depend on the circumstances of the individual case. It is unlikely that the court will deny the claimant the right to pursue a rightful and meritorious claim simply on the basis that he/she may have a possible claim against a third party particularly where the claimant is a vulnerable individual or a child (for an example, see *Re C (Deceased)* [1995] 2 FLR 24 (at para 3.5.3)).

3.5.8 Conscious decision not to make a claim

Where the applicant has been properly advised but seeks not to pursue a claim promptly or makes a conscious and informed decision not to pursue the claim and then changes his/her mind it is unlikely that an application for permission will succeed (see *Escritt v Escritt* (1982) 3 FLR 280 and para 3.5.4). In contrast in *Re C (Deceased)* (at para 3.5.3), the court took a different view on the facts and more particularly as the applicant was a child and dependent on the decision of her mother.

3.5.9 Claimant under disability

In the case of civil litigation, Limitation Act 1980, s 28(1) extends the limitation period where the claimant is a person under disability. The I(PFD)A 1975 does not make any special provision for a claimant who is physically or mentally disabled. The disabled claimant should not, however, be disadvantaged or prejudiced by the absence of any specific provisions since the court has an unfettered discretion under I(PFD)A 1975, s 4. In exercising its discretion, the court is obliged to have regard to all the circumstances, including human rights issues under the Human Rights Convention, and to consider whether it is reasonably clear that the extension of time is required in the interests of justice.

The constraints of time are often more pressing when the practitioner has to deal with a client under disability, particularly if the client has learning difficulties or otherwise lacks capacity or has a speech impediment or is hard of hearing. In the case of a claimant who has severe learning difficulties or lacks capacity, consideration should be given to the appointment of a litigation friend or a receiver or the intervention of the Court of Protection. In such a case, delay is likely, and steps must be taken to safeguard the interest of the claimant under disability. The duty and burden on the solicitor is necessarily a heavy one. Time may have begun to run or may have expired before advice is sought. It is essential that a meticulous note is kept of every step taken in the proceedings to show that the matter was dealt with expeditiously and efficiently. If there is any likelihood of delay before a claim can be issued, contact with the personal representatives or their solicitors must be maintained to ensure that they are kept informed and, if possible, to obtain an extension of time by agreement. In some cases it may be appropriate to apply for leave to issue the claim without the necessary supporting evidence, to protect the claim and then seek directions from the court or apply for a stay to enable the necessary inquiries and investigations to be made to pursue the claim.

Where delay has occurred and it is necessary to apply for an extension of time the principles set out above should be taken into account when preparing the supporting evidence. In addition, the extent and nature of the claimant's disability and the reason for the delay in making the claim are relevant factors, particularly if the delay is attributable to the claimant's disability. The claimant, through his/her solicitor, must set out any other factor which establishes that it would be just and fair for the court to exercise its discretion in his/her favour. Evidence which indicates that the matter was dealt with diligently, efficiently and expeditiously will be relevant.

The following are some of the cases where the court has waived the time limits, where the applicant has been a person under disability:

- *Re McNare, McNare v McNare* (at para 3.5.3), where the applicant was blind, crippled and 71 years of age and did not discover the death of the deceased until 5 months after the grant of probate had been issued to her son;
- *Re Wood (Deceased), Wood v Wood* [1982] LS Gaz R 774, where the deceased had died intestate in April 1980. She was survived by a severely mentally handicapped child and the deceased's husband who was not the child's natural father. The estate was valued at £26,737. The husband inherited £25,000, the child the balance. The husband died in January 1981 leaving his entire estate to his natural son. The child's application, brought out of time, was allowed;
- *Re C (Deceased)* (at para 3.5.3), where a claim on behalf of a child was allowed despite the fact that it was 2 years out of time and notwithstanding the fact that the mother of the child, who could have made the claim on behalf of the child on time, could not give any reason for the delay;
- *Stock v Brown* [1994] 1 FLR 840, where the applicant was 85 years of age when probate was granted and had not had the opportunity to obtain independent legal advice. Permission to bring a claim despite a delay of 6 years was granted due to the exceptional circumstances, the merits of the case and the fact that there was no prejudice to the beneficiaries.

3.5.10 Delay caused by application for public funding

Solicitors should be mindful of the fact that there is no guarantee that any delay in issuing a claim, resulting from the time taken by the Legal Services Commission to deal with an application for public funding, will be treated by the court sympathetically. It is the duty of the solicitor to ensure that the Legal Services Commission is made fully aware of the urgency when making the application and subsequently by sending regular reminders to the Commission that time is running out. If it appears that the application will take some time to process, then it would be advisable to seek an emergency certificate, or one limited to issuing the proceedings.

It is also well worth notifying the personal representatives or their solicitors of the application for public funding, keeping them informed at all times of the progress of the application, and seeking an extension by agreement. If all else fails, the solicitor should advise the client of the implications, with a view to ascertaining whether the client is able to meet the costs of issuing the claim out of his/her own resources. It is also possible to apply to the court for leave to issue the proceedings without the supporting evidence on the undertaking that the evidence will be filed upon the determination of the application for a public funding certificate.

3.5.11 Interests of justice – CPR

In determining whether to grant or withhold permission on application for permission to bring a claim under the I(PFD)A 1975 out of time, the court must have regard to all the circumstances including whether it is in the interests of justice to grant an extension of time. The CPR apply to claims under the I(PFD)A 1975. CPR r 1.1 provides that when considering any application the court must apply the 'overriding objective' to deal with the case justly. Dealing with the case justly includes so far as practicable:

(1)   ensuring that the parties are on an equal footing;

(2)   saving expense;

(3)   dealing with the case in ways which are proportionate: (a) to the amount of money involved; (b) to the importance of the case; (c) to the complexities of the issues; and (d) to the financial position of each party;

(4)   ensuring that it is dealt with expeditiously and fairly; and

(5)   allotting to it an appropriate share of the court's resources, while taking into account the need to allot resources to other cases.

The overriding objective was applied in *Hashtroodi v Hancock* [2004] EWCA 652, [2004] 1 WLR 3206 where, due to an oversight, the solicitors for the claimant had failed to serve the claim form before the due date. The court held that the application for permission had to be considered in the light of the overriding objective and therefore the reason for the delay was relevant. Where the reason for the delay in issuing proceedings was an oversight of the claimant or his/her legal advisers, although not an absolute bar to permission being granted, it would be a strong reason for refusing such an application.

The conduct of the parties prior to the proceedings being commenced will also be relevant. The size of the estate may also be a relevant consideration in applying the proportionality test. Where the size of the estate is insufficient to meet the competing claims and the costs of litigation the court may refuse the application (see *Gregory, Gregory v Goodenough* [1970] 1 WLR 1455 where the estate was worth about £2500).

When considering the merit of the claim the court may also apply the provision of CPR Part 24, which empowers the court as part of its case management duties to dispose of issues summarily without a trial. The test to be applied in such cases is whether the court considers that the claimant has a real prospect of succeeding on the claim or whether the defendant has no real prospect of successfully defending the claim and there is no other compelling reason why the case should be disposed of at a trial (see, further, para 3.5.3).

In addition, the court is under a duty to consider the provision of Human Rights Convention, Art 6.

3.6   PROCEDURE

An application under I(PFD)A 1975, s 4 for permission to bring an claim after the 6-month period has lapsed must be made in the claim form and supported by evidence (see Chapter 12).

3.7   BURDEN OF PROOF

The overall burden of proof rests on the applicant to establish that there are good grounds for the delay and that the interests of justice justify leave to be granted.

Chapter 4

Claimants

4.1 INTRODUCTION

I(PFD)A 1975, s 1(1), as amended by the Law Reform (Succession) Act 1995 and the CPA 2004, sets out the classes of person entitled to make an application for an order under s 2 for financial provision on the ground that the disposition of the deceased's estate effected by his/her will, or the law of intestacy, or the combination of his/her will and that law, is not such as to make reasonable financial provision for the applicant. These are:

    (1)   the spouse or civil partner of the deceased;

    (2)   a former spouse or civil partner of the deceased but no one who has formed a subsequent marriage or civil partnership;

    (3)   a cohabitant of the deceased;

    (4)   a child of the deceased;

    (5)   any person (not being a child of the deceased) who, in the case of any marriage or civil partnership to which the deceased was at any time a party, was treated by the deceased as a child of the family in relation to that marriage or civil partnership;

    (6)   any person (not being a person included in the foregoing classes) who, immediately before the death of the deceased, was being maintained, either wholly or partly, by the deceased.

4.2 SPOUSE OF THE DECEASED

In English law, for a marriage to be recognised as valid, it must be between a man and a woman. A marriage between two people of the same sex is not a marriage (see Matrimonial Causes Act 1973, s 11(c)). Until 4 April 2005 a male–female transsexual and a man could not claim a right to marry (see *Sheffield and Horsham v United Kingdom* (1998) 27 EHRR 163). The Gender

Recognition Act 2004 now enables a person who has undergone a gender realignment to be recognised in the acquired gender (see, further, below). Although same sex couples cannot enter into a marriage, their relationship is now recognised with similar rights as those enjoyed by heterosexual couples in a marriage, provided the couple have entered into a civil partnership (see para 4.3).

4.2.1   Proof of marriage

A claimant spouse of the deceased will have to establish that he/she was the spouse of the deceased and that the marriage was a valid marriage recognised under English law and was subsisting at the time of death.

There is usually no dispute about the identity of the person who was the wife or husband of the deceased immediately before death, and in most cases the production of a valid marriage certificate suffices. The parties remain married unless the marriage has been dissolved by a decree absolute. The remarriage of the widow or widower of the deceased after the claim under the I(PFD)A 1975 is issued but before the claim is finally determined does not affect the validity of the claim. It is, however, a factor which the court is entitled to consider when determining whether reasonable financial provision was made by the deceased and, if not, what orders the court should make having regard to all relevant circumstances of the case and the criteria set out in s 3.

In the case where the marriage was not celebrated in the United Kingdom, the provisions of Family Procedure Rules 2010 (SI 2010/2955) (FPR 2010), PD 7A provide that the validity of a foreign marriage may be established by the production of a certified copy of the foreign marriage where the existence and validity of the marriage is not in dispute.

Where there is any doubt about the validity of a foreign marriage, the claimant's evidence of the formalities of that marriage, the production of a certified copy of the marriage certificate, if available, and the evidence where appropriate of an expert in the local law to establish that the marriage certificate would be accepted in the country of origin of a valid marriage will be required.

Where a marriage certificate is not available, the claimant's evidence, corroborated by any witness who was present at the ceremony of the marriage, describing the formalities of the ceremony, and the evidence of an expert in the local or customary law to confirm that the formalities described would be accepted in the country of origin as evidence of a valid marriage, will be necessary.

Where the parties have gone through a ceremony of marriage in accordance with customary law, it is for the claimant to establish that the ceremony of marriage complied with customary law and would be recognised as a valid marriage in the country where the marriage occurred. It is possible to challenge the validity of a customary marriage on the ground that the ceremony did not comply with the customary law or on the basis that one of the parties to the marriage lacked the necessary intention to marry and that the actions of that party during the ceremony were equivocal (see *A-M v A-M (Divorce Jurisdiction: Validity of Marriage)* [2001] 2 FLR 6).

4.2.2   Separation by decree of judicial separation

The marriage of a claimant, who was separated from the deceased at the time of his/her death by a decree of judicial separation and remained separated at the date of the deceased's death, is considered to be subsisting and the survivor is regarded as the spouse of the deceased (see *Re Sehota, Surjit Kaur v Gian Kaur* [1978] 1 WLR 1506). If the decree was made within 12 months of the deceased's death the provisions of I(PFD)A 1975, s 14 apply, subject to the conditions set out in that section (see paras 4.4.2 and 4.5.2). Where the decree was made over 12 months before the deceased's death, the claimant will not be entitled to receive the same financial provisions which a widow/widower of the deceased would be entitled to receive. Where the separation was by agreement but a decree of judicial separation has not been obtained, the claimant will be entitled to make a claim as a spouse of the deceased.

4.2.3   Void marriages

A void marriage is one that is regarded, in any case in which the existence of the marriage is in issue, as never having taken place. It may be put in issue at any time, even after one or both parties to it has died.

Matrimonial Causes Act 1973, s 11 provides that a marriage is void on the following grounds only:

(a)   that it is not a valid marriage [in that]:
    (i)   the parties are within the prohibited degrees of relationship;
    (ii)   either party is under the age of sixteen; or
    (iii)   the parties have intermarried in disregard of certain requirements as to the formation of marriage;
(b)   that at the time of the marriage either party was already lawfully married;
(c)   that the parties are not respectively male and female;

(d)   in the case of a polygamous marriage entered into outside England
        and Wales, that either party was at the time of the marriage
        domiciled in England and Wales.

For the purposes of para (d), a marriage is not polygamous if, at its inception,
neither party had any spouse additional to the other.

4.2.4   Polygamous and potentially polygamous marriages

Where the deceased and the claimant entered into a polygamous marriage
overseas under a law which permits polygamy, the marriage is recognised in
England and Wales, and the claimant may pursue a claim under the I(PFD)A
1975 as a spouse of the deceased. In *Re Sehota (Deceased), Kaur v Kaur*
[1978] 1 WLR 1506, the claimant and the deceased were married in India in
1937. The marriage was potentially polygamous under Indian law. In 1948 the
deceased married again. The deceased and his two wives subsequently
acquired English domicile. In 1976 the husband died, leaving his entire estate
to his second wife. The first wife applied for an order for financial provision
as a wife of the deceased. She was adjudged to be the wife of the deceased
notwithstanding that the marriage was polygamous. It was held that s 1(1)(a)
should be construed in the light of Matrimonial Proceedings (Polygamous
Marriages) Act 1972, s 1, under which matrimonial relief may be granted in
cases where the marriage is polygamous.

Under Matrimonial Causes Act 1973, s 11(d) (before it was amended – see
below), a marriage celebrated after 31 July 1971 was considered void if it was
a polygamous marriage entered into outside England and Wales and either
party was, at the time of the marriage, domiciled in England and Wales. Thus,
in *Hussain v Hussain* [1982] 3 All ER 369, a man domiciled in England and
Wales married a woman domiciled in Pakistan, where the law permits a man
to take more than one wife but does not extend the like right to women. It was
held that since, under the law of domicile of both parties, neither could enter
into a second marriage, the marriage was monogamous. Had the woman been
domiciled in England and Wales and the man in Pakistan, the marriage would
have been potentially polygamous as the man would have been permitted
under the law of Pakistan to take a second wife.

Private International Law (Miscellaneous Provisions) Act 1995, s 5, has,
however, amended Matrimonial Causes Act 1973, s 11, to provide that a
marriage entered into outside England and Wales in a country which permits
polygamy, by parties, neither of whom is already married, and where either
party to the marriage is domiciled in England and Wales, will be recognised as
a valid marriage under the law of England and Wales. The effect is to render

void only a marriage entered into in a foreign country by a person domiciled in England and Wales which is actually polygamous, not one which is potentially polygamous.

If a party to a marriage who is already legally married and is domiciled in England and Wales at the time he/she enters into a second marriage outside England and Wales, that marriage will be void.

4.2.5 Rights of spouse to void marriage under the I(PFD)A 1975

The rights of a party to a void marriage, if that marriage is subsisting at the time of the deceased's death are preserved by the provision of I(PFD)A 1975, s 25(4) provided certain conditions are satisfied. Section 25(4) provides:

> (4)   For the purposes of this Act any reference to a wife or husband shall be treated as including a reference to a person who in good faith entered into a void marriage with the deceased unless either–
>
> (a)   the marriage of the deceased and that person was dissolved or annulled during the lifetime of the deceased and the dissolution or annulment is recognised by the law of England and Wales; or
>
> (b)   that person has during the lifetime of the deceased formed a subsequent marriage or civil partnership

4.2.6 Marriage entered into in good faith

As will be observed, the provisions of I(PFD)A 1975, s 25(4) only apply if the claimant entered into a void marriage with the deceased in good faith and that marriage has not been dissolved or annulled during the lifetime of the deceased or the claimant has not during the lifetime of the deceased entered into another later marriage. Thus the claimant must have believed that the ceremony entered into was one of marriage and did not know or have reason to believe that the marriage was not a valid one. If the claimant was aware or had reason to suspect that the marriage for whatever reason was not valid, the claimant will fail to establish that it was entered into in good faith. The issue of whether the marriage between the deceased and the claimant is void but was entered into in good faith will be determined on the facts. An example of a case which illustrates the effect of the provisions of s 25(4) is the case of *Ghandi v Patel* [2002] 1 FLR 603. In that case the claimant had undergone, at an Indian restaurant in London, a Hindu ceremony of marriage with the deceased who was separated from his first wife, but whose marriage to his first wife was still subsisting at the date of his marriage to the claimant. The marriage between the claimant and the deceased was conducted to comply with the rituals and requirements of the Hindu faith but no effort was made to comply with the English legal requirements to constitute a lawful marriage. Thereafter the claimant and the deceased had a stormy and troubled relationship and, following the birth of their second child, they lived separate lives. The claimant had, during the lifetime of the deceased, issued proceedings against the deceased seeking the transfer to her of one of the deceased's properties. In those proceedings she maintained that she was not married to the deceased. On his death, she applied for financial provision under the Act on the basis that, while she accepted that her marriage to the deceased was void by reason of the bigamy, she had nevertheless entered into the marriage with the deceased in good faith and was therefore entitled to claim as his spouse. On the facts, the court held that the claimant had not established 'good faith' within the meaning of s 25(4) because marriage requires the participation of two people – a man and a woman – and the ceremony must purport to be a marriage of the kind contemplated by the Marriage Acts and must comply with the requirements of English law or purport to do so. On the evidence adduced it was held that the Hindu ceremony did not comply with the requirements of English law and did not purport to do so. The Hindu marriage did not give rise to a void marriage. It was a 'non-marriage'. It was further held that even if the ceremony had created a void marriage, by reason of its bigamous nature, known to the claimant, she had not entered into the marriage in good faith. Her claim therefore failed.

4.2.7   Distinction between void marriage and non-marriage

A distinction needs to be made between a void marriage and a non-marriage. A void marriage is one which falls within the provisions of Matrimonial Causes Act 1973, s 11. A non-marriage is one which is conducted in England or Wales but the ceremony of marriage is not of a kind contemplated by the Marriage Acts. The case of *Ghandi v Patel* (above) is a good illustration of a non-marriage.

4.2.8   Effect of annulment of void marriage to claim under the I(PFD)A 1975

Where a void marriage has been annulled, a party to it who has not remarried may claim as a former spouse. If the decree of nullity was granted within 12 months of the death of the deceased, under the provisions of I(PFD)A 1975, s 14, the claimant may be able to claim for financial provision as a surviving spouse (see para 4.4.1).

4.2.9 Voidable marriage

Matrimonial Causes Act 1973, s 12 provides that a marriage is voidable on the following grounds:

(a) that the marriage has not been consummated owing to the incapacity of either party to consummate it;

(b) that the marriage has not been consummated owing to the wilful refusal of the respondent to consummate it;

(c) that either party to the marriage did not validly consent to it, whether in consequence of duress, mistake, unsoundness of mind or otherwise;

(d) that at the time of the marriage either party, though capable of giving a valid consent, was suffering (whether continuously or intermittently) from mental disorder within the meaning of the Mental Health Act 1983 of such a kind or to such an extent as to be unfitted for marriage;

(e) that at the time of the marriage the respondent was suffering from venereal disease in a communicable form;

(f) that at the time of the marriage the respondent was pregnant by some person other than the petitioner.

4.2.10 Marriage with transsexual – Gender Recognition Act 2004

Before 4 April 2005, where a person's biological and sexual characteristics at birth were congruent, those characteristics determined the person's sex for the purposes of marriage. It was for the court to determine, by assessing the facts of the individual case, whether a person was male or female. In his dissenting judgment in *Bellinger v Bellinger* [2001] EWCA Civ 1140, [2002] 2 WLR 394, Thorpe LJ considered that other factors, including psychological considerations, should be considered by the court; that the family justice system should be sufficiently flexible to accommodate social change; and that one of the objectives of statute law reform and of the family justice system in this field must be to ensure that the law reacts to and reflects social change in the construction of existing statutory provisions. On appeal ([2003] UKHL 21, [2003] 2 WLR 1174), the House of Lords confirmed that, in determining whether a person was male or female for the purposes of Matrimonial Causes Act 1973, s 11(c), the test set out in *Corbett v Corbett (Otherwise Ashley)* [1971] P 83, still applied; and that any change in the law was a matter for Parliament, particularly as the Government had already announced its intention to introduce primary legislation on the subject. The House of Lords also held, however, that the non-recognition of gender change for the purpose of marriage was incompatible with Human Rights Convention, Arts 8 and 12, and made a declaration to that effect in respect of Matrimonial Causes Act 1973, s 11(c).

See also *Goodwin v United Kingdom* (2002) 35 EHRR 18 and *I v United Kingdom* [2002] 2 FLR 518, where the European Court of Human Rights held that to deny legal recognition to transsexuals was no longer sustainable and was a violation of their rights under Arts 8 and 12. As a result, the Gender Recognition Bill was introduced into Parliament in November 2003 and led to the Gender Recognition Act 2004 (GRA 2004) receiving Royal Assent on 1 July 2004. The GRA 2004 came into force on 4 April 2005. The GRA 2004 made provision for the establishment of a gender recognition panel with authority to issue gender recognition certificates to transsexuals who no longer wish to be associated with their birth gender. For a person to qualify for a gender recognition certificate he/she must provide a declaration stating that he/she has lived in the new gender for a period of at least 2 years; to confirm whether he/she is married; and any other information required by the panel or the Secretary of State. The application must be supported by medical evidence from a general practitioner, practising in gender dysphoria and one other medical practitioner or a chartered psychologist practising in gender dysphoria.

4.3   CIVIL PARTNER OF THE DECEASED

The CPA 2004 enables same sex couples to register a civil partnership. Once the partnership is registered it gives the same sex couple the same legal rights as those enjoyed by heterosexual couples who enter into a marriage. A civil partnership may be terminated on the ground of nullity or the partnership may be dissolved by one partner issuing a petition for dissolution of the partnership or a legal separation or, where appropriate, applying for a presumption of death order. The same rules apply to the dissolution of a civil partnership as they do to the dissolution of a marriage.

4.3.1   Proof of civil partnership

The production of a civil partnership registration certificate will suffice to establish proof of the civil partnership.

A civil partnership formed at the British Consulate outside England and Wales, Scotland and Northern Ireland, or in the case of the armed forces personnel at their barracks, will be recognised as valid, provided the conditions set out in CPA 2004, s 210 in the case of the former and s 211 in the case of the latter are met. Where the civil partnership has been registered in a foreign country under the laws of that country it will be recognised as valid (CPA 2004, s 215) on the production of a certified copy of the registration document.

4.3.2 Separation by decree of judicial separation

A separation order may be obtained by a civil partner on similar grounds as those under the Matrimonial Causes Act 1973 (CPA 2004, s 179) with like effect as a judicial separation order obtained by a married heterosexual couple. If the separation order was made within 12 months of the deceased's death, the provisions of I(PFD)A 1975, s 14A apply, subject to the conditions set out in that section (see para 4.5.1). Where the separation order was made over 12 months before the deceased's death, the claimant will not be entitled to receive the same financial provisions which a widow/widower of the deceased would be entitled to receive. Where the separation was by agreement but a separation order has not been obtained, the claimant will be entitled to make a claim as a spouse of the deceased.

4.3.3 Void civil partnership

A nullity of the partnership may be obtained if the parties to the civil partnership were not eligible to register as civil partners or there was some irregularity in the registration of the partnership and both parties were aware of it at the time of registration.

A civil partnership will be considered void if the couple or either of them was not eligible to register as civil partners. CPA 2004, s 138(1) provides that two people are not eligible to register as civil partners of each other if:

(a) they are not of the same sex,
(b) either of them is already a civil partner or lawfully married,
(c) either of them is under 16,
(d) they are within prohibited degrees of relationship, or
(e) either of them is incapable of understanding the nature of the civil partnership.

For those who are within the 'prohibited degree of relationship', see CPA 2004, Sch 12.

A civil partnership will also be void where if at the time the parties entered into the civil partnership they both knew: (1) that the notice of proposed civil partnership has not been given; (2) that the civil partnership document has not been duly issued; (3) that the civil partnership document is void under CPA 2004, s 17(3) or s 27(2) (registration after end of time allowed for registering); (4) that the place of registration is a place other than that specified in the notices of proposed civil partnership and the civil partnership document; and

(5) that the civil partnership registrar is not present. It will also be void if the civil partnership document is void under CPA 2004, Sch 2, para 6(5).

4.3.4   Voidable civil partnership

A civil partnership will be considered voidable if:

(1)   either of the parties did not validly consent to its formation (whether as a result of duress, mistake, unsoundness of mind or otherwise);

(2)   at the time of its formation either of them, though capable of giving a valid consent, was suffering (whether continuously or intermittently) from a mental disorder of such a kind or to such an extent as to be unfit for civil partnership;

(3)   at the time of its formation, the respondent was pregnant by some person other than the applicant;

(4)   an interim gender recognition under the Gender Recognition Act 2004 has after the time of its formation been issued to either civil partner;

(5)   the respondent is a person whose gender at the time of its formation had become the acquired gender under the 2004 Act.

A nullity order will not however be granted where the applicant to such an order conducted him/herself in relation to the respondent to the application in such a way as to lead the respondent reasonably to believe that he/she would not seek to do so and that it would be unjust to the respondent to make the order (CPA 2004, s 51).

4.3.5   Civil partnership entered into in good faith

As in the case of a heterosexual couple, I(PFD)A 1975, s 25(4A) preserves the position of a person who entered into a void civil partnership in good faith. Section 25(4A) provides:

> For the purposes of this Act any reference to a civil partner shall be treated as including a reference to a person who in good faith entered into a void civil partnership with the deceased unless either–
>
> (a)   the civil partnership between the deceased and that person was dissolved or annulled during the lifetime of the deceased and the dissolution or annulment is recognised by the law of England and Wales; or

(b)   that person has during the lifetime of the deceased formed a
        subsequent civil partnership or marriage.

See, further, para 4.2.5.

4.3.6   Effect of dissolution or annulment of civil partnership

On the dissolution or annulment of the civil partnership civil partners are
entitled to apply for financial ancillary relief. The financial provisions to
which they are entitled mirror those which are available to heterosexual
couples on the dissolution or nullity of their marriage. Civil partners have the
same rights to make a claim under the I(PFD)A 1975 on the death of one of
the civil partners as heterosexual couples. The Act has been amended by the
CPA 2004 to give civil partners the same status and rights as a spouse.

4.3.7   Effect of marriage overseas between same sex couples

The effect of a marriage entered into by two people of the same sex in a
foreign country where such a marriage was recognised as valid was
considered by the English court in *Wilkinson v Kitzinger and another (No 2)*
[2006] EWHC 2022 (Fam), [2007] 1 FLR 295. The court held that where two
persons of the same sex, who are both domiciled in England and Wales, go
through a ceremony of marriage overseas in a country which recognises such a
marriage, the English courts will treat the relationship between the couple as a
civil partnership under CPA 2004, ss 212–218 and not a marriage.

In *Wilkinson v Kitzinger and another (No 2)* [2006] EWHC 2022 (Fam), [2007]
1 FLR 295, two women both domiciled in England and Wales went through a
ceremony of marriage in British Columbia, where such a marriage was valid.
Both women argued that the provision of Matrimonial Causes Act 1973, s
11(c) which only recognises a marriage between a man and woman violated
their rights under Human Rights Convention, Arts 8, 12 and 14. Alternatively,
it was submitted that the English court should recognise the marriage on the
basis that the capacity to marry was governed by the law of each party's
domicile prior to the marriage. Both arguments were rejected. The court held
that in making the provisions contained in the CPA 2004, Parliament had
created a legal framework to address the inequality of treatment to those in
same sex relationships by making the provisions contained in ss 212–218,
whilst enforcing the institution of marriage. The parties' rights under the
Convention had thus not been infringed.

4.3.8   Effect on claim made by surviving spouse or civil partner by the marriage or subsequent civil partnership before the claim is determined

To qualify as a spouse, or a former spouse, or surviving civil partner or former partner of the deceased, the claimant must not have remarried at the date when proceedings are issued. It matters not whether any such remarriage is void or voidable. I(PFD)A 1975, s 25(5) provides that:

> Any reference in this Act to the formation of, or a person who has formed, a subsequent marriage or civil partnership includes (as the case may be) a reference to the formation of, or to a person who has formed, a marriage or civil partnership which is by law void or voidable.

If, therefore, the surviving spouse or civil partner of the deceased remarries or enters into a subsequent civil partnership whilst an application under the I(PFD)A 1975 for financial provision is pending that will not affect his/her status as the surviving spouse or civil partner as long as the application was issued before the remarriage or subsequent civil partnership. It is however, likely to affect the decision of the court when it considers the factors which the court has to consider under s 3 (see Chapter 7) in determining whether the deceased made reasonable financial provisions for the applicant and if not, the extent of the provision which the court should provide in the circumstances.

4.4   FORMER SPOUSE OF THE DECEASED WHO HAS NOT REMARRIED

A 'former spouse' means a person whose marriage with the deceased was, during the lifetime of the deceased:

(1)   dissolved or annulled by a decree of divorce or of nullity of marriage granted under the law of any part of the British Islands; or

(2)   dissolved or annulled in any country or territory outside the British Islands by a divorce or annulment which is entitled to be recognised as valid by the law of England and Wales (I(PFD)A 1975, s 25, as amended by the MFPA 1984, as from 16 September 1985); and

(3)   that person has not remarried before the death of the deceased.

Where a decree nisi has been granted, but the deceased dies before the decree has been made absolute, the marriage is regarded as subsisting and the claimant is eligible to make a claim as the spouse of the deceased. The court is, however, entitled to have regard to any financial settlement reached between the parties or ordered by the court when considering what, if any, financial provision should be ordered (see, further, paras 4.4.2 and 4.4.5 and Chapter 7).

Family Law Act 1986, s 44(1) provides that:

> subject to section 52(4) and (5)(a) of this Act, no divorce or annulment obtained in any part of the British Islands shall be regarded as effective in any part of the United Kingdom unless granted by a court of civil jurisdiction.

4.4.1 Overseas divorce and talaq

The validity of an overseas divorce, annulment or legal separation obtained by means of proceedings must be recognised if the divorce, annulment or legal separation is effective under the law of the country in which it is obtained, and at the relevant date either party to the marriage (Family Law Act 1986, s 46(1)):

(a) was habitually resident in the country in which the divorce, annulment or legal separation was obtained; or

(b) was domiciled in that country; or

(c) was a national of that country.

The validity of an overseas divorce, annulment or legal separation obtained otherwise than by means of proceedings must be recognised if the divorce, annulment or legal separation is effective under the law of the country in which it was obtained, and at the relevant date (Family Law Act 1986, s 46(2)):

(a) each party to the marriage was domiciled in that country; or

(b) either party to the marriage was domiciled in that country and the other party was domiciled in a country under whose law the divorce, annulment or legal separation is recognised as valid; and

(c) neither party to the marriage was habitually resident in the United Kingdom throughout the period of one year immediately preceding that date.

In *Sulaiman v Juffali* [2002] 1 FLR 479, both parties were Saudi nationals of, and domiciled in, Saudi Arabia. They were married in Saudi Arabia. In 2001 the husband pronounced a bare talaq in England and then registered it with a Sharia court in Saudi Arabia, thus dissolving the marriage under Sharia law as applied in Saudi Arabia. The wife issued divorce proceedings in England. The husband contested the proceedings on a number of grounds including the fact the marriage had already been dissolved. It was held, applying the provisions of Family Law Act 1986, s 44(1) that, irrespective of the parties' domicile and religion, informal divorces obtained in England and Wales otherwise than by proceedings in a court of civil jurisdiction will not be recognised. A bare talaq pronounced in England does not therefore operate to dissolve the marriage because it is not obtained in any proceedings in a court of civil jurisdiction.

In *El Fadl v El Fadl* [2000] 1 FLR 175, however, it was held that the pronouncement of the talaq before witnesses, which was registered by a Lebanese Sharia court that was properly convened and took formal declarations, was a divorce obtained by means of proceedings, although the Sharia court did not have judicial jurisdiction to make it. See also *Wicken v Wicken* [1999] 1 FLR 293, where a letter of divorce was recognised.

For other cases where talaq has been considered, see *Quazi v Quazi* [1980] AC 744 (HL), *R v Secretary of State for the Home Department ex parte Ghulam Fatima* [1986] AC 527 and *Chaudhary v Chaudhary* [1985] Fam 19.

It should be noted that Family Law Act 1986, Part II does not apply where Council Regulation (EC) No 1347/2000 of 29 May 2000 on the jurisdiction, recognition and enforcement of judgments in matrimonial matters and in matters of parental responsibility for joint children [2000] OJ L160/19, Arts 14–20 apply. These Articles require that a judgment given in a Member State relating to divorce, annulment of marriage or legal separation is to be recognised in any other Member State without any special procedure being required; and that recognition may not be refused because the law of the Member State in which recognition is sought would not have allowed the dissolution or annulment of the marriage or a legal separation on the same facts (Art 18).

Article 15(1) of the Regulation provides:

> A judgment relating to a divorce, legal separation or marriage annulment shall not be recognised:
> (a)   if such a recognition is manifestly contrary to the public policy of the Member State in which recognition is sought;
> (b)   where it was given in default of appearance, if the respondent was not served with the document which instituted the proceedings or with an equivalent document in sufficient time and in such a way as to enable the respondent to arrange for his or her defence unless it is determined that the respondent has accepted the judgment unequivocally;
> (c)   if it is irreconcilable with a judgment given in proceedings between the same parties in the Member State in which recognition is sought;

(d)   if it is irreconcilable with an earlier judgment given in another Member State or in a non-Member State between the same parties, provided that the earlier judgment fulfils the conditions necessary for its recognition in the Member State in which recognition is sought.

Article 16 provides that a court of a Member State may, on the basis of an agreement on the recognition and enforcement of judgments, not recognise a judgment given in another Member State. Under Art 19, 'under no circumstances may a judgment be reviewed as to its substance'.

Prior to the enactment of the MFPA 1984, a person whose marriage was dissolved in a foreign country was not eligible to apply for financial provision under the I(PFD)A 1975 as a former spouse of the deceased. MFPA 1984, s 25 now enables a person whose marriage was dissolved outside England and Wales to apply for an order under I(PFD)A 1975, s 2.

4.4.2   Application of I(PFD)A 1975, section 14

In cases where, within 12 months from the date on which a decree of divorce or nullity has been made absolute, or a decree of judicial separation has been granted, a party to the marriage dies and an application for financial relief or property adjustment order under Matrimonial Causes Act 1973, ss 23 and 24 has not been made by the other party to the marriage, or such an application has been made but is pending at the time of the death of the deceased, the spouse may apply for an order under I(PFD)A 1975, s 2 and the court has power, if it thinks it just to do so, to treat the surviving spouse as if the decree of divorce or nullity of marriage had not been made absolute. Similar principles apply where a decree of judicial separation has been granted but only if at the date of death of the deceased the decree was in force and the separation was continuing (s 14).

4.5   FORMER CIVIL PARTNER OF THE DECEASED

A 'former civil partner' means a person whose civil partnership with the deceased was during the lifetime of the deceased either (I(PFD)A 1975, s 25(1)):

(a)   dissolved or annulled by an order made under the law of any part of the British Islands, or

(b)   dissolved or annulled in any country or territory outside the British
       Islands by a dissolution or annulment which is entitled to be
       recognised as valid by the law of England and Wales.

See, further, para 4.5.

4.5.2   Application of I(PFD)A 1975, section 14A

Similar provision as apply to heterosexual married couples has now been
included in the I(PFD)A 1975 to provide equality to civil partners. Section
14A provides that where in relation to a civil partnership one of the civil
partner dies within 12 months from the date on which a dissolution order,
nullity order, separation order or presumption of death order has been made,
and an application for financial relief or a property adjustment order under
CPA 2004, Sch 5, Part 1 or Part 2 has not been made by the other civil partner
or such an application has been made but the proceedings on the application
have not been determined at the time of the death of the deceased, then if an
application is made by the surviving partner for an order under I(PFD)A 1975,
s 2, the court has the power, if it thinks it just to do so, to treat the surviving
civil partner as if the civil partnership was subsisting save that in the case of a
separation order this principle would apply only if the separation order was
still in force at the date of the death of the deceased and the separation was
continuing.

4.6   HETEROSEXUAL COHABITANT OF THE DECEASED

I(PFD)A 1975, s 1(1)(ba) and (1A), introduced by the Law Reform (Succession)
Act 1995, extended the categories of person who may apply for financial
provision to include a cohabitant of the deceased. A cohabitant is, however,
eligible to apply as a cohabitant only if the deceased died on or after 1 January
1996, and, during the whole of the period of 2 years ending immediately before
the date when the deceased died, the person was living:

(1)   in the same household as the deceased; and
(2)   as the husband or wife of the deceased.

This provision was introduced in response to cases such as *Bishop v Plumley*
[1991] 1 WLR 582 (CA), where the claimant had to prove 'dependency' in
order to succeed. The revised provisions are, however, subject to certain
limitations. There are three conditions which must be satisfied to establish
eligibility, namely:

(1)　Cohabitation must have continued for the 'whole of the two years immediately before the death of the deceased'. There are two separate ingredients to this provision:
　　(a)　the whole of the period of 2 years; and
　　(b)　immediately before the death of the deceased.

(2)　The claimant must prove that he/she was living in the same household as the deceased (see *Re Watson*, below). This means living together as one unit, and does not include living in the same property but as two separate independent entities.

(3)　The claimant must prove that he/she was living 'as the husband or wife or as the civil partner of the deceased'.

4.6.1　Whole of the 2 years immediately before the date when the deceased died

The words 'whole of the two years' implies that there must have been continuous cohabitation without a break for the full 2 years and if this cannot be proved the claim will fail. It is submitted, however, that where the evidence establishes that, although the parties may have been physically apart, and their separation was not voluntary, the relationship was continuing and the household was being maintained as a single unit for both the deceased and the claimant, the claim should be allowed. To rule otherwise would mean a total disregard of social and economic changes which compel couples to be apart for short periods, for example, where one partner has to work away from home or is posted overseas for a short time, or one partner has to care for a sick relative or has, by agreement, taken a holiday without the other.

Likewise, the second ingredient, 'ending immediately before the date when the deceased died', should not, it is suggested, be applied too strictly. If the test relating to claimants under I(PFD)A 1975, s 1(1)(e) is applied (see para 4.9), where the language of the statute is 'immediately before the death of the deceased', then, if cohabitation has ceased, no matter for how short a period, s 1(1A) may not apply. It is submitted that a common sense approach should be taken and the provision interpreted to allow for circumstances beyond the parties' control which cause cohabitation to cease or to be interrupted immediately before the death of the deceased. The test applied under the Matrimonial Causes Act 1973, to cases of separation for 2 or 5 years, where the relationship is not regarded as at an end if separation has been brought about by illness, should be applied.

In *Jelley v Iliffe* [1981] Fam 128, Griffiths LJ held that:

The words 'immediately before the death of the deceased' in section 1(1)(e) cannot be construed literally as applying to the de facto situation at death but refer to the general arrangements for maintenance subsisting at the time of death. So that if, for example the deceased had been making regular payments to the support of an old friend, the claim would not be defeated if those payments ceased during a terminal illness because the deceased was too ill to make them.

An admission to hospital followed by death in hospital, for example, is a circumstance where the parties would be physically separated immediately before death but neither would have regarded their relationship as at an end. The break in the cohabitation could not be regarded as one of choice and should be disregarded as constituting an act of separation. The issue is not simply whether the deceased and the claimant were physically living together, but whether they remained bound together emotionally and socially and did not consider their relationship at an end (see *Gully v Dix*, below).

Although the above two issues were not argued in the case of *Re Watson* [1999] 1 FLR 878, the judgment of Neuberger J supports the view set out above. In *Re Watson*, the claimant and the deceased had had a relationship for over 30 years. From 1995 until April 1996, when the deceased died, the arrangement between them had been that the deceased provided the running living costs for both of them and the claimant looked after the home and contributed towards the service bills. They did not share the same bedroom and did not have a sexual relationship. The deceased was taken into hospital about 3 weeks before his death. Neuberger J (as he then was) held that:

> So far as s 1(1A) is concerned, it is not in dispute that during the whole of the period of two years ending immediately before the date when [Mr Watson] died Miss Griffiths was living ... in the same household as [Mr Watson]. The Treasury Solicitor has not argued that Miss Griffiths' application should fail because this condition was not satisfied during the last three weeks of Mr. Watson's life when he was in hospital, and it is right to record that, in my view, that is not an argument which could respectably have been advanced. In the first place as a matter of ordinary language, the fact that someone is in hospital for a period, possibly for a long period, at the end of which he dies, does not mean that, before his death, he ceased to be part of the household of which he was part, until he was forced by illness to go to hospital, and to which he would have returned had he not died. Secondly, even if it had involved straining the language of section 1(1A) of the Act to arrive at that result, it would appear to me to be appropriate so to do; it would be contrary to the whole purpose and thrust of the section, if someone, who otherwise fell within it, was wholly deprived of its benefit because the deceased had been forced to spend time in hospital immediately prior to his death. Even if the deceased had returned from hospital for his last few days of life, as not infrequently occurs, a person who otherwise fell within section 1(1A) of the Act might still be

deprived of its benefit if the Treasury Solicitor's concession is wrong, because it could then be argued that the deceased and the applicant were not 'living ... in the same household' for 'the whole of the period of two years ending with the death'.

This view has been applied in more recent cases. In *Baynes v Hedger and Others* [2008] EWHC 1587 (Ch), [2008] 2 FLR 1805, also at [2009] EWCA Civ 374, [2009] 2 FLR 767, CA (for the facts, see para 7.4), the court confirmed that where two people are living in the same household they will not necessarily stop doing so merely because they are temporarily separated.

In *Lindop v Agus, Bass and Hedley* [2009] EWHC 14 (Ch), [2009] Fam Law 808, the deceased and the claimant had begun a relationship in 2001 and in 2002 she moved in to live with the deceased in his house. However, she maintained a postal address at her father's house. In determining her claim as a cohabitant of the deceased the court held that there was nothing inconsistent in her relationship as a cohabitant of the deceased whilst at the same time maintaining a postal address elsewhere.

Guidance may also be found in the test applied in matrimonial cases where the court has had to determine whether the parties to a petition have lived separate and apart for the relevant period. Enforced periods of separation are brought about by external factors such as where the couple have spent time away from each other whilst on holiday or to get medical treatment, or where their circumstances compel one or both to live apart due to work commitments, or for example where the separation is due to the absence of the husband at sea (see *Lilley v Lilley* [1960] P 158). It implies the fact of physical separation as well as the intention to bring cohabitation between the parties to an end. (See *Santos v Santos* [1972] Fam 247 where the court considered the issue of whether the parties had been living separate and apart and when it could be inferred that they had made that decision.)

Much will depend on the factual circumstances, the evidence to support the case and the evidence adduced by those who wish to challenge the claim.

4.6.2 Living in the same household

The claimant must prove that he/she was living in the same household as the deceased (see *Re Watson*). This means living together as one unit, and does not include living in the same property but as two separate independent entities. The nature of their relationship will be the deciding factor.

The issue is not simply whether the deceased and the claimant were physically living together, but whether they remained bound together emotionally and socially and did not consider their relationship at an end:

> The relevant word is 'household' not 'house' . . . Thus they will be in the same household if they are tied by their relationship. The tie of that relationship may be made manifest by various elements, not simply their living together under the same roof, but the public and private acknowledgement of the mutual protection and support that binds them together. In former days one would possibly say one should look at the whole consortium vitae. For present purposes it is sufficient to ask whether either has demonstrated a settled acceptance or recognition that the relationship is in truth at an end. If the circumstances show an irrevocable breakdown of the relationship, then they no longer live in the same household and the Act is not satisfied. If, however, the interruption is transitory, serving as a pause for reflection about the future of a relationship going through difficult times but still recognised to be subsisting, then they will be living together in the same household and the claim will lie. (Ward LJ in *Gully v Dix* [2004] 1 FLR 918)

In *Gully v Dix*, the claimant, who had lived with the deceased for about 27 years, had left him following an incident when he had threatened her with a knife. She had then remained apart from him for about 3 months during which time the deceased had telephoned the claimant's daughter on several occasions to ask the claimant to come back. The daughter did not pass on the messages to her mother for fear that she would return to live with the deceased. It was held that on the facts the relationship had not ended. The deceased had genuinely wanted the claimant to return home and the claimant would have returned had she known of the deceased's telephone calls.

In *Re Watson* (above), where the couple had lived together and had sexual relations in the early years of that relation but in the latter they had abstained from sexual relationship, Neuberger J (as he then was) held that when considering whether a person falls within I(PFD)A 1975, s 1(1A) one must 'beware of indulging in too much over-analysis'. The court should take account of the multifarious nature of marital relationships and should 'ask itself whether, in the opinion of a reasonable person with normal perceptions, it could be said that the two people in question were living together as husband and wife'. The deceased's assumption of responsibility for the applicant and the nature and length of the relationship were relevant factors.

The claimant's continued links with his/her country of origin, the fact that he/she continued to retain a property there and had a child by a previous relationship are also relevant factors in considering whether the relationship between the deceased and the applicant was one as a cohabitants or simply as a dependant. In *Witkowska v Kaminiski* [2006] EWHC 1940 (Ch), [2007] 1 FLR 1547 on balance on the facts, the court found that the claimant had been cohabiting with the deceased before his death notwithstanding the fact that she had retained a property in Poland in which her son lived. Although she repeatedly returned to Poland the deceased had transferred funds to her and she and the deceased had conducted a close relationship for about 5 years before his death.

In an earlier case of *Kotke v Saffarini* [2005] EWCA Civ 221, [2005] 2 FLR 517, the court had held that the retention of a property which was used occasionally by the claimant was not in itself a barrier to establishing that the deceased and the claimant were cohabiting together as husband and wife unless it was clear that they had not committed themselves to such an arrangement. The fact that a couple have cohabited together but ceased to have sexual intercourse for 2 years and all communication between them has been conducted by written notes does not necessarily lead to the conclusion that their relationship has come to an end, but is comparable to a marriage in the last stages of breaking up (see *Adeoso v Adeoso* [1980] 1 WLR 1535, CA).

Cases decided under the Fatal Accidents Act 1976, the Rent Act 1977, the Housing Act 1988 and the Matrimonial Causes Act 1973 have been considered by the court when determining the issue of whether the deceased and the claimant were cohabiting in the same household immediately before the deceased's death.

It will be observed from the examples given above that success or otherwise of a claim under this head will depend very much on the circumstances of the individual case, the evidence adduced by both the claimant and those who are seeking to challenge the claim and the assessment of that evidence by the court.

4.6.3 As the husband and wife of the deceased

Third, the claimant must prove that he/she was living 'as the husband or wife or civil partner of the deceased'. The case of civil partnership is considered below.

This rules out cases where the parties were living in the same household but in a relationship other than that of a husband and wife. It is not necessary to prove that the claimant and the deceased were in a sexual relationship as long as they were in a relationship which was for all intents and purposes that of a couple cohabiting together. In *Re Watson* (above), Neuberger J (as he then was) held that when considering whether two people are living together as husband and wife it would be wrong to conclude that they do so simply because their relationship is one which a husband and wife would have. If the test were as wide as that, then, bearing in mind the enormous variety of relationships that can exist between husband and wife, virtually every relationship between a man and a woman living in the same household would fall within I(PFD)A 1975, s 1(1A). When considering whether the claimant was living as the wife or husband of the deceased the court should determine the matter by asking whether, in the opinion of a reasonable person with normal perceptions, it could be said that the two people were living together as husband and wife, although the multifarious nature of marital relationships should not be ignored.

In an earlier decision, *Adeoso v Adeoso* [1980] 1 WLR 1535 (CA), where the court was concerned with the provisions of Domestic Violence and Matrimonial Proceedings Act 1976, s 1(2), the parties were living together but had not had a sexual relationship with each other for 2 years. They slept in separate bedrooms. They had not spoken to each other and had communicated with each other only by way of notes. The applicant had stopped cooking and washing for the respondent. The Court of Appeal held that the parties' relationship was comparable to a marriage in the last stages of breakdown, and the fact that the parties had severed their living arrangements did not mean that they were living in different households (see, further, para 4.6.2).

4.6.4   Same sex cohabitants post-5 December 2005

By reason of the amendments made to the I(PFD)A 1975 by the CPA 2004 same sex couples who are in a relationship but have not entered into a civil partnership have the same rights as heterosexual couples if, for the whole of the period of 2 years ending immediately before the date when the deceased died, the person was living (I(PFD)A 1975, s 1(1B)):

    (a)   in the same household as the deceased, and
    (b)   as the civil partner of the deceased.

If these conditions are not met it may still be possible to make a claim under s 1(1)(e) (see para 4.8).

4.6.5   Same sex cohabitants pre-5 December 2005

The CPA 2004 came into force on 20 December 2007 so cases under the new provision are unlikely to surface for some time. Arguments raised in cases decided by the courts in statutory provisions other than the I(PFD)A 1975 will have to be relied upon and enforced with those brought about by the CPA 2004.

I(PFD)A 1975, s 1(1A) before its amendment, refers to the claimant living 'as the husband and wife of the deceased'. 'Cohabitant' is not defined in the Act as amended. There is no specific reference to gender in s 1(1A), and therefore the provision is capable of being construed as applying to both heterosexual and homosexual relationships. There are no decided cases on this issue under the Act, but Family Law Act 1996, s 62 defines 'cohabitants' as 'a man and a woman who, although not married to each other, are living together as husband and wife'. It is submitted that recent decisions under the Rent Act 1977, in matrimonial proceedings, and of the European Court of Human Rights under the Human Rights Convention, suggest that the I(PFD)A 1975 should apply to same sex relationships.

In the cases under the Rent Act 1977, the courts have overcome the problem by two separate routes. In *Fitzpatrick v Sterling Housing Association Ltd* [1998] Ch 304, the appellant and the tenant lived together for 17 years in a loving, faithful, monogamous homosexual relationship. When the tenant suffered a stroke the appellant gave up work and nursed him for 8 years. The issue for consideration was whether, as the homosexual partner of the lawful tenant, he was entitled to succeed to a statutory tenancy under Rent Act 1977, Sch 1, paras 2(2) and 3(1) as a 'person living with the original tenant as his or her wife or husband' or as 'a member of the original tenant's family'. The Court of Appeal, by a majority, held that the provisions applied only to heterosexual relationships and that only persons who were bound together by the ties of kinship could be regarded as 'member[s] of the original tenant's family'. Ward LJ, in his dissenting judgment, stated that if a gay couple was asked in what manner they lived together, the couple's answer would not be different from that given by a heterosexual couple save only in the one respect – that in their case their sexual relations were homosexual, not heterosexual:

> no distinction can sensibly be drawn between the two couples in terms of love, nurturing, fidelity, durability, emotional and economic inter-dependence – to name but some and by no means all of the hallmarks of a relationship between a husband and his wife with regard to the only distinguishing feature, sexual activity, that is a function of the relationship of a husband and wife, a man and his mistress and it is a function of homosexual lovers. That the activity takes place between members of different sexes or of the same sex is a matter of form not function ... I would say that there is no essential difference between a homosexual and a heterosexual couple and accordingly, I would find that the appellant had lived with the deceased tenant as his husband and wife ... The common man may be vaguely disapproving of the homosexual relationship which is not for him but having shrugged his shoulders, he would recognise that the relationship was to all intents and purposes a marriage between those partners. They lived a life akin to that of any husband and wife. They were so bound together that they constituted a family.

On appeal, the House of Lords (now the Supreme Court) concluded that the appellant could not be treated as the spouse of the deceased tenant because the language of the statutory provisions could be interpreted as referring only to heterosexual relationships, but stressed that this interpretation was confined to the particular provision of the Rent Act 1977. However, in *Mendoza v Ghaidan* [2002] EWCA Civ 1533, [2003] 1 FLR 468, the application of Rent Act 1977, Sch 1, para 2(1) as amended was considered again by the Court of Appeal in a case involving a same sex relationship. It was held that Sch 1, para 2(1) as construed by *Fitzpatrick v Sterling Housing Association Ltd* infringed Human Rights Convention, Art 14. Having regard to its duty under the Human Rights Act 1998, the court concluded that the words of the section 'as his or her wife or husband' should be read to mean 'as if they were his or her wife or husband'. On appeal, the House of Lords affirmed the decision of the Court of Appeal. In his leading judgment, Lord Nicholls of Birkenhead said, 'A homosexual couple, as much as a heterosexual couple, share each other's life and make their home together. They have an equivalent relationship. There is no rational or fair ground for distinguishing the one couple from the other in this context'.

The protection afforded to a cohabiting heterosexual couple is therefore equally applicable to the survivor of a homosexual couple. (See also *Saunders v Garrett* [2005] WTLR 749 (case under the I(PFD)A 1975) where the court applying the principles set out in *Fitzpatrick v Sterling Housing Association Ltd* concluded that the applicant who had been in a same sex relationship with the deceased was entitled to make the application for financial provision under I(PFD)A 1975, s 1(1)(ba).) As the law stood then, the court was obliged to take account of the Human Rights Convention and Human Rights Act 1998, s 3, which requires the court to read in words which change the meaning of enacted legislation, so as to make it Convention-compliant. The court can therefore modify the meaning of provisions to make it Convention-compliant. Hence it is possible in order to make the provisions of the I(PFD)A 1975 Convention-compliant to give it an interpretation which is expansive and which provides equality of treatment to same sex couples when there is no legitimate reason justifying discrimination. (See also *M v Secretary of State for Works and Pensions; Langley v Bradford Metropolitan District Council* [2004] EWCA Civ 1343, [2005] 1 FLR 498 where the court construed the words to read 'as if he had been the husband or wife of the deceased'.)

These cases and the duty to make any provision Convention-compliant justify pursuing a claim on the basis that the same sex claimant is eligible to make such a claim. In any event, such a claimant may have a good case under I(PFD)A 1975, s 1(1)(e) as a person who immediately before the death of the deceased was being maintained whether wholly or partly by the deceased.

4.7 CHILD OF THE DECEASED

A 'child' includes:

(1)   an illegitimate child;

(2)   a child *en ventre sa mere* (ie a child who has been conceived but not born at the death of the deceased (I(PFD)A 1975, s 25(1));

(3)   an adult child (see *Re Coventry, Coventry v Coventry* [1980] Ch 461 and *Re Callaghan (Deceased)* [1985] Fam 1);

(4)   an adopted child, that is, a child adopted in England and Wales or in any foreign country if the adoption is recognised in England and Wales.

4.7.1   Presumption of legitimacy

Where the parents of a child were married to each other at the time of his/her birth the presumption of legitimacy arises and the husband of the mother is presumed to be the father of the child unless the contrary is proved. The presumption can be relied on to prove parenthood until the presumption is rebutted. A certified copy of the claimant's birth certificate is regarded as sufficient evidence of legitimacy provided it contains the relevant information on parenthood. If an appropriate birth certificate is not available and there is no other evidence to prove the claimant's parenthood, an order for DNA profiling to be carried out could be applied for.

Where a child is born not later than the period of gestation after the marriage has been dissolved, the presumption of legitimacy may arise. In *Re Overbury (Deceased)* [1955] Ch 122, a child was born less than 9 months from the date when the mother's first marriage was dissolved but during the subsistence of her second marriage. On the basis of the common law presumption of legitimacy the child was presumed to be the child of both the former husband and the mother's current husband. The court ruled, on the evidence, that the child was the legitimate child of the first husband. Today, however, the matter would be established by DNA profiling, not by legal presumption or inference.

4.7.2   Legitimation

Where the parents of an illegitimate child marry then, provided that the father is domiciled in England and Wales at the time of the marriage, the child is legitimated at the date of the marriage (Legitimacy Act 1976, s 2). Where the father is not domiciled in England and Wales at the date of the marriage the child is legitimated if the law of the domicile of the father legitimates the child by marriage (Legitimacy Act 1976, s 3).

4.7.3   Legitimation and same sex female partners

The Legitimacy Act 1976 as amended by the HFEA 2008 now provides for a child born to same sex female couples who subsequently enter into a civil partnership to be legitimated. Legitimacy Act 1976, s 2A provides that where:

(a)   a person ('the child') has a parent ('the female parent') by virtue of section 43 of the Human Fertilisation and Embryology Act 2008 (treatment provided to woman who agrees that second woman to be parent);

(b)   at the time of the child's birth, the female parent and the child's mother are not civil partners of each other;

(c)   the female parent and the child's mother subsequently enter into a civil partnership; and

(d)   the female parent is at the date of the formation of the civil partnership domiciled in England and Wales,

the civil partnership shall render the child, if living, legitimate from the date of the formation of the civil partnership.

Where the female parent is domiciled outside England and Wales at the time of the formation of the civil partnership, Legitimacy Act 1976, s 3 as amended to include sub-section (2), now provides that where:

(a)   a person ('the child') has a parent ('the female parent') by virtue of section 43 of the Human Fertilisation and Embryology Act 2008 (treatment provided to woman who agrees that second woman to be parent);

(b)   at the time of the child's birth, the female parent and the child's mother are not civil partners of each other;

(c)   the female parent and the child's mother subsequently enter into a civil partnership; and

(d)   the female parent is not at the time of the formation of the civil partnership domiciled in England and Wales but is domiciled in a country by the law of which the child became legitimated by virtue of the civil partnership,

the child, if living shall in England and Wales be recognised as having been so legitimated from the date of the formation of the civil partnership notwithstanding that, at the time of the child's birth, the female parent was domiciled in a country the law of which did not permit legitimation by subsequent partnership.

4.7.4 Child of void marriage

Legitimacy Act 1976, s 1 as amended provides that a child of a void marriage, whenever born, shall, subject to I(PFD)A 1975, s 1(2) and Sch 1, be treated as the legitimate child of his/her parents if at the time of the insemination resulting in the birth, or where there was no such insemination, the child's conception (or at the time of the celebration of the marriage if later), both or either of the parties reasonably believed that the marriage was valid. For this provision to apply, the father of the child must be domiciled in England and Wales at the time of the birth or, if he died before the birth, he must have been so domiciled immediately before his death (s 1(2)).

The phrase 'child of a void marriage' does not extend to an illegitimate child born before the void marriage took place. Such a child is not the child of a void marriage but a child of his/her parents; the child is not legitimated by the subsequent void marriage of the parents. Section 1(1) applies only to a child born after a void marriage has been celebrated (see *Re Spence (Deceased)* [1990] Ch 652).

A child born or conceived during the subsistence of the marriage is legitimated notwithstanding the subsequent annulment of the marriage (Matrimonial Causes Act 1973, s 16).

4.7.5 Adopted child

A child of the deceased who is adopted after the death of his/her biological parent but before making a claim under the I(PFD)A 1975 is not a child of the deceased within the meaning of s 1(1)(c). This applies whether the adoption order was made under the Adoption Act 1976 or the Adoption and Children Act 2002. An adopted child is not eligible to make a claim under the I(PFD)A 1975 because, by virtue of Adoption Act 1976, s 39(2) and Adoption and Children Act 2002, s 67, an adopted child is treated in law as the child of the adopters and as such loses the right to make a claim against the estate of his/her biological parent. He/she is treated in law as the child of the adopters in all respects and a testamentary disposition made before the child was adopted by the adopters will be interpreted so as to give the adopted child inheritance rights under the disposition. An adopted child is thus eligible to make a claim under the I(PFD)A 1975 as the child of his/her adoptive parent.

The provisions of the Adoption Acts are not retrospective so that an illegitimate child who is adopted by his/her father cannot inherit under a will made prior to the statutory provisions coming into effect (see *Timothy Everard Upton v National Westminster Bank plc and Others* [2004] (Lawtel)).

However, this interpretation was not followed in *Pla and Puncernau v Andorra* [2004] 2 FCR 630 where the European Court of Human Rights held that any interpretation of a disposition which discriminates against an adopted child would be contrary to Human Rights Convention, Art 14 and that the disposition should be interpreted in the light of the social, economic and legal changes and the application of the Convention and not to the conditions which existed at the time when the will was made. In any event, the adopted child would be eligible to make a successful claim under the I(PFD)A 1975 against the estate of the deceased if the will is not interpreted in a way which is Convention-compliant.

Furthermore, Adoption Act 1976, s 42(4) and Adoption and Children Act 2002, s 42(4) do not confer on an adopted child an 'interest expectant', as he/she does not have an enforceable right against the estate of the deceased. The I(PFD)A 1975 merely confers a right to apply to the court for relief and thus he/she has a cause of action only (see *Re Collins (Deceased)* [1990] 2 All ER 47). The court in *Re Collins* was reinforced in this view by the decision in *Whyte v Ticehurst* [1986] Fam 64, where a wife who had applied for financial provision under the I(PFD)A 1975 died before the hearing of her claim. Her personal representatives applied to carry on with the proceedings on behalf of her estate. In dismissing the application, Booth J stated that the claim under the Act arose from the relationship of the two parties and was a personal one. On the death of the claimant it ceased to exist. In *Re Bramwell (Deceased), Campbell v Tobin* [1988] 2 FLR 263, it was held that the right to apply for financial provision under the Act was a mere hope or contingency and not a cause of action.

4.7.6   Child born as a result of infertility treatment

In view of the advancement in science in the development of human assisted reproduction, the law of parentage has evolved over the last two decades and is likely to continue to evolve. An outline of the various changes in the law is set out below simply as a quick guide to assist the practitioner. The issues of parentage of a child born as a result of reproductive treatment are set out in the following statutory provisions:

(1)   the Family Law Reform Act 1987;
(2)   the Human Fertilisation and Embryology Act 1990;
(3)   the Human Fertilisation and Embryology (Deceased Fathers) Act 2003;
(4)   the Human Fertilisation and Embryology Act 2008.

These statutes deal with the case where reproductive treatment is provided:

(1)   to those in a heterosexual married relationship;
(2)   to heterosexual unmarried couples;
(3)   to same sex female couples in a civil partnership;
(4)   to same sex female couples who are not registered as civil partners; and
(5)   for the posthumous use of sperm/embryo by all the above four categories.

The issue of surrogacy and parental orders and the parentage of a child when a parental order is made in favour of same sex male couples is considered at para 4.7.8.

There is a need to consider these provisions where a child has been conceived as a result of infertility treatment, such as artificial insemination, gamete intra-fallopian transfer (GIFT), or in vitro fertilisation (IVF), to identify the legal status of the child and to ascertain who in law are the child's parents.

Married heterosexual couples – Family Law Reform Act 1987

Where a child was born as a result of IVF or GIFT, or where sperm taken from the husband or partner of the mother was used to inseminate her (AIH), the legal relationship between the child and the parent can be established on the basis of blood ties. The child is the child of the mother and her husband or partner, and if the parents were married, the child would be legitimate.

Family Law Reform Act 1987, s 27 applied where a child was born to a married woman after 4 April 1988 in England and Wales as a result of artificial insemination of the woman (whose marriage had not at the time been annulled or dissolved), and she was artificially inseminated with the semen of some person other than her husband. In such a case, unless it was proved to the satisfaction of any court by which the matter had to be determined that the husband did not consent to the insemination, the child was treated in law as the child of the parties to the marriage. If the husband had not consented to the insemination of his wife, then he was not regarded as the child's father and the child was fatherless.

Married heterosexual couples – HFEA 1990

Family Law Reform Act 1987, s 27 was replaced, as from 1 August 1991, by the provisions of the Human Fertilisation and Embryology Act 1990 (HFEA 1990). Section 28 of that Act, headed 'Meaning of "father"', provided:

> (1)   This section applies in the case of a child who is being or has been carried by a woman as the result of the placing in her of an embryo or of sperm and eggs or her artificial insemination.
>
> (2)   If–
>
> (a)   at the time of the placing in her of the embryo or the sperm and eggs or of her insemination, the woman was a party to a marriage, and
>
> (b)   the creation of the embryo carried by her was not brought about with the sperm of the other party to the marriage,
>
> then, subject to subsection (5) below, the other party to the marriage shall be treated as the father of the child unless it is shown that he did not consent to the placing in her of the embryo or the sperm and eggs or to her insemination (as the case may be).
>
> (3)   If no man is treated, by virtue of subsection (2) above, as the father of the child but–
>
> (a)   the embryo or the sperm and eggs were placed in the woman, or she was artificially inseminated, in the course of treatment services provided for her and a man together by a person to whom a licence applies, and
>
> (b)   the creation of the embryo carried by her was not brought about with the sperm of that man, (*donor sperm*)
>
> then, subject to subsection (5) below, that man shall be treated as the father of the child.
>
> (4)   Where a person is treated as the father of the child by virtue of subsection (2) or (3) above, no other person is to be treated as the father of the child.
>
> (5)   Subsections (2) and (3) above do not apply–
>
> (a)   in relation to England and Wales and Northern Ireland, to any child who, by virtue of the rules of common law, is treated as the legitimate child of the parties to a marriage,
> ...
>
> (b)   to any child to the extent that the child is treated by virtue of adoption as not being the child of any person other than the adopter or adopters.
>
> (6)   Where–
>
> (a)   the sperm of a man who had given such consent as is required by paragraph 5 of Schedule 3 to this Act was used for a purpose for which such consent was required, or
>
> (b)   the sperm of a man, or any embryo the creation of which was brought about with his sperm, was used after his death,
>
> he is not to be treated as the father of the child.

(7)   The references in subsection (2) above to the parties to a marriage at the time there referred to–

(a)   are to the parties to a marriage subsisting at that time, unless a judicial separation was then in force, but

(b)   include the parties to a void marriage if either or both of them reasonably believed at that time that the marriage was valid; and for the purposes of this subsection it shall be presumed, unless the contrary is shown, that one of them reasonably believed at that time that the marriage was valid.

(8)   This section applies whether the woman was in the United Kingdom or elsewhere at the time of the placing in her of the embryo or the sperm and eggs or her artificial insemination.

(9)   In subsection (7)(a) above, 'judicial separation' includes a legal separation obtained in a country outside the British Islands and recognised in the United Kingdom.

Thus, a child born to a married woman after 1 August 1991 as a result of artificial insemination with the semen of someone other than her husband, is treated as the child of the woman and her husband unless it is shown that the husband did not consent to the artificial insemination (HFEA 1990, s 28(2)). Where, however, the parents remain married, the common law presumption of legitimacy arises, because s 28(5) provides that s 28(2) does not apply to any child who, by virtue of the rules of common law, is treated as the legitimate child of the parties to a marriage. If paternity is disputed, the dispute will have to be resolved by the court. If the presumption of legitimacy applies it can be rebutted by evidence which establishes that the person could not be the father, for example, that he was impotent, and if necessary by DNA profiling. In a case in France on 6 November 1997, a court in Paris ordered the exhumation of the body of Yves Montand, the French film actor who had died 6 years previously, to enable the applicant, who alleged that she was his daughter, to establish paternity.

Heterosexual married couples – HFEA 2008

The HFEA 2008 provides a definition for both the terms 'mother' and 'father'. It confirms the position under the HFEA 1990 that the woman who carries the child as a result of assisted reproduction anywhere in the world is the mother of the child unless that child is subsequently adopted or made the subject of a parental order (s 33).

Where the woman is married at the time of treatment when there was placed in her an embryo or the gametes involving donor sperm, her husband will be treated as the father of the child conceived as a result of the assisted reproduction unless it is shown that he did not consent to his wife's treatment. It matters not whether the woman was in the United Kingdom or elsewhere when she received the treatment (s 35). In this case no other person will be treated as the father of the child (s 38(1)) thus preserving the previous position of the donor that he cannot have the status of a father. Section 38(2) also confirms the presumption at common law that a child born to a married couple is the legitimate child of the parties to the marriage.

Unmarried woman and her male partner – HFEA 1990

Where an unmarried woman is artificially inseminated in the course of licensed treatment services provided for her and her male partner together, the partner will be treated in law as the father of the child (HFEA 1990, s 28(3)). Where the treatment was provided abroad, and therefore by a non-licence holder, the provisions of s 28(3) do not apply to confer paternity on the man. In such cases the issues which may arise include whether the treatment was provided 'together'; whether there was appropriate counselling; and whether the man was warned of the consequences and given a full opportunity to make an informed choice. Similarly, where treatment was provided to a couple together but is administered by a person who was not licensed under the Act (see *U v W (AG Intervening)* [1998] 1 FCR 526).

The question whether the treatment services were provided for the couple 'together' was considered in *Re B (Parentage)* [1996] 2 FLR 15, where the father had given sperm with which the mother was inseminated. At the time of insemination the relationship between the mother and the father had ended. The father accepted that he was the biological father of the twins born to the mother. The issues were whether the parties had been receiving treatment together, and whether the father had consented. On the facts, it was found that the father had not given his express consent, but it was held that he was deemed to have given his consent as he and the mother had been receiving treatment together and he had not at any stage before insemination withdrawn his consent.

For paternity to be established where the man has no biological connection with the embryo, the embryo must have been placed in the mother at a time when treatment services were being provided for the couple together. Thus, where the relationship between the couple had ended before the embryo was placed in the mother and the mother had misled the medical authority by falsely representing that the relationship with the man was subsisting, the man was held not to be the legal father of the child by reason of HFEA 1990, s 28(3) (see *Re R (IVF: Paternity of Child)* [2003] EWCA Civ 182, [2003] 1 FLR 1183).

In *Re Q (Parental Order)* [1996] 1 FLR 369, an unmarried mother acted as a surrogate mother for a married couple. She gave birth to a child created from the egg of the wife and fertilised by sperm from a donor under a licensed arrangement. Under HFEA 1990, s 28(6) the donor could not be treated as the father of the child. Section 28(3) did not apply as the husband had not received treatment services together with the woman. It followed that no man could be treated in law as the father of the child.

Unmarried woman and her male partner – HFEA 2008

The HFEA 2008 now makes provision for the male partner of an unmarried woman, who has no female partner, to be the father of a the child conceived by the woman using a donor sperm provided the 'fatherhood conditions' set out in s 37 are met and provided that:

(a)   the woman is treated in the United Kingdom by a person who is licenced to provide the treatment;

(b)   the 'fatherhood conditions' set out in s 37 are met;

(c)   the man remained alive at the time; and

(d)   the creation of the embryo carried by the woman was not that of her male partner.

The 'fatherhood condition' set out in HFEA 2008, s 37 which must be satisfied to enable the man to be treated as the father of the child are:

(a)   both the man and the woman must have given written notice that they both consent to the man being treated as the father of any child resulting from the treatment provided to the woman under the licence;

(b)   neither the woman nor the man has, since giving notice of their consent, given subsequent notice of the withdrawal of that consent;

(c)   the woman has not since giving her consent given a further notice that she consents to another man being treated as the father of any resulting child or that she consents to a woman being treated as a parent of the resulting child; and

(d)   the woman and the man must not be within the prohibited degrees of relationship in relation to each other

Same sex female couples – HFEA 2008

The HFEA 2008 in ss 42–44 makes new provisions to give same sex female couples similar rights as those which apply to heterosexual couples.

Where two females are in a relationship and one of them gives birth to a child conceived as a result of donor insemination, she alone will be considered the mother of the child (HFEA 2008, s 33(1)). In order to qualify as a parent of the child the other partner will need to satisfy certain conditions which vary according to whether or not the couple have entered into a civil partnership. These conditions mirror those which apply to heterosexual couples.

Same sex female couples in a civil partnership

If at the time the woman who received treatment was a party to a civil partnership she will be the mother of the child born to her as a result of donor insemination. Her partner will be a parent of the child unless she did not consent to the mother receiving the treatment (HFEA 2008, s 42(1)).

Same sex female couples not in a civil partnership

Where two women who are in a relationship have not entered into a civil partnership, the woman who carries the child will be the child's mother. Her partner will be treated as the legal parent provided certain conditions set out in HFEA 2008, s 43 and the 'female parenthood' conditions set out in s 44 are satisfied.

The conditions in HFEA 2008, s 43, are:

(a)   the embryo or the sperm and eggs were placed in the woman or the woman was inseminated, in the course of treatment services provided in a licenced clinic in the United Kingdom;

(b)   at the time when the treatment was provided the agreed female parenthood conditions set out in section 44 of the 2008 Act were met in relation to the other woman in relation to the treatment provided to the woman who will carry the child; and

(c)   the other woman remained alive at that time.

'Female parenthood' conditions

The 'female parenthood' conditions which much be satisfied by the woman who is not carrying the child are similar to those which apply to a male partner where the parties are in a heterosexual relationship. The conditions are as follows:

(1)   Both parties must have given to the person responsible for providing the treatment a written notice stating that they both consent to the other woman being treated as the parent of the resulting child.

(2)   Neither women has given a subsequent notice of withdrawal of consent to the person responsible for providing the treatment.

(3)   The woman must not have given a subsequent notice of consent to another woman being treated as the parent of the child.

(4)   The woman must not subsequently have given notice of consent to another man being treated as the child's father under HFEA 2008, s 37(1)(b).

(5)   The female couple must not be within the prohibited degree of relationship in relation to each other.

(6)   Where the above conditions are satisfied, the other woman will be treated as the parent of the child, and no man will be treated as the father of the child (s 45(1)).

Posthumous use of sperm (heterosexual couples) – HFEA 1990 as amended by the Human Fertilisation and Embryology (Deceased Fathers) Act 2003

Following the decision in *R v Human Fertilisation and Embryology Authority ex parte Blood* [1997] 2 FLR 742, the HFEA 1990 was amended to deal with the use of a deceased father's sperm. In *R v Human Fertilisation and Embryology Authority ex parte Blood* the claimant wished to be artificially inseminated with sperm taken from her husband at her request by doctors treating him when he was unconscious and receiving treatment in hospital. The sperm was stored in a licensed institution. The husband died. The Human Fertilisation and Embryology Authority refused to release the sperm to the applicant on the ground that no written consent had been obtained from the husband and he had not received counselling as required by the provisions of the Act. On appeal, it was held that the provisions of the Act had been breached and therefore the sperm should not have been preserved and stored. The court directed that in future those responsible for treating a man and a woman together should take the precaution of having the necessary consent not only to storage, but also to the continuation of treatment if the man should die before the sperm is used. Leave was, however, given for the sperm to be released so that the woman could receive treatment in Belgium. A child born as a result of such treatment is not considered the child of the husband (s 28(2) and (3)).

The Human Fertilisation and Embryology (Deceased Fathers) Act 2003 amended the HFEA 1990 to permit a man to be registered as the child's father if the child was conceived by using the man's sperm after his death or embryo created by using his sperm before his death.

Posthumous use of sperm – HFEA 2008

HFEA 2008, s 39 replaces the provision inserted in the HFEA 1990 by the Human Fertilisation and Embryology (Deceased Fathers) Act 2003 (see above) by setting out the conditions that must be satisfied before a man may be treated as the father of a child born to a woman by using the man's sperm after his death or using an embryo created with the man's sperm before his death but placed in the woman after his death, but only for the purposes of registering the birth of the child.

The conditions are:

(1)   the man must have consented in writing to the use of his sperm or embryo after his death and to being treated as the father of any resulting child for the purposes of registering the birth of the child;

(2)   the man must not have withdrawn his consent;

(3)   the woman must elect in writing not later than the end of the period of 42 days from the day on which the child was born for the man to be treated for the purposes of birth registration as the father of the child; and

(4)   no one else is to be treated:

(a)   as the father of the child by virtue of s 35 or s 36 or by virtue of s 38(2) or (3) (see paras 4.7.1 and 4.7.2: heterosexual married and unmarried couples and the provision of common law presumption of legitimacy);

(b)   no one else is to be treated as a parent of the child by virtue of s 42 or s 43 (see below); or

(c)   no one else is treated as a parent of the child by virtue of adoption.

Posthumous use of donated sperm where the couple are married

Where the child has been carried by a married woman as a result of placing in her of an embryo created by donated sperm and her husband died before the embryo was placed in the woman then the husband will be treated as the father of the resulting child provided the conditions set out in HFEA 2008, s 40 are satisfied.

The conditions are:

(1)   the woman must have been married when the embryo was created;

(2)   the husband died before the embryo was placed in the woman;

(3)   the husband must have consented in writing and not withdrawn his consent to the placing of the embryo in the woman after his

death and to being treated as the father of any resulting child for the purposes of birth registration;

(4) the woman has elected in writing no later than the end of the period of 42 days from the day on which the child was born for the man to be treated for the purposes of birth registration as the father of the child;

(5) no one else is to be treated as the father of the child by virtue of s 35 or s 36 (see above) or s 38(2) or (3); or as a parent of the child by virtue of s 42 or s 43 (see below);

(6) no one else is to be treated as a parent of the child by virtue of adoption.

Posthumous use of donated sperm where the couple are unmarried

Similar conditions as apply to married couples must be satisfied to ensure that the man is to be treated as the father of the resulting child. In addition, the woman must not have been a party to a marriage or a civil partnership at the time when the embryo was created, which must have been in the course of licensed treatment provided to the woman in the United Kingdom and immediately before the man's death, and the agreed 'fatherhood conditions' set out in HFEA 2008, s 37 must have been met in relation to treatment proposed to be provided to the woman in the United Kingdom by a licensed person (s 40(2)).

Same sex female couples in a civil partnership at the time of treatment – HFEA 2008

The HFEA 2008 for the first time introduces provisions providing for same sex female couples to have the same rights as those which apply to heterosexual couples.

HFEA 2008, s 42 provides that where, at the time of placing in her of the embryo or sperm and eggs or her artificial insemination, a woman was a party to a civil partnership, then the other party to the civil partnership is to be treated as a parent of the child unless it is shown that she did not consent to the mother's treatment. The woman who carried the child will be the child's mother (s 33(1)).

Same sex female couples not in a civil partnership

Where two women are in a relationship but they have not entered into a civil partnership the woman who carries the child will be the mother and her partner will be treated as a parent of the child provided that the 'female parenthood' conditions set out in HFEA 2008, s 44 are met.

The 'female parenthood' conditions are:

(1)   both parties must have given written notice of their respective consent to the other woman to be treated as the parent of any child resulting from treatment provided to the woman who is to carry the child;

(2)   neither of them must have withdrawn their consent

(3)   the woman must not have subsequently given notice that she consents to another woman being treated as a parent of any resulting child or a notice that she consents to a man being treated as the father of any resulting child;

(4)   the female couple must not be within the prohibited degrees of relationship in relation to each other

Posthumous transfer of embryo after death of civil partner

In line with the provisions in relation to heterosexual couples HFEA 2008, ss 46 and 40(2) provide for the registration of the deceased same sex female partner to be treated as a parent of the resulting child provided certain conditions are met.

HFEA 2008, s 46 provides that where a child has been carried by a woman as the result of the placing in her of an embryo which was created at a time when she was a party to a civil partnership and the other party to the civil partnership dies before the placing of the embryo in the woman, then provided the conditions set out in s 46(1)(d)–(f) are met the other party to the civil partnership is to be treated as a parent of the child for the purposes of birth registration. The conditions are:

(1)   that the other party consented in writing (and did not withdraw that consent) to the placing of the embryo in the woman after the death of the other party and to being treated as the parent of any resulting child for the purposes of birth registration;

(2)   the woman has elected in writing not later than 42 days from the day on which the child was born for the other party to the civil partnership to be treated for the purposes of birth registration as the parent of the child;

(3)   no one else is to be treated as the father of the child by virtue of s 35 or s 36 (conditions which apply to heterosexual married and unmarried couples) or s 42 or s 43 as a parent of the child by virtue or s 43;

(4)   no one else is to be treated as a parent of the child by virtue of adoption.

Posthumous transfer of embryo after death of same sex partner where the couple are not in a civil partnership

Where a child has been carried by a woman as a result of placing in her of an embryo and the embryo was not created at a time when the woman was a party to a marriage or civil partnership but was created in the course of licensed treatment provided to the woman in the United Kingdom, the woman's female partner may be treated as the parent of the resulting child provided the following conditions are satisfied:

(1)   the other female partner consented in writing (and did not withdraw that consent) to the placing of the embryo in the woman after her own death and to being treated as the parent of any resulting child for the purposes of registration of birth;

(2)   the other female partner died before the placing of the embryo in the woman;

(3)   immediately before the death of the other female partner, the agreed 'female parenthood' conditions set out in HFEA 2008, s 44 (see above) were met in relation to the licensed treatment provided in the United Kingdom to the woman bearing the child;

(4)   the woman carrying the child had elected in writing not later than the end of the period of 42 days from the day on which the child was born for the other woman to be treated as the parent of the resulting child for the purposes of registration;

(5)   no one else is treated as the father or parent of the child (see above);

(6)   if no one else is treated as the parent of the child by virtue of adoption then the other woman is to be treated as the parent of the child for the purposes of birth registration.

4.7.7   Mistaken transfer of sperm

Where, by mistake of the hospital authorities, the sperm used for IVF treatment was not, as intended, that of the woman's husband but of another man, the husband cannot be treated as the father of the child born to the mother as he had not consented to the use of the donor sperm. The presumption of legitimacy can be displaced by DNA tests to establish that the husband is not the father of the child born to the mother (see *Leeds Teaching Hospital NHS Trust v A & B* [2003] EWHC 259 (QB), [2003] 1 FLR 1091).

The law in this area is evolving and new scenarios will emerge. The statutory provisions and cases cited above are provided as an illustration of the difficulties that may arise and the hurdles to be crossed. It is not intended to be a full exposition of the law in this area. It is essential to be vigilant and aware of new developments. In case of doubt, advice from an expert in this field of law is advised.

4.7.8   A child who is the subject of a parental order

HFEA 1990, s 30 allowed a court to make a 'parental order' providing for a child, who is genetically the child of the husband or wife or both, but has been carried by a surrogate mother, to be treated in law as the child of the husband and wife. Before such an order could be made the court had to be satisfied that:

(1)   the husband and wife were married and had attained the age of 18 at the date of the making of the order;

(2)   they were domiciled in the United Kingdom or in the Channel Islands or the Isle of Man;

(3)   the child had had his home with the husband and wife;

(4)   the application for an order was made within 6 months of the birth of the child.

A child who is the subject of a parental order is treated as the child of the marriage of the couple in whose favour the order is made. The child is not regarded as illegitimate.

The HFEA 2008 repeals HFEA 1990, s 30 and replaces it by the provisions set out in HFEA 2008, s 54.

The first change that has been made by the new provision is to extend the categories of applicants who can apply for a parental order to civil partners, unmarried heterosexual couples and same sex couples who are not in a civil partnership.

The conditions that must be satisfied before a parental order can be made can be summarised as follows:

(1)   the application must be made by two people who must both be 18 years of age or over;

(2)   the applicants must be: (a) husband and wife; (b) civil partners of each other; (c) two persons who are living together in an enduring family relationship and are not within prohibited degrees of relationship in relation to each other;

(3)   the child must have been carried by a surrogate mother who is not one of the applicants;

(4)   the gametes of at least one of the applicants must have been used to bring about the creation of the embryo;

(5)   at the time of issuing the application and the making of the order either or both the applicants must be domiciled in the United Kingdom or in the Channel Islands or the Isle of Man;

(6)   the child must have his home with the applicants;

(7)   the application must be made within 6 months of the child's birth; and

(8)   the court must be satisfied that:

   (a)   the woman who carried the child and any other person who is a parent of the child but is not one of the applicants have freely and, with full understanding of what is involved, have agreed unconditionally to the making of a parental order;

   (b)   no money or other benefit (other than for expenses reasonably incurred) has been given or received by either of the applicants for or in consideration of the making of the order or any agreement required for the making of the application or the handing over of the child to the applicants, or the making of arrangements with a view to the making of the order unless authorised by the court;

   (c)   the agreement of the woman was given within 6 weeks of the birth of the child.

The agreement of a person who cannot be found or is incapable of giving consent is not required.

4.7.9   Declaration of parentage, legitimacy and legitimation

Any person may apply to the court for a declaration that:

   (a)   a person named in the application is or was his parent;
   (b)   he is the legitimate child of his parents;
   (c)   he has become a legitimated person;
   (d)   he has not become a legitimated person.

(Family Law Act 1986, as amended by the Family Law Reform Act 1987)

In order to make the application, the applicant must establish that he is domiciled in England and Wales on the date of the application, or has been habitually resident in England and Wales throughout the period of one year preceding the application.

The procedure to be followed is set out in FPR 2010, Part 8, Chapter 5. The application is made in Form C63 issued in the High Court, a county court or a magistrates' court. The application must contain the information set out in FPR 2010, r 8.21. A copy of the birth certificate of the person whose parentage is in issue, and a supporting statement which must be verified by a statement of truth, must accompany Form C63. The court may, at any stage of the proceedings, of its own initiative or on the application of any party to the proceedings, direct that the Attorney General be served with the proceedings.

The respondents to the application will generally be the parents, if alive, and the person whose parentage is in issue (if the application is not made by that person). In the case where a parent has died, the executors, the beneficiaries and any other person who may be affected by the declaration sought should be made a party to the application for the declaration. Service should be effected in accordance with FPR 2010, Part 6 and PDs 6A–6C. The respondents to the application should file an acknowledgement of service and any statement in answer within 14 days of service. The applicant may file a reply within 14 days of the respondents' statement.

The procedure set out in FPR 2010, Part 19 and PD 19A applies to an application for a declaration. The applicant must be heard by a judge. The court may give directions for scientific tests to be undertaken to determine paternity. If paternity is established, the court must make a declaration that the person named in the application is or was the parent of the person whose parentage is in issue.

A similar procedure is followed where a declaration of legitimacy or legitimation is sought under Family Law Act 1986, s 56. The FPR again apply to such an application. Any declaration made is in Form M31.

4.8   ANY PERSON TREATED AS A CHILD OF THE FAMILY

I(PFD)A 1975, s 1(1)(d), as amended by the CPA 2004 (with effect from 5 December 2005), provides that any application for an order under I(PFD)A 1975, s 2 may be made by 'a person who (not being a child of the deceased) in the case of any marriage or civil partnership to which the deceased was a party was treated by the deceased as a child of the family in relation to that marriage or civil partnership'.

The term 'child of the family' does not here, have the meaning given to it in the Matrimonial Causes Act 1973. The Family Law Act 1996 does not provide any new definition of 'child of the family'.

Unlike the case under the Matrimonial Causes Act 1973, there is no age limit. An adult child of the deceased has been regarded as a child of the family and entitled to claim under the I(PFD)A 1975. For a claim to proceed, however, the deceased must have been married or in a civil partnership, and the claimant must have been treated by him/her as a child of the family within that marriage or civil partnership. Whether a claimant falls within this category depends on the facts of the individual case, but the following examples of decided cases may assist.

In *Re Callaghan (Deceased)* [1985] Fam 1, the claimant was a step-son of the deceased. He was 6 years old when his natural father died. Three years later the deceased came to live in his mother's home as a lodger. Subsequently the deceased and the mother lived together as man and wife. The deceased treated the claimant as his son. In 1960, the claimant married, but continued to maintain a close relationship with his mother and the deceased. In 1972, the claimant's mother and the deceased married. The mother died in 1980. The claimant continued to care for the deceased until his death. In considering the claim, Booth J said:

> In this case the acknowledgement by the deceased of his own role of grandfather to the plaintiff's children, the confidences as to his property and financial affairs which he placed in the plaintiff, and his dependence on the plaintiff to care for him in his last illness are examples of the deceased's treatment of the plaintiff as a child, albeit an adult child of the family. All these things are part of the privileges and duties of two persons who, in regard to each other, stand in the relationship of parent and child; it is the existence of that relationship that enables the plaintiff to apply under section 1(1)(d) of the Act. My view is not altered by the fact that, in considering an application by a person coming within section 1(1)(d), the court is required to have regard to the education or training of the applicant and must also consider the extent to which the deceased has assumed responsibility for his maintenance.

In *Re Leach (Deceased), Leach v Leinderman* [1986] Ch 226, when the claimant's father remarried, the claimant was 32 years of age and was living away from home. The claimant never lived with her father and her stepmother in one household. The claimant's father died in 1974, and the stepmother died in 1981. The claimant applied for an order under I(PFD)A 1975, s 2 for a half share in the net estate. The claim was allowed because the stepmother had, after her marriage and on the death of her husband, expressly and impliedly assumed the position of a parent towards the claimant. Her treatment of the claimant after the death of the claimant's father was a consideration which the court could take into account as it stemmed from the marriage. In his judgment, Slade J said:

> I do not think it is necessary or appropriate to imply any similar temporal limitation in the construction of section 1(1)(d) of the 1975 Act, which is directing attention solely to the treatment of the child by one party to the marriage. The phrase used is not 'during the subsistence of the marriage', it is the wider phrase 'in relation to the marriage'. It seems to me that the treatment of an applicant by a surviving spouse after the death of the other spouse may be a relevant factor in deciding whether the applicant qualifies under section 1(1)(d), provided that such treatment is referable to or 'stems from' the marriage.

It seems therefore that the treatment by the step-parent of the claimant after the death of the natural parent may be a relevant factor provided that the treatment was 'in relation to the marriage' or now civil partnership as well.

Where grandparents or other relatives take on the responsibility of caring for a grandchild or a child related to them, that child may become a child of the family both within Matrimonial Causes Act 1973, s 52, and within the I(PFD)A 1975 (see *Re A (A Child of the Family)* [1998] 1 FLR 347, CA and *Re Debenham (Deceased)* [1986] 1 FLR 404, discussed at para 4.6.3). In such cases the court considers the matter objectively to determine the relationship between the grandparents/relative and the child, and whether the services were provided by him/her by way of support in an emergency, or whether he/she had assumed primary responsibility for the foreseeable future and cared for and treated the child as his/her own.

In a claim made under this head therefore, the applicant will need to establish that the deceased expressly or impliedly assumed the position of a parent towards the applicant with the attendant responsibilities, obligations and privileges of that relationship.

Where a couple are living together but are not married to each other or in a civil partnership, a child of one of them cannot be regarded as eligible under I(PFD)A 1975, s 1(1)(d) because, although there does not have to be a subsisting marriage or civil partnership, the conduct towards the claimant has to be in relation to marriage or a civil partnership. It matters not that the conduct relates to events after the death of one of the parties to the marriage or civil partnership.

To summarise therefore:

(1)   'child', for the purposes of this section, includes an adult child;

(2)   the relevant 'treatment' is the behaviour of the deceased towards the claimant;

(3)   the treatment must stem from the marriage, and the treatment of the claimant by the surviving spouse after the death of the natural parent is relevant;

(4)   the mere display of affection, kindness and hospitality by a surviving step-parent towards a step-child is not sufficient. Proof that the deceased expressly or impliedly assumed the position of a parent towards the claimant, with the attendant responsibilities and privileges of that relationship, may be relevant.

Note: the Law Commission in its Consultation Paper, *Intestacy and Family Provision Claims on Death* (Consultation Paper No 191), has sought views on whether an adult child should be given greater chance of success in applications under the Act and, if so, what criteria should be applied in such cases.

4.9   ANY PERSON (NOT BEING A PERSON INCLUDED IN THE FOREGOING PARAGRAPHS) WHO IMMEDIATELY BEFORE THE DEATH OF THE DECEASED WAS BEING MAINTAINED EITHER WHOLLY OR PARTLY BY THE DECEASED

This provision applies as a net to enable any other person who does not fall within the specific categories referred to above to make a claim, or who may not be able to establish such a relationship to make a claim in the alternative, provided it can be established that immediately before the death of the deceased, the person making the claim was being maintained wholly or partly, by the deceased. I(PFD)A 1975, s 1(3) requires the applicant to establish that the provision made for him/her was provided other than for full valuable consideration, and that it was substantially towards the reasonable needs of the applicant.

4.9.1   Being maintained

I(PFD)A 1975, s 1(3) provides that:

> for the purposes of section 1(1)(e) a person shall be treated as being maintained by the deceased, either wholly or partly, as the case may be, if the deceased, otherwise than for full valuable consideration, was making a substantial contribution in money or money's worth towards the reasonable needs of that person.

The I(PFD)A 1975 does not make any other reference to the meaning of 'being maintained', but s 3(4) requires the court when determining a claim under s 1(1)(e) to have regard to the extent to which and the basis on which the deceased assumed responsibility for the maintenance of the applicant and the length of time for which the deceased had discharged that responsibility.

These provisions read together identify what must be established. This includes:

(1)   the contribution made by the deceased must have been for the maintenance of the claimant and to provide for his/her reasonable needs;

(2)   the contribution must be substantial;

(3)   the payments must have been made immediately before the death of the deceased;

(4)   the payments must have been made otherwise than for full valuable consideration;

(5)   the nature, extent and purpose of the payments, and the length of time over which they were made, are matters which the court is required to take into account;

(6)   the deceased must have 'assumed responsibility' for the claimant.

4.9.2   Reasonable needs

In determining the issue of whether the deceased had maintained the claimant to provide for his/her reasonable needs it will be necessary for the court to consider the interaction between the provisions of I(PFD)A 1975, ss 1(3) and 3. The claimant will need to satisfy the court not only that he/she was being maintained either wholly or partly by the deceased immediately before his/her death but also the extent to which and the basis upon which the deceased had assumed responsibility for the claimant. An outright gift of a house many years before the death of the deceased would not constitute maintenance even if the claimed continued to live in the house, as it would be an asset over which the deceased had no control (see *Baynes v Hedger and Others* [2009] EWCA Civ 374, [2009] 2 FLR 767).

In considering the claim the court is required to look not at the de facto state of the maintenance existing at the moment of death but at the state and extent of the maintenance arrangement generally between the deceased and the claimant, using the date of death on which the arrangement would be considered. The issue of what constitutes a 'substantial contribution' and the 'assumption of responsibility' has been considered in a number of cases (see below for examples).

Case law provides some guidance on what would have to be proved to establish 'reasonable needs'. In *Re Coventry, Coventry v Coventry* [1980] Ch 461, Goff J referred to cases in which the meaning of maintenance was considered. He said:

> In particular, in this country there is *Re E, E v E* ([1996] 1 WLR 709, [1966] All ER 44), in which Stamp J said that the purpose was not to keep a person above the breadline but to provide reasonable maintenance in all the circumstances. If I may say so with respect, 'breadline' there would be more accurately described as 'subsistence level'. Then there was *Millward v Shenton* ([1972] 1 WLR 711, [1972] 2 All ER 1025) in this court. I think I need only refer to one of the overseas reports ... *Duranceau* ([1952] 3 DLR 714) where, in somewhat poetic language, the court said that the question is 'Is the provision sufficient to enable the dependant to live neither luxuriously or miserably, but decently and comfortably according to his or her station in life?'. What is proper maintenance must in all cases depend upon all the facts and circumstances of the particular case being considered at the time, but I think it is clear on the one hand that one must not put too limited a meaning on it; it does not mean just enough to enable a person to get by, on the other hand, it does not mean anything which may be regarded as reasonably desirable for his general benefit or welfare.

Reasonable needs may also mean reasonable requirements and in considering this the court must necessarily consider the factors which it is required to take into account under I(PFD)A 1975, s 3. In *Harrington v Gill* (1983) 4 FLR 265 (CA), the deceased and the claimant had cohabited together for 8 years before the deceased's death in the deceased's house. The claimant had retained the tenancy of her council flat. She carried out all the household duties and the deceased had paid all the outgoings. The claimant, who worked, also spent all her earnings on household extras, clothes and other necessaries. She made no contribution towards her board and lodgings. The deceased died intestate and his estate, worth about £65,000, went to his daughter, who was financially comfortable. At the date of the hearing the claimant was 74. Her income consisted of the state pension. She was living in the deceased's house but had surrendered the council tenancy. On appeal it was held that, in considering the needs of the claimant, the court will, among other things, consider the extent to which the deceased had undertaken responsibility for the claimant, the standard of living enjoyed by the claimant during the deceased's lifetime, and the extent to which the deceased contributed to that standard of living. Dunn LJ said:

> The scheme of the Act, as set out in the sections, is a little complicated, but at the end of the day the court must ask itself the question: What testamentary provision would a reasonable man in the position of this deceased have made for the plaintiff in all the circumstances, including the matters set out in section 3?

In *Re Watson (Deceased)* [1999] 1 FLR 878 where the deceased and the applicant had had a relationship over 30 years but they had not lived together until 1985 when they ceased to have the responsibility of caring for their elderly parents. Thereafter, the claimant moved in to live with the deceased until he went into hospital where he died. In considering her 'reasonable needs' and whether it requires the court to take into account the resources and assets of the applicant at the relevant time Neuberger J (as he then was) said, "I am not sure that that is a question which is capable of being answered unequivocally in the abstract. Bearing in mind the purpose of the Act it appears to be wrong, at least in general, to seek to fetter the meaning of any particular expression in it further than the legislature has done. However, it is fair to say that one would, on the face of it, expect the word 'needs' in section 1(3) to have the same meaning, for instance, as the word 'needs' in s 3(1)(a), (b) and (c) of the same Act"

But he pointed out that a contrast needs to be made between the provision of I(PFD)A 1975, ss 1(3) and 3 as the 'needs' referred to in s 1(3) related to the needs of the applicant at and a little time before the deceased's death, whereas the 'needs' referred to in s 3 referred to the needs at the date of the hearing and for the foreseeable future (s 3(5)).

In *Re Viner (Deceased), Kreeger v Cooper* [1978] CLY 3091, the claim was by a woman aged 74. She had been widowed for a year before her brother's death, and was left in difficult circumstances. The brother had been persuaded by another sister, to whom he was voluntarily paying £10 per week, partly to maintain the claimant. He agreed to divide the weekly payments of £10 between his two sisters, and grudgingly paid £5 per week to the claimant for 6 months prior to his death. By his will the deceased left an annuity to his unmarried sister but nothing to the claimant. The residue of his estate was left to a person with whom he had worked. On the facts the claimant succeeded.

In *Rees v Newbery and the Institute for Cancer Research* [1988] 1 FLR 1041, for almost 10 years before the death of the deceased the claimant had lived in a flat owned by the deceased. He had paid to the deceased rent below the market rent. The deceased had given instructions for a new will which was to provide that the claimant should continue living at the property under the existing arrangements for life. Before the will could be executed, the deceased died. The claim was allowed because the deceased had not only expressly indicated his intention, but the arrangement between the deceased and the claimant before death led to the inference that the claimant had been maintained by the deceased, that he had assumed responsibility for the claimant's maintenance, and that he was making a substantial contribution towards the reasonable needs of the claimant.

4.9.3 Otherwise than for full valuable consideration

The provision made by the deceased for the claimant must be otherwise than for full valuable consideration. I(PFD)A 1975, s 25(1) defines 'full valuable consideration' to exclude 'marriage or a promise of marriage'. This will also exclude a civil partnership or a promise to enter into a civil partnership with the claimant. Where some valuable consideration was accepted by the deceased from the claimant for meeting the claimant's needs, the nature and extent of the consideration he/she received will be relevant. *Rees v Newbery and the Institute for Cancer Research* (above), where the claimant had paid to the deceased rent below the market rent and the deceased had clearly expressed his intention that this arrangement should continue after his death for life, is a good example of a case where it was held that the deceased had maintained the claimant and that the rent received could not be said to be in 'full' consideration of that privilege.

In *Re Wilkinson (Deceased), Neale v Newell* [1978] Fam 22, Arnold J, when assessing the value of the contributions made by the claimant, said:

> It is not very easy, when one is dealing with the question of what is full valuable consideration, to measure in purely financial terms the sort of things which the applicant was doing for the deceased and the sort of thing which the applicant represented to the deceased … Somehow it seems to me I have to measure those matters in order to see whether, fairly looked at, they were a full valuable requital or return for that which the applicant received from the deceased.

In *Re Wilkinson*, the sister of the deceased had left her employment at the age of 61 to look after the deceased. The deceased had paid for all the food and met the household expenses. The claimant had done the light housework and the cooking. The heavier tasks were carried out by a home help and a sister-in-law. Having carried out a balancing exercise, the court held that the deceased had made a substantial contribution to the claimant's needs, and that the duties that the claimant performed for the deceased could not be regarded as full valuable consideration in return for the contribution made by the deceased. See, also, para 4.9.4.

4.9.4 Substantial contribution and assumption of responsibility

I(PFD)A 1975, s 1(3) requires that the contribution made by the deceased towards the maintenance of the claimant must be 'substantial' and s 3 requires the claimant to establish that the deceased had 'assumed responsibility' for him/her.

Whether the deceased made a substantial contribution to another's reasonable needs depends, therefore, on the circumstances of the parties and their relationship. The deceased's motives or intentions are relevant only when the court is considering the matters set out in I(PFD)A 1975, s 3(4) and determining whether or not to make any orders for financial provision for the claimant: 'the benefactor's motives or intentions are irrelevant except insofar as s 3(4) makes them relevant to the court's task of deciding whether or not to make provision for the claimant and if so in what form and what scale' (per Walker LJ in *Bouette v Rose* [2001] 1 FLR 363, see below).

In determining whether the deceased had made a 'substantial contribution' to the claimant's needs, the court must approach the problem in the round, apply a common sense approach, and avoid fine balancing computations involving the value of normal exchanges of support in the domestic sense (see *Bishop v Plumley* [1991] 1 WLR 582).

The court must balance what the deceased was contributing against what the claimant's contributions were. Where the claimant was contributing more than the deceased or where the contributions were equal, there would be no dependency. Where there is doubt about the balance tipping in favour of the deceased's contribution being the greater then the claimant is entitled to succeed (see *Jelley v Illife* [1981] Fam 128). In *Jelley v Illife*, Griffiths LJ in his judgment said, 'the court must use common sense and remember that the object of Parliament in creating this extra class of persons who may claim benefit from an estate was to provide relief for persons of whom it could truly be said that they were wholly or partially dependent on the deceased'. And:

> Each case will have to be looked at carefully on its own facts to see whether common sense leads to a conclusion that the applicant can fairly be regarded as a dependant.
>
> As a general rule, the fact that the claimant was being maintained by the deceased under an arrangement subsisting at the time of the deceased's death and the deceased was making a substantial contribution in money or money's worth to the reasonable needs of the claimant will raise an inference that the deceased had undertaken to maintain the claimant and had assumed responsibility for the maintenance of the claimant. In such circumstances there would be no need to establish any other overt act to demonstrate the 'assumption' of responsibility.

All the contributions made, whether in kind or otherwise, are taken into account. In *Jelley v Illife*, the claimant was a widower, and had lived with his daughter before he went to live with the deceased. The deceased lived in a house which had been conveyed to her by her children on the understanding that she would leave it to them on her death. The claimant and the deceased shared the accommodation and pooled their resources. The claimant also did the household jobs and the gardening. He lived in the house rent-free. On her death the deceased left all her property to her children and nothing to the claimant. His claim was allowed.

The following cases provide a guide on the approach taken by the court on the issue of whether the deceased had made a 'substantial contribution' and assumed responsibility for the claimant.

In *Re Beaumont (Deceased), Martin v Midland Bank Trust Co Ltd* [1980] Ch 1144, the male claimant and the deceased began living together in 1940 in the deceased's bungalow. In 1964, the deceased retired. In 1966, the claimant retired from full-time work, but continued to work part-time for about 10 years. Thereafter he received his state pension. He made regular weekly payments to the deceased for his accommodation and shopping expenses. In all other respects they pooled their resources. The deceased also made it clear to the claimant that the bungalow belonged to her and she paid all the outgoings. She also paid the claimant for any decorating work that he did for her. In dismissing the claim, the court held that on the true construction of the section the court was required to look not at the de facto state of maintenance existing at the moment of death, but at the 'substantial and enduring' basis or arrangement existing between the parties and the degree of maintenance existing normally and habitually under the arrangement; it must be shown that the deceased had 'made a substantial contribution in money or money's worth towards the reasonable needs of the applicant otherwise than for full valuable consideration'. Full consideration was not limited to consideration provided under a contract but extended to any contribution. Thus if a couple living together made equal contributions towards the maintenance of each other by bearing one half of the cost, then, although both would be making a contribution towards the reasonable needs of the other they would be doing so for full valuable consideration, and each would be barred from making a claim against the estate of the other.

To satisfy the provision of I(PFD)A 1975, s 3(4) that the deceased had assumed responsibility for the claimant, it is not enough to establish a mere fact of maintaining someone. The assumption of responsibility requires an act on the part of the deceased demonstrating that he had undertaken or assumed some 'legal or moral responsibility' for the claimant. In *Re Beaumont*, Sir Robert Megarry VC said:

> The word 'assumes', too, seems to me to indicate that there must be some act or acts which demonstrate an undertaking or responsibility or the taking of the responsibility on oneself. It may be that in some cases where there is neither a negation of responsibility nor a positive undertaking of it, it will be possible to

infer from the circumstances attending the act of maintenance that there has indeed been an assumption of responsibility. But it is for the plaintiff to establish that there has been an assumption of responsibility, and for the defendant to have to rebut any presumption of an assumption of responsibility which is to be drawn from the bare fact of maintenance.

To establish that the deceased had assumed responsibility for the claimant's maintenance, the applicant must show that the deceased had regarded himself as discharging the responsibility to maintain the claimant (see *Re B* [1999] Ch 206). It is the settled basis or general arrangement between the parties as regards maintenance during the lifetime of the deceased which must be considered, not the actual, perhaps fluctuating, variations of it which exist immediately before the death of the deceased. The court has to consider whether the deceased, otherwise than for valuable consideration, was in fact making a substantial contribution in money or money's worth towards the reasonable needs of the applicant on a settled basis or arrangement, which either was still in force immediately before the deceased's death, or would have lasted until death but for the approach of death and the consequent inability of either party to continue to carry out the arrangement.

In *Re Beaumont (Deceased)* (above), the court had held that the claimant had to establish some action on the part of the deceased to show that he had undertaken responsibility for the claimant before the claim could succeed, whereas the decision in *Rees v Newbery* (at para 4.9.2) suggests that it is open to the court to infer the assumption of responsibility from the surrounding facts, unless the circumstantial evidence suggests that the deceased had made it clear that he did not assume such responsibility or that his actions should not be taken to mean that the support afforded to the claimant would continue. It is not necessary, however, to prove that the deceased had intended to maintain the claimant after his death. Such an intention may be inferred from the conduct of the deceased, particularly where the conduct was such that the claimant had been made wholly or partly dependent on the deceased, as was the case in *Graham v Murphy* [1997] 1 FLR 860. There, the deceased and the claimant had lived together from 1976 until 1993 when the deceased died. The deceased had a substantial income, whereas the claimant was a lorry driver with an average wage of £160 per week. By reason of the deceased's income the couple were able to live a comfortable life including eating out and going for holidays abroad which were paid for by the deceased. In 1990 the deceased became ill. Throughout her illness until her death the claimant cared for and provided support for the deceased. The claim was allowed, although the court referred to it as 'quite close to borderline'. The provisions of Law Reform (Succession) Act 1995, s 2 were then not in force. Had they been, the claimant would have succeeded in any event as a cohabitant of the deceased.

A situation similar to that in *Graham v Murphy* arose in *Bishop v Plumley* (at para 4.6). In *Re Haig, Powers v Haig* [1979] LS Gaz R 476, the claimant had lived with the deceased as his wife for 3 years preceding his death. She was given the right to occupy his house rent-free.

In *Malone v Harrison* [1979] 1 WLR 1353, where the deceased had failed to make any provision for his second mistress, who had been wholly supported by the deceased, she was awarded a lump sum.

In *Bouette v Rose* [2001] 1 FLR 363, the deceased had suffered severe mental and physical disabilities due to medical negligence at birth, for which she had been awarded damages of £250,000. Her financial affairs were managed by the Court of Protection and her mother, who was the claimant, was appointed receiver. The Court of Protection provided the mother with regular payments in her capacity as receiver for the deceased's maintenance. The deceased died intestate. Her estate passed on intestacy to the mother and father in equal shares. The mother made a claim under the I(PFD)A 1975. On the father's application, the claim was struck out on appeal from the master's decision; the judge held that the Court of Protection had made payments solely for the deceased's maintenance and that the deceased had not assumed responsibility for her mother's maintenance. On the mother's appeal, the Court of Appeal held that it must have been obvious to the Court of Protection that the payments made to the mother would necessarily be used to meet the mother's financial and material needs, particularly as, on the facts, the mother had made no contribution toward the household expenses. There was nothing absurd in the notion of the Court of Protection acting as the conscience of the patient and making provision for those to whom the patient would have felt a moral obligation if the patient had been of full capacity. On the facts, it would have been obvious to the Court of Protection that the payments made to the mother were also providing the financial and material needs of the mother throughout the deceased's life.

Recently in *Lindop v Agus, Bass and Hedley* [2009] EWHC 14 (Ch), [2009] Fam Law 808, the claimant, in addition to claiming that she and the deceased had lived together as husband and wife, also claimed in the alternative that she had been maintained by him as he had provided her a home for which he had paid all the outgoings until his death and that he had also provided her with transport to travel to and from work and had also paid for her holidays and her wardrobe.

See also *Harrington v Gill* (1983) 4 FLR 265 (CA) and *Re Viner (Deceased), Kreeger v Cooper* [1978] CLY 3091 (at para 4.9.2) and determining whether or not to make any orders for financial provision for the claimant, 'the benefactor's motives or intentions are irrelevant except insofar as section 3(4) makes them relevant to the court's task of deciding whether or not to make provision for the claimant and if so in what form and what scale' (per Walker LJ in *Bouette v Rose* (above)).

4.9.5   Immediately before the death of the deceased

In claims under I(PFD)A 1975, s 1(1)(e), the relationship between the deceased and the claimant must have been continuing at the date of the death, and the claimant must show that the deceased was maintaining the claimant immediately before the death of the deceased. If the arrangement had ceased before the date of death, the claim will fail no matter how short the period. Thus, where cohabitation between the deceased and the claimant had ended 2 years before the death of the deceased, the claim failed (see *Layton v Martin* [1986] 2 FLR 227).

Where the deceased had left his mistress 9 days before he died, it was held that she was not being maintained by him immediately before his death and the claim failed (see *Kourkgy v Lusher* (1983) 4 FLR 65).

In *Sen v Headley* [1991] Ch 425, the claimant was obliged to make a claim under the doctrine of *donatio mortis causa* as she was not being maintained by the deceased immediately before his death.

On the other hand, the court does have regard to the circumstances which led to the break. Dependence is not measured in days or weeks, particularly where the separation has been forced or is involuntary, for example where the deceased becomes terminally ill and has to be admitted to hospital. In *Re Beaumont* (at para 4.9.4), Megarry VC said:

> If one is to reject a mere examination of the de facto state of affairs existing at the instant of death, and seek to discover something more substantial and enduring than that, then an assumption by the deceased of responsibility for the maintenance of the applicant seems to me to be the relationship which has to be considered. If immediately before the death of the deceased such an assumption of responsibility by the deceased for the applicant was in existence, and under it the applicant was being maintained, wholly or partly, by the deceased, then the applicant may claim under the Act. In such a case the degree of maintenance would not be whatever degree existed at the instant before death but whatever degree normally and habitually existed under the assumption of responsibility which was then in existence.

In *Re Kirby (Deceased), Hirons v Rolfe* (1982) 3 FLR 249, the court applied the test of 'the settled pattern of arrangements between the parties ignoring any transitory interruption owing to changes of circumstances occurring immediately before the death and possibly in anticipation of it'. In *Re Watson* (at para 4.9.3), although the point was not raised by the Treasury Solicitor, Neuberger J said that if it had, it was not an argument which in his view could respectably have been advanced, and that as a matter of ordinary language, the fact that someone is in hospital for even a long period at the end of which he dies does not mean that 'he ceased to be part of the household of which he was a part until he was forced by illness to go to hospital and to which he would have returned had he not died'.

It would seem, therefore, that the court will not apply the words of the section strictly, but consider the facts and the circumstances which led to the separation, and the parties' relationship, and take a broad and practical decision (see, further, para 4.6.1).

Chapter 5

Forfeiture

5.1 INTRODUCTION

The forfeiture rule is a common law rule of public policy which, in certain circumstances, precludes a person who has unlawfully killed another from acquiring a benefit in consequence of the killing. It applies to succession under wills and intestacy.

Such an offender may not take any benefit which would otherwise accrue to him/her under a disposition made in the victim's will, or on the victim's intestacy. The whole of any disposition in favour of the offender fails. The offender and his/her successors in title are prevented from acquiring any benefit under any disposition made by the deceased in his/her will or under the laws of intestacy. Thus where the offender is the only child of the victim his/her inheritance goes to other relatives. All descendants of the offender are excluded, eg his/her child and the grandchild of the victim, as occurred in *Re DWS (Deceased)* [2001] Ch 568, CA, where a person killed both his parents neither of whom left a will. The offender was not allowed to inherit from them by reason of the forfeiture rule. The Court of Appeal decided that not only he but also his son was excluded from inheriting and the deceased's estate passed to other relatives.

The Forfeiture Act 1982 has modified and mitigated to some extent this rule. It has limited the operation of the rule in respect of claims made under the I(PFD)A 1975 in cases where the claimant is convicted of unlawful killing, after 13 October 1982, the date the Forfeiture Act 1982 came into force. The Forfeiture Act 1982 enables a person who has unlawfully killed another to make a claim under any of the provisions of the I(PFD)A 1975 for financial provision from the estate of the deceased.

Following the decision in *Re DWS (Deceased)* (see above), the Law Commission
was asked to consider the law on this rule and it made recommendations in 2005
which have not as yet been implemented.

5.2   ORDER MODIFYING THE EFFECT OF THE RULE

Forfeiture Act 1982, s 2(1), empowers the court, when determining a claim
under I(PFD)A 1975, s 2, to make an order modifying the effect of the
forfeiture rule. Forfeiture Act 1982, s 2 provides as follows:

> (1)   Where a court determines that the forfeiture rule has precluded a
> person (in this section referred to as 'the offender') who has
> unlawfully killed another from acquiring any interest in property
> mentioned in subsection (4) below, the court may make an order
> under this section modifying the effect of that rule.
>
> (2)   The court shall not make an order under this section modifying the
> effect of the forfeiture rule in any case unless it is satisfied that,
> having regard to the conduct of the offender and of the deceased
> and to such other circumstances as appear to the court to be
> material, the justice of the case requires the effect of the rule to be
> so modified in that case.
>
> (3)   In any case where a person stands convicted of an offence of which
> unlawful killing is an element, the court shall not make an order
> under this section modifying the effect of the forfeiture rule in that
> case unless proceedings for the purpose are brought before the
> expiry of the period of three months beginning with his conviction.
>
> (4)   The interests in property referred to in subsection (1) above are–
> (a)   any beneficial interest in property which (apart from the
>   forfeiture rule) the offender would have acquired–
>   (i)   under the deceased's will ... or the law relating to
>   intestacy or by way of *ius relicti, ius relictae* or
>   *legitim*;
>   (ii)   on the nomination of the deceased in accordance
>   with the provisions of any enactment;
>   (iii)   as a *donatio mortis causa* made by the deceased; or
>   (iv)   under a special destination (whether relating to
>   heritable or moveable property); or
> (b)   any beneficial interest in property which (apart from the
>   forfeiture rule) the offender would have acquired in
>   consequence of the death of the deceased, being property
>   which, before the death, was held on trust for any person.
>
> (5)   An order under this section may modify the effect of the forfeiture
> rule in respect of any interest in property to which the
> determination referred to in subsection (1) above relates and may
> do so in either or both of the following ways, that is–

(a)   where there is more than one such interest, by excluding the application of the rule in respect of any (but not all) of those interests; and

(b)   in the case of any such interest in property, by excluding the application of the rule in respect of part of the property.

(6)   On the making of an order under this section, the forfeiture rule shall have effect for all purposes (including purposes relating to anything done before the order is made) subject to the modifications made by the order.

(7)   The court shall not make an order under this section modifying the effect of the forfeiture rule in respect of any interest in property which, in consequence of the rule, has been acquired before the coming into force of this section by a person other than an offender or a person claiming through him.

(8)   In this section–
'property' includes any chose in action or incorporeal moveable property; and
'will' includes codicil.

It will be observed that the court's powers are limited in the following respects:

- The court's power is discretionary (s 2(2)).
- The court cannot make an order modifying the effect of the rule unless it is 'satisfied, having regard to the conduct of the offender and of the deceased and to such other circumstances as appear to the court to be material, that the justice of the case requires the effect to be modified' in that case. The moral culpability of the offender and the justice of the case are matters which are relevant (s 2(2)).
- The court cannot make an order modifying the effect of the rule unless proceedings for the modification of the rule are commenced before the expiry of 3 months from the date of the offender's conviction. There is no power to extend the time limit (s 2(3)).
- The court cannot modify the rule in respect of any interest in property which, in consequence of the rule, has been acquired before the coming into force of s 2 by a person other than the offender or a person claiming through him/her (s 2(7)).
- The court has no power to modify the effect of the rule if the offender has been convicted of murder.
- The court may modify the rule by totally or partially excluding the forfeiture rule's application to relevant property or interest.
- Property includes all benefits by way of succession.
- The time limit for making the application is 3 months from the date of death. The court does not have any power to extend the time limit.

If the court decides that relief should be granted it may:

(1)   order that the forfeiture rule should not apply to any of the property, thus allowing the property to devolve as if no cause for forfeiture existed; or

(2)   reject the application of the rule to the whole of the property (see *Dalton v Latham* [2003] EWHC 796 (Ch));

(3)   apply the rule to some parts of the property and to others by identifying the particular assets, interests or property or percentage of the estate; or

(4)   make other provisions for the property, for example order that the proceeds of an insurance policy be put into a trust for a child (see *Re S (Deceased) (Forfeiture Rule)* [1996] 1 WLR 235).

Forfeiture Act 1982, s 3 provides that the forfeiture rule shall not be taken to preclude any person from making an application under the I(PFD)A 1975. This appears to include an unlawful killing including murder.

5.3   THE CASES

The following cases illustrate how the courts have interpreted these provisions.

In *Re Royse (Deceased), Royse v Royse* [1985] Fam 22, the claimant had been convicted of the manslaughter of her husband and committed to hospital under Mental Health Act 1959, s 60. On 31 March 1981, she was discharged from hospital and returned to live in the former matrimonial home, which was valued at £30,000, and which comprised the major part of the net estate of £32,000. The claimant was the sole beneficiary of the deceased's estate under his will. Letters of administration with the will annexed were first granted to the deceased's mother, and, on her death, to the brother and sister of the deceased. The claimant applied for financial provision to be made for her, because she was precluded from acquiring any benefit by reason of the forfeiture rule. In October 1982, after the claim had been made, the Forfeiture Act 1982 came into force. The application failed because the absence of reasonable financial provision was a consequence of a rule of public policy which precluded her from receiving any benefit under the will. The claimant's application under the Forfeiture Act 1982 also failed since the I(PFD)A 1975 was not in force when she made the claim. This would not apply today by virtue of the Forfeiture Act 1982. It would also be considered as Convention non-compliant and, by reason of Human Rights Act 1998, s 3, the court is under an obligation to construe statutory provisions, in this case the Forfeiture Act 1982, in a way which makes it Convention-compliant.

In *Re K (Deceased)* [1985] Ch 85, there had been a history of ill-treatment of the wife by the deceased during their marriage. On 30 September 1982, during an altercation, the deceased was killed at short range by a shotgun held by the wife. The wife was charged with murder but pleaded guilty to manslaughter. She was placed on probation. The deceased had bequeathed his residuary estate on trust to his widow for life and thereafter to four named beneficiaries. The estate was worth £412,000. The matrimonial home was held on a joint tenancy so the widow was entitled to the deceased's half share. The residuary beneficiaries contended that, notwithstanding the provisions of Forfeiture Act 1982, s 7(4), which enabled the court to modify the operation of the forfeiture rule, and whether the killing occurred before or after the I(PFD)A 1975 came into force, the court could not make an order under the Act in respect of an interest in property which had been acquired before the Act came into force. Vinelott J held that, on the true construction of Forfeiture Act 1982, s 2(7), an interest in property acquired before the coming into force of the I(PFD)A 1975 denoted property which had actually been transferred to the person entitled to it by virtue of the operation of the forfeiture rule, or who had acquired an indefeasible right to have it transferred to him/her. It did not include property which, at the time the section came into force, was held by the personal representatives who had not completed the administration; such property could therefore be the subject of an order under the Forfeiture Act 1982.

Although by reason of the wife's conduct the forfeiture rule applied, the purpose of the I(PFD)A 1975 was to require the court to form a view of the culpability attending the killing, in order to see whether, in the particular case, the effect of the rule should be modified. On the facts, since the widow had been a loyal wife, who had been subjected to violence by the deceased, and since there were no other persons to whom the deceased owed a moral obligation, it was held that it would be unjust for the widow to be deprived of the benefits which the deceased had conferred on her by his will and those which had accrued to her by survivorship. The rule was modified and she was allowed to take under the will. The conduct of the deceased towards his wife would also be a relevant consideration under Forfeiture Act 1982, s 2(3).

In *Re S (Deceased)* [1996] 1 WLR 325, a husband, who had entered into a joint insurance endowment policy with his wife, was convicted of her manslaughter. They had one son. The wife died intestate and her estate therefore passed to the son. The husband sought an order under the Forfeiture Act 1982 in respect of the policy on the ground that it came within s 2(4)(b), and was held on trust before the death of the wife pursuant to Married Women's Property Act 1882, s 11. The court held that the insurance policy could be treated as two separate policies for the husband and wife individually, for the benefit of each other. But for the application of the forfeiture rule, the beneficial interest under the policy would have passed to the husband. However, the policy constituted property held on contingent trust for him which had existed before the wife's death and thus came within Forfeiture Act 1982, s 2(4)(b). In the circumstances, the court held that it would be appropriate to apply the proceeds of the policy to a trust set up for the benefit of the son.

In *Re Jones, Jones v Midland Bank Trust Co Ltd* [1998] 1 FLR 246 (CA), the testatrix's will provided that her entire estate should pass to her son; if he predeceased her, then her two nephews were to take in equal shares. The son killed his mother and was convicted of her manslaughter. He was sentenced to a community rehabilitation order. The son applied for relief under the Forfeiture Act 1982. A preliminary issue was raised whether the residuary estate was to be held for those entitled on the deceased's intestacy, or for her two nephews. On appeal, applying the decision in *Re Sinclair, Lloyds Bank plc v Imperial Cancer Research Fund* [1985] FLR 965 (CA), it was held that the estate should devolve as on the deceased's intestacy as the gift over could take effect only if the son had predeceased the testatrix. It was not possible to speculate what provisions she would have made had she known that her son would kill her and forfeit his claim unless the court exercised its discretion.

In *Jones v Roberts* [1995] 2 FLR 422, the applicant was suffering from mental illness and killed both his parents. He pleaded guilty to manslaughter on the grounds of diminished responsibility. He was ordered to be detained under Mental Health Act 1983, s 37. The parents had died intestate. The claimant applied to the court for a determination whether, in view of his mental illness, he was precluded from taking on his father's intestacy. *Gray v Barr (Prudential Assurance Co Ltd, third party)* [1971] 2 QB 554, was relied on in support of a submission that the forfeiture rule did not apply automatically in every unlawful killing case, but only where the claimant had been guilty of deliberate and intentional manslaughter, violence or threats of violence. In rejecting the submission, the court distinguished the other cases cited. It found that the claimant's case was not one of insanity, nor of accident or recklessness. The defence of diminished responsibility reduced the charge of murder to manslaughter but the defendant was still criminally liable for his action. His application was refused.

In *Dalton v Latham* [2003] EWHC 796 (Ch), (2003) 147 Sol Jo LB 537 the claimant was convicted of manslaughter and sentenced to a term of imprisonment. He had a history of mental illness. His application was refused on the grounds that his conviction for manslaughter on the grounds of diminished responsibility had resulted simply in the claimant's responsibility for his actions being 'reduced not extinguished' but he still remained criminally liable for his actions and that the interests of justice did not require that the forfeiture rule should be modified. His plea that he had taken care of the deceased was rejected, the court finding that he had taken advantage of the deceased.

In *Dunbar v Plant* [1998] Ch 412, which was a case of suicide, the claimant's son (the deceased) and the defendant were lovers. They had purchased a property in joint names with a collateral insurance policy. The son had a like policy for the benefit of the defendant. They had planned to marry. The defendant was then accused of fraud and decided to commit suicide. She told her fiancé (the deceased) of her decision. They agreed to commit suicide together. On the third attempt the claimant's son (the deceased) died and the defendant survived. It was held that the forfeiture rule applied to offences under the Suicide Act 1961, but the court had a discretion under the Forfeiture Act 1982 to modify the rule and had to consider s 2(2) when doing so. On the facts, the court directed that the forfeiture rule should not apply and granted the defendant full relief.

5.4 SUMMARY

In summary, therefore, the language of Forfeiture Act 1982, s 2(2) is wide in its terms and the court is required to consider the justice of each case. In so doing, it will consider:

- the intention of the offender, particularly of the survivor of a suicide pact, as a relevant factor;
- the wishes of the beneficiaries, which are also material and must be given weight (see *Re K* (above));
- the conduct of the offender and the deceased;
- any moral obligation the deceased owed to the applicant and any other beneficiaries, which will be given due weight;
- in the case of property held on constructive trust, giving effect to the trust so as to provide a benefit to a third party, for example, a son of the deceased;
- the applicant's culpability, as a relevant factor;
- the fact that the forfeiture rule will not be modified in cases where a charge of murder has been reduced to manslaughter by reason of diminished responsibility;

- the fact that the Forfeiture Act 1982 does not apply to a claim made before the I(PFD)A 1975 came into force;
- as per the court's duty, what would be just in all the circumstances.

5.6   THE LAW COMMISSION'S RECOMMENDATIONS

In July 2003 following the decision in *Re DWS (Deceased)* (above), the Department for Constitutional Affairs (now renamed the Ministry of Justice) asked the Law Commission to review the relationship between the forfeiture rule and the law of succession. In its report at para 5, its recommendations in so far as it related to the forfeiture rule were that:

> 5.1   There should be a statutory rule that where a person forfeits the right to inherit from an intestate through having killed that intestate, the rules of intestate succession as laid down in sections 46 and 47 of the Administration of Estates Act 1925 (as amended), should be applied as if the killer had died immediately before the intestate.
>
> 5.2   Where a person forfeits a benefit under an intestacy through having killed a deceased, but as a result of our reforms property devolves on or is held for a minor descendant of the killer, the court should have power to order that the property be held by the Public Trustee, who should administer it so as to avoid benefit to the killer.
>
> 5.3   Where a person forfeits a benefit under a will through having killed the testator, the will should be applied as if the killer had died immediately before the testator, unless the will contains a provision to the contrary.
>
> 5.4   Where a person forfeits a benefit under a will through having killed the deceased, but as a result of our reforms, property devolves on or is held for a minor of the killer, the court should have power to order the property to be held by the Public Trustee, who should administer it so as to avoid benefit to the killer.

The Law Commission Report has attached to it a draft of the proposed Bill for legislation but it has not been implemented.

Chapter 6

Basis of the Claim

6.1 GROUNDS ON WHICH A CLAIM MAY BE MADE

There is only one ground upon which a claim under the I(PFD)A 1975 may be made, namely that (s 1(1)):

> the disposition of the deceased's estate effected by his will or the law relating to intestacy, or the combination of his will and that law, is not such as to make reasonable financial provision for the applicant.

When determining whether the disposition is such as to make reasonable financial provision for the claimant, the court must have regard to the matters set out in I(PFD)A 1975, s 3; these are discussed in detail in Chapter 7 and the material in this chapter should be read in conjunction with Chapter 7.

6.2 MEANING OF 'REASONABLE FINANCIAL PROVISION' FOR CLAIMS MADE BY SPOUSE OR CIVIL PARTNER OF THE DECEASED

The statutory definition of 'reasonable financial provision' is provided in I(PFD)A 1975, s 1(2) as amended by the CPA 2004. A distinction is drawn between a claimant who is a surviving spouse or civil partner of the deceased and all other categories of claimants.

In respect of a surviving spouse (except where the marriage or civil partnership with the deceased was the subject of a decree of judicial separation or separation order and at the date of death the decree was in force and the separation was continuing), 'reasonable financial provision' means (I(PFD)A 1975, s 1(2)(a)):

such financial provision as it would be reasonable in all the circumstances of the case for a husband or wife to receive, whether or not that provision is required for his or her maintenance

It will be observed that the section makes an exception in relation to a surviving spouse who was separated from the deceased under a decree of judicial separation which was in force at the date of death. Such a spouse/civil partner is excluded from receiving the wider financial provision which applies to a spouse/civil partner of the deceased and comes within the provision which applies to all other claimants (see below).

If, however, despite the decree of judicial separation or separation order (in the case of a civil partnership) the parties were living together and therefore the decree of judicial separation or separation order was not in force and the separation was not continuing, then the claimant would be entitled to receive financial provision as set out under I(PFD)A 1975, s 1(2)(a) above.

The I(PFD)A 1975 makes one further exceptional provision in respect of a claimant who is a former spouse/civil partner of the deceased. This exception is set out in ss 14 and 14A, as amended by the CPA 2004.

I(PFD)A 1975, s 14 deals with the exception provided in respect of a surviving former spouse. Where the deceased dies within 12 months of the decree absolute of divorce or dissolution of the civil partnership or nullity or decree of judicial separation or separation order but where:

(1)   an application for a financial provision order under Matrimonial Causes Act 1973, s 23 or a property adjustment order under s 24 of that Act has not been made by the other party to that marriage, or

(2)   such an application has been made but the proceedings theron have not been determined at the time of the death of the deceased,

then if an application for an order under I(PFD)A 1975, s 2 is made the court shall, notwithstanding anything in s 1 or s 3, have power if it thinks it just to do so, to treat that party for the purposes of the application as if the marriage was still subsisting save that in the case of a judicially separated spouse the provision will not apply if the decree of judicial separation remains in force and the separation is continuing.

In the case of civil partners, the I(PFD)A 1975 has been amended by CPA 2004, Sch 4, para 20 to add a new s 14A which provides that where:

(1)   a dissolution order, nullity order or presumption of death order has been made under the CPA 2004, chapter 2 in relation to a civil partnership,

(2)   one of the civil partner dies within 12 months from the date on which the order is made, and

(3)   either an application for a financial provision order under CPA 2004, Sch 5, Part 1 or a property adjustment order under Part 2 of that Schedule has not been made by the other civil partner, or such an application has been made but the proceedings on the application have not been determined at the time of death of the deceased,

then if an application is made for an order under I(PFD)A 1975, s 2 by a surviving civil partner, notwithstanding anything in ss 1 and 3, the court shall have power, if it thinks just to do so, to treat the surviving former civil partner as a surviving partner.

There are four matters of note within these two sections. The first is that provided the conditions are satisfied, a former spouse and civil partner's claim for financial provision will be considered on the basis of what the outcome would have been in the matrimonial proceedings. Second, that although the provision is drafted in mandatory terms by the use of the words 'the court shall', on closer scrutiny it will be observed that the court is given a discretion by the words, 'if it thinks just' whether or not to treat such a claimant as a surviving spouse or civil partner. Third, in the case where there has been a judicial separation or, in the case of a civil partner, a separation order which was in force, and the separation was continuing at the date of the death of the deceased, any claim made by the surviving spouse or civil partner of the deceased will be limited to financial provision which would be reasonable in all the circumstances of the case for the claimant to receive for his/her maintenance and not the generous provisions which apply to a surviving spouse or civil partner. Thus in the case of a surviving spouse or civil partner the claim for financial provision is not limited to maintenance. The governing criterion is what the court considers to be reasonable provision unqualified by consideration of maintenance, although there may be cases where the order made will be restricted to maintenance in such cases. Finally, in the case of a civil partnership, I(PFD)A 1975, s 14A refers to an additional order, namely that of a 'presumption of death order' which is not referred to in s 14 and does not apply to a surviving spouse.

6.2.1   Meaning of 'reasonable financial provision' in the case of all other claimants

In the case of all other claimants 'reasonable financial provision' means:

> such financial provision as it would be reasonable in all the circumstances of the case for the claimant to receive for his maintenance
> (I(PFD)A 1975, s 1(2)(b))

6.3   REASONABLE FINANCIAL PROVISION FOR SURVIVING SPOUSES/CIVIL PARTNERS AND THOSE WHO COME WITHIN I(PFD)A 1975, SECTIONS 14 AND 14A

In the case of a surviving spouse and a spouse who comes within I(PFD)A 1975, s 14, the statutory definition makes clear that the court's considerations are not restricted to what would be reasonable for the spouse to receive by way of 'maintenance'. In the words of Oliver LJ in *Re Besterman, Besterman v Grusin* [1984] Ch 458:

> The Inheritance (Family Provision) Act 1938, which first introduced the concept of reasonable testamentary provision into English Law, was an Act to provide for the maintenance of dependants. The present Act remains such an Act in relation to dependants other than surviving spouses, but this section expressly provides that in the case of a surviving spouse the governing criterion is to be what the court considers to be 'reasonable' provision unqualified by any such consideration. There may, of course, be cases where that reasonable provision in all the circumstances might be restricted to maintenance, but the sub-section makes it clear that the court, in making such reasonable provision, is not to be inhibited by what I may call 'the 1938 concept' that maintenance is the only criterion or, indeed, even that that is the dominant consideration.

In *Re Besterman*, the deceased and the claimant were married in 1958 and lived together until the deceased's death in 1976. The deceased had been extremely wealthy, and his wife had enjoyed a very high standard of living. Under the deceased's will the widow received personal chattels and a life interest in war stocks, which produced an income of £3,500 per annum. The principal beneficiary was Oxford University. The widow had no financial resources, other than a state pension. She applied for financial provision to be made for her. An interim order was made, granting her a lump sum of £75,000 to purchase a property, and interim periodical payments of £15,000 per annum. At the substantive hearing a lump sum of £259,000 was awarded to her. The widow appealed on the ground that the provision made for her was considerably less than she might reasonably have expected to receive under the Matrimonial Causes Act 1973, which was a factor the court was required, by I(PFD)A 1975, s 3(2), to have regard to when calculating reasonable financial provision. On appeal, the lump sum was increased to £378,000 (see, also, Chapter 7).

The following cases further illustrate how the court has dealt with this special provision in respect of a surviving spouse:

• In *Re Bunning (Deceased), Bunning v Salmon* [1984] Ch 480, the claimant had married the deceased when she was 35 and he was 56. Soon after the marriage, the claimant had given up her job; she had found it impossible to continue working and to run a home and give assistance to the deceased in his business. In 1971 the deceased retired. In 1978 the claimant left him. Between 1968 and 1973 the deceased had given the claimant various capital funds. On his death in 1982 he left various legacies, including legacies to the Royal Society for the Protection of Birds and the Department of Veterinary Medicine at Cambridge University. At the time of his death the widow's assets were estimated at £98,000 and her income consisted of an investment income, the state pension and other pensions. She had an earning capacity. There were no dependants. In considering her claim, the court had regard, as required by I(PFD)A 1975, s 3(2), to the lump sum she would have been awarded on an application under the Matrimonial Causes Act 1973. The court also had regard to her age and the likely length of widowhood, and took into account the fact that the assets had been built up largely by the deceased's own efforts before the marriage. In determining what the wife would have received under the 1973 Act the court took into account the husband's likely future needs and on that basis the maximum the widow would have received would have been £36,000. The court would not interfere with the deceased's right to dispose of his assets as he willed, save to make reasonable provision for the wife. She was awarded £60,000 which, added to her existing assets, gave her about one half of the total assets of the parties.

• In *Re Rowlands (Deceased)* [1984] FLR 813, the claimant widow was 90. She had lived apart from the deceased for about 43 years when the deceased died in 1981. She lived with her daughter and son-in-law. The deceased left his entire estate, worth about £100,000, to his two sons. On her application, the widow was awarded £3,000. She appealed. The court, in dismissing her appeal, took into account her special position as a surviving spouse and the matters set out in I(PFD)A 1975, s 3(2), but found that she was not able to formulate what her needs were and what she would do if a substantial award was made in her favour. There was no indication how her life would be enhanced if periodical payments or a lump sum were awarded to her.

- In *Stead v Stead* [1985] FLR 16, the claimant and the deceased had married when they were 55 and 63 respectively. The deceased had two children by his first marriage. The parties worked in their farming business and the claimant also worked as a nursery nurse. On their retirement they sold the farm and purchased a new home, and thereafter the claimant took in paying guests. The deceased was 88 when he died. By his will, he gave his widow a life interest in the home on condition that she discharged all the outgoings, and bequeathed a sum of £60,000 on trust to be invested to give her an income for life. On her claim under the I(PFD)A 1975 she was awarded a lump sum and periodical payments of £1,500 per year.

- In *Re Krubert* [1997] Ch 97 (CA), by his will, the deceased left his widow £10,000 and a life interest in the matrimonial home and in the residuary estate. The trustees were required to hold the residuary estate in trust for the deceased's sister and brother in equal shares. At first instance the widow received what was in effect 85 per cent of the net estate and the brother and sister received legacies of £7,000 each. On appeal, it was held that, in considering an appropriate award for a surviving spouse, the figure resulting from what would have been a s 25 exercise in ancillary relief proceedings under the Matrimonial Causes Act 1973 was merely one of the factors to which the court must have regard, subject to the overriding consideration of what was reasonable in all the circumstances. The Court of Appeal preferred the approach in *Re Besterman*, stating that it was more in accordance with the intention of the I(PFD)A 1975 read as a whole.

It will be noted from the above decisions that the court has used the matrimonial concept as a yardstick when determining a claim by a surviving spouse. However, as was pointed out in *Re Krubert*, this approach is merely one of the factors to which the court must have regard, subject to the overriding consideration of what was reasonable in all the circumstances. It is submitted that there is nothing in the statutory provisions which suggests that this factor should be given importance or more weight than other factors referred to in I(PFD)A 1975, s 3. More recent decisions suggest that the *Besterman* test should be approached with caution and that the 'divorce comparison' referred to is only one of the factors to be taken into account by the court in determining a claim by a surviving spouse/civil partner.

In *Moody v Stevenson* [1992] Ch 486, a notional divorce provision was treated as the starting point. In *P v G, P and P (Family Provision: Relevance of Divorce Provision)* [2004] EWHC 2944 (Fam), [2006] 1 FLR 431, Black J (as she then was) pointed out that the provisions of the I(PFD)A 1975 which relate to a surviving spouse/civil partner do not contemplate the playing out of the entire fictional ancillary relief case. To do so would involve the court in a spurious exercise. The court should, however, 'reach sufficient of a conclusion about how it would have been resolved to take that factor into account in considering what would be reasonable financial provision' under the Act.

In *Fielden and Graham v Cunliffe* [2005] EWCA Civ 1508, [2006] 1 FLR 745, the Court of Appeal took the view that the approach adopted in ancillary relief cases should be used and that result then checked against the yardstick of equality of division in cases under the I(PFD)A 1975, but pointed out that there was no presumption that the division of the assets should be in favour of an equal division. The court in cases under the Act had to carry out a balancing exercise between the various factors which had be to be taken into consideration when determining a claim under the Act. Referring to *Re Besterman*, Wall LJ said that the case should be 'viewed with a substantial element of caution not least because Oliver LJ giving the leading judgment, warned against using it as basis for drawing general decisions of principle to be applied in other and probably quite different cases'. Reference was also made to the fact that the case predates the amended provision of Matrimonial Causes Act 1973, s 25, the decision in *White v White* [2000] 2 FLR 981 (HL) and the *Duxbury* calculations (see *Duxbury v Duxbury* [1992] Fam 62).

More recently in *Baker v Baker (Financial Provision: Divorce Comparison)* [2008] EWHC 977 (Ch), [2008] 2 FLR 1956, the court applied *Fielden and Graham v Cunliffe* (see above). The court confirmed that the concept of equality had to be approached with caution in the context of family provision. Whilst acknowledging that in the case of a spouse the financial provision was not confined to reasonable maintenance, the court nevertheless had to take into account other factors. On the facts of the case, the impact of any order on other beneficiaries, on the continuation of the family business which was in the instant case run by the deceased's sons, and the difficult 'circumstances which prevailed in extricating the estate's interest in the business, together with the fact that the parties had agreed that there was a need for a clean break, were all considered to be relevant factors which the court took into account when deciding what financial provision would be appropriate for the widow. Similar views were expressed in *Barron v Woodhead* [2008] EWHC 810 (Ch), [2009] 1 FLR 747, where on the facts the court's principal concern was to ensure that the claimant had a roof over his head and sufficient means for his everyday needs.

In *Moor v Holdsworth and Others* [2010] EWHC 683 (Ch), [2010] 2 FLR 1501, in evaluating the widow's claim against the estate, the court took account of s 3 factors together with the divorce comparator. The court concluded that it was unlikely that she would have received the whole estate as she claimed. The court struck a balance and awarded her a life interest.

To summarise, therefore, in claims made by a surviving spouse the court will have regard to the following:

- that what is reasonable financial provision for a surviving spouse should not be restricted to maintenance;
- that there may be circumstances where what is reasonable financial provision may be restricted to maintenance;
- that the divorce comparator is only one of the relevant factors, not the paramount factor in determining the competing claims;
- that the I(PFD)A 1975 does not contemplate the playing out of the whole matrimonial ancillary relief exercise but its use merely as a yardstick against which to measure what would be the appropriate reasonable financial provision for the surviving spouse or civil partner;
- that the other factors set out in s 3 must be considered alongside the divorce comparator in achieving a just result;
- that unlike an application for ancillary relief under the Matrimonial Causes Act 1973, where the court is only concerned with striking a balance between two living spouses where one or both may have earning capacity, in a claim under the I(PFD)A 1975 the court is concerned with striking a balance between the surviving spouse or civil partner and the competing claims of other beneficiaries from the estate;
- that the test applied in *Re Besterman* should be applied with a 'substantial element of caution', and to note that that case was one of a blameless widow of a wealthy man who was, on the facts, entitled to financial security commensurate to the lifestyle she had enjoyed;
- that the overriding consideration is what would be reasonable in all the circumstances of the case;
- that where the surviving spouse/civil partner is unable to formulate what his/her needs are and what he/she would do if a substantial award were to be made in his/her favour, it would be difficult for the court to allow a claim for a substantial award (see *Re Rowlands* [1984] 1 FLR 813 and *Gregory, Gregory v Goodenough* [1970] 1 WLR 1465).

6.3.1   Claim by surviving husband

The I(FP)A 1938 makes no distinction between a claim by a surviving husband and a claim by a surviving wife. In the early cases, however, the courts appeared to be disinclined, save in exceptional circumstances, to grant relief where the claim was made by a surviving husband. This is illustrated by two cases in particular. In *Re Sylvester, Sylvester v Public Trustee* [1941] Ch 87, the parties were married in 1931. The husband subsequently gave up his employment and thereafter did all the housework and nursed his wife during her illness. The wife had her own income. The husband had none. She died in 1940. She bequeathed to him an annuity of £525 per annum and gave her residuary estate to a number of charities. The husband made a claim against the estate for his maintenance under the I(FP)A 1938. Farwell J, in allowing the husband's claim and awarding him 3 shillings a week, stated:

> I do not consider that, in the ordinary way, applications by husbands for this sort of assistance should be readily entertained. Prima facie a husband should be able to maintain himself, and ought not to ask the court to give him, out of his wife's estate, more than she thought fit to provide for him. There are, of course, exceptional cases in which such an application may be justified, but personally I should not be very willing to assist husbands in cases of this sort, unless the circumstances were indeed exceptional.

In *Re Styler, Styler v Griffiths* [1942] Ch 387, the deceased had made an agreement with her second husband that, on his making a will in her favour, she would make a will leaving the income of her estate to him for life. They both made wills in accordance with the agreement. Subsequently, the wife made another will leaving all her estate to her daughter by her first marriage. On the wife's death, the husband applied for reasonable provision. In refusing his application, Morton J approved the judgment of Farwell J in *Re Sylvester* (above) and criticised his own decision in *Re Pointer* [1941] Ch 60. He stated, 'Having now had more experience of administering the Act since I decided that case, I do not think that I should now make any provision, as I did there for a husband with a pension of £180 a year, an annual income of £124 from investments and £25 a year net from property, unless the circumstances were exceptional'.

It is submitted that the court's approach today would be different, having regard to decisions concerning applications for financial relief under the Matrimonial Causes Act 1973, and more particularly to the decisions in *White v White* [2001] 1 AC 596 (HL) and *Cowan v Cowan* [2001] EWCA Civ 679, [2002] Fam 97. In *White v White*, Lord Nicholls of Birkenhead stated, 'There is one principle of universal application which can be stated with confidence. In seeking to achieve a fair outcome, there is no place for discrimination between husband and wife and their respective roles' (see, further, Chapter 7). (See also *Barron v Woodhead* [2008] EWHC 810 (Ch), [2009] 1 FLR 747, where in a claim made by a surviving husband, the court was concerned with providing the claimant with the security of a roof over his head.)

6.3.2 Judicially separated spouse/civil partner and former spouse/civil partner

A surviving spouse or civil partner who is judicially separated from the deceased, and a former spouse or civil partner, are placed in the same category as other claimants. This distinction may well have been made because a judicially separated or divorced spouse/civil partner would have been entitled to apply for ancillary relief under the Matrimonial Causes Act 1973 and the CPA 2004 respectively, and such an application would have been considered and dealt with under the very wide jurisdiction provided by both Acts. It will thus be difficult for such a clamant to satisfy the court that the deceased's will or the law of intestacy or the combination of the will and that law has failed to make reasonable financial provision for the claimant. Any claim for financial provision made under the I(PFD)A 1975 by such a spouse or civil partner would therefore be additional to the relief already obtained in the matrimonial proceedings (but see I(PFD)A 1975, s 15, which entitles the court to exclude such a claimant from seeking an order under the Act; see para 7.10.1). The court in those circumstances will be reluctant to interfere with the deceased's disposition of his/her estate. It will only do so if it is satisfied that the deceased has not been reasonable and will decide the issue 'by ordinary canons of human behaviour and decency balancing generosity against parsimony, and the duty to a family against the claim of an ex-wife' (*Re Talbot* [1962] 1 WLR 1113).

Some confirmation for the basis of this distinction can also be found in the special and exceptional provision made by I(PFD)A 1975, ss 14 and 14A in respect of a claimant whose marriage/civil partnership was dissolved or annulled, or who was granted a decree of judicial separation, within 12 months of the date of the deceased's death and the application under the Matrimonial Causes Act 1973 or the CPA 2004 has not yet been made or is still pending.

In view of the court's powers, under the Matrimonial Causes Act 1973 and the CPA 2004, to make capital adjustments between spouses and civil partners on a divorce dissolution, annulment of marriage/civil partnership or judicial separation or separation, there will be few cases in which it will be possible for a former spouse/civil partner to satisfy the condition that the deceased's will or the law of intestacy, or the combination of his/her will and that law, failed to make reasonable financial provision for the former spouse/civil partner. The former spouse/civil partner will have to show exceptional circumstances. These exceptional circumstances were referred to by Ormrod and Purchas LJJ in *Re Fullard (Deceased)* [1981] 3 WLR 743. Purchas LJ said:

There must be some exceptional developments or conditions present which would make the analysis of what is reasonable as at the date of the death, which is the time when considerations under the Act must be made, different from the circumstances which existed at the dissolution of the marriage when these matters were carefully canvassed and resolved. There may well, of course, be developments which would enable an ex spouse to seek relief with some chances of success under this Act. Where there has been a long period of time since the dissolution of the marriage in circumstances in which a continuing obligation to support the ex spouse has been established by an order of the court, by consent, or otherwise, under which periodical payments have been, and continue to be made up to the date of death there may be circumstances such as envisaged by counsel for the applicant, where the death itself unlocks a substantial capital sum of which the testator should have been aware and from which had he made a will, at the time immediately before his death, he ought, within the criteria of the 1975 Act have made provision. There may be other incidents of further accretion of wealth but I doubt that the mere fact of accretion of wealth after the dissolution of the marriage would justify an application. An application would only be justified if all the circumstances of the case and all the considerations set out in the Act, made it reasonable that the testator should have made some provision as at the time of his death for the applicant.

The test in such cases is whether the former spouse/civil partner is reasonably provided for, and it is only if he/she is not so provided for that the court will interfere. See also *Whiting v Whiting* [1988] 2 FLR 189.

The following are some of the cases in which a claim made by a former spouse was considered. They illustrate the distinctly different principles which apply to such claims:

- In *Re Talbot* (above), the claimant was 52. Her marriage to the deceased had been annulled and on her application for ancillary relief an order by consent was made in her favour for her maintenance at the rate of £432 per annum. A year later she gave birth to a child of whom the deceased was not the father. The deceased nevertheless continued to maintain the claimant. The deceased remarried and had three children by his second wife, all of whom were minors at the date of his death. His estate, worth £19,397, was left to his second wife. When dismissing the claimant's claim Baker J said:

  Before I sit in the testator's chair to amend his last will, I must be satisfied that he has not been reasonable in his solution to the dilemma which faced him. Would any testator have done other than did the deceased in the circumstances which existed immediately before his death? I think not. Such a man would regard interference with his disposition as an unwarranted statutory and judicial defeat of his intentions. It may be said that all testators who fail to make provision for a former wife are unreasonable if a substantial maintenance order is suddenly to be cut off at death. But that problem should be decided by the ordinary canons of human behaviour and decency, balancing generosity against parsimony and the duty to a family against the claim of an ex-wife.

- In *Re Eyre* [1968] 1 WLR 530, when allowing the claimant's claim, Lane J had regard in particular to:

  - the fact that there was an order for secured maintenance in her favour;
  - whether the first wife should be accorded financial equality with the widow. He came to the view that there was no such general rule, even when there was nothing to choose between them so far as conduct was concerned, as there were many other factors to be considered; and
  - the fact that an accretion of wealth to the estate had occurred since the first marriage ended.

- In *Lusternik v Lusternik* [1972] Fam 125, the claim succeeded because the deceased had not made a full, frank and honest disclosure of his means.
- In *Re Crawford (Deceased)* (1983) 4 FLR 273, the deceased and his former wife were divorced in 1968. A consent order was made, under which the deceased was required to pay the claimant, by way of maintenance, one third of his gross salary less the mortgage and the insurance on the former matrimonial home, where the claimant lived. In addition, the deceased was obliged to pay the outgoings on the property. In 1975 the former matrimonial home was sold and another property purchased for the claimant. The deceased thereafter failed to make the payments under the order. The deceased remarried and had two children, who were both dependants at the date of his death. On his retirement, the deceased received a lump sum of £69,767, which was paid into a joint account with his second wife. He also received an index-linked pension. In 1979, on the deceased's suggestion, the claimant made an application for a lump sum order on a 'clean break' basis. Before the application was heard the deceased died. The claimant did not receive anything from his estate. The trustees of the pension fund, however, paid to the widow £72,402.12, which did not form part of the net estate. She also received an index-linked pension, as did her two children; again, these did not form part of the net estate. Her pension was £10,369, and the children's was £8,644.92. She also received £46.27 state pension per week and £10.50 child allowance per week. In addition, the widow had an interest in one half of the former wife's house and a life interest in the other half under the will. She also

had capital of £69,767.21 and the lump sum from the pension fund. The claimant had capital of £1,500 and state benefits of £34.28 per week.

It was conceded that the deceased had failed to make reasonable financial provision for the claimant and that a lump sum should be awarded. The issue related to the amount which should be awarded, and in deciding the amount the questions were:

- whether the court should take into account the financial benefits accruing to the beneficiaries of the estate of the deceased or to the claimant by reason of the death of the deceased but which did not form part of his estate;
- whether there were any special principles to be applied by the court in determining whether or not to exercise its discretion under I(PFD)A 1975, s 9 to treat the severable share in joint property as part of the net estate (see para 9.8.3);
- if the court decided to exercise its discretion under s 9, whether the former wife's house should be treated differently from the net estate merely by virtue of its being joint property; and
- if the needs of the former wife remained the same, whether it was reasonable for her to receive the same provision out of the estate as was agreed or ordered by the court during the deceased's lifetime.

The court held that:

- I(PFD)A 1975, s 3(1)(c) directed the court to take into account the financial resources and financial needs which any beneficiary of the estate of the deceased had, so that the lump sum of £72,402 paid to the second wife, the pension of £10,369 per annum that she received and the capital of £69,767 which she had in the building society were financial resources which the court was entitled to take into consideration in deciding the claim;
- there were no special principles which ought to guide the court in considering its discretion under s 9, as that section sets out everything which is necessary for the purpose of guiding the court;
- if the court exercised its discretion and ordered the deceased's share in the joint property to be treated as part of the net estate, it should not be treated differently;
- it should not be assumed that provision for a former wife under the Act was the same as a periodical payments order under the Matrimonial Causes Act 1973, as different considerations applied under the two enactments. In assessing the amount to be awarded to

the former wife, the court had to look at all the matters set out in
s 3(1)(a)–(g) and s 3(2)(a) and (b);
– on the facts of the case, the former wife needed an annuity of £4,000
per annum, which would cost £35,000 and, in the circumstances, an
order under s 9 was justified.

See also *Re Farrow (Deceased)* [1988] 1 FLR 205.

Where, however, a former wife's claims for income and capital have been
finally settled, she is unlikely to succeed in obtaining an order under I(PFD)A
1975, s 2. In *Brill v Proud* [1984] Fam Law 59 (CA), the parties had obtained,
upon a decree, a consent order in full and final settlement of their claims for
financial relief. The former wife had, under the terms of the settlement,
received the former matrimonial home in return for a small lump sum. Her
income was higher than her husband's. On his death she made a claim which
failed.

In *Cameron v Treasury Solicitor* [1996] 2 FLR 716, the claimant's marriage to
the deceased had been dissolved in 1971. They had no children. The claimant
had received a lump sum payment on the dissolution of the marriage by way
of a clean break provision. The deceased died intestate and the estate devolved
on the Crown as *bona vacantia*. The former wife's claim under the I(PFD)A
1975 failed on appeal despite the fact that she was in difficult financial
circumstance and in poor health on the grounds that the clean break order had
been obtained over 19 years before the death of the deceased and there was no
evidence that he had had any continuing obligation towards her and she had
not made out a case that it was not reasonable for the deceased to have not
made any financial provision for her.

In *Barrass v Harding* [2001] 1 FLR 138 (CA), following a divorce between
the claimant and the deceased there had been a clean break settlement in 1964.
The deceased remarried but his second wife predeceased him. He made a will
leaving his estate to his sister in law. The former wife was living with her son
in poor circumstances. Her claim failed.

Although not a case under the I(PFD)A 1975, in *Benson v Benson* [1996]
1 FLR 692, within 6 months of financial settlement in divorce proceedings the
wife died. The husband by way of an appeal sought to have the order set aside
on the grounds that the order was still executory. The appeal was dismissed on
the grounds that where the parties had been legally represented and the
agreement reached between them which had led to the order was clear,
unambiguous and made for good consideration, the court would not interfere
with the consent order. The death of the wife was not an event which was

contemplated by the parties and in any event the appeal was lodged over a year after the wife's death.

6.4 MEANING OF 'MAINTENANCE'

There is no definition of the term 'maintenance' in the I(PFD)A 1975, but case law provides guidance on the approach of the courts on what can be regarded as reasonable maintenance:

- 'Maintenance' includes payments which directly or indirectly enable the claimant in the future to discharge the cost of living. It does not include a capital sum to enable the claimant to discharge his/her tax liability (see *Re Dennis (Deceased), Dennis v Lloyds Bank* [1981] 2 All ER 140).
- The fact that the claimant is in necessitous circumstances is not enough (see *Re Coventry (Deceased), Coventry v Coventry* [1980] Ch 461 (CA)). In *Re Coventry*, the claimant was the only child of the deceased. He returned home when he was 26. Shortly afterwards, the mother left home and she lived separately from the deceased. The son looked after the home, did all the tasks and contributed towards the general outgoings. When he married, his wife took over the task, but the marriage broke down. A year later the deceased died intestate. His entire estate passed to his widow. The son, who was on a low income and had no savings, made a claim. His claim failed.
- 'Maintenance' does not mean whatever may be desirable for the claimant's general benefit or welfare (see *Re Coventry*).
- 'Maintenance' means what is sufficient to enable the claimant to live decently and comfortably according to the station in life to which he/she has been called. It does not merely mean enough to bring the claimant to subsistence level, but it does not mean sufficient to give the claimant a life of luxury (see Ewbank J in *Re Debenham (Deceased)* [1986] 1 FLR 404, adopting the decision in *Re Duranceau* [1952] 3 DLR 714). In *Re Debenham*, the claimant was an unwanted child of the deceased, who had always been aloof, distant and cruel to the claimant. The claimant was brought up by her grandparents in South Africa. When she was 21 she came to England to see her mother but she was totally rejected by her. Subsequently, the mother had led her to believe that she would be 'all right' if anything happened to the mother. The deceased left the claimant a legacy of £200, and most of the residue of her estate was left to six charities. The claimant was 58, an epileptic and a sick woman. She and her husband lived on a pension of £500 per annum and state benefits. In allowing her application the

court had regard to the matters set out in s 3; the fact that there were no other claimants; and the fact that the deceased had no obligations or responsibilities to the charities. The court considered that the deceased owed the claimant a moral obligation and responsibility and awarded her a lump sum of £3,000 and periodical payments of £4,500 per annum. The case was distinguished from that of *Re Coventry* (above).

- 'Maintenance' means no more or less than the claimant's and his/her family's way of life and well-being, his health and financial security. In *Graham v Murphy* [1997] 1 FLR 860, on the facts, it was decided that maintenance did not mean that the claimant should be provided with a lavish lifestyle or such as would relieve him/her from working, or such as would provide him with a high standard of life for the rest of his/her life. See also *Re Scott-Kilvert (Deceased), Robinson v Bird* [2003] 2 All ER (D) 190, on luxury items not coming within the meaning of 'maintenance'.

- An award of a lump sum to pay off past debts does not fall within the concept of 'maintenance' unless the payment of such debts enable the claimant to derive a future income, or the debts represented living expenses since the death of the deceased (see *Baynes v Hedger and Others* [2009] EWCA Civ 374, [2009] 2 FLR 767).

- Some moral obligation of maintenance over and above blood ties must be established. In *Re Goodchild, Goodchild v Goodchild* [1997] 1 WLR 1216, the deceased and his wife had executed simultaneous wills in favour of the survivor of them and then in favour of their adult son. After his wife's death the deceased remarried and made a new will leaving his entire estate to his second wife. On the son's claim, it was held that the wills were not mutually binding but that when the first wife made her will it had been on the clear understanding that her husband would give effect to their mutual intention. That gave rise to a moral obligation to provide for the son. The deceased was in breach of that obligation which left the son in financial difficulties; in those circumstances the court had to ensure that adequate financial provision was made for the son to provide for his reasonable needs for maintenance and support.

- It is not enough to establish relationship and necessity. A child must also establish special circumstances, which must be relevant to the issues before the court. Moral obligation is the most obvious special circumstance although not the only one (see *Re Abrams* [1996] 2 FLR 379). In *Re Pearce (Deceased)* [1998] 2 FLR 705 (CA), the deceased's son had worked hard on the deceased's farm without pay and was told repeatedly by the deceased that he would leave the farm to him. The deceased and his wife divorced and the deceased started cohabiting with the defendant. The deceased made a will leaving all his property to her. She subsequently moved out but the deceased did not alter his will. The son was on a low income. He had five children and lived in a property which required considerable improvement. The court found that the deceased owed a moral obligation to his son and had not made reasonable financial provision for him.

- In *Re Hancock (Deceased)* [1998] 2 FLR 346, the deceased did not make any provision for one of his daughters because sufficient funds were not available, but stipulated that, in the event of his wife's predeceasing him, his money was to be divided between his beneficiaries, which included his daughter. The deceased's assets included a plot of land, which was valued at £100,000, and which he left to his other children. The land was sold at a price higher than had been expected and the children received a windfall. The daughter's claim succeeded on the basis that the deceased's will clearly indicated that he would have made provision for her if he had believed he had sufficient assets available. A periodical payments order of £3,000 per annum was awarded.

  For other examples where an award was made, see *Rees v Newbery and the Institute for Cancer Research* [1988] 1 FLR 1041 and *Re Watson* [1999] 1 FLR 878 (see Chapter 4).

- Failure by the deceased to provide for the claimant during the claimant's minority does not entitle the claimant to apply for financial provision from the deceased's estate when he/she becomes an adult (see *Re Jennings (Deceased)* [1994] Ch 286 (CA)).

- In *Re Christie (Deceased), Christie v Keeble* [1979] Ch 168, an order was made to redress the balance between the two children of the deceased. The court interpreted s 1(2)(b) thus:

  In my judgment, the financial provision that is thus contemplated is not necessarily financial provision that would be 'required' for the applicant's maintenance. The contrast between paragraphs (a) and (b) of section 1(2), in my judgment, makes it clear. Nor in my judgment does the use of the word 'maintenance' carry with it any implication that the applicant, in order to qualify, must be in any way in a state of destitution or financial difficulty. Nor in my judgment, is it useful to refer to the test as being an objective test, whatever that word may mean, in the context of this Act which directs the court to consider the particular and personal matters set out in section 3. In my judgment the word 'maintenance' refers to no more and no less than the applicant's way of life and well-being, his health, financial security and allied matters such as the well-being, health and financial security of his immediate family for whom he is responsible.

Other cases where the court has made an award include cases where the claimant is mentally disabled and on state benefits. State benefits have been disregarded in considering whether reasonable financial provision had been made for the claimant by the deceased. In *Re Collins* [1990] Fam 56, the deceased died intestate. The claimant was her daughter who was mentally subnormal, unemployed and on state benefit. She was awarded £5,000 and her entitlement to state benefit was disregarded.

The fact that the claimant is on state benefit should not preclude the person from seeking or being granted an award unless, as occurred in *Re E, E v E* [1966] 1 WLR 709, the estate is so small that it would not benefit anyone to make any awards. Since those under disability, particularly those with mental disability, are often treated in the community, an award can provide them with some basic needs and comfort which would otherwise not be available. See *Hanbury v Hanbury* [1999] 2 FLR 255, where an award of £39,000 was settled on a discretionary trust. Where a person is on benefits, and particularly where the recipient of such benefit is under some disability, it is essential to ascertain the maximum capital which a person is entitled to have and still remain eligible for benefit.

In *Gold v Curtis* [2005] WTLR 673, the deceased had left her entire estate to her daughter indicating that she had not made any provision for her son as he had had enough from her during her lifetime and that they had been estranged. The son had in fact received only two modest payments from his mother of £1,200 and £600 Before her death they had become reconciled and the deceased saw her grandchildren during their childhood. One of the grandchildren was mentally disabled and would remain dependent on her father. On the facts it was held that the deceased had not made reasonable financial provision for her son having regard to his inadequate circumstances and the fact that his disabled child would remain wholly dependent on him (see, also, *Myers v Myers* [2004] EWHC 1944 (Fam), [2005] WTLR 851).

In deciding the reasonableness of the provision made by the testator the court will apply the objective test. However, having regard to the fact that the court has to consider the factors set out in I(PFD)A 1975, s 3 it is submitted that the court's decision will involve some degree of a subjective test.

Practitioners' attention is drawn to the Law Commission's Report, *Cohabitation: The Financial Consequences of Relationship Breakdown*, Law Com No 307 (TSO, 2007), 207, which recommends the need for the removal of the 'maintenance' ceiling in relation to cohabitants and extending it to cover what would be reasonable in all the circumstances of the case irrespective of whether the provision is required for the applicant's maintenance, ie to bring it in line with the test applied in claims made by spouses and civil partners. It also recommend that a person should be entitled to apply for provision under the I(PFD)A 1975 where the applicant was living in the same household as the deceased immediately before the deceased's death: (1) either: (a) the applicant and the deceased had lived for a period of 2 years immediately before the deceased's death, or (b) the applicant and the deceased had a child together; and (2) that the court should not have discretion to dispense with these requirements. The Law Commission has also suggested that a person who had cohabited with the deceased, but whose relationship ended shortly before the deceased's death, should be entitled to make a claim.

Chapter 7

Matters to which the Court is to Have Regard

7.1 INTRODUCTION

Once the court is satisfied on the preliminary issues, namely that the application has been made within the time limit, or if out of time, leave to apply has been considered, that the deceased died domiciled in England and Wales and that the claimant comes within the categories of persons who are eligible to make a claim against the estate, it can go on to consider:

(1) whether the disposition of the deceased's estate effected by his/her will or the law of intestacy, or the combination of his/her will and that law, is such as to make reasonable financial provision for the claimant. In determining whether the deceased has failed to make reasonable financial provisions for the claimant the court must apply the factors set out in I(PFD)A 1975, s 3;

(2) if the court considers that reasonable financial provision has not been made, in determining whether and in what manner and to what extent it should exercises its powers under s 2 it must again have regard to the factors set out in s 3. When determining a claim for an order under s 2, the court must therefore proceed to determine:

    (a) whether the disposition of the deceased's estate effected by his/her will or the law of intestacy, or both, makes reasonable financial provision for the claimant. The issue for determination is not whether the deceased acted unreasonably but whether, looked at objectively, and having taken into account all the factors under s 3, the provisions made or the lack of disposition produce an unreasonable result in not making any or inadequate provision for the claimant;

(b)   if reasonable financial provision has not been made, the
        court must decide whether or not to exercise its powers
        under the Act; and

(c)   if it does decide to exercise its powers, it must decide in
        what manner and to what extent it should do so (see
        Chapter 8).

The requirements of I(PFD)A 1975, s 3 are mandatory. In determining the issues,
the court must take into account all the matters set out in s 3(2) and have regard to
those facts as known at the date of the hearing (s 3(5)) (see *Re Coventry, Coventry
v Coventry* [1980] Ch 461 and *Re Rowlands (Deceased)* [1984] FLR 813). The
court, will therefore require up-to-date information about the parties'
circumstances and the values of all assets, including those of the parties. It is thus
important to ensure that the evidence is updated to reflect the changes in the
circumstances of the parties between the commencement of the proceedings and
the date of the hearing. Where the claimant lives overseas, evidence of the cost of
living in the foreign country should be adduced (see *Witkowska v Kaminski* [2006]
EWHC 1940 (Ch), [2007] 1 FLR 1545). The value of the estate should also be
updated as the court is unlikely to allow any orders to be set aside and the matter
to be reheard where there has been a fluctuation of the valuation of the assets (see
Myerson v Myerson (No 2) [2009] EWCA Civ 282, [2009] 2 FLR 147).

When dealing with the claim, the court should not:

> interfere with a testatrix's or testator's disposition merely because the judge
> may think that he would have been inclined, if he were in the position of the
> testator or testatrix, to make some provision for a particular person. I think that
> the court has to find that it was unreasonable on the part of the testatrix or the
> testator to make no provision for the person in question, or that it was
> unreasonable not to make a larger provision.
>
> (*Re Styler, Styler v Griffiths* [1942] Ch 387, per Morton J)

See also *Re Talbot* [1962] 1 WLR 1113, 'Nothing in the 1975 Act undermines
the basic proposition that a citizen of England and Wales is at liberty at his
death to dispose of his own property in whatever way he pleases'. There is no
concept of 'forced heirship' (see *H v J's Personal Representatives, Blue
Cross, RSPB and RSPCA* [2009] EWHC 3114 (Fam), [2010] 1 FLR 1613,
where on appeal a daughter's claim against her mother's estate for financial
provision was dismissed, but on further appeal to the Court of Appeal, the
court reversed the decision and found that the district judge was entitled to
find the deceased's failure to make provision for her daughter to be
unreasonable and that the district judge's decision should not have been
disturbed unless it was shown to be plainly wrong. The district judge had fully
and clearly explained his exercise of his discretion to award her financial

in the foreseeable future (see *Re Besterman* (above) and *Re Debenham* (above));

(4) any obligations and responsibilities which the deceased has towards any claimant for an order under s 2 or towards any beneficiary of the estate of the deceased (see *Rajabally v Rajabally* (above));

(5) the size and nature of the estate of the deceased (for the definition of 'net estate', see Chapter 9 and see *Re Besterman* (above));

(6) any physical or mental disability of any claimant for an order under s 2 or any beneficiary of the deceased;

(7) any other matter, including the conduct of the claimant or any other person, which in the circumstances of the case the court may consider relevant;

(8) the age of the claimant and the duration of the marriage/civil partnership, or, in the case of a cohabitant, the length of the period during which the claimant lived as the husband or wife or civil partner of the deceased and in the same household;

(9) the contribution made by the claimant to the welfare of the family of the deceased, including any contribution made by looking after the home or caring for the family.

7.2.3 Child of the deceased

In the case of a claim by a child of the deceased the criteria in I(PFD)A 1975, s 3(1) and (3) are as follows:

(1) the financial resources and financial needs which the claimant has or is likely to have in the foreseeable future;

(2) the financial resources and financial needs which any other claimant for an order under s 2 has or is likely to have in the foreseeable future (see *Re Debenham* (above));

(3) the financial resources and financial needs which any beneficiary of the estate of the deceased has or is likely to have in the foreseeable future (see *Re Besterman* (above) and *Re Debenham* (above) and Chapter 5);

(4) any obligations and responsibilities which the deceased has towards any claimant for an order under s 2 or towards any beneficiary of the estate of the deceased (see *Rajabally v Rajabally* (above));

(5) the size and nature of the estate of the deceased (for the definition of 'net estate', see Chapter 9, and see *Re Besterman* (above));

(6)   any physical or mental disability of any claimant for an order under s 2 or any beneficiary of the deceased;

(7)   any other matter, including the conduct of the claimant or any other person, which in the circumstances of the case the court may consider relevant;

(8)   the manner in which the claimant was being, or in which he/she might have expected to be, educated or trained.

7.2.4   Person treated as a child of the family

Where the claim is made by a person (not being a child of the deceased) who was treated by the deceased as a child of the family, the court must take into account (I(PFD)A 1975, s 3(1) and (3)):

(1)   the financial resources and financial needs which the claimant has or is likely to have in the foreseeable future;

(2)   the financial resources and financial needs which any other claimant for an order under s 2 has or is likely to have in the foreseeable future (see *Re Debenham* (above));

(3)   the financial resources and financial needs which any beneficiary of the estate of the deceased has or is likely to have in the foreseeable future (see *Re Besterman* (above) and *Re Debenham* (above) and Chapter 5);

(4)   any obligations and responsibilities which the deceased has towards any claimant for an order under s 2 or towards any beneficiary of the estate of the deceased (see *Rajabally v Rajabally* (above));

(5)   the size and nature of the estate of the deceased (for the definition of 'net estate', see Chapter 9, and see *Re Besterman* (above));

(6)   any physical or mental disability of any claimant for an order under s 2 or any beneficiary of the deceased;

(7)   any other matter, including the conduct of the claimant or any other person, which in the circumstances of the case the court may consider relevant;

(8)   the manner in which the claimant was being, or in which he/she might have expected to be, educated or trained;

(9)   whether the deceased had assumed any responsibility for the claimant's maintenance and, if so, the extent to which and the basis upon which the deceased assumed that responsibility, and the length of time for which the deceased discharged that responsibility;

(10) whether, in assuming and discharging that responsibility, the deceased did so knowing that the claimant was not his/her own child; and

(11) the liability of any other person to maintain the claimant.

7.2.5 Any other person who was being maintained by the deceased

In the case of a claim by any other person who, immediately before the death of the deceased, was being maintained, either wholly or partly, by the deceased, the court must have regard to (I(PFD)A 1975, s 3(1) and (4)):

(1) the financial resources and financial needs which the claimant has or is likely to have in the foreseeable future;

(2) the financial resources and financial needs which any other claimant for an order under s 2 has or is likely to have in the foreseeable future (see *Re Debenham* (above));

(3) the financial resources and financial needs which any beneficiary of the estate of the deceased has or is likely to have in the foreseeable future (see *Re Besterman* (above) and *Re Debenham* (above));

(4) any obligations and responsibilities which the deceased has towards any claimant for an order under s 2 or towards any beneficiary of the estate of the deceased (see *Rajabally v Rajabally* (above) and at para 7.2.1);

(5) the size and nature of the estate of the deceased (for the definition of 'net estate', see Chapter 9, and see *Re Besterman* (above));

(6) any physical or mental disability of any claimant for an order under s 2 or any beneficiary of the deceased;

(7) any other matter, including the conduct of the claimant or any other person, which in the circumstances of the case the court may consider relevant;

(8) the extent to which, and the basis upon which, the deceased assumed responsibility for the maintenance of the claimant, and the length of time for which the deceased discharged that responsibility.

7.3   FINANCIAL RESOURCES AND FINANCIAL NEEDS – I(PFD)A 1975, SECTION 3(1)(A)–(C)

In all cases the court must take account of the financial resources and financial needs of the claimants and beneficiaries. There is no formal definition provided in the I(PFD)A 1975 for the terms 'financial resources' and 'financial needs' but s 3(6) provides that in considering the 'financial resources' of any person the court must take into consideration the person's earning capacity, and in considering the 'financial needs' of any person account must be taken of that person's 'obligations and responsibilities'.

7.3.1   Financial resources

The I(PFD)A 1975 requires the court to take account of not only the present financial resources of the claimant/s and beneficiaries but also their foreseeable future resources. This therefore includes information not only about current earnings, but about future prospects. Earnings from investments, such as dividends from shareholdings, interest on savings and income from other sources, must be provided. In respect of a person receiving state benefits, it is necessary to consider the different types of benefit and the amounts of each type to which the person is entitled. Any pension rights, whether under a state pension or an occupational or private pension, are relevant. Information about, and valuations of, capital and other assets, including real property, savings, shareholdings and any other item of value, must be disclosed. Any entitlement under an insurance policy should be disclosed, including the surrender value and its value on maturity.

In relation to earning capacity and future earnings, much will depend on the individual circumstances of the claimant and or beneficiary, but merely because the claimant is in necessitous circumstances will not be sufficient to entitle the claimant to seek a variation in the dispositions made by the deceased particularly when the circumstances are brought about by the action of the claimant, for example in choosing not to work when he/she has an earning capacity: see *H v J's Personal Representatives, Blue Cross, RSPB and RSPCA* [2009] EWHC 3114 (Fam), [2010] 1 FLR 1613, and the reversal of the decision by the Court of Appeal in *Ilot v Mitson* (see para 7.1).

The court is likely to consider these issues in the same way as it does when assessing claims for damages in personal injury cases and in proceedings for ancillary relief under the Matrimonial Causes Act 1973. The age, health and skills of the individual will be relevant (see below). In the case of claimants with young children, personal circumstances, the availability or otherwise of a support network and the prospect of the person obtaining employment when the children are older are all relevant issues. Depression in the labour market in any specific area of employment in which the claimant's skill lies or evidence of the effect of recession on the labour market generally may also be relevant.

Form E, which is used in applications for ancillary relief, provides a good guide to the information required and can be referred to in s 2 claims cases as a way of ensuring all the relevant evidence is collected. Form E is available on the website of HM Courts Service at www.courtservice.gov.uk. Preparation of a schedule of assets, income and expenditure in the form usually prepared in matrimonial cases will be a good guide and starting point, and beneficial to the court. Similarly, it would also be useful both in terms of considering the nature of the evidence which may be relevant and to get a 'bird's eye view' of the merits of the case and the possible orders which may be appropriate to prepare a schedule similar to that which is prepared in civil actions such as personal injury claims.

7.3.2   Financial needs

'Financial needs' means reasonable requirements, and in assessing this factor the court may take into account the standard of living enjoyed by the claimant during the lifetime of the deceased, and the extent to which the deceased contributed to that standard (see *Harrington v Gill*, at para 4.9.2, *Malone v Harrison*, at para 4.9.4, *Stead v Stead*, at para 6.3 and *Re Besterman* and *Re Bunning*, at para 6.3).

The needs of a claimant or beneficiary depend on his/her standard of life and the extent to which the deceased provided for that standard. In a claim by a surviving spouse or cohabitant, the lifestyle enjoyed by the claimant and the deceased, to which the deceased contributed, is highly relevant. Whether those needs can be met will depend on the size of the estate and the competing claims of other claimants and beneficiaries. It is not the function of the court to re-write the deceased's will, but to carry out a balancing exercise between the competing interests, while giving effect to the deceased's intention.

What is reasonable is relative and much will depend on the individual facts of each case. However, in *White v White* [2000] 2 FLR 981, the House of Lords (now the Supreme Court) disapproved any evaluation of a wife's needs solely or even largely by reference to 'reasonable requirements' on the basis that the Matrimonial Causes Act 1973 does not refer to an entitlement being assessed in that manner. The only yardstick that the court can now use is that of fairness between the parties with the objective of achieving a fair outcome. In *Miller v Miller; McFarlane v McFarlane* [2006] UKHL 24, [2006] 1 FLR 1186, Lord Nicholls stated that the hopes, aspiration and expectations of the parties were not an appropriate basis on which to assess financial needs. Baroness Hale made the observation that, 'the court has to take some account of the standard of living enjoyed during the marriage: section 25(c). The provision should enable a gentle transition from that standard to the standard that she could expect as a self-sufficient woman'.

Both the above cases relate to financial provision following a dissolution of marriage but the decisions are relevant in claims under the I(PFD)A 1975 where the claimant is a surviving spouse or civil partner, although only as a starting point. In a claim under the Act the court has to balance the needs of the claimant against the needs of any beneficiary, not simply those of the spouses/civil partners.

The I(PFD)A 1975 requires the court to consider both present and foreseeable future needs. It is under this head that information relating to the parties' future prospects, in terms of both income and capital, is relevant. In addition, the needs of those for whom the claimant or beneficiary is and will continue to be responsible, for example, children, an adult disabled child and other members of the family, are relevant. Any other liability which the claimant or a beneficiary has is also a relevant factor. Where a claimant or beneficiary or his/her dependant is suffering ill-health, medical evidence should be provided about the person's present condition and the prognosis; in appropriate cases it may be useful to adopt the approach taken in personal injury cases (see *Hanbury v Hanbury* [1999] 2 FLR 255, for the facts, see para 8.5).

When considering whether the deceased has made reasonable financial provision for the claimant, the court is concerned with whether the provisions made or not made were reasonable in the circumstances as they existed, and not as the deceased may have thought they existed. (See *Millward v Shenton* [1972] 1 WLR 711, where the claimant was suffering from *dystrophia syotonica* and was an invalid living on benefits. His mother made no provisions for any of her six children as she believed they were self-supporting.)

7.4   DECEASED'S OBLIGATIONS AND RESPONSIBILITIES – I(PFD)A 1975, SECTION 3(1)(D)

The obligations and responsibilities which the deceased had towards the claimant or beneficiary, to be taken into account when considering a claim, must have existed immediately before the death of the deceased. A claim by an adult child of the deceased, without any evidence to show special circumstances, will generally fail. Failure by the deceased to provide for his/her child during the child's minority does not entitle the child, when he/she is an adult, to found a claim. The fact that an adult child of the deceased is in necessitous circumstances does not in itself justify a conclusion that the deceased failed to make reasonable provision for his/her child (see *Re Coventry, Coventry v Coventry* (above)). Where the claimant is of working age with a job or capable of obtaining a job which would be available to him/her but chooses not to work, he/she is unlikely to succeed unless there are some special circumstances to justify the conclusion that the failure to make any or insufficient provision for the claimant was unreasonable (see *Ilot v Mitson* (para 7.1), which reversed the decision in *H v J's Personal Representatives, Blue Cross, RSPB and RSPCA* [2009] EWHC 3114 (Fam), [2010] 1 FLR 1613). But where the claimant had given up employment to care for the deceased and had long been out of employment, that was considered a relevant factor in considering whether in the circumstances the deceased had failed to discharge his obligation. In *Espinosa v Bourke* [1999] 1 FLR 747, when the deceased was 79 he and his grandson moved in with his adult daughter who gave up her part-time employment to care for him and his grandson. When the deceased was 87, the daughter left to marry, leaving the deceased to be cared for by his grandson and a cleaner. The deceased left his estate including the portfolio of shares he had inherited from his wife to the grandson and excluded his daughter despite the fact that he had promised his wife that he would leave the shares to the daughter. In allowing the appeal against the decision of the trial judge who had dismissed the daughter's claim, it was held that the trial judge had focused too much on the requirement that an adult child must show moral obligation and her conduct in leaving the deceased and had failed to take account of the criteria in I(PFD)A 1975, s 3 into the balancing exercise. The judge had failed to take account of the claimant's age and the fact that she had been out of employment for a long time. He had also failed to take account of the promise he had made to leave his wife's portfolio of shares to the daughter. She was awarded £60,000 (see, also, below).

In *Re Jennings (Deceased)* [1994] Ch 286, the claimant's father had not made any financial contribution for the claimant's maintenance during his minority and had had no contact with him. The father died without leaving any other children or other dependants. He left his estate to remote relatives and three charities. The claimant lived comfortably. At first instance, the judge had held that he was entitled to take into account the deceased's total failure to fulfil his financial and moral obligations towards the claimant during his minority and awarded the claimant £40,000 to enable him to reduce his mortgage. On appeal, it was held that Parliament had not intended that the I(PFD)A 1975 should revive defunct obligations and responsibilities as a basis for a claim under the Act. As a general rule, the obligations and responsibilities of the deceased referred to in s 3(1)(d) are those which the deceased had immediately before his death, and if the claim did not come within para (d) it could not be brought under the general provision of s 3(1)(g). Blood relationship between a parent and child did not impose a continuing moral obligation which could found a claim under the Act. Furthermore, on the facts, the claimant had failed to satisfy the test in s 1(1)(b) that the provision was necessary for his maintenance to enable him to discharge the cost of his daily living at the standard appropriate to him. See, also, *Williams v Johns* [1988] 2 FLR 475.

In *Re Jennings (Deceased)* [1994] Ch 286 (CA), an adult son's claim against the estate of his father, based on the fact that the father had failed to discharge his responsibilities towards him during this minority, failed.

In *Adams v Lewis* [2001] WLTR 493, although the deceased's daughters were on state benefits, had little if any savings and lived modestly, their claim against the estate failed. The court found that there was no moral or other obligation on the deceased to provide for the daughters.

In *H v J's Personal Representatives, Blue Cross, RSPB and RSPCA* [2009] EWHC 3114 (Fam), [2010] 1 FLR 1613, where the claimant was estranged from her mother since she was 17 and three attempts at reconciliation had failed, the daughter's claim against the estate failed although she was in necessitous circumstances relying mainly on state benefits for income. The claimant did not work and her husband worked only part-time. The mother had set out her reason for not making any provision for her daughter in a letter. On appeal, the court held that necessitous circumstances could not in itself be a reason to alter the disposition made by the deceased particularly as the claimant had the ability to work but had chosen not to do so. 'The ordinary family obligations of a mother towards her only child who was an independent adult' was not a weighty factor and on the facts there was no obligation on the part of the deceased to make provision for her daughter. However, on further appeal to the Court of Appeal, the court reversed the decision. The court held that the issue of whether the mother's failure to make financial provision for her estranged daughter was a value judgment, and the district judge's decision should not be disturbed when the reasons for the exercise of his discretion had been fully and clearly explained, unless it was plainly wrong (*Ilot v Mitson* (see para 7.1)).

Similarly, in *Garland v Morris* [2007] EWHC 2 (Ch), [2007] 2 FLR 528, a claim made by an adult daughter, who had not spoken to her father for 15 years, against her father's estate failed. In *Baynes v Hedger and Others* [2009] EWCA Civ 374, [2009] 2 FLR 767 it was held that the deceased who was the claimant's godmother did not have obligations or responsibility to make provisions for her goddaughter. She had fulfilled her obligations to her goddaughter during her lifetime by providing financial assistance to her in her lifetime.

As shown by the above cases, the morality of a claim, or the deceased's moral obligation, though not always enough to substantiate a claim, may be relevant when weighing up all the other factors under I(PFD)A 1975, s 3 and carrying out the balancing exercise. In the case of an adult child, it is not necessary to show exceptional circumstances. While a claim by an adult child who is able to support him/herself, without any other relevant circumstances, is unlikely to succeed, it does not follow that a claim by an adult child will always fail. The test is whether, after applying the s 3 criteria to the particular facts of the case, which include the deceased's obligations towards the claimant, it is established that the deceased did not make such provision as would be reasonable in all the circumstances of the particular case for the claimant to receive for his/her maintenance. The Act does not in any way restrict the interpretation to be given to the word 'obligations'.

Re Coventry, Coventry v Coventry [1980] Ch 461 is often cited as authority that an adult child of the deceased is not entitled to make a claim unless it can be shown that there are exceptional circumstances; reliance for this proposition is placed on the judgment of Oliver J where he said, 'applications for maintenance by able-bodied and comparatively young men in employment and able to maintain themselves must be relatively rare and need to be approached, I would have thought, with a degree of circumspection'. But the learned judge also said:

> It cannot be enough to say, 'Here is a son of the deceased; he is in necessitous circumstances; there is property of the deceased which could be made available to assist him, but which is not available if the deceased's dispositions stand: therefore those dispositions do not make reasonable provision for the applicant'. There must it seems to me, be established some sort of moral claim by the applicant to be maintained by the deceased, or at the expense of his estate, beyond the mere fact of a blood relationship, some reason why it can be said that, in the circumstances, it is unreasonable that no or no greater provision was in fact made.

In *Re Debenham (Deceased)* [1986] 1 FLR 404, the deceased had never recognised her obligations towards the claimant, her daughter, whom she had rejected since her birth, and consistently repulsed efforts by the daughter to form a relationship with her, although she had indicated to the claimant that she would be well provided for in her will. The deceased left the claimant £200, even though she was aware that her daughter was an epileptic and unable to work; her life expectancy was lower than average and she and her husband lived on a small income. The deceased left the rest of her estate to six animal charities to whom she had no obligations. It was held that although the deceased did not owe any legal obligation to the claimant who was an adult, she owed her a moral obligation and responsibility.

Case law supports the view that the deceased's moral obligation to the claimant justifying an award may be established where promises were made; or where the deceased took advantage of the services of the claimant; or by evidence of the deceased's conduct towards the claimant, as occurred in *Re Debenham* (above); or where the deceased had said that he/she owed the claimant such an obligation. In *Re Abrams (Deceased)* [1996] 2 FLR 379, a claim was made by an adult son of the deceased. The son had worked for the deceased in the family business for many years at a low wage in expectation that one day it would be his. He had been forced by the mother's ill-treatment of him to leave the business. The court found that moral obligation was the most obvious circumstance to be taken into account and that, on the facts of the case, the deceased's moral obligation or special circumstances and failure to make provision had been overwhelmingly established to justify an award.

In *Re Pearce* [1998] 2 FLR 705, the claimant, the deceased's son, had worked hard on the deceased's farm without pay and was told by the deceased that he would leave the farm to his son on his death. The deceased, on his divorce, formed a relationship with the defendant. He made a will leaving all his property to the defendant. She then left him and did not live with him again. The deceased did not change his will. The claimant was on a low income and lived with his wife and five children in a home which was in need of substantial improvements. It was held that the deceased had a moral obligation to his son to make financial provision for him.

In *Espinosa v Bourke* [1999] 1 FLR 747, an award was made even though the claimant had left her father when he was aged 87, to be cared for by his grandson and the cleaner. The court made the award on the basis that, in considering the criteria in I(PFD)A 1975, s 3, it had to consider that the claimant had initially left her employment to care for her father for 8 years, had not been in formal employment for a considerable period and was in financial need. The deceased had also promised his wife that he would leave the wife's portfolio of shares to his daughter and he therefore had an obligation arising from that promise to make provision for his daughter.

See, also, *Re Callaghan (Deceased)* [1985] Fam 1, where the deceased, who had been cared for by his adult step-son, was held to have owed the step-son considerable obligations.

In *Re Rowlands (Deceased)* [1984] FLR 813, a daughter of the deceased had cared for her mother, who was bed-ridden, in very difficult circumstances. The court held that, although the deceased owed an obligation towards his wife, the daughter's claim failed.

In *Re Hancock* [1998] 2 FLR 346, the deceased, when not making any provision for the claimant, who was one of his daughters, had expressed that he would have done so if there had been sufficient money available, and had made provision that if his wife predeceased him, his money was to be divided between his children, including the claimant. The estate received a windfall as a result of the sale of a plot of land. It was held that, in determining the claim, the windfall should be taken into account, along with the expressed obligation of the deceased.

It may be possible to establish a claim grounded in moral obligation on the basis of estoppel, where the deceased's actions led and encouraged a person to act in the belief thereby arising, as occurred in *Re Goodchild, Goodchild v Goodchild* (at para 6.4).

Moral obligation is also owed by the deceased where the claimant is mentally disabled or suffers from disability, or where the claimant cared for a disabled child. See *Hanbury v Hanbury* [1999] 2 FLR 255 (at para 6.4), where the claimant, an adult child of the deceased, was physically and mentally disabled and the deceased had deliberately taken steps to avoid a claim by his daughter. See, also, *Re Wood (Deceased), Wood v Wood* [1982] LS Gaz R 774 and *Bouette v Rose* (at para 4.9.4).

In the case of a claim by a former spouse, the deceased does not owe any obligation or responsibility where there has been a 'clean break' settlement by agreement or court order; indeed the court may specifically have directed, pursuant to I(PFD)A 1975, s 15, that neither party is entitled, on the death of the other, to apply for financial provision under s 2. Where, however, a continuing obligation has been imposed by an order made on marriage breakdown, or it becomes evident that the deceased had not given a full and frank disclosure of his/her assets, it could be argued that the deceased owed the former spouse obligations and responsibilities (see, further, Chapter 4).

To summarise some of the points raised above, there is unlikely to be any obligations in the following circumstances:

- necessitous circumstances in itself will not be sufficient to justify an award;

- failure by a parent to provide for an adult child during his/her minority will not suffice to raise a special obligation owed by the deceased to an adult child;
- the fact that a claimant is on state benefit will not raise a moral or legal obligation on the deceased to make provision;
- where an adult child has made a choice not to pursue employment it does not raise any legal or moral obligations on the part of the deceased;
- blood ties alone are insufficient to found a claim;
- where the adult child is self-sufficient, independent and has a comfortable standard of living;
- where the claimant's conduct towards the deceased has been reprehensible;
- where the adult child and deceased parent have been estranged it may reduce the weight of the obligation owed by the deceased;
- where a marriage or civil partnership has ended with a clean break settlement, the court is unlikely to find a continuing obligation unless there was a continuing financial order.

Legal and moral obligation on the part of the deceased may arise:

- where the claimant or any beneficiary is physically and or mentally disabled;
- where an adult child has cared for a deceased parent or step-parent;
- where the deceased had wholly or partially supported and maintained the claimant and undertaken responsibility for the claimant;
- where promises have been made by the deceased to the claimant;
- where the conduct of the deceased gives rise to an equitable obligation or constructive trust (see para 7.7.3);
- where the deceased has taken advantage of the services of the claimant or by his/her conduct has led the claimant to act to his/her disadvantage or led the claimant to an expectation;
- where the deceased has expressly acknowledged to the claimant that he/she has an obligation towards him/her;
- where the doctrine of estoppel arises;
- towards a former spouse or civil partner in certain circumstances and particularly where the financial provision order on the dissolution of the marriage or civil partnership imposes a continuing obligation.

7.5 SIZE AND NATURE OF THE NET ESTATE – I(PFD)A 1975, SECTION 3(1)(E)

For the meaning of 'net estate', see Chapter 9.

The net estate includes the deceased's interest in any foreign property (see *Beekhun v Williams* [1999] 2 FLR 229). Where the estate is large, there may not be much difficulty in meeting the competing claims of the claimants and the beneficiaries, particularly where the deceased did not owe any obligations or responsibilities to beneficiaries, as where the beneficiary is a charity (*Re Besterman* and *Re Debenham* (at para 6.3) or a remote relative. Where, however, the estate is modest, with insufficient funds available to meet the competing claims, particularly having regard to the cost of litigation, the court will be slow to deprive the testator of his/her freedom to dispose of his/her estate as he/she willed (see *Re Gregory, Gregory v Goodenough* [1970] 1 WLR 1455, where the estate was worth about £2,500 and *Re Harker-Thomas* [1969] P 28, where it was worth about £6,082). Difficulties may also arise where it is not possible to realise the 'book' value of assets, or where an asset is tied as in the case of the matrimonial home which provides a home for, say, a child.

7.6 PHYSICAL AND MENTAL DISABILITY OF ANY CLAIMANT OR BENEFICIARY – I(PFD)A 1975, SECTION 3(1)(F)

The cases of *Re Debenham* [1986] 1 FLR 404, where the claimant was an epileptic and unable to work (see para 6.4), *Hanbury v Hanbury* [1999] 2 FLR 255, where the deceased's daughter was physically and mentally disabled with a mental age of about 12 and had been cared for by the deceased but where the deceased had deliberately taken steps to avoid making provision for her (see para 6.4), *Re Wood, Wood v Wood* [1982] LS Gaz R 774, where the claimant was a severely mentally disabled step-child of the deceased for whom he had not made any financial provision, *Millward v Shenton* [1972] 1 WLR 711, where the claimant was suffering from *dystrophia syotonica* and was an invalid, and *Re McNare, McNare v McNare* [1964] 1 WLR 1255, where the applicant was blind and crippled and 71 years of age, are good examples of cases in which an award was held to be justified.

In *Gold v Curtis* [2005] WTLR 673, the mother of the claimant had left the bulk of her estate to her daughter. She had stated that she had been estranged from him and in any event she had given him financial assistance in her lifetime. Some years prior to her death they had become reconciled but she had failed to alter her will. The claimant suffered from depression and had a mentally disabled child. His income was insufficient to provide the family with a sustainable standard of living whereas the daughter had substantial assets and her income exceeded her needs. The court struck a balance between the competing claims of both siblings.

In *Myers v Myers* [2004] EWHC 1944 (Fam), [2005] WTLR 851, the daughter of the deceased suffered from depression, mental health problems and a personality disorder. She was unable to find employment. Her claim against her father's estate was allowed.

Inheritance claims, like personal injury claims, should be meticulously prepared, so that the court is provided with all appropriate medical evidence and evidence about the costs of care. Where appropriate, joint medical and employment experts should be instructed to assess the claimant's disability, earning capacity or lack of it and needs where the disability is profound.

7.7   ANY OTHER MATTER INCLUDING CONDUCT – I(PFD)A 1975, SECTION 3(1)(G)

I(PFD)A 1975, s 3(1)(g) provides that the court must take into account any other matter, including the conduct of the claimant and any other person which, in the circumstances of the case, the court may consider relevant. 'Other relevant matters' may include the deceased's reasons for disposing of his/her estate as he/she did, the deceased's wishes in respect of his/her assets, and mutual wills.

7.7.1   The deceased's reasons

I(FP)A 1938, s 1(7), as amended, had required the court to consider the testator's reasons 'so far as ascertainable' for making the dispositions contained in his/her will (if any), for refraining from disposing of his/her estate, or for not making any provision for a dependant. The court could admit documentary evidence, other evidence of facts, and oral statements by the deceased for the purpose of ascertaining or inferring the deceased's reasons for making or not making financial provision for the claimant. The court was not obliged, however, to comply with the deceased's wishes. This is demonstrated by the following cases, in which the court considered evidence of the deceased's reasons but rejected them when determining a claim for financial provision from the deceased's estate. The cases may also be a useful guide on the nature of the evidence which may be relied on in claims under the I(PFD)A 1975 where the deceased's reasons are regarded as relevant to the issues before the court.

In *Re Vrint, Vrint v Swain* [1940] Ch 920, the court permitted a document, which had been formulated by the deceased's solicitors and approved by the deceased in connection with his former wife's application for maintenance in the magistrates' court, to be adduced in evidence for the purposes of inferring the deceased's reasons for not making any provision for her.

In *Re Pugh, Pugh v Pugh* [1943] Ch 387, the deceased by his will left his farm, worth £5,000, to his grandson and the residue, valued at about £1,800, to his widow. In support of her claim, the widow sought to rely on the evidence that, about 4 months before his death, the deceased had told his solicitors that he intended to alter his will. Thereafter, he had told the claimant that he intended to leave everything to her. That intention was repeated by him on many occasions, including as he was passing into unconsciousness, just before his death. It was held that the statements amounted to statements of intention and could not be described as the deceased's reasons for not making any further provision.

In *Re Smallwood, Smallwood v Martins Bank* [1951] Ch 369, on the widow's application for financial provision under the I(FP)A 1938, a statement by the son of the deceased about what the deceased had said to him about the claimant was admitted, on the basis that s 1(7) extended to evidence of facts from which the court could infer the deceased's reasons for making or not making any provision.

In *Re Clarke, Clarke v Roberts* [1968] 1 WLR 415, the deceased had agreed with his wife, the claimant, that they would live with his mother as a temporary measure. The mother's conduct, however, forced the claimant to leave the home, but she told the deceased that they ought to have their own home. The deceased did not respond. He died leaving a legacy of £1,000 to the claimant and the residue to his mother. His reasons for not making any further provision for the applicant were that she had agreed that the matrimonial home should be his mother's home, and that she had left and set up home on her own. The court considered those reasons, but found that it was the deceased who had broken the terms of the agreement and that the deceased's moral obligation to the claimant as his wife had not ceased.

In *Re Preston, Preston v Hoggarth* [1969] 1 WLR 317, the deceased gave, as his reasons for not making any provision for his wife, the fact that she was responsible for their separation by returning to Australia with her daughter. Notwithstanding the reasons given, the claimant was awarded a lump sum.

See also *Re Gregory, Gregory v Goodenough* (at para 7.5) and *Millward v Shenton* (at para 7.3).

The I(PFD)A 1975, by contrast with the I(FP)A 1938, does not provide that the deceased's reasons for making or not making any provision is a factor to be considered by the court when determining a claim under s 2. Section 3(1)(g), however, requires the court to have regard to 'any matter which in the circumstances of the case the court may consider relevant'. This is wide enough to include the deceased's reasons for making or not making any financial provision in his/her will for a claimant, but such considerations must be taken in the context of all the circumstances of the case. If the court considers it relevant, it will weigh that evidence against all the other factors which the court is enjoined to take into account.

Goff LJ referred to the deceased's reason as a relevant factor in *Re Coventry*, in the following terms, 'Indeed I think any view expressed by a deceased person that he wishes a particular person to benefit will generally be of little significance because the question is not subjective but objective. An express reason for rejecting the applicant is a different matter and may be relevant to the problem'.

In *Re Leach (Deceased), Leach v Linderman* [1986] Ch 226, the claimant obtained an award against her deceased's step-mother's estate despite the fact that she had never lived in her step-mother's household and was never maintained either wholly or partly by her. One of the factors in her favour was that there was considerable evidence that the deceased intended to make a will in the step-daughter's favour.

In *Re Hancock (Deceased)* [1998] 2 FLR 346 (at para 7.4), the deceased had recorded that, had there been sufficient funds available, he would have made provision for the claimant, and a clause in the will expressed his wish that his widow should make provision by her will for the claimant. A plot of land forming part of the deceased's estate was sold for development for a substantial sum of money, by the beneficiaries under his will. The Court of Appeal accepted the approach adopted in *Re Coventry* by Goff LJ and said:

> That principle of course governs the approach of the court to the assessment required to be made by the court of the reasonableness of the provision or lack of provision. A good reason to exclude a member of the family has to be a relevant consideration. However, in my view, the recognition by the testator of the status of members of his family and his goodwill towards them and in this case towards the plaintiff are factors which it is proper to take into account under s 3(1)(g) and it is for the court to give such weight to those factors as may in the individual case be appropriate.

In *Myers v Myers* [2004] EWHC 1944 (Fam), [2005] WTLR 851, the deceased's reasons that he had not included his daughter in his will because he considered that he had made adequate provision for her during his lifetime were disregarded.

In *Gold v Curtis* [2005] WTLR 673, the deceased's reasons that she had excluded her son and his family as he had had enough during the lifetime of both his parents and that he had been estranged from her were disregarded. However, in *H v J's Personal Representatives, Blue Cross, RSPB, RSPCA* [2009] EWHC 3114 (Fam), [2010] 1 FLR 1613, the deceased had set out in a letter of her reasons for excluding her daughter from any benefit the fact that she had been estranged from her and expressed the pain that she had been caused by the daughter's conduct. She had also informed her daughter of her decision and the reasons for it and the daughter had not had any expectation of receiving any benefit. The daughter's claim was allowed at first instance but failed on appeal as the testator had clearly expressed her intention and given her valid reasons for so doing. It was not for the court to interfere with those intentions and the testator's right to dispose of her will as she pleased. The court considered the criteria in I(PFD)A 1975, s 3 but, on the facts, came to the conclusion that none of them weighed sufficiently heavily to justify interfering with the deceased's intention. On further appeal, the Court of Appeal reversed the decision and confirmed the decision of the district judge (reported as *Ilot v Mitson* (see para 7.1)).

It seems therefore that, in appropriate cases, a statement of the deceased's wishes or reasons for making or not making financial provision may be a relevant factor which the court will consider in weighing up all the matters set out in I(PFD)A 1975, s 3 and carrying out a balancing exercise.

7.7.2 Claimant's wish to pass assets to beneficiaries of choice

In claims under the I(PFD)A 1975, particularly where the claimant is a surviving spouse/civil partner of the deceased the claim may seek an award which includes sufficient assets to enable the claimant to bequeath some of it to beneficiaries of his/her choice. This is not a factor set out in s 3 which the court is required to consider. It is also not a factor which is set out in Matrimonial Causes Act 1973, s 25, but it has been considered as a legitimate issue which the court should take into account (see *Page v Page* [1981] 2 FLR 198, *Preston v Preston* [1982] Fam 17 and *Re Besterman v Grusin* [1984] 3 WLR 280) and confirmed in the judgment of Lord Nicholl in *White v White* [2000] 2 FLR 981 in the following passage:

I agree that a parent's wish to be in a position to leave money to his or her children would not normally fall within paragraph (b) as a financial need, either of the husband or of the wife. But this does not mean that this natural parental wish is wholly irrelevant to the section 25 exercise in a case where resources exceed the parties' financial needs. In principle, a wife's wish to have money so that she can pass some on to her children at her discretion is every bit as weighty as a similar wish by a husband. A *Duxbury* type fund is intended to provide money for living expenses but not more. The amount of the *Duxbury* fund is calculated on the basis that the capital as well as the income will be used. The calculation assumes that nothing will be left when the wife dies ...

In my view, in a case where resources exceed needs, the correct approach is as follows. The judge has regard to all the facts of the case and to the overall requirements of fairness. When doing so the judge is entitled to have in mind the wish of a claimant wife that her award should not be confined to living accommodation and a vanishing fund of capital earmarked for living expenses which would leave nothing for her to pass on. The judge will give to that factor whatever weight, be it much or little or none at all, he considers appropriate in the circumstances of the particular case

Such an award was made in *Re Adams v Lewis* [2001] WLTR 493. The court made that allowance by applying the test in I(PFD)A 1975, s 1(2)(a), under which there is no requirement that the award be restricted to the reasonable maintenance of the surviving spouse; and on the basis of s 3(2) which requires the court to have regard to the provision which the surviving spouse might have expected to receive if, on the day on which the deceased died, the marriage, instead of being terminated by death, had been terminated by a decree of divorce. The court also considered *White v White* [2001] AC 596 (HL), stating that where the estate of the deceased is substantial and there is a surplus of assets, the application of the principles in *White v White* may be appropriate and may not do injustice to those who may have competing claims, but where the estate is modest or small, it would create injustice to do so.

It is suggested that these decision should not be taken as laying down a principle that in claims under the I(PFD)A 1975 in assessing the surviving spouse's or civil partner's claim this should be taken account of as a rule. It is suggested that it should be an exception and only where the estate is substantial. Consideration has to be given to the fact that, notwithstanding s 3(2), where the marriage has terminated by divorce, there are only two parties to the proceedings whose interests the court has to consider, subject to the claims of the minor children if any; and the parties, or one of them, may have the earning capacity to increase the assets from which the payments may be made.

In claims under the I(PFD)A 1975 the assets from which an award may be made are limited to the net estate, and the interests of other beneficiaries have to be considered. Of the criteria set out in s 3, no one factor has greater significance or priority than any other. The court's duty is to strike a balance between the competing claims of the surviving spouse; any other claimants, who may be minor children of the deceased; a cohabitant of the deceased; disabled children, both adult and minor; and other beneficiaries. It is not the court's function to rewrite the deceased's will or to make what it considers to be an equitable distribution of the estate. To use the divorce comparison particularly where the estate is modest would, it is submitted, be inappropriate (see *Fielden and Graham v Cunliffe* [2005] EWCA Civ 1508, [2006] 1 FLR 745 and *P v G, P and P (Family Provision: Relevance of Divorce Provision)* [2004] EWHC 2944 (Fam), [2006] 1 FLR 431 (para 7.9)).

7.7.3   Conduct

I(PFD)A 1975, s 3(1)(g) specifically refers to conduct of the parties as a relevant factor. The 'conduct' under the Act does not have the same meaning as it does under the Matrimonial Causes Act 1973. In relation to a claim made by a surviving spouse or civil partner conduct cannot be relied on as part of the 'divorce comparison'. In *Miller v Miller; McFarlane v McFarlane* [2006] UKHL 24, [2006] 1 FLR 1186 (HL), it was held that it was not open to the courts to redraw the line in relation to conduct under the guise of having regard to all the circumstances of the case. It could only become relevant if the circumstances were such that it would be regarded as inequitable to disregard it. Baroness Hale said that it would only be taken into account if one party has been very much more to blame than the other and it was both 'obvious and gross'. (See, also, *Barron v Woodhead* [2008] EWHC 810 (Ch), [2009] 1 FLR 747.)

Examples of cases where 'conduct' has been considered a relevant factor include:

- *Talbot v Talbot* [1962] 1 WLR 1113, where the claimant had given birth to a child after the termination of her marriage, her unchastity was considered a relevant though not a decisive factor. It is questionable whether this would now be considered as a relevant factor.
- *Re W* (1975) 119 Sol Jo 439, where after obtaining a divorce on the ground of desertion the wife had not applied for maintenance as the husband had been secretive about his financial position. On his death the wife was in receipt of state benefits and dependent on charity. The deceased had left his residual estate to two female friends in equal shares. Rees J took account of the deceased's secretive conduct; the fact that he had accumulated capital at the expense of the claimant; the

claimant's precarious financial position; and the effect on her of the breakdown of her marriage. Her claim succeeded. In *Re Harker-Thomas* [1969] P 28, the wife had concealed her financial position and had continued to receive maintenance at a higher level than that to which she would have been entitled. (See, also, *Re Basham* [1986] 1 WLR 1498.) In *Re Rowlands* [1984] FLR 813, the widow's separation for a period of about 48 years was regarded as conduct which was relevant to diminish her entitlement.

- *Ghandi v Patel* [2002] 1 FLR 603, where although the surviving widow's claim failed on the issue of the validity of the marriage, the court observed that had the claim succeeded the court would not have considered the deceased to have made reasonable financial provision for the claimant, but that there was a possibility that the award she would have received would have been reduced by reason of the allegations of unsatisfactory conduct in her relationship with the deceased. Conduct after the death of the deceased and in relation to proceedings may never the less be relevant.
- *Baynes v Hedger and Others* [2008] EWHC 1587 (Ch), [2008] 2 FLR 1805, where the court at first instance took into account the claimant's conduct towards the deceased in pressurising the deceased with financial demands which led to the deceased making payments to the claimant of £171,000 during the 4 years immediately preceding her death. On appeal, it was observed that conduct alone should not exclude an otherwise meritorious claim.
- See also *H v J's Personal Representatives, Blue Cross, RSPB, RSPCA* (above), where the court considered the claimant's behaviour towards her mother as a relevant factor in weighing up the I(PFD)A 1975, s 3 factors when dismissing the claimant's claim.

7.7.4   Proprietary estoppel

The conduct of the deceased in encouraging the claimant to believe that he/she would acquire an interest in his/her estate and thereby, upon that belief, to act to his/her detriment, can give rise to estoppel upon which a claim may be based. In order to establish proprietary estoppel, whereby a court of equity would prevent a person from relying on his/her legal rights when it would be unconscionable for him/her to do so, the claimant must prove:

(1)   that the claimant had a belief at all material times that he/she would receive the property which is the subject of the action;
(2)   that that belief was encouraged by the deceased; and
(3)   that, in reliance on that belief and assurance, the claimant acted to his/her detriment.

Although the case of *Re Basham (Deceased)* [1986] 1 WLR 1498, was not a claim under the I(PFD)A 1975, it concerned the question of family provision, the conduct of the deceased and the assurances he gave during his lifetime. The circumstances and the result of the case, however, may be of relevance in claims under the Act. The claimant was the step-daughter of the deceased. She had lived with the deceased from the age of 15 when her mother married the deceased, and, together with the claimant's husband, they had formed a very closely knit family. The claimant, her husband and their children had assisted the deceased in his business and had worked for the deceased for no reward. The deceased had given the claimant assurances that he would leave her all his estate and that she and her family should have no worries about money. Her understanding was that she would inherit his property. When the claimant's husband wished to move to Lincolnshire to a better job, he was persuaded not to do so by the deceased. He was also persuaded by the deceased not to apply for planning permission on a plot of land he owned with a view to selling it. The claimant also cooked and cleaned for the deceased for the rest of his life and spent a considerable amount of time and money on him. Allowing the claimant's claim, Edward Nugee QC, sitting as a deputy High Court judge, said:

> Where a person (A) has acted to his detriment on the faith of a belief, which was known to and encouraged by another person (B), that he either has or is going to be given a right in or over B's property, B cannot insist on his strict legal rights if to do so would be inconsistent with A's belief. The principle is commonly known as proprietary estoppel, and since the effect of it is that B is prevented from asserting his strict legal rights it has something in common with estoppel. But in my judgment, at all events, where the belief is that A is going to be given a right in the future, it is properly to be regarded as giving rise to a species of constructive trust, which is the concept employed by a court of equity to prevent a person from relying on this legal rights where it would be unconscionable for him to do so. The rights to which proprietary estoppel gives rise and the machinery by which effect is given to them, are similar in many respects to those involved in cases of secret trusts, mutual wills and other comparable cases in which property is vested in B on the faith of an understanding that it will be dealt with in a particular manner.

The doctrine of proprietary estoppel was applied. In *Wayling v Jones* [1995] 2 FLR 1029 (CA), the doctrine was applied where the claimant had been in a homosexual relationship with the deceased over a long time and had worked for the deceased on the assurance that he would inherit the deceased's estate (see also *Greasley v Cooke* [1980] 3 All ER 710).

In *Negus v Bahouse* [2007] EWHC 2628 (Ch), [2008] 1 FCR 768, an application made by the claimant, who had been in a relationship with the deceased for 12 years, for a declaration that she had a beneficial interest in the flat owned by the deceased but in which she had lived with the deceased on the ground of proprietary estoppel, failed. The court held that in order to succeed the claimant had to show: (1) an agreement or an assurance by the deceased that the property was to be shared beneficially; (2) that the claimant had relied on the assurance; and (3) that the claimant had suffered a detriment as a result of relying on the assurance given to her – the fact that the deceased had told her that she could live in his home was not in itself, sufficient to establish an agreement in relation to the property. The claimant, however, succeeded in establishing a claim under the Act on the basis that the deceased had not made reasonable financial provision for her maintenance. The court ordered that the flat should be transferred to the claimant free of mortgage and awarded her a lump sum to enable her to provide a pension policy for herself. See *Walsh v Singh* [2009] EWHC 3219 (Ch), [2010] 1 FLR 1658 for a recent decision in which the principles set out in *Negus v Bahouse* applied, although that case was not cited in the judgment). See also *Kernott v Jones* [2010] EWCA Civ 578, [2010] 2 FCR 372 where a claim based on constructive trust failed.

In contrast in *Taylor v Dickens* [1998] 1 FLR 806, the court applied a stricter test to a claim by the claimant for a declaration that he was entitled to the residuary estate of the deceased or alternatively, damages. The facts were that the claimant had worked for an elderly widow who had told him that she would leave her house to him. On this basis, the claimant had not charged her for his services. She made a will which accorded with the assurances that she had given him. However, as she became more frail she needed the services of other carers. She subsequently changed her will leaving the house to one of the carers but did not tell the claimant of the change. The court refused his claim and held that in order to found a case on estoppel, the claimant had to show that the deceased had created a belief or expectation on the part of the claimant that the deceased would not withdraw from the agreement. It was also held that there was no contract between the deceased and the applicant that she would not change her will. The agreement was that she would make a will in the claimant's favour, which she had done. Furthermore, the agreement was a contract relating to land and as such would have had to be in writing. The court thus drew a distinction between a case where the promise was to make a will and no such will is made, and those cases where a will is made but subsequently the will is changed, and the deceased has not created and encouraged a belief by the applicant that he/she would not change the will. It is submitted that the distinction made is an artificial one, and the court in making that distinction has given greater weight to the procedural aspect than to the substance and nature of the promise, understanding or assurance given by one person which has encouraged the belief in another, and leads that other to act to his/her detriment. As a result of the decision in *Taylor v Dickens*, the test which the court in future will apply is now unclear. It is submitted that the test laid down in *Re Basham* and applied in *Wayling v Jones* is to be preferred. See also the judgment in *Gillett v Holt* [2000] 2 All ER 289 (CA), where the decision in *Taylor v Dickens* was criticised, and *Jennings v Rice* [2002] EWCA 159, [2002] WTLR 367.

In *Q v Q* [2008] EWHC 1874 (Fam), [2009] 1 FLR 935, in a claim for ancillary relief, the court applied the strict test and found that the husband and wife had acted to their detriment in reliance of the agreement between the father of the husband and the husband's brother, by investing both capital and their efforts on renovating the property on the assurance that the property would become theirs. The shared intentions of all the relevant parties had been clear from the agreement and the supporting documents which showed that the husband or the husband and wife were to receive the beneficial interest in the property. In both *Walsh v Singh* and *Kernott v Jones* (above), the claim relied on the doctrine of proprietary estoppel/constructive trust and evidence of common intention coupled with an action that was detrimental to establish a beneficial interest in property.

In the recent case of *McDonald v Frost* [2009] EWHC 2276 (Ch), the deceased's two daughters brought a claim in estoppel against the estate of their deceased father. They had each been making monthly payments to him and his first wife of £100 and each received money and property worth £20,000 from him. After the deceased's first wife died he remarried, but the daughters continued to make the monthly payments. In his will the deceased left his entire estate to his second wife. The daughters brought a claim against the estate asserting that the deceased had repeatedly assured them that they would benefit from his estate. The court dismissed the claim on the grounds that on the evidence there had not been any express assurances or promises after the deceased remarried. There was also no particular reason for the deceased to have made such promises. Two further decisions which, although not concerned with family disputes, are relevant because they set out the principles which apply in cases where estoppel is raised. In *Revenue and Customs Commissioners v Benchdollar Ltd* [2009] EWHC 1310 (Ch), [2010] 1 All ER 174, it was held that:

(1)   it was not enough that the common assumption was understood by the parties; it had to be expressly shared between them;

(2)   the expression of the common assumption by the party alleged to be estopped had to be such that he might properly have assumed some responsibility for it and in conveying to the other party an understanding that he expected the other party to rely on it;

(3)   the other party must have relied upon the common assumption to a sufficient extent;

(4)   that reliance had to have occurred in connection with some subsequent dealings between the parties; and

(5)   the person alleging the estoppel must have acted upon and suffered some detriment or some benefit thereby must have been conferred on the person alleged to have been estopped. The benefit must be sufficient to establish that it would be unjust or unconscionable for that person to assert his legal position.

In *Thorner v Majors and Others* [2009] UKHL 18, [2009] 3 All ER 945, the House of Lords (now the Supreme Court) set out the conditions which must be satisfied before a claim based on proprietary estoppel could succeed. These are:

(1)   the relevant assurances must be clear and unequivocal and must appear to have been intended to be taken seriously and might reasonably be expected to be relied upon by the person to whom it was made;

(2)   the assurances given to the claimant whether expressly or impliedly or tacitly should relate to identified property owned by the defendant.

In *Evans v HSBC Trust Co (UK) Ltd* [2005] WTLR 1289, two brothers claimed the whole of the estate of the deceased who was unrelated to them but whom she had treated as if they were her grandchildren. They relied upon the principle of proprietary estoppel to support their claim. They maintained that she had also repeatedly given them assurances that they would inherit the whole of her estate and they had acted to their detriment on those assurances by purchasing property which they would not have purchased but for the assurances given to them and had also incurred liabilities. The court found that in the circumstances it would be unconscionable to revoke those assurances. However, the court took account of the fact that the deceased was survived by three blood relatives and adjusted the claim to make allowances for them.

A good example of a case where the essential elements to establish proprietary estoppel were considered is *Stallion v Albert Stallion Holdings (Great Britain) Limited* [2009] EWHC 1950 (Ch), [2010] 2 FLR 78. The case concerned a divorced woman who had agreed not to contest the divorce proceedings and not to seek ancillary relief in return for her husband's promise that she would have the right for life to live rent-free in property owned by her husband's company, to have secure employment with his company and the use of a car. The agreement also provided that if her husband were to die and the property had to be sold or she was required to vacate the property, she would be entitled to receive £55,000 from the estate. After the divorce and when the now former husband had remarried, he attempted to renegotiate the agreement and served her with a notice to quit but she asserted her rights under the original agreement. When the former husband died, he left his estate to his wife who then moved into the property with the claimant. The company wished to develop the property and wanted both women out of the property. The claimant applied for a declaration that she was entitled to live in the property for life and to have exclusive right to do so. The company sought a possession order on the basis that the claimant had no interest in the property. On the facts, it was held that no representation or assurance had been made to the claimant that she would have exclusive rights to possession of the property and that she had not enjoyed such rights. The history of the occupation of the property indicated that she had not had exclusive rights over the property and that she had not enjoyed such possession. However, she had been induced to consent to the divorce and not to claim ancillary relief on the basis of the agreement and she had acted upon that agreement as a result of which she had not pursued a claim for financial relief and had thus suffered considerable detriment in not applying for an order. The court in those circumstances had to stand back and consider whether in all the circumstances it would be 'unconscionable' for the estate to avoid the representations made to her and upon which she had acted to her detriment. On the facts, the court held that given that the claimant had occupied the property rent-free for about 15 years and having regard to the circumstances of the other parties to the dispute, it would be unconscionable if the agreement was avoided. Furthermore, the evidence did not establish that events referred to in the saving clause contained in the agreement had arisen. Therefore until such an event/s occurred the claimant was entitled to remain at the property.

Constructive trust

A claim may be made against the estate of the deceased where the deceased had entered into an arrangement or agreement with another under which he/she held the property which formed part of his/her estate in trust for the claimant. In *Staden v Jones* [2008] EWCA Civ 936, [2008] 2 FLR 1931 the appellant, who was the daughter of the deceased, sought to enforce a trust arising from an agreement reached between her parents on their divorce which had led her mother to agree to transfer her share in the property to her father on the basis that it would pass to her. On the basis of the agreement in which the father had given a signed undertaking to that effect, the mother had executed the transfer for no consideration. The father subsequently remarried and transferred the property into the joint names of himself and his second wife, who on his death acquired the beneficial interest in the property by survivorship. The Court of Appeal, in allowing the appeal, held that it was clear from the intention of the parties that the deceased was to hold the property on the basis that he would hold half the beneficial interest in the property for the daughter subject to his right to occupy it. The daughter's interest did not lie only in the proceeds of the sale of the property.

In *Q v Q* (above), the documentary evidence in relation to the property which was the subject of the dispute was found to be sufficient to give rise to a constructive trust. In *Hameed v Qayyum* [2009] EWCA Civ 352, [2009] 2 FLR 962, the court on the evidence approached the issue on what the position would have been in equity if the application had been one for the rescission of the agreement on the basis of innocent misrepresentation.

7.7.5   Doctrine of mutual wills

The doctrine applies only where the agreement to enter into mutual wills is reinforced by undertakings that the wills shall not be revoked. If the first testator dies having made a will in compliance with the agreement, the agreement becomes binding on the second testator, and gives rise to an equitable obligation to give effect to the mutually agreed disposition(s). A 'floating trust' is created, and the personal representatives of the second testator are obliged to administer it.

The legal principles which apply to mutual wills were considered recently in *Charles v Fraser* [2010] EWHC 2124 (Ch) and the law was summarised as follows:

- Mutual wills are made by two or more persons, usually in substantially the same terms and conferring reciprocal benefits, following an agreement between them to make such wills and not to revoke them without the consent of the other.
- For the doctrine to apply there has to be what amounts to a contract between the two testators that both wills will be irrevocable and remain unaltered.
- The mere execution of wills which mirror each other does not imply an agreement either as to revocation or non-revocation (see also *Re Goodchild* (above)).
- For the doctrine to apply it is not necessary that the second testator should have obtained a personal financial benefit under the will of the first testator.

Where the legal formalities relating to mutual wills have not been complied with, but the parties believed that they had created mutually binding wills, a constructive trust is implied to prevent the second testator from dealing with the deceased's assets in a way which is incompatible with the agreement (see *Healey v Brown* [2002] EWHC 1405 (Ch), [2002] 19 EG 147, [2002] WTLR 849). The case of *Re Goodchild* (above) illustrates the practical difficulties which arise in relation to such wills.

7.8 FACTORS RELEVANT TO A SURVIVING SPOUSE, FORMER SPOUSE AND CIVIL PARTNER AND COHABITANTS

7.8.1 Age

The age of a surviving spouse/civil partner is relevant in assessing his/her earning capacity. Also relevant is whether and, if so, the extent to which, the surviving spouse is caring for a minor child. If the surviving spouse/civil partner was not gainfully employed during the marriage or civil partnership, age will be relevant in considering whether that person could train or retrain so as to earn an income to meet some or all of his/her own needs. In such a case provision may be made for a modest sum to enable the spouse to adjust to the new situation and to take up or resume gainful employment. Cases decided under the Matrimonial Causes Act 1973 should be considered as examples of how the courts have dealt with this issue. For example, in *Khan v Khan* [1981] 2 FLR 131, an order limited in time was made while the wife trained and obtained employment; and in *Attar v Attar (No 2)* [1985] FLR 653, a wife was given a lump sum representing 2 years' maintenance. Where the surviving spouse or civil partner is middle-aged or elderly, it will be relevant whether or not that spouse/civil partner has lost the potential to earn income or is disadvantaged in the labour market (see *Robertson v Robertson* (1983) 4 FLR 387, where a wife had not lost the potential to work). In *Fielden and Graham v Cunliffe* [2005] EWCA Civ 1508, [2006] 1 FLR 745, the age of a widow was a relevant consideration in assessing her ability to gain and remain in full-time employment and obtain pension rights and meet her needs.

7.8.2 Duration of marriage, civil partnership and cohabitation

The duration of marriage is a significant relevant factor in assessing what is reasonable financial provision for the surviving spouse/civil partner. Where the marriage or civil partnership has lasted a long time, with the parties living together and bringing up a family, a substantial award may be justified. Where the surviving spouse/civil partner is not young, although the marriage or civil partnership may have been short, the effect on the spouse or civil partner is relevant in assessing an award which is just in all the circumstances of the case. The surviving spouse or civil partner may have given up employment or lost pension rights and other benefits in order to care for the deceased.

Where the surviving spouse or civil partner is young and the marriage or civil partnership was short, whether or not there are children, the short duration of the marriage or civil partnership is a relevant consideration. Premarital cohabitation and any contribution made during that period should also be taken into account. Conversely, any period during which the spouses or civil partners were separated should be deducted in calculating the length of the marriage. Much will depend on the facts of the individual case, the competing claims of any beneficiaries and the size and nature of the deceased's estate

Where the marriage is long but the parties had lived separate and apart, although not divorced, the period of separation will be a relevant factor (see *Re Rowlands deceased* [1984] FLR 813 where the separation had lasted 43 years). In *GW v RW* [2003] EWHC 611 (Fam), [2003] 2 FLR 108, a period of pre-marriage cohabitation and a period of estrangement during the marriage were both taken into account in calculating the length of the marriage; it was stated that a 12-year period of marriage with two children could not be regarded as a long marriage, but a 20-year marriage would fall into that category. Pre-marriage cohabitation is as relevant as cohabitation after marriage. In *Co v Co (Ancillary Relief: Pre-marriage Cohabitation)* [2004] EWHC 287 (Fam), [2004] 1 FLR 1095, it was held that to ignore pre-marriage cohabitation would be to fly in the face of the principal statutory duty of the court to have regard to all the circumstances of the case in exercising its powers. In that case Coleridge J said:

> Committed, settled relationships which often endure for years in the context of cohabitation (often but not always with children) outside marriage must, I think, be regarded as every bit as valid as those where parties have made the same degree of commitment but recorded it publicly by civil registration, ie by marriage. This has nothing to do with striving to achieve financial fairness as between a couple at a particular stage in society's development.

This decision will also be relevant in claims made by cohabitants.

In *Fielden and Graham v Cunliffe* [2005] EWCA Civ 1508, [2006] 1 FLR 745, Wall LJ (as he then was) approached the case with a 'divorce comparison' and considered the interplay between the provision of the Matrimonial Causes Act 1973 and the provisions of I(PFD)A 1975, s 3(2), and the application of the principles laid down in *White v White* [2000] 2 FLR 981 (HL) and its relevance when the marriage was a short one. His Lordship observed that in such cases caution had to be exercised when applying the principles laid down in *White v White* to a case under the Act and drew a distinction between the two principles as follows:

(1) Divorce involves two living former spouses to each of whom the provisions of Matrimonial Causes Act 1973, s 25(2) apply whereas in cases under the I(PFD)A 1975, a deceased spouse who leaves a widow is entitled to bequeath his estate to whomsoever he pleases; his statutory obligation is to make reasonable financial provision for his widow. In such cases, depending on the value of the estate, the concept of equality may bear little relation to such provision.

(2) Divorce involves a conscious decision by one or both of the spouses to bring the marriage to an end. That process leaves two living former spouses, each of whom have resources, needs and responsibilities. In such a case the length of the marriage and the parties' respective contribution to it assume a particular importance when the court is striving to reach a fair financial outcome. Where a marriage is dissolved by death the widow is entitled to say that she entered into it on the basis that it would be of indefinite duration and in the expectation that she would devote the remainder of the parties' joint lives to being his wife and caring for him. The fact that the marriage has been prematurely terminated by death after a short period may, therefore, render the length of the marriage a less critical factor than it would be in the case of a divorce.

(3) There is a clear difference between a widow who had been married for many years and who had made an equal contribution to the family of the deceased and one who like the claimant had been married only a year and who had not made such a contribution. Therefore, the duration of a marriage/civil partnership or even cohabitation before marriage or the formal civil partnership and the 'divorce comparison' is likely to be relevant in considering housing needs.

In *Aston v Aston* [2007] WTLR 1349, in a claim brought by the widow of the deceased the court held that the 'divorce fiction' referred to in I(PFD)A 1975, s 3(2) was relevant to the specific facts of the case because the marriage had effectively ended well before the death of her husband. She was thus better off than she would have been on a divorce as she had received a lump sum under an insurance policy; she had an earning capacity of £18,000 plus benefits; and a civil service pension as the deceased's widow. Her claim for half the share in the home and half the capital in the estate was refused.

The House of Lords' decision in *Miller v Miller; McFarlane v McFarlane* [2006] UKHL 24, [2006] 1 FLR 1186 considered the approach to be adopted in short marriage cases but in the context of a divorce. The former wife in *McFarlane v McFarlane* where the marriage had lasted for only two and a half years received a substantial award. The House of Lords did not follow the pre-*White* line of cases which confined the former wife to her needs, but Lord Nicholls observed that in big money cases the court should decide what would be a fair division of the available assets having regard to their financial needs and the need for compensation and all the circumstances of the case and consider whether there are good reasons for departing from equality. In a short marriage there will often be a good case for departing substantially from equality with regard to non-matrimonial property.

It should be noted that the cases of *Miller v Miller* and *McFarlane v McFarlane* were not claims under the I(PFD)A 1975 and since the emphasis in a claim under the Act is to achieve fairness, the application of the general principle will depend on the facts of the individual case. In every case, therefore, the result will be very much fact specific and this is particularly the case in claims under the Act. In every case the court strives to achieve a fair outcome having regard to the facts and it is more likely than not, particularly where the estate is modest in size and there are competing claims of other claimants and beneficiaries to be taken into account, that equality cannot be achieved so the stakes should not be raised too high.

In the case of cohabitants, the length of the period of cohabitation will be as relevant as it is in marriage and civil partnership cases particularly where there are children as a result of the relationship and it is established that the cohabitant and the children were wholly or substantially maintained by the deceased, ie that they were dependent on him/her. Evidence of the nature and extent of that dependency and the standard of living enjoyed by the family will be essential to establish a case for an award (see *Negus v Bahouse* [2007] EWHC 2628 (Ch), [2008] 1 FLR 381). In *Webster v Webster* [2008] EWHC 31 (Ch), [2009] 1 FLR 1240, the court applied the case of *Negus*. There the parties had lived together for 27 years and had two children. The home in which they lived was in the man's sole name and he paid the mortgage whilst the claimant paid some of the outgoings of the home. Both parties worked but the man earned substantially more than the woman. The man died intestate. The estate fell to be divided under the intestacy laws between his children from his former marriage and the two children from his relationship with the claimant. She made a claim under the I(PFD)A 1975 for an interest in the family home and the company shares in the man's name. On the facts and the evidence adduced before the court in respect of the claimant's circumstances at the date of the hearing the court transferred the home to her outright and ordered the estate to pay the mortgage on the property. The award combined with the sums already paid to the claimant out of the estate amounted to about the same as a *Duxbury* capitalisation of an income of £1,500 per annum, which was equivalent to the fall in the amount of the family income consequent on the death of the man.

The Law Commission's Consultation Paper, *Intestacy and Family Provision Claims on Death*, recommends the removal of the 2-year qualifying period where there are children of the relationship between the cohabitant and the deceased.

7.8.3 Claimant's contribution to the welfare of the family

The contribution made by a spouse or civil partner and cohabitants by looking after the home and caring for the family is given as much weight as that of the spouse or civil partner who goes out to work. Greater value should not be placed on the contribution of the breadwinner than that of the homemaker as a reason for an unequal division of assets between the spouses/civil partners. Sterile suggestions that the breadwinner's contributions were greater than the homemaker's should be avoided. The nature of the contributions made by each party may be different and incommensurable and each should be recognised as of no less value than the other (see *Lambert v Lambert* [2002] EWCA Civ 1685, [2003] 1 FLR 139). Contribution made by a wife/civil partner to the business of the husband or the other civil partner which assisted in making the business prosperous must be given due weight (see *Conran v Conran* [1997] 2 FLR 615). Similar principles will apply to cohabitants.

See the recommendation of the Law Commission's Paper referred to in the previous paragraph.

7.8.4 Financial contribution

I(PFD)A 1975, s 3 does not refer to financial contribution but, in cases decided under the Matrimonial Causes Act 1973, financial contribution made by a spouse or civil partner has been a relevant factor in so far as a party seeking to receive an uplift in the award made on the ground that the contribution was exceptional (see *Conran v Conran* (above)). The court has also departed from the concept of equality where the husband's or civil partner's special contribution to the marriage or civil partnership was as a result of the exceptional business acumen, which, in *Sorrell v Sorrell* [2005] EWHC 1717 (Fam), [2006] 1 FLR 497, was referred to as amounting to genius and it was held that it would be unfair not to recognise this special contribution in the final division of the family assets. It was also indicated that the case of *Lambert v Lambert* (above) did not establish any new test in relation to special circumstances. The decision in *Lambert* has tightened the criteria to the 'most exceptional and limited circumstance' but it has not provided or suggested any guidelines on the issue. Some guidance on the approach which the courts should adopt when assessing financial contribution as a factor can be found in the judgment of Lord Nicholls in *Miller v Miller; McFarlane v McFarlane* [2006] UKHL 24, [2006] 1 FLR 1186, where he said, 'Parties should not seek to promote a case of "special contribution" unless the contribution is so marked that to disregard it would be inequitable. A good reason for departing from equality is not to be found in the minutiae of married life'.

Baroness Hale supported this interpretation to some extent when she said that Matrimonial Causes Act 1973, s 25(2)(f):

> does not refer to the contribution which each has made to the parties' *accumulated wealth* but to the contribution they have made and will continue to make to the *welfare of the family*. Each should be seen as doing their best in their own sphere. Only if there is such a disparity in their respective contributions to the *welfare of the family* that it would be inequitable to disregard it should this be taken into account in determining their shares.

It will, however, be observed that the emphasis of the two judgments is on different issues on what should be considered as sufficient to justify a departure from the principle of equality, so although some guidance may be obtained it is not clear how the issue will be approached in future.

In *McCartney v Mills McCartney* [2008] EWHC 401 (Fam), [2008] 1 FLR 1508, however, where the marriage was short and the assets had been in the main acquired by the husband before the marriage, the court departed from the equality principle and in arriving at its decision applied the 'needs' test as a relevant and important factor.

Pre-nuptial agreements

Where the parties have entered into a pre-nuptial agreement to protect assets acquired before the marriage, the Supreme Court in *Radmacher (formerly Granatino) v Granatino* [2010] UKSC 42, [2011] 1 All ER 373 has held that it is for the court to determine the appropriate financial relief to be awarded on the breakdown of a marriage and the parties cannot by agreement oust the jurisdiction of the court, but the court should consider and determine what weight should be attached to such an agreement and whether it was fair or just to depart from it. The court should give effect to a nuptial agreement that is freely entered into by each party with a full appreciation of its implications unless in the circumstances prevailing it would not be fair to hold the parties to their agreement. The agreement must therefore have been entered into without undue influence or pressure and with knowledge of its implications. It was important that the parties had disclosure of all the relevant material to enable the parties to make an informed decision and to seek advice before making the decision, and that both parties understood and intended that the agreement should govern the financial consequences in the event of the marriage coming to an end. Factors such as duress, fraud and misrepresentation would negate the agreement. Unconscionable conduct would also be likely to have an adverse effect. Other relevant factors which may reduce or eliminate the weight to be attached to the agreement include conduct such as exploitation, unfair advantage, the parties' emotional state, the circumstances of the parties at the time of the agreement and the question whether the marriage would have gone ahead without the agreement.

Once the court is satisfied that the agreement was entered into freely it would then have to consider whether it was just and fair to hold it as binding. That issue would be dependent on the facts of the particular case. The Supreme Court gave some guidance on the issue of fairness as follows:

- a nuptial agreement could not be allowed to prejudice the reasonable requirements of any children of the family;
- the court should accord respect to the decision of a married couple as to how they wished to regulate their financial affairs;
- the distinction between matrimonial and non-matrimonial property was significant and the preservation of non-matrimonial property may be justified;
- a significant change in the parties' circumstances may make it unfair to hold the parties to their agreement;
- needs and compensation were the strands that could most readily render the agreement unfair but where these considerations did not apply fairness might not require a departure from the agreement. It was in relation to the sharing principle that the court would be most likely to make a order in the terms of the nuptial settlement in place of the order that it would otherwise have made.

The Supreme Court disapproved the decision of the Privy Council in *Macleod v Macleod* [2008] UKPC 64, [2009] 1 FLR 641 which distinguished between pre-nuptial agreements and post-nuptial agreements, and suggested that there should not be any difference between them. It concluded that post-nuptial agreements were contracts and were thus not contrary to public policy and that the same principle should apply to pre-nuptial agreements. Both agreements should be enforceable.

The court went on to state that the test for varying a maintenance agreement under Matrimonial Causes Act 1973, s 3 and that in *Edgar v Edgar* [1981] 2 FLR 19 were appropriate for a separation agreement but not necessarily so for post-nuptial agreements.

The decision in *Radmacher (formerly Granatino) v Granatino* (above) was a majority decision of the Supreme Court and hence it is important to refer in summary to the dissenting judgment of Baroness Hale.

Lady Hale in her dissenting judgment took the view that:

• pre-nuptial agreements were not legally enforceable contracts;
• it was for Parliament with the help of the Law Commission to review and reform the law and not for the court to hold that such agreements are legal contracts and enforceable;
• the test applied by the majority was an impermissible gloss on the courts' statutory duties in that it introduced a presumption or starting point;
• the test should be 'Did each party enter into an agreement, intending it to have legal effect and with a full appreciation of its implication? If so the circumstances as they now are, would it be fair to hold them to their agreement?';
• the husband's appeal should have been allowed as although there was nothing in the circumstances which rendered the agreement unfair, the husband's role as father to the children was a relevant factor even though the children had attained the age of majority to justify providing a home for him for life;
• the Court of Appeal had erred in principle in treating a parent who had been married to the other parent as they would treat a parent who had not.

Having regard to the decision in *Radmacher (formerly Granatino) v Granatino*, it is likely that pre-nuptial agreements will be entered into more frequently in future, even in cases where the assets are not substantial and more particularly where the parties are entering into a second or third marriage. Hence, as stated above, the dissenting judgment of Baroness Hale should be read and given consideration. The judgment also raises questions on what is likely to be considered as unfair, what the court is likely to do in such cases, whether the court will take account of it merely as a factor to be taken into account or whether it will ignore the agreement completely and determine the issues between the parties applying the provisions of Matrimonial Causes Act 1973. Since most pre-nuptial agreements are entered into by couples where one of the parties has substantial assets, future contested cases may clarify how the test of fairness will be applied by the courts.

7.9 WHAT SURVIVING SPOUSE/CIVIL PARTNER MIGHT REASONABLY HAVE EXPECTED TO RECEIVE ON DIVORCE/DISSOLUTION – DIVORCE COMPARISON TEST

I(PFD)A 1975, s 3(2) provides that, in a claim by a surviving spouse of the deceased, the court should, unless at the date of death a decree of judicial separation was in force and the separation was continuing, have regard to the provision which the claimant might reasonably have expected to receive if, on the day on which the deceased died, the marriage, instead of being terminated by death, had been terminated by divorce. This implies an exercise under Matrimonial Causes Act 1973, s 25, although this provision is not the only, or the paramount, factor to be considered by the court. It is one of eight other factors among all the other circumstances of the individual case. The House of Lords' decision in *White v White* [2000] 2 FLR 981 and *Miller v Miller; McFarlane v McFarlane* [2006] UKHL 24, [2006] 1 FLR 1186 set out the principles which now form the basis of the courts' approach to applications for financial relief under the Matrimonial Causes Act 1973, although it should be noted that both cases were 'big money cases' and the principles set out there should not be applied inflexibly, but tailored to the individual circumstances of each case and to the value of the assets available for distribution. This is particularly significant in cases under the I(PFD)A 1975. The general principles which emerge from these decisions, bearing in mind that in these cases the assets substantially exceeded the needs, and the court's observations were made in that context, are:

(1)   the objective of the court is to achieve a fair outcome;

(2)   in seeking to achieve a fair outcome, there is no place for discrimination between husband and wife and their respective roles. Whatever the division of labour between the spouses, fairness requires that this should not prejudice or advantage either party;

(3)   the non-financial contributions made to the welfare of the family and the loss of opportunity to acquire and develop money-earning qualifications and skills should be recognised;

(4)   where the wife has made a non-financial contribution to the family she is entitled to a fair settlement which is not confined to her reasonable needs;

(5)   the '*Duxbury* calculations' (see *Duxbury v Duxbury* [1992] Fam 62) are not always a reliable guide and do not take account of the parental wish to pass money to the next generation;

(6)   property acquired before marriage, inherited property or property acquired from sources external to the marriage should

be treated differently from assets acquired by the joint efforts of the spouses, referred to as 'matrimonial property';

(7)   a presumption of equal division would not be an impermissible judicial gloss on the statute;

(8)   equality of division should be the yardstick and, as a general rule, should be departed from only if there are good reasons for doing so. Good reasons for departing from equality should be articulated;

(9)   a pre-nuptial agreement freely entered into with full appreciation of its implications should be given effect unless it would not be fair to do so.

Since these decisions, further guidance on the interpretation of these principles has been given in a number of cases. In *Dharamshi v Dharamshi* [2001] 1 FLR 736, the wife received between 35 per cent and 41 per cent of the assets. In *H v H* [2001] EWCA Civ 653, [2001] 3 FLR 628, she received 42 per cent. In *D v D (Lump Sum: Adjournment of Application)* [2001] 1 FLR 633, the principles in *White* were applied. In *N v N (Financial Provision: Sale of Company)* [2001] 2 FLR 69, the court ordered the sale of the husband's business, which was an income-producing asset. In *Foster v Foster* [2003] EWCA Civ 565, [2003] 2 FLR 299, the Court of Appeal upheld the district judge's attempts to give back to the parties what they had brought into the marriage at the value at the date of the marriage, and divide equally the proceeds generated during the marriage from property dealings. In *GW v RW* (at para 7.8.2), a period of cohabitation before the marriage was treated as equivalent to marriage; it was accepted that some departure from equality was justified as the husband had brought to the marriage a developed career and high earnings capacity, which was unmatched by anything the wife had contributed, and the husband's assets had grown during the separation. The wife was awarded 40 per cent of the assets.

The equality principle has been applied in a number of other cases, but in each of these cases the assets were substantial. It is submitted that these cases may impact on cases under the I(PFD)A 1975 where the estate is large and there is a surplus available. Where the estate includes assets acquired before the marriage, or acquired by inheritance or sources outside the marriage, applying *White v White*, such assets ought to be treated differently from 'matrimonial assets'. Where the estate is sufficiently large it may be appropriate to apply this principle, but where the funds are insufficient to meet the claims, it may not be.

All the above cases relate to decisions made following the breakdown of the marriage. There are, however, two cases which were dealt with under the I(PFD)A 1975 where the 'divorce comparison test' was considered. In *Fielden and Graham v Cunliffe* [2005] EWCA Civ 1508, [2006] 1 FLR 745, Wall LJ (as he then was) said:

19. The correct approach for the court to adopt, following the decision of the House of Lords in *White v White* ... is to apply the statutory provisions to the facts of the individual case with the objective of achieving a result which is fair, and non-discriminatory. Having undertaken that exercise, a way of assessing the fairness and non-discriminatory nature of the proposed result is to check it against the yardstick of equality of division. There is, however, no presumption of equal division of assets, but as a general guide, in the words of Lord Nicholls of Birkenhead, 'equality should be departed from, only if, and to the extent that, there is a good reason for doing so'. He added: 'The need to consider and articulate reasons for departing from equality would help the parties and the court to focus on the need to ensure the absence of discrimination ...'.

20. With appropriate adjustments based on the different statutory provisions, I see no reason, in principle, why the *White v White* approach to marital financial claims should not be applied to proceedings under the 1975 Act brought by a widow, not least because, in any case brought under section 1(1)(a) of the 1975 Act, section 3(2) imposes a statutory cross-check of its own to the provision which Mrs Cunliffe might reasonably have expected to receive if on the day on which the deceased died the marriage, instead of being terminated by death, had been terminated by a decree of divorce. This sub-section assumes a particular importance in the instant case due to the brevity of the marriage.

21. Caution, however, seems to me necessary when considering the *White v White* cross-check in the context of a case under the 1975 Act. Divorce involves two living former spouses, to each of whom the provisions of section 25(2) of the Matrimonial Causes Act 1973 apply. In cases under the 1975 Act, a deceased spouse who leaves a widow is entitled to bequeath his estate to whomsoever he pleases: his only statutory obligation is to make reasonable financial provision for his widow. In such a case, depending on the value of the estate, the concept of equality may bear little relation to such provision.

In that case, the court considered this factor with all the others set out in I(PFD)A 1975, s 3, particularly the short length of the marriage which the court considered was a powerful argument against an equal division (see above), the claimant's housing and her earning capacity and financial needs and in this context found the *Duxbury* approach a useful guide. Wall LJ (as he then was) advised that caution should be given in following the case of *Re Besterman*, and the 'cushion' advocated to be provided for the claimant, as it predates the changes brought about by *White v White* and *Duxbury v Duxbury*.

In *P v G, P and P (Family Provision: Relevance of Divorce Provision)* [2004] EWHC 2944 (Fam), [2006] 1 FLR 431, Black J observed that there is an uneasy interplay between the obligation of the court under I(PFD)A 1975, s 3(2) which required the court to have regard to the provision which the claimant might reasonably be expected to receive if the marriage had been terminated by divorce rather than death, and the obligation to take account of the facts as they are known at the hearing. In relation to the valuation of assets, she did not consider that the intention of the statute was that the court should embark on a 'most sterile and wasteful of exercises in which valuations of assets in an Inheritance Act claim by a spouse should be carried out on two bases' with the resulting costs of valuers and accountants. As regards the factors set out in Matrimonial Causes Act 1973, s 25, she said that an ancillary relief judge having considered these would have used equality of division as his cross-check for fairness. She did not think that:

> it is helpful to go further with the divorce fiction and to attempt to translate the percentage division of the categories of asset into more precise figures. One has only to begin upon the process, as I have done before abandoning it, to realise that any appearance of accuracy and precision in such an exercise is spurious; an over-exact approach to s 3(2) would provide a thoroughly undesirable opportunity to spend the assets of the estate on litigation rather than on provision for the family without, I think materially assisting the court it its task under the I(PFD)A 1975.

The learned judge concluded:

> Ultimately I have concluded that what the statute contemplates in a case such as this is not that the entire fictional ancillary relief case should be played out within the Inheritance Act claim but that the court should simply reach sufficient of a conclusion about how it would have been resolved to take that factor into account in considering what would be reasonable financial provision under the 1975 Act.

However, in considering the authorities which refer to the difference between divorce where there are two surviving spouses for whom to make provision, and death where there is only one, Black J said:

> it seems to me probable that this difference will not infrequently be reflected in greater provision being made under the 1975 Act than would have been made on divorce and that this may legitimately be so even where the estate is a relatively large one, as it is here. In saying this I have not ignored the importance of testamentary freedom. The wish to be in a financial position to make provision by will for adult children, whilst not a financial need as such for the purposes of s 25 of the Matrimonial Causes Act 1973, was recognised in *White v White* as a valid consideration where resources exceed need.

Both the above decisions make it clear that in a claim under the I(PFD)A 1975 the court is not required to carry out a detailed and precise inquiry to assess what relief the claimant would have received. The approach should be to consider that in matrimonial proceedings the court seeks to achieve a result that is fair and non-discriminatory and tests that against the yardstick of equality of division and applies a similar approach in I(PFD)A 1975 claims, subject to the fact that there is no presumption of an equal division and the fact that the court in a claim under the Act is required to carry out a balancing exercise between different factors and the claims of others. The precise extent of the division must still be decided on a case-by-case basis.

Where the estate is small or modest it is difficult to see how the 'divorce comparison' test can provide a fair result if it outweighs the needs of other claimants and beneficiaries. It can only be considered as one of the many factors which the court is required to take into account. It is suggested that in claims under the I(PFD)A 1975 the court should first consider whether, viewed objectively the provision made is unreasonable. If the court finds that it is, it should then go on to consider what would be a reasonable provision for the claimant applying the criteria set out in s 3 and consider what a family judge would have ordered if divorce instead of death had separated the couple and what in the circumstances is reasonable, viewed objectively. It is not for the court to interfere with the disposition so as to make an equitable distribution of the estate.

7.10 FACTORS WHICH APPLY TO A FORMER SPOUSE/ CIVIL PARTNER OR COHABITANT

In the case of a claim by a former spouse, civil partner or cohabitant, the matters to which the court must have regard are, save for the deemed marriage issue, the same as for a surviving spouse/civil partner (see above). Where a 'clean break' settlement was made, it will be rare for a claim under the I(PFD)A 1975 to be made, or, if made, to succeed, unless there is a continuing liability, or a secured provision order has been made, or there are exceptional circumstances (see *Barrass v Harding* [2001] 1 FLR 138). See, also, *Parnall v Hurst and Others* [2003] WTLR 997, where a former wife, whose marriage to the deceased was dissolved after 29 years and the deceased was ordered to make periodical payments of £500 per year, issued a claim under the I(PFD)A 1975. An application to strike out was refused as the claim was not regarded as 'doomed' to fail.

Where the claimant is able to establish that, following an ancillary relief order, the parties had entered into an agreement that, in return for the wife foregoing her periodical payments, the husband would forego his charge on the matrimonial home and that she had thus acted to her detriment, a case for constructive trust/proprietary estoppel may be made out (see *S v S and M* [2006] EWHC 2892 (Fam), [2007] 1 FLR 1123). See, also, *Stallion v Stallion*

Holdings Ltd [2009] EWHC 1950 (Ch), [2010] 2 FLR 78, in which the parties had, following their divorce, agreed that the wife could live rent-free at a particular property and on that basis she had not proceeded with her application for ancillary relief. It was held that she had thereby acted to her detriment and was entitled to remain in the property as agreed.

7.10.1 Matrimonial proceedings and disentitlement orders under I(PFD)A 1975, sections 15, 15ZA, 15A and 15B

I(PFD)A 1975, s 15 provides that where a court in England and Wales grants a decree of divorce, a decree of nullity of marriage or a decree of judicial separation, it may, either then, or at any time thereafter, if it considers it just to do so, exclude the right of the parties to apply for an order under s 2.

In the case of a decree of divorce or nullity of marriage the order may be made before or after the decree is made absolute. If it is made before the decree has been made absolute, it does not take effect until the decree has been made absolute (s 15(2)).

In the case of a s 15 order made on the grant of a decree of judicial separation, with respect to any party to a marriage, then if the other party dies while the decree is in force and the separation is continuing, the court cannot entertain any application for an order under I(PFD)A 1975, s 2 by the surviving party.

Thus, where, on an application for ancillary relief in matrimonial proceedings, a 'clean break' provision is made, consideration should be given to whether an order, disentitling the parties from making any claim for an order under I(PFD)A 1975, s 2 against the estate of the other, would also be appropriate.

CPA 2004, s 71, Sch 4, Part 2, para 21 has extended this restriction to a dissolution, nullity order, separation order or presumption of death order to civil partners with the same consequences by inserting in the I(PFD)A 1975 an additional s 15ZA.

MFPA 1984, s 25 amended the I(PFD)A 1975 by inserting s 15A which gives the court power to make an order similar to that under s 15 to marriages which have been dissolved or annulled overseas; where the parties have been legally separated; and where a court in England and Wales has made an order for ancillary relief under MFPA 1984, s 17. On the making of an order under MFPA 1984, s 17 in respect of a marriage which has been dissolved or annulled overseas, or where there has been a decree of judicial separation, the court, if it considers it just to do so, may, on the application of either or both parties to the marriage, order that the other party to the marriage shall not, on the death of the other, be entitled to apply for an order under I(PFD)A 1975, s 2.

Where an order under I(PFD)A 1975, s 15, s 15ZA, s 15A or s 15B has been made, with respect to any party to a marriage or civil partnership, then on the death of the other party to that marriage or civil partnership the court cannot entertain any application under s 2 against the estate of the deceased by the surviving spouse or civil partner.

There are two conflicting decisions of the Court of Appeal on how the court should approach an application for an order under any of the above sections of the I(PFD)A 1975. In *Re Fullard (Deceased)* [1982] Fam 42, when considering the implications of I(PFD)A 1975, s 15 in an application under the Act, Ormrod LJ stated:

> I regard section 15 as a form of insuring against applications under the 1975 Act which some people may very reasonably wish to do, having made financial provision of a capital nature for the former spouse. People obviously have other commitments – second wives (or husbands) and children and so on. I do not regard section 15 as materially affecting the question the court has to answer as the condition precedent to these applications.

In *Whiting v Whiting* [1988] 2 FLR 189, however, following the divorce of the parties, a consent order was made for financial provision for the wife and children. Subsequently the husband applied, under Matrimonial Causes Act 1973, s 31(7), for a variation of the order for periodical payments for the wife and for an order under I(PFD)A 1975, s 15(1). His application was dismissed. On appeal it was held that, before the court can consider it just to make an order, it must be presented with some indication of what the estate is likely to consist of and some details of the person(s) whom the applicant considers to have a prior claim on the estate. Balcombe LJ said:

> For the court to make an order under section 15(1) it must consider it just to do so. In my judgment, before the court can consider it just to make an order depriving a divorced spouse of an opportunity to claim financial provision from the estate of the other spouse, it should be given some indication of what that estate is likely to consist of and some details of the persons whom the applicant considers to have a prior claim on his estate in the event of his decease. I am prepared to accept that the husband's capital asset is his interest in his present house and that this is likely to be the only asset of substance in his estate. It is a reasonable inference that he considers his present wife and, presumably his children, to have a prior claim on his estate in the event of his death, but nowhere in his evidence does he say so. The whole of his evidence is directed towards supporting his application for a discharge of the 1979 order, and he (or those advising him) appear to have assumed that his application under section 15 of the

1975 Act will stand or fall with that other application. In these circumstances it is hardly surprising that the judge made no mention of this limb of the husband's application. For my part, I would dismiss the appeal on the simple ground that the husband has not made out a case to support his application under section 15 of the 1975 Act. That is not to say that he may not be able to do so, and accordingly I would dismiss this part of the appeal without prejudice to the husband's right to renew the application under section 15.

It is submitted that, of the two decisions, that of Ormrod LJ in *Re Fullard* is to be preferred. The decision in *Whiting* fails to take account of social changes, including the increasing independence of women, the growing divorce rate and the fact that divorcing couples tend to be young and move on to form other relationships and have second families. It also disregards the concept of a final and clean break settlement on divorce. It is unrealistic, in the majority of cases, to expect divorcing couples to be able to give the details described in *Whiting*. To require an applicant under I(PFD)A 1975, s 15 to provide details of those he/she considers would have a prior claim to his/her estate on his/her death some decades in the future is almost impossible to fulfil; if such a requirement were to be applied strictly, the provision would, in time, become redundant.

Practitioners should nevertheless ensure that there is full and frank disclosure where the court is considering financial provision, particularly where a clean break settlement is sought. If an order is made under I(PFD)A 1975, s 15, s 15ZA, s 15A or s 15B and it is subsequently challenged on the basis that the court did not have the required information when it made the order; or if, in the absence of such an order, a claim is made under s 2, it does not follow that the claim under s 2 will necessarily succeed, because the claimant will still have to satisfy the court that the requirements under the Act are met. Where a former wife's claims under Matrimonial Causes Act 1973, ss 23 and 24 have been fully considered and a final order has been made, it is unlikely, save in exceptional circumstances, that a claim for an order under I(PFD)A 1975, s 2 would succeed. (For an example of exceptional circumstances, see *Re Fullard* (above).)

This issue was raised in *Cameron v Treasury Solicitor* [1996] 2 FLR 716, where, on the claimant's divorce, a clean break order was made by consent, requiring the deceased to pay the claimant a lump sum of £8,000. About 20 years later the husband died intestate. His estate, amounting to about £7,677, passed as *bona vacantia* to the Crown. The former wife applied for an order under I(PFD)A 1975, s 2. She was then suffering from ill-health and was in very straitened circumstances; there were no competing claims. At first instance, it was held that the fact of the clean break did not preclude her from making the claim and she was awarded the whole of the net estate. On appeal, it was held that the first task of the claimant in such cases is to make out a case that she is entitled to some relief under the Act. To do this she must satisfy the court that the disposition of the deceased's estate, effected by the law of intestacy in this case, was not such as to make a reasonable financial provision for her. In the present case, a clean break order had been obtained by consent some 19 years before; the deceased had not since then offered any financial support to the claimant; there were no grounds to show that he owed her a moral obligation; nor were there any special circumstances to establish entitlement to an order. The court also expressed the view that it is now the practice of the court to include a s 15 direction in all clean break orders, and an order which did not include such a direction would suggest a fundamental error in drafting.

It is rare for the parties not to be legally represented in applications for financial relief following the breakdown of their marriage or civil partnership when final orders are made. There is provision for a full disclosure of information within those proceedings. Where there is a clean break order which includes a direction under any of the above sections, then that order should be respected. Where such a direction is not included, there is usually a good reason for its absence from the order.

Where the s 15 direction is not made, it should not be assumed that its absence is an error. The court should consider any claim for an order under I(PFD)A 1975, s 2 on its merits. Since the claimant has to establish that the disposition of the deceased's estate is not such as to make reasonable financial provision within the meaning of s 1(2)(b), the circumstances at the time the ancillary relief order was made and the circumstances since then would have to be considered in the light of the factors the court is required to have regard to under s 3. The claimant would have to jump over several hurdles to succeed. In some cases a trial of the preliminary issue may in the long run avoid delay and expense. Furthermore, although the decision in *Cameron v Treasury Solicitor* seems to suggest that a s 15 direction is inserted in all clean break orders as a matter of practice, the reality is that, although such a direction is usually considered seriously by practitioners who advise divorcing or separating couples, the court has to approve any settlement of the matrimonial proceedings which includes such an order. A claimant who seeks to challenge a s 15 order in a claim under the Act would need to establish some very exceptional circumstance in order to succeed.

It should also be noted that the provisions of I(PFD)A 1975, ss 15(3) and (4), 15ZA(3) and (4), 15A(2) and (3), and 15B(2) and (3) are all mandatory. It would therefore be open to the court, of its own motion, or on application by a defendant in a claim under the Act, to strike out the claim on the basis that the court does not have the power to entertain the claim by virtue of the aforesaid provisions.

In summary, case law suggests that the following matters are relevant to a claim under the I(PFD)A 1975 by a former spouse/civil partner:

(1)   a clean break settlement where there is no continuing obligation;

(2)   whether there was a relationship between the deceased and the former wife since the divorce which could suggest a moral obligation to provide for her;

(3)   special or exceptional circumstances;

(4)   the time that has elapsed since the parties separated and since the divorce and the final settlement;

(5)   whether there is any evidence to suggest that a full and frank disclosure was not made, or that the deceased has been secretive about his financial affairs which led the former wife to receive less than she might have received;

(6)   whether a s 15, s 15ZA, s 15A or s 15B order has been made in ancillary relief proceedings.

The following have been found not to amount to special circumstances or reasons to allow a claim:

(1)   that the former wife received less under different legislation than she might have received when the deceased died;

(2)   that the deceased's estate is substantial;

(3)   that the former wife is in straitened circumstances or suffering ill-health.

7.11   CLAIM BY SURVIVING HUSBAND

The I(PFD)A 1975 makes no distinction between a claim by a surviving husband and a claim by a surviving wife. In the early cases, however, the courts appeared to be disinclined, save in exceptional circumstances, to grant relief where the claim was made by a surviving husband. This is illustrated by two cases in particular. In *Re Sylvester, Sylvester v Public Trustee* [1941] Ch 87, the parties were married in 1931. The husband subsequently gave up his employment and thereafter did all the housework and nursed his wife during her illness. The wife had her own income. The husband had none. She died in 1940. She bequeathed to him an annuity of £525 per annum and gave her residuary estate to a number of charities. The husband made a claim against the estate for his maintenance under the I(FP)A 1938. Farwell J, in allowing the husband's claim and awarding him 3 shillings a week, stated:

> I do not consider that, in the ordinary way, applications by husbands for this sort of assistance should be readily entertained. Prima facie a husband should be able to maintain himself, and ought not to ask the court to give him, out of his wife's estate, more than she thought fit to provide for him. There are, of course, exceptional cases in which such an application may be justified, but personally I should not be very willing to assist husbands in cases of this sort, unless the circumstances were indeed exceptional.

In *Re Styler, Styler v Griffiths* [1942] Ch 387, the deceased had made an agreement with her second husband that, on his making a will in her favour, she would make a will leaving the income of her estate to him for life. They both made wills in accordance with the agreement. Subsequently, the wife made another will leaving all her estate to her daughter by her first marriage. On the wife's death, the husband applied for reasonable provision. In refusing his application, Morton J approved the judgment of Farwell J in *Re Sylvester* (above) and criticised his own decision in *Re Pointer* [1941] Ch 60. He stated, 'Having now had more experience of administering the Act since I decided that case, I do not think that I should now make any provision, as I did there for a husband with a pension of £180 a year, an annual income of £124 from investments and £25 a year net from property, unless the circumstances were exceptional'.

It is submitted that the court's approach today would be different, having regard to decisions concerning applications for financial relief under the Matrimonial Causes Act 1973, and more particularly to the decisions in *White v White* [2001] 1 AC 596 (HL) and *Cowan v Cowan* [2001] EWCA Civ 679, [2002] Fam 97. In *White v White*, Lord Nicholls of Birkenhead stated, 'There is one principle of universal application which can be stated with confidence. In seeking to achieve a fair outcome, there is no place for discrimination between husband and wife and their respective roles'.

7.12 CLAIMS BY CHILDREN OF THE DECEASED AND CHILDREN OF THE FAMILY – I(PFD)A 1975, SECTION 1(1)(C) AND (D)

I(PFD)A 1975, s 3(3) requires the court to have regard to whether the deceased had assumed responsibility for the maintenance of a child who was not his biological child, and if so the extent to which, the basis on which and the length of time that responsibility was undertaken. Where appropriate the court is also required to take account of the manner in which the child of the deceased and a child for whom he had assumed responsibility was being or in which he might expect to be educated or trained.

7.13 CLAIMS BY PERSON MAINTAINED BY THE DECEASED – I(PFD)A 1975, SECTION 1(1)(E)

There are three factors which the court is required to consider in relation to those claimants who allege that they were being maintained by the deceased immediately before his/her death. These are:

(1)   the extent to which the deceased assumed responsibility for the claimant;

(2)   the basis on which the deceased assumed responsibility for the maintenance of the claimant; and

(3)   the length of time for which the deceased discharged that responsibility.

See, further, Chapters 4 and 7, paras 4.9.2 and 7.4, *Baynes v Hedger and Others* [2009] EWCA Civ 374, [2009] 2 FLR 767, *Bouette v Rose* [2001] 1 FLR 363, *Malone v Harrison* [1979] 1 WLR 1353 and *Graham v Murphy* [1997] 1 FLR 860 as some examples where these issues were dealt with.

7.14 ASSUMPTION OF RESPONSIBILITY BY THE DECEASED – I(PFD)A 1975, SECTION 3(3) AND (4)

I(PFD)A 1975, s 3(4), which requires the court when determining a claim under s 1(1)(e) to have regard to the extent to which and the basis on which the deceased assumed responsibility for the maintenance of the applicant and the length of time for which the deceased had discharged that responsibility, must be read alongside the provision of s 1(3).

As a general rule, the fact that the claimant was being maintained by the deceased under an arrangement subsisting at the time of the deceased's death and the deceased was making a substantial contribution in money or money's worth to the reasonable needs of the claimant will raise an inference that the deceased had undertaken to maintain the claimant and had assumed responsibility for the maintenance of the claimant. In such circumstances there would be no need to establish any other overt act to demonstrate the 'assumption of responsibility'. All the contributions made, whether in kind or otherwise, will be taken into account.

In *Jelley v Illife* (above), Griffiths LJ in his judgment said:

> the court must use common sense and remember that the object of Parliament in creating this extra class of persons who may claim benefit from an estate was to provide relief for persons of whom it could truly be said that they were wholly or partially dependent on the deceased.

And:

> Each case will have to be looked at carefully on its own facts to see whether common sense leads to a conclusion that the applicant can fairly be regarded as a dependant.

The court will consider, for example:

- the circumstances of the claimant and to what extent the contribution made by the deceased affected those circumstances and how it affected the claimant's position (see *Rees v Newbery and Institute for Cancer Research* [1988] 1 FLR 1041);
- the extent to which the claimant had altered his/her situation based on the actions taken and the contribution made by the deceased (see *Re Wilkinson (Deceased), Neale v Newell* [1978] Fam 22);
- whether the deceased had made any promises, given assurances and/or whether there had been any agreement between the parties;
- whether the deceased had expressed his/her motives or intention, the circumstances of the claimant and the deceased and the nature of their relationship (eg as in *Bouette v Rose* [2001] 1 FLR 363 and *Bishop v Plumley* [1991] 1 All ER 236);
- the extent of the contribution made by the deceased, which has to be substantial. This may not necessarily be quantification in monetary terms. It may involve considering the circumstances of the claimant and the difference the contribution made to the claimant's family, social, working and financial life. The assessment will be made not on a fine arithmetical computation but on a broad common-sense approach. If contributions were made both by the claimant and the deceased the court will consider the extent of the contributions in the light of each party's circumstance and the effect on both of the overall arrangement.

See, further, paras 4.9, 4.9.3 and 7.9.4.

It should also be noted that the Law Commission in its Consultation Paper No 191 has suggested that the 'assumption of responsibility' as a qualifying factor in relation to claimants should be discontinued (para 6.10).

Chapter 8

Powers of the Court to Make Orders

8.1 INTRODUCTION

Once the court is satisfied that the claimant is eligible to make a claim under the I(PFD)A 1975 and that the disposition of the deceased's estate effected by his/her will or the law of intestacy, or the combination of his/her will and that law, is not such as to make reasonable financial provision for the claimant, the court must decide the extent and nature of the financial provision which should be provided for the claimant.

The orders which the court may make are set out in I(PFD)A 1975, ss 2, 5, 6–11 and 16–19. The court's powers relate not only to making financial provisions but include the power to make orders for the purpose of facilitating the making of those provisions by making orders for property to be brought into the estate so that it is available for the necessary financial provisions to be made. The Act has also been amended to include the changes brought about as a result of the provisions of the CPA 2004 as from 5 December 2005. Section 2(1)(g) has been amended to enable the court to vary any settlement made during the subsistence of a civil partnership formed by the deceased or in anticipation of the formation of such a partnership. Sections 16–18 have been amended to take account of orders that can be made in relation to maintenance agreements between civil partners or former civil partners and following the dissolution of a civil partnership.

This chapter deals with the powers set out in I(PFD)A 1975, ss 2, 5, 6, 7 and 16–19. The orders which relate to making property available where the estate is insufficient to make the necessary provision or where the deceased had disposed of property during his/her lifetime for the purpose of defeating or reducing a possible claim under ss 10–13 are dealt with in Chapter 10.

I(PFD)A 1975, s 2 empowers the court to make any one or more of the following orders:

(1) an order for the making to the applicant, out of the net estate of the deceased, of such periodical payments and for such term as may be specified in the order;

(2) an order for the payment to the applicant, out of that estate, of a lump sum of such amount as may be specified;

(3) an order for the transfer to the applicant of such property comprised in that estate as may be specified;

(4) an order for the settlement, for the benefit of the claimant, of such property comprised in that estate as may be specified;

(5) an order for the acquisition, out of property comprised in that estate, of such property as may be specified and for the transfer of the property so acquired to the applicant, or the settlement thereof for his benefit;

(6) an order varying any ante-nuptial or post-nuptial settlement (including such a settlement made by will) made on the parties to a marriage to which the deceased was one of the parties, the variation being for the benefit of the surviving party to that marriage, or any child of that marriage, or any person who was treated by the deceased as a child of the family in relation to that marriage;

(7) an order varying any settlement made:

(a) during the subsistence of a civil partnership formed by the deceased, or

(b) in anticipation of the formation of a civil partnership by the deceased.

In certain circumstances, the court may make an interim order for periodical payments and a lump sum out of the net estate (I(PFD)A 1975, s 5). The financial provisions to meet these orders may be made out the net estate as defined in s 25(1) including property which forms part of the net estate pursuant to orders made under ss 8–12.

8.2 PERIODICAL PAYMENTS – I(PFD)A 1975, SECTION 2(1)(A)

An order for periodical payments must specify the term for which the order is to run (I(PFD)A 1975, s 2(1)).

When making a periodical payment the court may (I(PFD)A 1975, s 2(2)):

(1) specify in the order the amount to be paid;

(2)   express the amount to be paid to be such sum as is equivalent to the whole, or a specified portion, of the income of the net estate;

(3)   direct that a specified part of the net estate be appropriated or set aside for meeting periodical payments, and express the amount of such periodical payments to be equivalent to the whole of the income of such part of the net estate.

No larger part of the net estate than is sufficient, at the date of the order, to produce the income required may be set aside or appropriated (I(PFD)A 1975, s 2(3)). The power of appropriation is in addition to any power conferred by the deceased's will or given by the court to the personal representatives under its jurisdiction to make consequential orders and give directions. Alternatively, the court may provide for the amount of the periodical payments, or any of them, to be determined in any other way as the court thinks fit (s 2(2)).

8.2.1   Commencement date

There are three possible dates from which an order for periodical payments can commence:

(1)   the date of the deceased's death, when the right to make the claim accrued;

(2)   the date when proceedings were commenced, when the right to make the claim was exercised;

(3)   the date the order is made, when the court finally determines the merit of the claim.

There is no rule that an order for periodical payments must be backdated to commence from the date of the deceased's death. I(PFD)A 1975, s 19(1) provides that, where an order is made under s 2 then, for all purposes, including the purposes of the enactments relating to inheritance tax, the will or the law of intestacy, or both the will and the law relating to intestacy, as the case may be, shall have effect and be deemed to have had effect as from the deceased's death subject to the provisions of the order.

The commencement date of a periodical payment order or any other order is in the discretion of the court. In the absence of exceptional circumstances, the court will be reluctant to backdate the order to a date earlier than the date the proceedings were commenced. Even when backdating is considered appropriate, the court would be mindful not to backdate the order to such an extent that it results in a substantial lump sum having to be paid.

In order to obviate the need to backdate an order for periodical payment the court may consider it appropriate to make an order for a small capital sum to be paid (see *Re Debenham (Deceased)* [1986] 1 FLR 404 and *Re Farrow (Deceased)* [1988] 1 FLR 205). Where the claimant has no financial resources and is in receipt of state benefits, it is a matter for the court's discretion whether or not to backdate the order. Each case turns on its own facts, but orders have been made notwithstanding the fact that the claimant was in receipt of state benefits and may have had to pay back the benefits received. The case of *Lusternik v Lusternik* [1972] Fam 125 is an example where an order was backdated although the claimant had been in receipt of state benefits. In that case the deceased and the claimant were divorced and an order for periodical payments of £6 per week was made following the divorce. The claimant continued to maintain both a social and a business relationship with the deceased. The deceased made a will in 1960 leaving his share in a company to the claimant for life. Six weeks before his death in December 1964 he revoked his will by codicil and left her a legacy of £500 and the residue to his executrix. The net estate was valued at £10,000. When the claimant made her application she was unable to work and in ill-health. When her appeal was heard she was in receipt of retirement pension and supplementary benefit of £9.60 per week. The trial judge made an order in her favour of £6 per week backdated to February 1970. On appeal the order was increased to £8 per week. On the issue of backdating, Cairns LJ said:

> As to backdating, I do not accept the contention of counsel for the applicant that there is any rule that prima facie the payments should be backdated to the death. This was certainly not laid down as a rule in the case he cited, *Askew v Askew*. There Marshall J held that it was a matter of discretion in each case; and indeed I think that is the necessary wording of the Act. Where an applicant has not brought proceedings until several years after probate was granted, I should not, in the absence of very special circumstances consider it right to backdate the order to a date earlier than that of the originating summons. And again where, as here, the proceedings have extended over some four years from the date of the originating summons to that of the order, I should not consider it right to backdate the order to the date of the summons unless it is shown that there had been some deliberate obstruction by the respondent in the course of the proceedings. One should I think guard against backdating the order for periodical payments to such an extent as in effect to add to it a lump sum order substantial in relation to the size of the estate. In this case, if there had been no provision at all for the applicant in the will, I should have been disposed to backdate the order for two years or perhaps two and a half years. But taking account of her legacy of £500, I think that the registrar and the judge were right here in choosing the shorter period. By my reckoning, the arrears calculated (now) at £8.00 per week and making an allowance for the interim payments which were ordered and which I understand were made between February and May 1971, will be about £480, payable within a week or two, and I do not think it would be fair to the respondent to increase that sum.

In *Askew v Askew* [1961] 1 WLR 725, the court was directly concerned with the question of whether the fact that the former wife had been receiving state benefits afforded a ground for postponing the commencement date of the payments ordered. Marshall J said:

> It falls to the court to consider whether in the section itself there is any indication or guide to the proper date from which the payments should be made out of the estate. The right which the former wife has established is described in s. 3(1) as a right of 'reasonable provision for her maintenance after his death' and I have no doubt whatever that a court in its discretion would if the circumstances of any particular case warrants it, make an order that there is a right arising immediately after death in all circumstances. In my judgment this section gives the court a discretion, and it would be incumbent on the court to consider all the factors in the case before deciding on any date from which the first payment under the section should be made.

In *Re Goodwin (Deceased), Goodwin v Goodwin* [1969] 1 Ch 283, however, the court, in exercising its discretion, considered the matter on the basis that if the will had made reasonable provision, that provision would have taken effect from the testator's death. Accordingly, the court ordered that payments should commence from the death of the testator. The court treated any state benefits which were received by the claimant as a matter which was extraneous to the issue before the court. See also *Stead v Stead* [1985] FLR 16, where payments were backdated to the day after the testator's death; and *Re Farrow (Deceased)* [1988] 1 FLR 205, where, in backdating the payments, the court took into account all the relevant factors.

The decision in *Re Goodwin* was not cited in *Lusternik v Lusternik* and appears to suggest that, generally speaking, the discretion should be exercised in favour of backdating the order to the date of death. Since, however, the I(PFD)A 1975 is silent on the date from which an order for periodical payments should commence, and the court's power is any event discretionary, it is submitted that, in exercising its discretion, the court should have regard to all the circumstances of the case, including any delay in issuing proceedings; any delay resulting from deliberate obstruction by the respondent to the claim; any payments made to the claimant under an interim order; and any benefits received by the claimant under the will. The provision which the will should have made is and should be one of the considerations, and not the premise from which the court ought to start.

When an immediate order is not required, but it is anticipated that provision will be required in the future, the court may adjourn the application (see *Re Franks, Franks v Franks* [1948] Ch 62).

8.2.2   Setting aside and appropriation of property – I(PFD)A 1975, section 2(3)

I(PFD)A 1975, s 2(3) gives the court power to direct that such part of the net estate as may be specified be set aside or appropriated for the making, out of the income from such property, of the payments ordered by the court. But the section also restricts the court's power to anticipate the future needs of the claimant, in that it prohibits setting aside or appropriating any part of the net estate larger than would be sufficient at the date of the order to produce, from the income thereof, the amount ordered by the court. The future needs of the claimant must, therefore, be dealt with by an application for variation of the periodical payments order (see para 8.11), but when varying the order, the court has no power to bring in new property to meet any increase.

Thus the court may order that part of the net estate be set aside for the making of the payments out of the income it produces or, should the payments ordered fall into arrears, they can be discharged from the property/capital ordered to be set aside (see para 8.2.4). Note, however, the restriction imposed by this provision that the court cannot set aside any part of the net estate larger than is necessary to meet the needs of the claimant at the date when the order is made. The court cannot, therefore, anticipate the future needs of the claimant and set aside funds to meet those future needs.

8.2.3   Supplementary orders and conditions

By virtue of I(PFD)A 1975, s 2(4), the court may make such consequential and supplementary provisions to an order as it thinks necessary or expedient for the purposes of giving effect to the order, or for securing that the order operates fairly as between the beneficiaries of the estate of the deceased.

The court may attach conditions to an order for periodical payments, as it did in *Re Lidington, Lidington v Thomas (No 2)* [1940] Ch 927, where, on making provision for periodical payments for the widow of the deceased, the court required her to undertake to maintain the children during their minority. In *Re Pointer, Pointer v Shonfiel v Edward* [1941] Ch 60, the court awarded the daughter of the deceased the income of one fifth of the residuary estate or the sum of 30 shillings per week, whichever was the smaller, during her life, subject to I(FP)A 1938, s 1(2)(b), namely in the particular circumstances of her disability ceasing, but subject to the condition that her daughter should inform the trustees if she received at any time a sum in excess of 200 shillings from any source.

8.2.4   Secured periodical payments order

Matrimonial Causes Act 1973, s 23(1)(b) makes provision for a periodical payments order to be secured for such term as may be specified in the order. The I(PFD)A 1975 does not specifically make any provision for a secured periodical payments order. However, I(PFD)A 1975, s 2(4) confers on the court unlimited power to make such other consequential and supplemental provisions for the purpose of giving effect to its order and for the purpose of securing that the order operates fairly. It is suggested that, as in matrimonial financial relief applications, a secured periodical payments order could be made if the court considers it is justified, necessary or expedient to make those provisions to ensure that payments under the order will be met. It is also suggested that in appropriate cases, the court may consider making provision for an annuity to be set up. See para 8.12 for variation of a secured periodical payments order made under the Matrimonial Causes Act 1973.

8.2.5   Duration of periodical payments order

The order for periodical payments should specify the term for which the order is to run. In the case of an order or interim order in favour of a former spouse or civil partner of the deceased or where there is a judicial separation order or separation order in force, I(PFD)A 1975, s 19(2) provides that:

> Any order made under section 2 or 5 of this Act in favour of–
>
> (a)   an applicant who was [the former spouse or former civil partner] of the deceased, or
>
> (b)   an applicant who was the husband or wife of the deceased in a case where the marriage with the deceased was the subject of a decree of judicial separation and at the date of death the decree was in force[, at the date of death, a separation order under the Family Law Act 1996 was in force in relation to the marriage with the deceased][1] and the separation was continuing, [or
>
> (c)   an applicant who was the civil partner of the deceased in a case where, at the date of death, a separation order under Chapter 2 of Part 2 of the Civil Partnership Act 2004 was in force in relation to their civil partnership and the separation was continuing,]
>
> shall, in so far as it provides for the making of periodical payments, cease to have effect [on the formation by the applicant of a subsequent marriage or civil partnership, except in relation to any arrears due under the order on the date of the formation of the subsequent marriage or civil partnership].

---

[1]   Inserted by Family Law Act 1996, s 66(1), Sch 8, para 27(7).

Two matters arise from this provision. First, it appears that although the order will automatically cease on the formation of a subsequent marriage or civil partnership of a former spouse or civil partner the I(PFD)A 1975 is silent in relation to the former spouse or civil partner forming a subsequent relationship which leads to cohabitation. Second, the Act does not make any like provision for the termination of the order in the case of the formation of a subsequent marriage or civil partnership by a surviving spouse or civil partner or the cohabitation of the spouse or civil partner with another person.

Matrimonial Causes Act 1973, s 28(2) provides for a periodical payments order or secured periodical payments order in favour of a party to the marriage to cease on the remarriage of or formation of a civil partnership by that party except in relation to any arrears due under it on the date of the remarriage or formation of the civil partnership. The order is usually expressed to last 'during the parties' joint lives or the petitioner's earlier remarriage or further order'. It is also now the practice, on the making of an order for periodical payments in matrimonial proceedings, to provide that the order will cease on the cohabitation of the recipient of the payment with another person. It is therefore suggested that an order for periodical payments made under the I(PFD)A 1975 in favour of a widow(er) or the surviving civil partner should likewise provide for such a cut-off date, ie on the formation of a subsequent marriage or civil partnership. It should also provide that the order in favour of the surviving spouse, civil partner, former spouse or civil partner should also cease on the spouse/civil partner's cohabitation with another.

In relation to an order in favour of a child, the I(PFD)A 1975 does not specifically provide the maximum term for which the order should last. Matrimonial Causes Act 1973, s 29(1) provides that no financial order and no order for a transfer of property shall be made in favour of a child beyond the age of 18 unless the child remains in education or training or there are special circumstances which justify the order lasting beyond the age of 18 years (s 29(3)). Special circumstances may arise for example where the child suffers from physical or mental incapacity. The order in favour of a child is expressed to last 'until the said child attains the age of 17 or ceases full-time (secondary/tertiary) education, whichever is the later'. It is suggested that, when making an order under the I(PFD)A 1975, the court should follow the same principle. This would ensure that distribution of the estate can take place without delay. The Act makes provision for an application for a variation of the order to be made if the circumstances justify this (for variation and suspension of orders see, further, para 8.11).

8.3   LUMP SUM ORDER – I(PFD)A 1975, SECTION 2(1)(B)

An order for a specified lump sum to be paid out of the net estate may be made on a claim under the I(PFD)A 1975. It can also be made on an application under s 6 for the variation or discharge of an order for periodical payments (see para 8.11.2). A lump sum ordered under s 6, however, may be made only out of any 'relevant property', to the original claimant or to any such person who has applied or would, but for s 4, be entitled to apply for an order under s 2.

In claims under the I(PFD)A 1975 it is more common for the court to award a lump sum payment rather than periodical payments. This is because a lump sum provides finality for both the claimant and the other beneficiaries, and allows the personal representatives to administer the estate without the additional costs of operating trusts, which would have to be created to provide income to meet a periodical payments order.

8.3.1   Instalment order

Pursuant to I(PFD)A 1975, s 7(1), where a lump sum is ordered under s 2(1)(b) or s 6(2)(b), the court has power to order that the lump sum be paid by instalments of such amount as may be specified in the order.

8.3.2   Variation of order

The court also has power to vary a lump sum order, whether made under I(PFD)A 1975, s 2 or s 6, but the power is limited in that the order may be varied only on the application of:

(1)   the person to whom the lump sum is payable;

(2)   the personal representatives of the deceased; or

(3)   the trustees of the property out of which the lump sum is payable.

Further, the order may be varied only by altering:

(1)   the number of instalments payable;

(2)   the amount of any instalment; and

(3)   the date on which any instalment becomes payable.

8.3.3   Assessing amount to be awarded

The factors taken into account in arriving at the amount to be awarded under a lump sum order depend on the circumstances of each case, and in particular the matters set out in I(PFD)A 1975, s 3 (see Chapter 7).

Where a capital sum is provided to produce an income, an important factor to be taken into account in assessing the amount to be awarded is the fact that the claimant is forgoing the right to apply for variation; an adjustment in favour of the claimant should therefore be made to compensate for the loss of that right. This is particularly likely to be the case where the estate is large. Other factors for which the court should make allowance are inflation and future contingencies. In the words of Oliver LJ in *Re Besterman (Deceased), Besterman v Grusin* [1984] Ch 458:

> ... houses decay, circumstances change, the cost of living increases and the value of money falls, or certainly the history of the last ten years leads us to believe. Furthermore, although, happily, the plaintiff appears in good health, there is an inevitable health hazard with advancing age, and having regard to the fact that this lady is the widow of a more than ordinarily wealthy man, reasonable provision would in my judgment require that she should have access to a sufficient sum of money to ensure beyond any reasonable doubt that she is relieved of any anxiety for the future. It is a criticism of the annuity purchase approach to the problem that the income which it is intended to provide is provided only if an annuity is actually purchased which is not, in general, a course which a prudent adviser would advise in an age of inflation and that postulates that there can be no resort to capital in the event of emergency ... The relevant consideration is the extent of the lump sum and that ought (at any rate where as here the estate is ample for the purpose and scarcity of funds is not an inhibiting factor) to take account of the fact that the plaintiff is (whether or not of her volition) giving up the right to return to the court for a variation of the provision in the event of unforeseen contingencies. I think that the absence, which is inherent in a lump sum order, of an opportunity to return to the court does mean that, in assessing the lump sum, the court must take rather greater account than might otherwise be the case of contingencies and inflation. I accept the submission of junior counsel for the plaintiff that reasonable provision, in the case of a very large estate such as this and wholly blameless widow who is incapable of supporting herself, should be such as to relieve her of anxiety for the future. I say 'in the case of a very large estate' not because there is any difference in principle but simply because the existence of a large estate makes that which is desirable also practically possible. It has been pointed out more than once that the calculation in cases of this sort is, of necessity, not one where any precision is possible, but for my part I take the view that reasonable provision in this case would dictate that in addition to the secure roof over her head, the widow should have available to her a capital sum of sufficient size not simply to enable her to purchase an adequate annuity

according to her present needs but to provide her with the income which she needs and a cushion in the form of available capital which will enable her to meet all reasonable foreseeable contingencies. What that sum is, is a matter for judgment but I think that in it we are entitled to take into account that, though the plaintiff is quite content with her present residence it is in fact somewhat more modest than she might be thought to be entitled to expect to be provided for her by a husband in the financial position of the deceased.

The fact that a lump sum may enable the claimant to provide for someone else should not govern the amount ordered to be paid. In *Preston v Preston* [1982] Fam 17 (a case under the Matrimonial Causes Act 1973), Brandon J said that the lump sum awarded to the wife should not include an amount for the future maintenance of her son (see paras 7.7.2 and 7.7.6).

In assessing the amount of the lump sum to be awarded the court has sometimes capitalised periodical payments which it has awarded. In *Malone v Harrison* [1979] 1 WLR 1353, the court used a multiplier and multiplicand as applicable in personal injuries actions. In *Re Besterman v Grusin* [1984] Ch 458, the court used the amount of capital which would be needed to generate the income required to satisfy the claimant's needs. See also *Re Bunning (Deceased), Bunning v Salmon* [1984] Ch 480. If the circumstances justify it, it may be appropriate to apply the *Duxbury* calculations (see *Duxbury v Duxbury* [1992] Fam 62) or the Ogden Tables (Michael Ogden, *Actuarial Tables with Explanatory Notes for Use in Personal Injury and Fatal Accident Cases* (Stationery Office Books, 1994)) to achieve the right result.

It should be borne in mind that no hard-and-fast rule has been applied and there is no case which sets out any guidelines. The court's decision turns on the particular facts of the case before it and the application of the principles set out in I(PFD)A 1975, s 3.

8.4   TRANSFER OF PROPERTY ORDER – I(PFD)A 1975, SECTION 2(1)(C)

I(PFD)A 1975, s 2(1)(c) empowers the court to order the transfer to the claimant of such property comprised in the net estate as may be specified in the order. 'Property' is defined in s 25(1) to include 'any chose in action'. This power is similar to that contained in Matrimonial Causes Act 1973, s 24. As in matrimonial proceedings, there is no power to order a transfer of property on an application for periodical payments, but on a variation of a periodical payments order the court may order a transfer of property under s 6(2)(c) (see, further, para 8.11.2).

Where an order for transfer of property in favour of a claimant is justified, but would mean that the needs of the other beneficiaries would not be met because the other assets are insufficient, the court may order the transfer subject to a legacy in favour of a beneficiary or subject to a charge over the property. In *Rajabally v Rajabally* [1987] 2 FLR 390, the testator, who was survived by his widow, their two sons and a son of his first marriage, left his estate, consisting of the former matrimonial home, to his widow and the three children in equal shares. The widow lived in the house with two of her sons. The eldest son suffered from mental illness, lived in council accommodation and his only source of income was state benefits. The widow made a claim under the I(PFD)A 1975. During the proceedings the eldest son was prepared to take the provision made under the will by being bought out at a valuation. The two younger children were prepared to give assurances that they would not insist on their rights under the will. The court took the view that the widow should be provided with real security in the house, but that account had to be taken of the limited means and uncertain future of the eldest son. The balance was struck by transferring the house to the widow absolutely, but subject to a legacy in favour of the eldest son to be raised by a mortgage on the property. See, also, *Re Christie (Deceased), Christie v Keeble* [1979] Ch 168.

8.5   SETTLEMENT OF PROPERTY ORDER – I(PFD)A 1975, SECTION 2(1)(C)

The power to order property comprised in the net estate to be settled for the benefit of the claimant is derived from I(PFD)A 1975, s 2(1)(c). There is no power to vary or discharge such an order once made. If it is envisaged that the purpose of the settlement may alter in the future, powers of appointment and variation, and the power to invest and purchase property, can be provided. The deed of trust should be tailored to meet the particular circumstances of the case and the deed should be drafted with care to cover contingencies and changes of circumstances which may occur in the future. Where the interests of others need to be protected it would be advisable for the deed of trust or settlement to be drafted by experienced Chancery lawyers.

The nature of the settlement which the court may order will depend on the circumstances of the case. Where the settlement is in favour of a child, it will provide for the needs of the child during his minority. In the case of a widow it could be limited until such time as she remarries or cohabits. In the case of a civil partner it would be limited until a subsequent partnership is formed by the surviving partner.

The power to settle property is particularly useful where the deceased did not make provision for a mentally disabled child, particularly an adult child, in the belief that the child would be adequately provided for by the state. In view of the policy of providing care in the community for those who are disabled, a financial provision order in the form of a settlement would provide for a better quality of life within the community than would otherwise be possible. In such cases the court should consider making a settlement of property order; and, if necessary, an order for the acquisition of property and its settlement upon a discretionary trust so as to permit the whole or any part of the income from the trust fund to be applied for the maintenance, care and benefit of the claimant as the trustees in their discretion deem fit.

In *Hanbury v Hanbury* [1999] 2 FLR 255, the deceased's daughter was physically and mentally disabled with a mental age of about 12. She was living with and cared for by her mother, supported by social services. At the time of his death the deceased was making maintenance payments under a court order to the daughter, but he had, from choice, not had any contact with her since she was four years old. Having sought legal advice on how to defeat his daughter's claim, the deceased had transferred his property into, and acquired investments in, the joint names of himself and his second wife and had arranged for investment trust holdings to be bought in the second wife's sole name. Applying the powers it had under I(PFD)A 1975, ss 9 and 10, the court treated the severable share of the jointly owned property as part of the net estate of the deceased and took the net estate to include a one-half share of the investment holding and of the joint accounts. The court took into account the fact that the daughter's needs would eventually be met by placement in a residential home. It ordered the costs of such placement to be met by settling £39,000 in a discretionary trust, with the daughter as principal beneficiary, so that her state benefits by way of income support would not be prejudiced.

Re Abrams (Deceased) [1996] 2 FLR 379 is another case where the court used the power to settle property to make appropriate provision for a claimant out of the net estate. In *Re Abrams*, at the date of the hearing, the claimant's business had failed and he had entered into an individual voluntary arrangement under Insolvency Act 1986, Part VIII. It was a term of the individual voluntary arrangement that any capital sum received by the claimant's estate should be paid to the creditors. The claimant's home had been repossessed and he was unemployed. To ensure that the provision ordered by the court was received by the claimant, the court ordered a settlement to be effected under I(PFD)A 1975, s 2(1)(d) whereby 50 per cent of the estate would be settled on the claimant for life on protective trusts, the life interest importing the statutory trusts under Trustee Act 1925, s 33, so that the income would be paid to the claimant for life; but if he became bankrupt or sought to alienate his interest, the life interest would be determined and replaced by a discretionary trust for the claimant and his immediate family.

8.6   ACQUISITION OF PROPERTY ORDER – I(PFD)A 1975, SECTION 2(1)(E)

I(PFD)A 1975, s 2(1)(e) gives the court power to make an order for the acquisition of property comprised in the net estate, and for the acquired property to be transferred to the claimant; or for the settlement of such property for the benefit of the claimant. Once made the order may not be varied (s 6(9)). This power can be useful where the claimant is a person who suffers from physical or mental disability (see Chapter 4) or is a child and needs a home. Where this power is used, the order may also provide for the settlement of the acquired property for the benefit of the claimant. There is no restriction on the type of property which may be acquired but it is likely to be one that satisfies the needs of the claimant.

8.7   VARIATION OF NUPTIAL SETTLEMENT – I(PFD)A 1975, SECTION 2(1)(F) AND (G)

I(PFD)A 1975, s 2(1)(f) provides that the court may vary any ante-nuptial or post-nuptial settlement (including such a settlement made by will) made on the parties to a marriage to which the deceased was one of the parties, the variation being for the benefit of the surviving spouse to that marriage, or any child of that marriage, or any person who was treated by the deceased as a child of the family in relation to that marriage.

Similar provision is made in I(PFD)A 1975, s 2(1)(g) giving the court power to vary any settlement made during the subsistence of a civil partnership formed by the deceased or in anticipation of the formation of a civil partnership by the deceased.

These provisions mirror those which are set out in Matrimonial Causes Act 1973, s 24(1)(c) and in CPA 2004, Sch 5, para 7.

As with variation of settlement orders in the context of divorce and nullity of marriage proceedings and the dissolution and nullity of civil partnerships, the I(PFD)A 1975 requires any settlement to be varied to have a 'nuptial' element and the court's power to vary such a settlement is limited to:

(1)   a party to a marriage or civil partnership;
(2)   a child of that marriage or a child of both the civil partners; or
(3)   a child who was treated by the deceased as the child of the
       family in relation to that marriage or civil partnership.

8.7.1   Has there been a settlement?

In considering whether to exercise its powers under this provision the court
will first need to determine whether there has been a settlement. The I(PFD)A
1975 does not define an ante-nuptial or post-nuptial settlement. In the case of
an ante-nuptial settlement, the agreement to settle property must have been
made prior to that marriage or civil partnership. In the case of a post-nuptial
settlement, it may result from an agreement made before or after the marriage
or civil partnership but settled after the marriage or civil partnership has taken
place. In *Hargreaves v Hargreaves* [1926] P 42, such a settlement was defined
as one which was made 'in contemplation of, or because of, marriage and with
reference to the interests of married people and their children'.

The term 'settlement', in most cases, has been given a wide meaning. In
Brooks v Brooks [1995] 2 FLR 13, Lord Nicholls of Birkenhead said:

> The authorities have consistently given a wide meaning to settlement in this
> context, and they have spelled out no precise limitations. This seems right,
> because this approach accords with the purpose of the statutory provision.
> Financial provision that is appropriate so long as the parties are married will
> often cease to be appropriate when the marriage ends. In order to promote the
> best interests of the parties and their children in the fundamentally changed
> situation, it is desirable that the court should have power to alter the terms of
> the settlement. The purpose of the section is to give the court this power. The
> object does not dictate that settlement should be given a narrow meaning. On
> the contrary, the purpose of the section would be impeded, rather than
> advanced, by continuing its scope. The continuing use of the archaic
> expression 'ante-nuptial' and 'post nuptial' does not point in the opposite
> direction. These expressions are apt to embrace all settlements in respect of the
> particular marriage, whether made before or after the marriage. In this
> connection, it should be noted in passing that a settlement may be made in
> respect of a particular marriage even though in certain circumstances the wife
> or husband by a subsequent marriage might be the person to take. *Lort-*
> *Williams v Lort-Williams* [1951] P395 affords an illustration of this.

In *Ben Hashem v Al Shayif* [2008] EWHC 2380 (Fam), [2009] 1 FLR 115,
Munby J (as he then was) stated that:

> one of the classic statements of what is meant by a nuptial settlement for this
> purpose is to be found in the judgment of Hill J in *Prinsep v Prinsep* [1929] P

225 at 232: 'Is it upon the husband in the character of husband or in the wife in the character of wife, or upon both in the character of husband and wife? If it is, it is a settlement on the parties within the meaning of the section. The particular form of it does not matter. It may be a settlement in the strictest sense of the term, it may be a covenant to pay by one spouse to the other, or by a third person to a spouse. What does matter is that it should provide for the financial benefit of one or other or both of the spouses as spouses and with reference to their married state'.

Thus, the settlement need not be a classic marriage settlement, nor is it necessary for the settlement to be expressed to be a marriage settlement. It is the substance of the settlement which is significant. The particular form of the settlement does not matter as long as it provides for the financial benefit of one or other of the spouses or civil partners as spouses/civil partners with reference to their married/civil partnership relationship.

It is also irrelevant who the settlor of the settlement is or what the motive of the settlor was when the settlement was made (see *Prescott (formerly Fellowes) v Fellowes* [1958] P 260). What matters is the substance of the arrangements and whether it related to that marriage, not marriage generally, and whether it made continuing provision for the husband, wife, the civil partners and or their child or a child of the family. (See, also, *N v N and F Trust* [2005] EWHC 2908 (Fam), [2006] 1 FLR 856 and *C v C (Ancillary Relief: Nuptial Settlement)* [2004] EWCA Civ 1030, [2005] Fam 250, *sub nom Charalambous v Charalambous* [2004] 2 FLR 1093.) In *K v K (Ancillary Relief: Deed of Appointment)* [2007] EWHC 3485 (Fam), [2009] 2 FLR 937, the court on the facts adopted a more restrictive approach. In *K v K*, the trust had been settled by the husband's mother for the benefit of her two children and remoter issue and their spouses, widows and widowers. The trustees had an overriding power of appointment. At a later date the trust was varied by two deeds of appointment, both revocable with the prior consent of the husband, which excluded the husband's brother and his issue. Both at the time of the original trust and the two subsequent deeds of appointment, the husband was single. He married the woman with whom he had been in a relationship for 24 years after his mother, the settlor, died, so that the children of their relationship could be legitimated and included as beneficiaries under the trust. After the marriage, another deed of appointment was executed by the trustees again excluding the husband's brother and his family as beneficiaries. The marriage broke down and the wife sought a variation of the trust contending that it was a post-nuptial settlement. The court held that the sole purpose of the deed made after the marriage was an administrative exercise to ensure that the husband's brother and his family could never benefit from the trust and therefore he had not revoked the deed made before the marriage and there was nothing in the deed to suggest that there had been any intention to confer an irrevocable benefit on the wife.

The acquisition by a husband and wife or civil partners of a matrimonial home in their joint names constitutes a post-nuptial settlement, but a disposition which confers 'an immediate and absolute interest in an item of property does not constitute a settlement of that property' (see *Brooks v Brooks* (above) and see, also, *Thompson v Thompson* [1986] Fam 38 and *Dinch v Dinch* [1987] 1 WLR 252 (HL)). In *E v E (Financial Provision)* [1990] 2 FLR 233, during the course of the marriage, a property for which the husband's father had provided the funds was settled on discretionary trusts of which the husband and the wife were beneficiaries; it was held that the settlement constituted a post-nuptial settlement. For a review of what constitutes settlement, see *Ben Hashem v Al Shayif* [2008] EWHC 2380 (Fam), [2009] 1 FLR 115.

To determine whether a nuptial settlement has been made, the court will take into account all the relevant facts to identify the substance of the transaction and whether such a settlement was made will depend very much on the facts of the individual case.

8.7.2   How should the court exercise its discretion?

Once it is confirmed that a settlement is a 'nuptial' settlement the court will then need to identify the property comprised in the settlement/trust and consider how it should exercise its discretion.

In *Dixit v Dixit*, CAT, 23 June 1988 (CA), the testator made no provision in his will for his widow or for the children of his second marriage. There was, however, an investment property, which was held in trust, the effect of which was to give the widow a life interest in one half and, contingent on their attaining the age of 18 years, the other half to the two children of the testator's second marriage. Waite J gave the widow a full life interest in the property and provided for the children by granting them an interest in another property which passed under the will of the deceased. The Court of Appeal held that the order made by the judge could not stand as he had failed to consider the tax implications, but did not decide whether Waite J had power under I(PFD)A 1975, s 2(1)(f) to 'switch' the trusts. This appears to be the only case under the Act on the point.

In general the power of variation will be exercised to benefit the surviving spouse/civil partner provided the settlement related to that marriage or civil partnership.

In *Ben Hashem v Al Shayif* [2009] EWHC 864 (Fam), [2009] 1 FLR 115, Munby J (as he then was) when dealing with the variation of a settlement under Matrimonial Causes Act 1973, s 24(1)(c) held that:

- The court has unfettered and in theory unlimited discretion, as between husband and wife, to rearrange the 'family assets' but 'there is no such general jurisdiction to take away – in plain language to confiscate – the children's property, let alone the step children's property to meet clams brought by a wife.
- The court should have regard to all the circumstances and in particular to the matters listed in section 25 with the objective so far as it is possible to make it, to achieve a result which is fair to both parties looking to the effect of the order considered as a whole.
- The court ought to be very slow to deprive innocent third parties of their rights under the settlement. If their interests are to be adversely affected then the court, looking at the wider picture, will normally ensure that they receive some benefit, which, even if not pecuniary, is approximately equivalent, so that they do not suffer substantial injury.
- If and in so far as the variation would affect the interests of the child, it should be permitted only if, after taking into account all the terms of the intended order, all monetary considerations and any other relevant factors, however intangible, it can be said, on the while, to be for the benefit or, at least, not to their disadvantage.
- The court when exercising its discretion in favour of the spouse/civil partner and contemplating depriving a third party and particularly a child to meet the claims of a spouse/civil partner should look for fairness and justice and ask itself why a third party and more particularly a child should be deprived of their interest in order to meet the claims of a spouse/civil partner.

Where the marriage or the civil partnership has been dissolved but the provisions of I(PFD)A 1975, s 14 apply (see paras 4.4.2–4.5.2), the court has power under s 14 to treat the former spouse/civil partner of the deceased in the same category as a surviving spouse and to vary an appropriate settlement for that claimant's benefit.

In proceedings for ancillary relief following a dissolution of a marriage or civil partnership the court can, pursuant to the provisions of the Matrimonial Causes Act 1973, as amended by Welfare Reform and Pensions Act 1999, Sch 3, para 3, make a pension sharing order, but there is no such power in respect of a claim under the I(PFD)A 1975. It has been suggested that the decision in *Brooks v Brooks* could be applied to a claim under the Act but there is no direct authority on the subject.

The Law Commission in its Consultation Paper 191 has considered the issue of pension assets and its unavailability in proceedings under the I(PFD)A 1975. The view expressed at para 7.80 is that 'resort to pension assets should in practice be limited to those cases, where there are insufficient other assets in the estate from which provision can be made for deserving applicants for family provision', but the Commission has invited further responses on whether this is a serious problem that needs to be addressed and whether there are any technical implications. The Consultation Paper has asked consultees to consider whether they would favour reform of the Act to the effect that benefits from a pension fund, whether lump sums or periodical payments, could be the subject of family provision orders made by the court and whether legal or practical difficulties would result if benefits from a pension fund could be the subject of family provision order and, if so, what these might be.

8.8   CONSEQUENTIAL AND SUPPLEMENTAL ORDERS – I(PFD)A 1975, SECTION 2(4)

When making any of the orders referred to under I(PFD)A 1975, s 2(1), the court also has power, under s 2(4), to make such consequential and supplemental provisions as it thinks necessary or expedient for the purposes of:

(1)   giving effect to the order;

(2)   securing that the order operates fairly as between one beneficiary of the deceased and another.

There are no limitations on the very wide scope which the court has under this provision. Without in any way restricting the court's power under this subsection, I(PFD)A 1975, s 2(4) particularises four specific orders which the court can make under this provision, namely:

(1)   to order any person who holds any property which forms part of the net estate of the deceased to make such payment, or transfer such property, as may be specified in the order;

(2)   to vary the disposition of the deceased's estate effected by the will or the law of intestacy, or by both the will and the law relating to intestacy, in such manner as the court thinks fair and reasonable having regard to the provisions of the order and all the circumstances of the case;

(3)   to confer on the trustees of any property which is the subject of an order under s 2 such powers as appear to the court to be necessary or expedient.

The powers given under this provision can be used to impose conditions on a substantive order made under I(PFD)A 1975, s 2 to define, restrict or regulate the order made. For instance, where a periodical payments order is made the court may direct the claimant to inform the personal representatives of any change in the financial circumstances of the claimant, or it may grant the claimant the right to occupy a property subject to making payment for use and occupation. The specific power under s 2(1)(d) enables the court to extend the authority given to trustees under the will to meet the particular requirements of the case.

The court's power under I(PFD)A 1975, s 2(4) to make consequential directions for the purpose of giving effect to the order, or to secure that the order operates fairly between the beneficiaries, enables the court to apportion the incidence of any orders between different classes of beneficiary or between the same class. Usually, the awards are made out of the residuary estate, but where this is not possible the court is likely to apportion the burden between pecuniary legatees and residuary legatees. See *Bunning, Bunning v Salmon* [1984] Ch 480 and *Malone v Harrison* [1979] 1 WLR 1353.

The court is not bound by any express declaration of the deceased as to how an award should be borne; although awards are usually made out of the residuary estate this is not always the case. In *Re Preston, Preston v Hoggarth* [1969] 1 WLR 317, the testator provided in his will that in the event of his widow making a claim, it was his wish that the award should be discharged out of the provision made for his grandchildren. The court held that it had power not only to apportion the burden of the award as regards respective classes of beneficiary, but also to throw the burden unequally between beneficiaries in the same class.

In exercising its discretion, the court should have regard to the claims of beneficiaries who would be claimants under the I(PFD)A 1975 and those who do not qualify. It should also have regard to the intention of the deceased, whether expressed or presumed (see *Re Simson, Simson v National Provincial Bank* [1950] Ch 38). Finally, the court should have regard to the matters which influence the court in deciding whether or not the deceased has made reasonable financial provision for the claimant.

In addition to these wide powers the court also has the powers it can exercise under CPR Part 25, to preserve any property until the conclusion of the proceedings, to grant injunctions and freezing orders and orders to prevent the dissipation of assets or disposition of property intended to defeat or reduce a claim under the I(PFD)A 1975.

The court may also make orders for the disclosure of information under CPR r 25.1(1)(g) directing a party to provide information about the location of relevant property or assets or to provide information about relevant property or assets which are or may be the subject of an application for a 'freezing order'. Practitioners are advised to consider the orders which are available under the CPR. An application for disclosure of information may also be sought before proceedings are begun under CPR r 31.16 and for a direction for accounts or inquiries to be undertaken or made under Part 24, PD 24.6.

8.9 INTERIM ORDERS – I(PFD)A 1975, SECTION 5

On an application under I(PFD)A 1975, s 2 the court has power to order interim payments to be made, out of the net estate, of such sum or sums, and if more than one, at such intervals, as the court thinks reasonable.

8.9.1 Conditions precedent

Before the court can make an interim order it must be satisfied that:

(1) the claimant is in immediate need of financial assistance but it is not yet possible to determine what order (if any) should be made under s 2; and

(2) property forming part of the net estate of the deceased is or can be made available to meet the needs of the claimant.

Since the power to make the order is discretionary, the claimant must also prove that it would be just in all the circumstances of the case for the court to exercise its discretion. For a case where both a periodical payments order and a lump sum order were made on an interim application, see *Re Besterman (Deceased)* (above).

In *Re Ralphs, Ralphs v District Bank* [1968] 1 WLR 1522, the deceased's second wife had left him after a marriage which had lasted about 9 years. By his will the deceased left her the income from a sum of £8,000. To his daughter he left an income of £13,000 and capital of £3,000 and the residue he left to his son. The daughter was destitute. The second wife applied for financial provision. An interim order was made in her favour, the court holding that in the great majority of cases where some benefit is given to the claimant by the will there can be no good reason for withholding it pending the hearing of the summons.

8.9.2 Matters to be considered

I(PFD)A 1975, s 5(3) provides that in determining what order, if any, should be made under the section, the court shall, so far as the urgency of the case admits, have regard to the same matters as those to which the court is required to have regard under s 3 (see Chapter 7). In exercising its discretion, the court has regard to the fact that the purpose of any order it makes is to hold the situation as reasonably and fairly as possible until the determination of the final application.

8.9.3   Orders that can be made

The court's power to make interim orders is limited to ordering such sum or sums as the court thinks reasonable. This would include an order for periodical payments and a lump sum order, but not a property transfer order. The court may, however, make an order for a lump sum payment to enable the claimant to purchase a home, as occurred in *Re Besterman* (above). The court may impose conditions and restrictions, and determine the duration of any interim orders it may make. It may order that any sum paid to the claimant shall be treated, to such an extent and in such manner as may be provided, as having been paid on account of any payment provided for by that order (I(PFD)A 1975, s 5(4)). When making an interim order therefore, the court may seek an undertaking that if, say, the claimant's financial circumstances change, the claimant should notify the personal representatives so that an application for variation of an interim order can be applied for.

The court has power to vary an interim order under the provisions of I(PFD)A 1975, s 5(1).

By virtue of I(PFD)A 1975, s 5(2), when making an interim order, the court may provide for:

(1)   payments of such amount as may be specified in the order;

(2)   payments equal to the whole of the income of the net estate or of such portion thereof as may be specified;

(3)   payments equal to the whole of the income of such part of the net estate as the court may direct to be set aside or apportioned for the making out of the income thereof of interim payments, or may provide for the payments or any of them to be determined in any other way as the court thinks fit.

8.9.4   Personal representatives and interim orders – I(PFD)A 1975, section 20(2)

I(PFD)A 1975, s 20(2) provides that where the personal representative of a deceased person pays any sum directed by an order under s 5 to be paid out of the net estate, he/she shall not be under any liability by reason of the estate's not being sufficient to make the payment, unless at the time of making the payment he/she had reasonable cause to believe that the estate was not sufficient. In *Re Ralphs, Ralphs v District Bank* (above), Cross J laid down the following guidelines for personal representatives faced with an application for an interim order:

> They should form their own view, with the assistance, of course, of their legal advisers, as to the payments which can properly be made, and if they are not prepared to make such payments on their own responsibility they should ask the parties who might conceivably be affected – whether applicant of residuary legatee – for their consent. If such consent is not forthcoming the executors can apply to the court for leave to make the payment in question and the court, if it thinks that any withholding of consent was unreasonable, could throw the costs of the application on the party to blame.

8.10 INJUNCTIONS

In *Andrew v Andrew* [1990] 2 FLR 376, it was held that the court does not have power to restrain tortious conduct in relation to an application under the I(PFD)A 1975. The substantive issues raised in the proceedings were not for assault, trespass or any other cause of action based on tort or an invasion of a legal right; therefore the applicant was not, under County Courts Act 1984, s 38, entitled to any injunctive relief. Section 38 has since been amended by the Courts and Legal Services Act 1990 to confer wide injunctive powers on the county court. It now provides that, subject to certain exceptions, the county court may make any order which could be made by the High Court if the proceedings were in the High Court. Any such order may be made either unconditionally or on such terms and conditions as the court thinks just.

In addition, the CPR now govern practice and procedure across all jurisdictions and the procedural rules in relation to claims made under the I(PFD)A 1975 are governed by those rules. The court, therefore, is empowered to make such orders as may be appropriate under CPR Part 25, to preserve any property until the conclusion of the proceedings, to grant injunctions and freezing orders, and to grant orders to prevent the dissipation of assets or disposition of property intended to defeat or reduce a claim under the I(PFD)A 1975.

The court may also make orders for the disclosure of information under CPR r 25.1(1)(g) directing a party to provide information about the location of relevant property or assets in the form of a mandatory injunction which may be enforced, if necessary by a committal order provided the order has been endorsed with a penal notice and is personally served on the person to whom it is directed.

It is submitted that the provisions of I(PFD)A 1975, s 2(4) (see para 8.8) are wide enough to include injunctions.

Furthermore, in *Burris v Azadani* [1995] 1 WLR 1372, it was held that both the High Court and county courts have jurisdiction to grant injunctions in wide terms to restrain conduct that was not in itself tortious or otherwise unlawful if such an order was reasonably regarded as necessary for the protection of a claimant's legitimate interests.

Since the I(PFD)A 1975 provides for a transfer of property order, the court would have jurisdiction to make any orders to prevent any dealing with property and to make any orders which would ensure that property is preserved until the claim before the court is finally disposed of. Before making such an order, the court will need to be satisfied that the claimant has an arguable case for an order under s 2, and that it would be just in all the circumstances of the case to exercise the court's discretion.

8.11 VARIATION, DISCHARGE, SUSPENSION AND REVIVAL OF ORDERS – I(PFD)A 1975, SECTION 6

Where the court has made an order for periodical payments under I(PFD)A 1975, s 2(1)(a) (the 'original order'), it has power to vary or discharge that order; to suspend any provision of it temporarily; and to revive the operation of any provision so suspended (s 6(1)). An application to vary an order may be made only in respect of a periodical payments order. Section 7 makes provision for a lump sum order to be varied but only in respect of instalments (see para 8.3.2). For variation of orders made under the Matrimonial Causes Act 1973, see ss 16–18, paras 7.12–7.14. An order varied once may be varied again (see *Frickler v Personal Representatives of Frickler* (1982) 3 FLR 288).

8.11.1 Who may apply?

An application under I(PFD)A 1975, s 6 for variation, discharge, suspension or revival of an order for periodical payments may be made by any one of the following persons (I(PFD)A 1975, s 6(5)):

(1)   a person who has applied for an order under s 2, or who would have been entitled to apply for an order under s 2 were it not for the time limit for applications imposed by s 4;

(2)   the personal representatives of the deceased;

(3)   the trustees of any 'relevant property' (see *Frickler v Frickler* (above));

(4)   any beneficiary of the estate of the deceased.

8.11.2   Orders that can be made – I(PFD)A 1975, section 6(2)–(4)

On an application for variation of the original order the court may:

(1)   provide for the making, out of any relevant property, of such periodical payments and for such term as may be specified in the order, to any person who has applied, or would but for I(PFD)A 1975, s 4 be entitled to apply, for an order under s 2 (whether or not, in the case of any claim, an order was made in favour of the claimant);

(2)   provide for the payment, out of any relevant property, of a lump sum of such amount as may be specified, to the original recipient or to any such person as is mentioned in (1) above;

(3)   provide for the transfer of the relevant property, or such part thereof as may be specified, to the original recipient or to any such person as is referred to in (2) above (s 6(2));

(4)   make orders under s 6(3) (see below);

(5)   give consequential directions as it thinks necessary and expedient having regard to the provisions of the order (s 6(8)).

There is no power, on an application for variation under I(PFD)A 1975, s 6, to make any of the following orders:

(1)   a settlement of property under s 2(1)(d);

(2)   an order for the acquisition of specified property out of the net estate (s 2(1)(e));

(3)   a variation of an ante-nuptial or post-nuptial settlement (s 2(1)(f));

(4)   dealing with the deceased's severable share of property on a joint tenancy under s 9;

(5)   dealing with dispositions intended to defeat applications for financial provision under s 10;

(6)   under s 11 in respect of contracts to leave property by will.

Where an order for periodical payments is to cease:

(1)   on the occurrence of an event (other than the remarriage of a former spouse) specified in the order, or

(2)   on the expiration of a period specified in the order,

and no application for variation has been made before the occurrence of the specified event or the expiration of the specified period, as the case may be, then if, before the end of the period of 6 months from the date of the occurrence of that event or of the expiration of that period, an application is made for variation, discharge, suspension or revival, the court may make any order which it would have had power to make if the application had been made before that date. The order in such an instance may be made in favour of:

    (1)   the original recipient;

    (2)   any other person who has applied for an order under s 2; or

    (3)   any person who would have been entitled to apply for an order under s 2 were it not for the time limits for application imposed by s 4.

It appears from I(PFD)A 1975, s 6(3) and (5) that a person who was debarred from making an application under s 2 by reason of the limitation period imposed by s 4, or a person whose original application was unsuccessful, may nevertheless apply for the variation of an order made in favour of another.

In an application falling within I(PFD)A 1975, s 6(3), the court has power to make any order which it would have had power to make if the application had been made in time. An order varying the original order may be made only within the limits of the 'relevant property' available. It follows that an increase in periodical payments or other variation can occur only in limited circumstances, such as:

    (1)   if there is an increase in income available from the relevant property;

    (2)   if another recipient dies, thus releasing the payments in respect of him/her; or

    (3)   there is a reduction in payments to another recipient.

8.11.3 Meaning of 'relevant property'

I(PFD)A 1975, s 6(6) defines 'relevant property' as follows:

    (a)   property the income of which is at the date of the order applicable wholly or in part for the making of periodical payments to any person who has applied for an order under this Act, or

    (b)   in the case of an application under subsection (3) above in respect of payments which have ceased to be payable on the occurrence of an event or the expiration of a period, property the income of which was so applicable immediately before the occurrence of that event or expiration, as the case may be ...

8.11.4 Matters to be considered

In exercising the power to vary, the court must have regard to all the circumstances of the case, including any change in those circumstances and any change in the matters to which the court was required to have regard under I(PFD)A 1975, s 3 when making the original order (s 6(7)).

Lewis v Lewis [1977] 1 WLR 409 concerned the construction of Matrimonial Causes Act 1973, s 31, which gives the court power to vary or discharge a periodical payments order in divorce proceedings. It was held that, in considering an application for variation, the court is not confined to looking at any change in the means of the parties since the original order was made, but is required to look at the actual means of the parties as they stand at the time when the case is before the court, and to approach the matter as it were fixing the payment *de novo*.

An order can be varied to take account of inflation (see *Frickler v Frickler* (1982) 3 FLR 288).

8.11.5 Time limits

Save for the limitation in I(PFD)A 1975, s 6(3), an application for the variation, discharge, suspension or revival of the original order may be made at any time. Section 6(3) relates to periodical payments which are to cease on the occurrence of an event or the expiry of a specified period. An application relating to such an order must be made within 6 months of the event's occurring or the expiry of the specified period. There is no power to extend this period. In all other cases, however, the court is entitled to consider any delay which has occurred in making the application. Some or all of the matters set out in Chapter 3 may be relevant where the application is made by a person who had failed to apply within the time limit set out in s 4. It is unlikely that a claimant who had been refused leave to apply out of time will succeed in bringing a claim by using this provision unless there are exceptional reasons.

8.11.6 Commencement of the order

An order made by virtue of I(PFD)A 1975, s 6(3) may be directed to take effect from:

(1) the date of the occurrence of the specified event;
(2) the expiration of the specified period; or
(3) such later date as may be specified by the court.

8.12 VARIATION AND DISCHARGE OF SECURED PERIODICAL PAYMENTS ORDERS MADE UNDER MATRIMONIAL CAUSES ACT 1973 – I(PFD)A 1975, SECTION 16

Matrimonial Causes Act 1973, s 31(6) provides that, where a person liable to make payments under a secured periodical payments order has died, an application relating to that order (and to any order made under s 24A(1) which requires the proceeds of sale of property to be used for securing those payments) may be made by the person entitled to payments under the periodical payments order or by the personal representatives of the deceased person, for variation or discharge of the order, or the suspension of the order temporarily, or to revive the operation of any provision so suspended. Such an application must be made within a period of 6 months from the date on which representation in regard to the estate of the deceased person is first taken out unless the court grants permission to make the application out of time.

I(PFD)A 1975, s 16 incorporates a similar provision, enabling an application by the person entitled to secured periodical payments, or the personal representatives of the deceased, to apply to vary or discharge that periodical payments order or to revive the operation of any provision thereof which has been suspended under Matrimonial Causes Act 1973, s 31. The powers exercisable by the court under this section in relation to an order are also exercisable in relation to any instrument executed in pursuance of the order (I(PFD)A 1975, s 16(3)). The personal representatives of the deceased will not be liable for distributing the estate prior to an application being made, if it is made after the 6-month time limit has elapsed.

In *Re Eyre* [1968] 1 WLR 530, although the court was not directly concerned with the provisions of I(PFD)A 1975, s 16, it took into account the fact that there was an order in favour of the applicant, who was the former spouse of the deceased, for secured periodical payments. On the facts, it was concluded that, 'an order for secured maintenance should not properly be treated as a pre-determination of what a survivor is to receive after the death of a former spouse, although it is necessarily an important factor to be considered in every application under section 26'. (Note that this was a pre-I(PFD)A 1975 decision.)

8.12.1 Who may apply?

Both under Matrimonial Causes Act 1973, s 31(6) and I(PFD)A 1975, s 16 the application may only be made by:

(1)　the person entitled to the secured provision;
(2)　the personal representatives of the deceased.

Time limit

The application must be made within 6 months of the date on which representation with regard to the estate was taken out, unless the court extends that time limit.

Matters to be considered

In exercising its powers under I(PFD)A 1975, s 16, the court must have regard to all the circumstances of the case, including any order which the court proposes to make under s 2 or s 5 and any change (whether resulting from the death of the deceased or otherwise) in any of the matters to which the court is required to have regard when making a secured periodical payments order (s 16(2)).

Orders that can be made

The court may make the following orders under I(PFD)A 1975, s 18(2):

- Where an application is made under Matrimonial Causes Act 1973, s 31(6) for a variation or discharge of the secured periodical payments order or for the revival of the operation of any provision of that order which has been suspended, the court has power to direct that the application made under s 31(6) is deemed to have been accompanied by an application for an order under I(PFD)A 1975, s 2.
- On the making of the order that the application under Matrimonial Causes Act 1973, s 31(6) be deemed to be accompanied by an application for financial provision under the I(PFD)A 1975, the court may give such directions as it has power to make under the Act as if the application had been made jointly with an application for an order for financial provision under I(PFD)A 1975, s 2.
- The court also has power to give such consequential directions as may be necessary for enabling it to exercise any of the powers available to it under the I(PFD)A 1975 (see paras 7.8 and 7.10).

8.12.2　Provisions of Children Act 1989, Schedule 1

Children Act 1989, Sch 1, para 7 makes comparable provisions whereby secured periodical payments orders in favour of children which continue after the death of the payer may be varied after the death of the payer, on the application of the surviving parent or guardian of the child or any person in whose favour a residence order in respect of the child is in force. The personal representatives of the deceased also have a right to apply.

In exercising its powers the court must have regard to all the circumstances of the case, including the changed circumstances resulting from the death of the payer (Children Act 1989, Sch 1, para 7(5)).

8.13 Variation and revocation of maintenance agreements – I(PFD)A 1975, section 17

Where a claim for an order under I(PFD)A 1975, s 2 is made to the court by any person who was, at the time of the death of the deceased, entitled to payments from the deceased under a maintenance agreement which continues after the death of the deceased, the court has power to vary or revoke the agreement if an application is made under s 17 by either the payee or the personal representatives (s 17(1)). This subsection identifies the persons who may apply for an order under this section namely:

(1)   the payee; and
(2)   the personal representatives.

8.13.1 Meaning of 'maintenance agreement'

I(PFD)A 1975, s 17(4), as amended, now takes account of those who are in a civil partnership relationship and defines 'maintenance agreement' as follows:

> In this section 'maintenance agreement' in relation to a deceased person means any agreement made, whether in writing or not whether before or after the commencement of this Act, by the deceased with any person with whom he formed a marriage or civil partnership, being an agreement which contained provisions governing the rights and liabilities towards one another when living separately of the parties to that marriage or of the civil partners (whether or not the marriage or civil partnership has been dissolved or annulled) in respect of the making or securing of payments or the disposition or use of any property, including such rights and liabilities with respect to the maintenance or education of any child, whether or not a child of the deceased or a person who was treated by the deceased as a child of the family in relation to that marriage or civil partnership.

To fall within the definition, the agreement must be one made between parties to a marriage or civil partnership.

Children Act 1989, Sch 1, para 10 contains provisions whereby a maintenance agreement in favour of a child, which provides for the continuation of payments after the death of one of the parties, may be varied or revoked by the High Court or the county court on the application of the surviving party or the personal representatives of the deceased. The application must not, however, except with the leave of the court, be made after the end of the period of 6 months beginning with the day on which representation in regard to the estate of the deceased is first taken out (Sch 1, para 11(3)). A grant limited to settled land or to trust property is left out of account when calculating when representation was first taken out, unless a grant limited to the remainder of the estate has previously been made or is made at the same time (Sch 1, para 11(2)).

8.13.2 Orders that can be made

I(PFD)A 1975, s 17(1) limits the court's power where an application is made under s 17 to:

- vary the agreement;
- revoke that agreement.

8.13.3 Criteria to be applied by the court

I(PFD)A 1975, s 17(2) requires the court in exercising its powers under s 17 to have regard to all the circumstances of the case, including any order the court proposes to make under s 2 or s 5, and any change (whether resulting from the death of the deceased or otherwise) in any of the circumstances in the light of which the agreement was made.

8.13.4 Effect of the order

If the maintenance agreement is varied by the court under I(PFD)A 1975, s 17 the effect of the variation will be 'as if the variation had been made immediately before the death of the deceased by agreement between the parties and for valuable consideration' (s 17(3)).

8.14 COURT'S POWERS IN RELATION TO APPLICATIONS UNDER MATRIMONIAL CAUSES ACT 1973, SECTIONS 31 AND 36 – I(PFD)A 1975, SECTION 18

Where on the death of a person against whom a secured periodical payments order was made under the Matrimonial Causes Act 1973, an application is made under s 31(6) for the variation or discharge of that order or for the revival of the operation of any provision thereof which has been suspended or where a party to a maintenance agreement within the meaning of s 34 dies, then if the agreement provided for the continuation of payments under the agreement after the death of one of the parties and an application is made under s 36 for the alteration of the agreement under s 35, the court has power to direct that the application made under s 31(6) or s 36(1) is deemed to have been accompanied by an application for an order under I(PFD)A 1975, s 2 (I(PFD)A 1975, s 18(1)(a) and (b)).

Where the court gives a direction under I(PFD)A 1975, s 18(1)(a) or (b) that the application under the Matrimonial Causes Act 1973 is deemed to be accompanied by an application for an order under I(PFD)A 1975, s 2, it has power, in the proceedings on the application under Matrimonial Causes Act 1973, s 31(6) or s 36(1), to make any order which the court would have had power to make under the I(PFD)A 1975 if the application under s 31(6) or s 36(1) had been made jointly with an application for an order under I(PFD)A 1975, s 2. The court also has power to give such consequential directions as may be necessary for enabling the court to exercise any of the powers available to the court under the I(PFD)A 1975 in the case of an application under s 2 (I(PFD)A 1975, s 18(2)).

Note that when it is dealing with an application under I(PFD)A 1975, s 18 the court has wide powers:

- to direct that the application made under Matrimonial Causes Act 1973, s 31(6) or s 36(1) be deemed to have been accompanied by an application for an order under I(PFD)A 1975, s 2 (I(PFD)A 1975, s 18(1));
- to make any order which it would have power to make under the I(PFD)A 1975 (I(PFD)A 1975, s 18(2)); and
- to give such consequential directions as may be necessary for enabling it to exercise any of the powers available to the court under the I(PFD)A 1975 when an application is made for an order under I(PFD)A 1975, s 2 (I(PFD)A 1975, s 18(2)).

But it does not have the power to direct that an application under Matrimonial Causes Act 1973, ss 31(6) and 36(1) is deemed to have been accompanied by an application for an order under I(PFD)A 1975, s 2 if an order under s 15(1) is in force with respect to a marriage (I(PFD)A 1975, s 18(3)) (see Chapter 7).

8.14.1 Time limit

The application must not, except with the leave of the court, be made after the end of the period of 6 months beginning with the day on which representation in regard to the estate of the deceased is first taken out (Matrimonial Causes Act 1973, ss 31(6)–(9) and 36(2)–(6)).

8.15 EFFECT, DURATION AND FORM OF ORDERS – I(PFD)A 1975, SECTION 19

I(PFD)A 1975, s 19(2) makes provisions for any order made under s 2 or s 5 for the making of periodical payments in favour of an applicant who was the former spouse or civil partner of the deceased or where the marriage or civil partnership was the subject of a judicial separation, or separation order as the case may be, and the order was in force at the date of death and the separation was continuing at the date of death of the deceased, to cease to have effect on the remarriage or subsequent formation of a civil partnership (see, further, para 8.2.5).

I(PFD)A 1975, s 19(4) provides that every order made under the Act other than an order made under s 15(1) or s 15ZA(1) (see para 7.10.1) must be sent to the Principal Registry of the Family Division for entry and filing, and a memorandum of the order must be endorsed on, or permanently annexed to, the probate or letters of administration under which the estate is being administered.

Chapter 9

The Net Estate

9.1 INTRODUCTION

I(PFD)A 1975, s 2 gives the court power to make orders for financial provision out of the net estate of the deceased. The definition of 'net estate' under the Act is set out in s 25(1) and replicates the definition in I(FP)A 1938, s 5(1), but is wider in scope in three respects (I(PFD)A 1975, ss 10 and 11):

(1)   any property may be treated as part of the net estate if the court considers it just so to order;

(2)   'net estate' includes property held on a joint tenancy which can be treated as forming part of the net estate by the court, overriding the law of survivorship (s 9); and

(3)   the court may order that 'net estate' also includes any property which forms part of a transaction intended to defeat an application for financial provision.

I(PFD)A 1975, s 25(1) nevertheless restricts the meaning of 'net estate'. This chapter deals with the definition of 'net estate' in s 25(1), and the provisions which permit the court to treat certain property as part of the net estate if necessary to make an award for financial provision under the Act. These include nominated property and *donatio mortis causa* which comes within the definition of net estate by virtue of s 8, and property held jointly by the deceased and another which is included in the net estate pursuant to s 9. Any property which may be included in the net estate by reason of the deceased disposing of it with a view to defeating or decreasing a claim is dealt with in Chapter 10.

9.2   DEFINITION – I(PFD)A 1975, SECTION 25(1)–(3)

I(PFD)A 1975, s 25(1) defines the 'net estate' from which any order for financial provision may be made as follows:

(a)   all property which the deceased had power to dispose of by his will (otherwise than by virtue of a special power of appointment), less his funeral, testamentary and administration expenses, debts and liabilities, including any inheritance tax payable out of his estate on his death;

(b)   any property in respect of which the deceased held a general power of appointment (not being a power exercisable by will) which has not been exercised;

(c)   any sum of money or other property which is treated for the purposes of the Act as part of the net estate of the deceased by virtue of section 8(1) or (2) of this Act;

(d)   any property which is treated for the purposes of this Act as part of the net estate of the deceased by virtue of an order made under section 9 [see para 9.8];

(e)   any sum of money or other property which is, by reason of a disposition or contract made by the deceased, ordered under section 10 or 11 of this Act to be provided for the purpose of the making of financial provision under this Act [see Chapter 10].

'Property' is defined as including any chose in action.

9.3   PROPERTY WHICH THE DECEASED HAD POWER TO DISPOSE OF BY WILL

This category corresponds to that set out in I(FP)A 1938, s 5(1). Creditors take priority over beneficiaries and dependants. Property subject to a special power of appointment is excluded.

I(PFD)A 1975, s 25(2) provides that, for these purposes, a person who is not of full age and capacity is treated as having power to dispose by will of all property of which he/she would have had power to dispose by will if he/she had been of full age and capacity.

I(PFD)A 1975, s 25(3) provides that any reference in the Act to provision out of the net estate of a deceased person includes a reference to provision extending to the whole of that estate.

Any property which the deceased owned but which was disposed of during his/her lifetime in order to avoid a claim under the I(PFD)A 1975 or to avoid a claim by a third party during the deceased's lifetime may be brought into question and included into the net estate by challenging the validity of such a disposition as is possible in proceedings under the Matrimonial Causes Act 1973.

9.4 PROPERTY UNDER GENERAL POWER OF APPOINTMENT

Where the deceased had a general power of appointment which he/she could have exercised by will, and either he/she did not exercise the power, or did so by will, in either case, the property subject to the power forms part of the net estate of the deceased. Note, however, that the definition specifically excludes the deceased's interest in a special power of appointment.

9.5 WHAT MAY BE DEDUCTED FROM THE NET ESTATE?

The following may be deducted from the net estate:

- Funeral expenses.
- Testamentary and administrative expenses.
- Debts and liabilities.
- Inheritance tax.

9.6 NOMINATED PROPERTY – I(PFD)A 1975, SECTION 8(1)

I(PFD)A 1975, s 8(1) provides that where a deceased person has, in accordance with the provision of any enactment, nominated any person to receive any sum of money or other property on his/her death, and that nomination is in force at the time of his/her death, that sum of money, after deducting any inheritance tax payable thereon, or that property to the extent of the value thereof at the date of death of the deceased after deducting any inheritance tax payable, is treated as part of the net estate of the deceased.

I(PFD)A 1975, s 8(1) also provides that nothing in the section renders any person liable for having paid that sum or transferred that property to the person named in the nomination in accordance with the directions given in the nomination. This provision exempts from liability the person transferring property on a nomination, but such transfer should not be made until 6 months after the grant was first taken out.

Two conditions apply to any nomination made by the deceased before it can be treated as forming part of the net estate. These are that the nomination must be in force at the time of the deceased's death and must be in accordance with the provision of any enactment.

9.6.1   Insurance policies and pension schemes

A nominated policy under an insurance scheme which is effected pursuant to a contract does not form part of the net estate. Under such a policy, a member of the scheme may nominate a beneficiary, within a designated class of permitted beneficiaries, to whom the benefit is payable on the member's death. The nominations under these schemes are not effected pursuant to any statute, and the benefits payable therefrom fall outside the definition of net estate. If the benefits under such a scheme automatically fall into the estate of the deceased they form part of the net estate. If the pension benefits automatically pass to the deceased's widow or widower they are not included in the net estate.

Private occupational pension schemes are not operated pursuant to any enactment and so fall outside I(PFD)A 1975, s 8. It is debatable whether public sector schemes fall within the ambit of s 8. Any capital or income, however, which is paid to a beneficiary in consequence of a pension scheme will be considered by the court when it takes into account the financial resources and financial needs of a beneficiary of the estate.

This point was raised in *Re Cairnes (Deceased), Howard v Cairnes* [1983] FLR 225. The preliminary issue was whether, on the true construction of I(PFD)A 1975, s 25(1), a death benefit fell within the meaning of net estate. The claimant was the deceased's mistress. The defendant and the deceased were married in 1954. They were divorced in 1976. After the divorce, the deceased lived, on and off, with his former wife and with the claimant, until his death. On the divorce the deceased had agreed with his wife that he would give her £80 per month and that he would share the household expenses of the matrimonial home while he lived there. In addition, he gave her £18 per week and paid the hire instalments on the television and the washing machine. The deceased's employment was pensionable. Under the terms of the pension scheme a member could nominate a beneficiary, within a designated class, to whom benefits would accrue on the member's death. The designated classes were:

(1)   a member's wife; and
(2)   any person who, in the opinion of the insurance company, was, immediately prior to the member's death, in receipt of any

regular weekly or monthly voluntary payment from the member for the ordinary necessities of life.

The deceased had nominated his wife as beneficiary. The nomination of the beneficiary or its cancellation required the trustees' consent, as did any variation of the nominated beneficiary.

On the deceased's death the claimant, the deceased's mistress, applied for an order under the I(PFD)A 1975. She contended that the proper time for determining whether a beneficiary fell within the designated class was at the time of death, and therefore the nomination of the former wife as beneficiary was no longer effective and the fund fell into the residuary estate. Further, in any event, under the terms of s 25(1), the words 'net estate' were to be construed as widely as possible. The court rejected these submissions on the grounds that:

(1)   even if the entitlement to the death benefit vested only at the testator's death, the former wife was still within the designated class of beneficiary because she was receiving regular payments from the deceased and was dependent upon him, within (2) above;

(2)   the death benefit did not come within para (a) of the definition of 'net estate' in s 25(1) because the power of the testator to dispose of the death fund was circumscribed. He did not have the power to dispose of the fund which was in the control of the trustees;

(3)   the death benefit could not be construed as part of the net estate within para (c) of the definition because s 8(1) required the nomination to be 'in accordance with the provision of any statute'.

Accordingly, on the preliminary issue, it was held that the death benefit was not part of the net estate.

Monies due under a life insurance policy of the deceased or under a pension scheme are not excluded and form part of the net estate.

9.7   *DONATIO MORTIS CAUSA* – I(PFD)A 1975, SECTION 8(2)

Donatio mortis causa is a gift made by a person in contemplation of death but which does not take effect until the death of the donor.

I(PFD)A 1975, s 8(2) provides that where any sum of money or other property is received by any person as *donatio mortis causa* made by the deceased, that sum of money, after deducting any inheritance tax payable, or that other property, to the extent of the value thereof at the date of the death of the deceased after deducting any inheritance tax payable, is treated for the purposes of the Act as part of the net estate of the deceased.

For a gift to be regarded as *donatio mortis causa*, four conditions need to be satisfied:

(1)   the gift must be made in contemplation of the death of the donor;

(2)   the gift must be made on condition that it becomes absolute and irrevocable only on the death of the donor;

(3)   the subject matter of the gift, or something that represents the gift, must have been delivered to the donee or someone on his/her behalf, with the intention of parting with it;

(4)   the property must be capable of passing by *donatio mortis causa*. Any property which can be transferred by delivery or some suitable document can be given.

Donatio mortis causa of land is now possible (see *Sen v Headley* [1991] Ch 425).

If the gift is made unconditionally, it does not form part of the net estate unless it can be proved that it was made with the intention of defeating a claim for financial provision under the I(PFD)A 1975 (see Chapter 10).

I(PFD)A 1975, s 8(2) exempts from liability any person who has paid a sum of money or transferred property in order to give effect to the *donatio mortis causa*.

On whether a *donatio mortis causa* of movable property outside the jurisdiction forms part of the net estate, see Dicey and Morris, *The Conflict of Laws* (Sweet & Maxwell, 14th edn, 4th Supplement, 2010).

I(PFD)A 1975, s 20 absolves the personal representatives from liability for having distributed any part of the estate of the deceased after 6 months from the date of the grant. By analogy it could be submitted that the same principle applies where payment is made or property transferred in accordance with a nomination or *donatio mortis causa*. It would, however, be advisable for the persons responsible for giving effect to the *donatio mortis causa* or the nomination to ensure that a grant has been obtained and that there is no potential claim under the I(PFD)A 1975 before making the payment.

9.8 PROPERTY HELD ON JOINT TENANCY – I(PFD)A 1975, SECTION 9

I(PFD)A 1975, s 9(1) provides that where a deceased person was immediately before his/her death beneficially entitled to a joint tenancy of any property, then if, before the end of the period of 6 months from the date on which representation with respect to the estate of the deceased was first taken out, an application is made for an order under s 2, the court for the purposes of facilitating the making of financial provision for the applicant under the Act may order that the deceased's severable share of that property, at the value thereof immediately before his/her death, shall, to such extent as appears to the court to be just in all the circumstances of the case, be treated for the purposes of the Act as part of the net estate of the deceased.

There are a number of matters which must be considered if an application under I(PFD)A 1975, s 9 is intended to be made:

(1) What is the time limit for making the application and does the court have power to extend the time limit?

(2) What does 'property' include?

(3) Was the property held by the deceased *jointly* with another immediately before his/her death?

(4) In what circumstances will the court consider it appropriate to make an order under s 9?

(5) What criteria will the court apply when considering such an application?

(6) What is meant by the term 'at the value thereof immediately before his death'?

(7) The valuation of the deceased's severable share.

9.8.1 Time limit

I(PFD)A 1975, s 9(1) makes it clear that an application under s 9 must be made 'before the end of the period of six months from the date on which representation with respect to the estate of the deceased was first taken out'. Unlike the provision of s 4, the court does not have any power to extend this time limit. So practitioners should beware of falling into what has been referred to as 'the section 9 trap' and finding out that it is too late to bring in to the net estate possible assets which may make the difference to the extent of the family provision which the court may order. If in doubt, it is best to play safe, particularly where it appears that the size and nature of the estate may be either small or modest, and include the application for a s 9 order in the substantive application. If, when disclosure has taken place, the issue is not relevant the application may be withdrawn. On the other hand, if an issue arises on whether there is any merit in pursuing the application this may be dealt with as a preliminary issue. The advantage of dealing with this issue at an early stage is that until the matter can be resolved, interlocutory orders or undertakings may be sought to preserve the assets in question. It also puts on notice any person who has an interest in the jointly owned property not to dispose of it until the court has ruled on it. Where there are limited assets, the merit of the s 9 application may be argued on the basis of the s 3 criteria and the fact that one of the factors that the court has to consider under s 3 is the nature and size of the net estate and therefore this additional asset in appropriate cases cannot be ignored and must be preserved until the substantive application is determined.

Another reason for taking this step is the fact that I(PFD)A 1975, s 9(3) specifically provides that the person dealing in any way with such an asset is not liable for anything done by him/her before the order was made.

It should also be noted that the Law Commission Consultation Paper No 191, *Intestacy and Family Provision Claims on Death,* has recommended a review of the effect of this rule and has sought consultation on whether the court should have discretion in an appropriate case to exercise its powers under I(PFD)A 1975, s 9 even where the application is brought more than 6 months after the grant (see Consultation Paper, paras 7.57–7.60).

9.8.2   Meaning of 'property'

I(PFD)A 1975, s 9(4) provides that there may be a joint tenancy of a chose in action. 'Property' therefore includes not only real property but also monies held in a joint account (see *Powell v Osborne* [1993] 1 FLR 1001), a joint insurance policy and other joint investments.

9.8.3   Severance

I(PFD)A 1975, s 9 applies only to property which is subject to a joint tenancy at the date of the deceased's death. If the joint tenancy was severed before death then the provisions of s 9 do not apply. A joint tenancy may be severed by notice in writing or by any act done which has the effect of severing the joint tenancy. The question whether or not the joint tenancy has in fact been severed may be raised as an issue. The following cases are provided as illustrations of the evidence needed to establish severance.

In *Hawkesley v May* [1956] 1 QB 304, a settled fund was held on a trust which provided that, on attaining the age of 21, the applicant and his sister would became absolutely entitled to the fund as joint tenants. The question was whether the joint tenancy had been severed, and the sister's share transferred to her, when she wrote a letter requesting that the dividends be paid into her bank account. Holding that the tenancy had been severed, Havers J stated:

> there are a number of ways by which a joint tenancy may be severed. In *Williams v Hensman* [1861] Sir W Page Wood VC in the course of his judgment said 'a joint tenancy may be severed in three ways: in the first place, an act of any one of the persons interested operating upon his own share may create severance as to that share. The right of each tenant is a right by survivorship only in the event of no severance having taken place of the share which is claimed under the *jus accrescendi*: each one is at liberty to dispose of his own interest in such manner as to sever it from the joint fund – losing, of course, at the same time, his own right by survivorship. Secondly, a joint tenancy may be severed by mutual agreement. And in the third place, there may be severance by any course of dealing sufficient to intimate that the interests of all were mutually treated as constituting a tenancy in common. When a severance depends on an inference of this kind without any express act of severance it will not suffice to rely on an intention, with respect to the particular share, declared only behind the backs of the other persons interested. The first method indicated, namely an act of any one of the person interested operating upon his own share, obviously includes a declaration of intention to sever by one party.

In *Re Draper's Conveyance, Nihan v Porter* [1969] 1 Ch 486, property was conveyed to a husband and wife as joint tenants in October 1951. The parties divorced and the decree absolute was made in March 1966. On 11 February 1966 the wife issued proceedings under Married Women's Property Act 1882, s 17 for an order for sale of the property and the division of the net proceeds. It was held that the joint tenancy was severed by the issue of the proceedings, coupled with the affidavit in support of it which clearly evinced an intention on the part of the wife to sever the tenancy.

In *Harris v Goddard* [1983] 1 WLR 203, the issue was whether a prayer in a petition for divorce for a property adjustment order operated as a notice in writing to sever the joint tenancy. Before the application was heard the husband died in a road traffic accident. The executors and the children of the deceased's first marriage sought a declaration that the tenancy had been severed and that they were entitled to one half of the net proceeds of sale. In holding that the prayer in the petition did not take effect as a severance notice, Lawton LJ said:

> When notice in writing of a desire to sever is served pursuant to s 36(2) [of the Law of Property Act 1925], it takes effect forthwith. It follows that a desire to sever must evince an intention to bring about the wanted result immediately. A notice in writing which expresses a desire to bring about the wanted result at some time in the future is not, in my judgment, a notice in writing within s 36(2). Further, the notice must be one which shows an intent to bring about the consequences set out in section 36(2), namely that the net proceeds of the statutory trust for sale shall be held upon trust which would have been requisite for giving effect to the beneficial interests if there had been an actual severance. I am unable to accept the submission of counsel for the plaintiffs that a notice in writing which shows no more than a desire to bring the existing interest to an end is a good notice. It must be a desire to sever which is intended to have the statutory consequences. Paragraph 3 of the prayer of the petition does no more than invite the court to consider at some future time whether to exercise its jurisdiction under section 24 of the 1973 Act, and if it does, to do so in one or more of three different ways. Orders under section 24(1)(a) and (b) could bring co-ownership to an end by ways other than by severance.

Dillon LJ stated:

> Joint ownership is a form of co-ownership or concurrent ownership of property. Its special feature is the right of survivorship, whereby the right to the whole of the property accrues automatically to the surviving joint tenant or joint tenants on the death of any one joint tenant. Severance is, as I understand it, the process of separating off the share of a joint tenant, so that the concurrent ownership will continue but the right of survivorship will no longer apply. The parties will hold separate shares as tenants in common. The joint tenancy may come to an end through other acts which destroy the whole ownership e.g. if one joint tenant acquires the entire beneficial interest of the other joint tenant(s) so as to become solely and absolutely entitled beneficially to the property, or by all the joint tenants joining in resettling the property on other trusts not involving concurrent ownership; but such acts do not involve severance and would not be called severance of the joint tenancy. In *Draper's Conveyance* the relief claimed by the originating summons which had been issued and by the affidavit in support included, as Lawton LJ has pointed out, a claim that the property might be sold and the proceeds be divided equally in accordance with the rights of the parties. This plainly involved severance of the beneficial joint tenancy as I understand the term 'severance'.
>
> In the present case, however, paragraph 3 of the prayer in the petition merely seeks relief in the most general and unparticularised terms under Matrimonial Causes Act 1973, s 24. Apart from the fact that any relief for Mrs Harris under s 24 lay in the future and was contingent on the court exercising its discretion

under the section in her favour, she had not yet specified what she desired by the time Mr Harris died, and the general prayer in her petition could have been satisfied by relief which did not involve severance, eg an order extinguishing Mr Harris's interest in the property and directing that the property be vested in Mrs Harris as sole absolute beneficial owner, or an order directing a resettlement of the property on Mr and Mrs Harris successively and not as concurrent owners. Therefore the petition in this case cannot be notice of a desire to sever the joint tenancy.

Where on an application for ancillary relief following a divorce or dissolution order an agreement is reached between the parties for the sale of the former matrimonial home and the division of the proceeds of sale, the joint tenancy is severed so that if one of the parties dies before the agreement is approved by the court and an order made, the joint tenancy remains severed by the agreement. The agreement does not have to be enforceable provided it indicated a common intention to sever (see *Hunter v Babbage* [1994] 2 FLR 806).

Where a deceased person's estate is found to be insolvent, administration takes place under Insolvency Act 1986, s 421 and the matter is governed by the Insolvent Estates of Deceased Persons Order 1986 (SI 1986/1999). However, the making of an insolvency administration order does not relate back to sever the deceased's beneficial interest in property owned by the deceased and his wife immediately before the deceased's death as the deceased's interest in the property passes to the widow by survivorship at the moment of death (see *Re Palmer (A Debtor)* [1994] 2 FLR 609 (CA)).

9.8.4   Circumstances in which an order will be considered

The court is given a discretion to consider bringing into the net estate the severable share of a jointly owned asset. It can, however, use its discretion only for the purposes of facilitating the making of financial provision for the claimant. This will usually occur where the net estate is insufficient to meet the claims made by the claimant/s as well as honour the wish of the deceased expressed in his/her will towards other beneficiaries.

9.8.5   Criteria which will be applied

I(PFD)A 1975, s 9(1) and (2) refers to four factors which the court should take into account when dealing with an application under s 9 for the severance of the deceased's share in jointly owned property. These are:

- The court should exercise its discretion only to the extent as appears to be just in all the circumstances.
- If it is necessary to facilitate the making of financial provision for the claimant.
- The value of the asset immediately before the deceased's death.
- In determining the extent to which any severable share is to be treated as part of the estate the court must have regard to any inheritance tax payable in respect of the severed share (s 9(2)).

9.8.6 Facilitating the making of financial provision/and appears to be just

The language of I(PFD)A 1975, s 9 is so broadly phrased that it gives the court a very wide discretion in respect of the matters it may take into account when determining the issue. The objective is to ensure that justice is done. This must mean justice not only to the claimant/s but also to other beneficiaries and any other respondent who may have an interest in the asset. If severance would lead to hardship to the surviving joint owner, in order to deal with the application justly the court will need to balance the needs of the claimant against those of the other party. Although the provisions of the section appear not to refer to any other criteria, in order to determine whether severance is necessary and just, it would appear that the court will have to consider the s 3 factors (see Chapter 7 and below).

The court may only exercise its discretion if it is satisfied that it is necessary for the purposes of facilitating the making of financial provision and then only to the extent that it appears to the court to be just in all the circumstances of the case. The severance may relate to part of the severable share of the deceased in the assets and not the whole. Whether or not the court exercises its discretion, the factors which will weigh in that exercise and the extent to which that discretion is exercised will depend on the circumstances of the individual case. The following cases may offer some guidance on the criteria used by the court when determining an application for a s 9 order.

In *Kourkgy v Lusher* (1983) 4 FLR 65, Wood J stated that the words 'facilitating and making financial provision for the applicant' should not be understood to narrow the broad discretionary power given by s 9. In considering the application the court will necessarily take into account the financial needs and resources of the parties. With the increase in divorce and cohabitation, it seems inevitable that the courts will be concerned with cases where the property which is the subject matter of the application provides a home for the deceased's families, or with assets which provide, as far as possible, financial security for such families and step-families. Since the court's duty when exercising its discretion is to impart justice having regard to all the circumstances of the case, it seems unlikely that the courts will take from Peter to give to Paul where the assets are inadequate. The discretion is to be exercised at each stage of the proceedings applying the provisions of the section (see *Kourkgy v Lusher* (1983) 4 FLR 65, 80 and 81 and *Re Crawford* (1983) 4 FLR 273, 280 (both judgments of Eastham J)).

In *Re Crawford* (1983) 4 FLR 273 (for the facts, see para 6.3.2), the court applied the provisions of I(PFD)A 1975, s 3 and took into account financial benefits to the beneficiaries under the will of the deceased. In *Kourgky v Lusher* (above), Wood J approached the exercise of discretion by considering the matters set out under Matrimonial Causes Act 1973, s 25. Although those matters resemble those under I(PFD)A 1975, s 3, they are not identical in all respects. It is submitted that it is questionable whether it is appropriate to introduce the provisions of the Matrimonial Causes Act 1973, which concern matters following the breakdown of a marriage, to claims for financial provision under the I(PFD)A 1975, where the circumstances are necessarily different, and the statutory bases for determining the applications are set out in different enactments.

In *Jessop v Jessop* [1992] FLR 591, the property was owned jointly by the deceased and his mistress. The value of the property had risen considerably between the death of the deceased and the date of the final hearing. Although the value to be taken into account is the value immediately before the death, in determining the claim, Nourse J took into account the income, expenditure and capital resources of the parties when making an order for the payment of £10,000 to the deceased's widow. It would appear that, where the court is asked to take into account the deceased's severable share in any property, it does not follow that the whole of the property will be treated as part of the net assets of the deceased. Whether the court will treat the severable share as part of the net estate, and if so, to what extent, will depend on the particular circumstances and what appears, in those circumstances, to be just. In some cases part of the value may be sufficient to meet the justice of the case. In others, as in *Hanbury v Hanbury* [1999] 2 FLR 255 (for the facts, see para 8.5), the whole of the share may be treated as part of the net estate.

Where the deceased had an interest in property abroad, much will turn on the laws of succession of the country in question, and whether the deceased made a valid will according to the law of that country or died intestate. Where the property is overseas the court does not have jurisdiction over it unless the property is brought within the jurisdiction of the court or the person who has control over the property is within the jurisdiction which would then enable the court to direct any order it makes to that person.

9.8.7 Meaning of 'at the value thereof immediately before [the deceased's] death'

The meaning of the words 'at the value thereof immediately before his death' was considered by the Court of Appeal in *Zulekha Bibi Dingmar v Dingmar* [2006] EWCA Civ 942, [2007] Ch 109, where the appellant widow of the deceased had appealed against the decision of the trial judge who had awarded her one half of the value of the matrimonial home as at the date of death. The property had been owned jointly by the appellant's husband and a third party who became the sole owner of the property by survivorship when the husband died in 1977. After his death the widow continued to live in the property until her two children reached majority in 2004, when the third party claimed possession. The widow then obtained letters of administration and made a claim under the I(PFD)A 1975 for financial provision and an application under s 9 for the deceased's severable share in the property to be treated as part of his net estate. It was agreed that at the date of death the house was valued at £40,000 but its value had increased to £95,000 when the application was heard. She was awarded one half of the value at the date of death. The widow appealed on the grounds that the words of s 9 should not be taken to restrict the court's discretionary power to make reasonable financial provision for her. Ward and Jacob LJJ gave different reasons for allowing the appeal. Jacob LJ considered three different interpretations and concluded that 'value' does not refer to monetary value but to a proportionate value of the property as this interpretation fits in best with the purpose of the Act. He opined that to view otherwise would lead to irrationalities and Parliament could not have intended the irrational. His Lordship also stated that another possible explanation may lie in tax consideration and the words are there to define the value for tax reasons and to inform that the value to be assessed for tax purposes is the value at the date of death.

Ward LJ's interpretation of the provision was as follows:

(a) even though a value has to be given to that share at a particular point in time, the subsection does not require that the sum of money representing that value be treated as part of the net estate. The emphasis is on the property not a sum of money equal to its value which is clawed back into the net estate. Giving the share a value is merely a descriptive of the share;

(b) the use of commas at the beginning and end of the phrase puts the phrase in parenthesis. If there had not been any punctuations the word 'value' would have acquired a more intrinsically important feature not the incidental one suggested by the use of commas;

(c) tax reasons:

To treat the value immediately before death as creating a cap is to give the element of value an importance it does not seem to me to deserve. It has the consequence that the value placed on the severable interest dominates and controls the property interest to the extent that it changes the nature of the severable share itself from something certain to something uncertain. If the value was to have such defining influence I would have expected "net estate" for s. 9 purposes to be defined in s. 25(d) as "any sum of money, being the value of the share before death"...

...

Reading the Act as a whole there is enough ambiguity for the court to override what may be a literal meaning when its result is to produce palpably absurd and self-evidently capricious consequences. A construction of the Act must be favoured which eliminates the ambiguity and anomaly by allowing common-sense and justice to prevail. ... Such a conclusion seems to me to fully give effect to paragraph 140 of the Law Commission Report...

> "justice requires that in all cases where property whether real or personal was held by the deceased on a beneficial tenancy, *the interest which passes by right of survivorship should be available for family provision.*"

Lloyd LJ in his dissenting judgment relied on the literal interpretation applying the general principle of construction. He did not consider that it is legitimate to ignore the words and deprive them of meaning or effect because the court may regret the effect that they would have in this case, or may suppose that if Parliament or the draftsman had thought harder about their effect the words would not have been included. It is not a case in which those words make nonsense of the provision as a whole even though they limit, in a way which the court may consider unfortunate, the beneficial effect of the statute. He could not accept that Parliament would not have considered the sort of situation presented by the case. The purpose of imposing a cap on the relevant value was to protect the surviving joint tenant or tenants, particularly as the issue would normally arise soon after the death. In his view the words in the section are prescriptive and not descriptive as suggested by Ward LJ.

On the majority judgment, the words do not operate as a cap and do not prevent the court from awarding a claimant a half share in the house of which the deceased was a joint tenant.

The unsatisfactory terminology in I(PFD)A 1975, s 9 relating to the valuation of the deceased's share has been considered by the Law Commission in its Consultation Paper No 191. The Paper refers to the decision in *Zulekha Bibi Dingmar v Dingmar* (above) and the dissatisfaction of the three appeal court judges with the terminology with particular reference to Jacob LJ's observations that 'there is an inherent contradiction which must be overcome somehow' and Ward LJ's interpretation that the words were 'descriptive and

Inheritance Act Claims

not prescriptive' and that a literal interpretation would produce 'palpably absurd and self evidently capricious consequences'. The Law Commission also referred to Lloyd LJ's comment that s 9 'might have achieved the Law Commission's avowed purpose more effectively if the question of value had been treated in different words'.

In the light of those observations, the Law Commission in paras 7.64 and 7.65 proposes as follows:

> In the light of these comments we think it is right to review section 9 to ensure that the plain meaning of the section accords with the actual result reached in *Dingmar*. Similar wording appears in section 8(2) which concerns gifts made in contemplation of death. Such cases are unusual but we nevertheless consider that the wording of section 8 should be consistent with any changes to section 9.
> We provisionally propose that the value for the purposes of sections 8 and 9 of the Inheritance (Provision for Family and Dependants) Act 1975 should be their value at the date of the application not at the date of death.

Since, when dealing with an application under the I(PFD)A 1975, the court has to consider the circumstances of the parties at the date of the hearing and one of the factors under s 3 that is relevant to the determination of the application is the size and nature of the net estate, an up-to-date valuation of all property which is the subject of the proceedings must be provided. Valuation of the property at the time of death will be relevant to assess the inheritance tax payable on such property to obtain the net value and then the valuation at the date of the application and at the date of the hearing will be an important consideration to determine what would be reasonable financial provision for the claimant, as occurred in *Jessop v Jessop* (see above).

Where the property is subject to a charge, the value of the outstanding debt/mortgage must be deducted from the valuation but if the charge/mortgage was protected by a collateral endowment policy the value of that policy at the time immediately before the death must be accounted for and set off against debt (see *Powell v Osbourne* [1993] 1 FLR 1001 (CA)), where the deceased and his wife were divorced but the decree nisi had not been made absolute as there were pending ancillary relief proceedings. The deceased lived with his mistress. About 2 months before the deceased's death he and his mistress purchased a property as beneficial joint tenants. The property was subject to a substantial mortgage. There was also a joint collateral endowment policy. The house was the only property out of which any provision for the widow could be made. It was argued that, immediately before the death of the deceased, the policy had no surrender value. It acquired a value on death and therefore should be disregarded in valuing the deceased's assets. The Court of Appeal rejected this argument on the basis that it is at the moment immediately before death that a joint tenancy can be severed, and that if death were certain the value of the policy immediately before the death of the deceased would be equal to the proceeds of the policy when it matures.

It follows from this decision that the value of the property for the purposes of making an order under I(PFD)A 1975, s 2 will be assessed after setting off the value of the policy at death against the mortgage debt on the property.

Chapter 10

Dispositions Intended to Defeat Financial Provision

10.1 INTRODUCTION

Provision is made in the I(PFD)A 1975 to prevent a person from defeating frustrating or reducing claims made under the Act on his/her death by making dispositions of his/her assets during his/her lifetime or contracting to do so after his/her death. The powers of the court in respect of such evasion or avoidance, and the duties of personal representatives and the protection afforded to them, are set out in ss 10–13. Section 10 deals with disposition made during the life time of the deceased and s 11 with contracts made to bequeath property in a will. Sections 12 and 13 make supplementary provisions relating to applications made under ss 10 and 11. Section 12 makes provisions which include how the court can determine the intention to defeat any consequential order it can make when dealing with issues arising from applications made under either s 10 or s 11, and s 13 deals with powers of the court to make orders against trustees of such property.

The provisions under I(PFD)A 1975, ss 10 and 11 may be invoked only if the court is satisfied that the exercise of its powers under s 10 would facilitate the making of financial provision for the claimant.

10.2 *INTER VIVOS* DISPOSITION

Where a claim for financial provision is made under I(PFD)A 1975, s 2, the claimant in those proceedings may apply to the court for an order under s 10(2) that the donee of an *inter vivos* disposition (whether or not at the date of the order he/she holds any interest in the property disposed of to him/her or for his/her benefit by the deceased) provide, to the claimant, for the purposes of making that financial provision, such sum of money or property as may be specified in the order. Thus any order made by the court will be directed to the donee to provide the 'money or other property'.

10.2.1   Condition precedent for an order

Before the court may make an order under I(PFD)A 1975, s 10(2), it must be satisfied that:

(1)   less than 6 years before the date of his/her death, the deceased, with the intention of defeating an application for financial provision under the Act, made a disposition; and

(2)   full valuable consideration for that disposition was not given by the donee to whom, or for the benefit of whom, the disposition was made, or by any other person; and

(3)   the exercise of the power conferred by s 10 would facilitate the making of financial provision for the claimant under the Act.

10.2.2   Meaning of 'disposition'

The section is wide in its terms. I(PFD)A 1975, s 10(7) defines 'disposition' to include:

> any payment of money (including the payment of a premium under a policy of assurance) and any conveyance, assurance, appointment or gift of property of any description, whether made by an instrument or otherwise.

On the other hand, the I(PFD)A 1975 specifically excludes:

(1)   any provision in a will, any such nomination as is mentioned in s 8(1) (see para 8.6) or any *donatio mortis causa* (see para 8.7); or

(2)   any appointment of property made, otherwise than by will, in the exercise of a special power of appointment.

The transactions under (1) (above) are excluded because they form part of the 'net estate' pursuant to other provisions in the I(PFD)A 1975. Property which is the subject of a special power of appointment and is disposed of *inter vivos* is excluded by reason of the fact that it was never part of the deceased's 'net estate'.

In *Clifford v Tanner*, unreported, CAT, 10 June 1986, the deceased had a right under a covenant to occupy a house belonging to his daughter. He released the right to his daughter without full valuable consideration. It was held that the release of the right to occupy came within the definition of disposition, as a 'gift of property of any description'.

I(PFD)A 1975, s 10(8) also excludes any disposition made in respect of any property before the commencement of the Act on 1 April 1976.

10.2.3 Full valuable consideration

I(PFD)A 1975, s 25(1) provides that 'valuable consideration does not include marriage or a promise of marriage'. A civil partnership or a promise to enter into a civil partnership will now also be excluded.

The consideration need not, however, have been provided by the donee. It could have been provided by 'any other person' (I(PFD)A 1975, s 10(2)(b)).

The consideration has to be 'full', ie not nominal or at a value well beyond the market price. An example where the court held that the disposition had not been for full consideration can be found in *Dawkins v Judd* [1986] 2 FLR 360 (at para 10.2.4) where the deceased had transferred the matrimonial home to his daughter for £100.

10.2.4 Intention of defeating a claim

For a disposition to come within the provisions of I(PFD)A 1975, s 10 the claimant must satisfy the court that, in making the disposition, the deceased had the intention of defeating a claim for financial provision under the Act (s 10(2)). Section 12(1) of the Act provides that this condition should be fulfilled if the court is of the opinion that, on a balance of probabilities, the intention of the deceased (though not necessarily his/her sole intention) in making the disposition was to prevent an order for financial provision being made under the Act, or to reduce the amount of the provision which might otherwise be granted.

Three issues are highlighted by taking the provisions of I(PFD)A 1975, ss 10(2) and 12(1) together. These are that:

- The intention to defeat a claim need not be the sole intention but there must be some evidence of an intention to defeat a claim for financial provision under the Act.
- The standard of proof is the civil standard of proof, namely 'the balance of probabilities'.
- The intention of the deceased in making the disposition was either:

- to prevent an order for financial provision being made, or
- to reduce the amount of the provision which might be granted.

The issues raised above can be illustrated by the following cases.

The intention to defeat a claim need not be the sole intention, but there must be some evidence of an intention to defeat such a claim. The intention also need not necessarily be in relation to a claim under the I(PFD)A 1975. In *Re Kennedy (Deceased), Kennedy v Official Solicitor* [1980] CLY 2820, the deceased transferred his house to his mistress in consideration of natural love and affection. The deceased's wife issued proceedings for divorce in which she indicated her intention to apply for ancillary relief, but before the decree nisi was pronounced, he died. A few months later the mistress died too. It was held that it was not essential to show that the Act or its provisions were present in the mind of the deceased when he entered into the transaction which was called into question, but there had to be evidence that he intended to defeat a claim made after his death against the estate.

In *Dawkins v Judd* [1986] 2 FLR 360, the deceased had transferred the matrimonial home to his daughter by his first marriage for £100, a year before he indicated to his wife that he wanted a divorce. He left a will leaving his entire estate to the daughter. He died 2 years after making the transfer. Evidence was adduced that the deceased had sought legal advice on how he could preserve the property for his daughter in the event of his death. Bush J had no difficulty, when applying the test set out in I(PFD)A 1975, s 12, in reaching the conclusion that the sale of the house to the daughter was entered into with the intention, though not necessarily the sole intention, of defeating a claim for financial provision.

In *Hanbury v Hanbury* [1999] 2 FLR 255, having sought legal advice on how to defeat his disabled daughter's claim under the I(PFD)A 1975, the deceased transferred his property into the joint names of himself and his second wife and arranged for investments to be bought in the sole name of his second wife (see Chapter 8). Intention to defeat was proved by disclosure given during the proceedings of the legal advice the deceased had sought. (For further information on disclosure, see CPR Part 31.)

To summarise:

- The evidence of such an intention therefore need not be in writing.
- It may be by way of oral statements made by the deceased or evidence of the legal advice sought or it can be derived from the circumstances of the disposition.

- The following matters are relevant and must be taken into account:
  - the value of the property in issue at the time of the disposition;
  - the value of any consideration given for the property; and
  - the relationship between the deceased and the donee.

10.2.5 Matters the court will take into consideration

In determining whether to exercise its powers under I(PFD)A 1975, s 10(2), and in what manner to exercise its powers, the court must have regard to the following matters (I(PFD)A 1975, s 10(6)):

(1)   the circumstances in which the disposition was made;
(2)   the valuable consideration which was given;
(3)   the relationship, if any, of the donee to the deceased;
(4)   the conduct of the donee;
(5)   the financial resources of the donee; and
(6)   all the other circumstances of the case.

The cases set out in para 10.2.4 illustrate how the court has determined the issue of 'intention'. It should also be noted that the court is under a duty to have regard to and consider the above factors when an issue of intention to defeat a claim arises in an application under the I(PFD)A 1975. The provision of s 10(6) is mandatory.

10.2.6 Orders that can be made

If the conditions referred to above are satisfied, and subject to the provisions of I(PFD)A 1975, ss 12 and 13, the court's order will be directed to the donee to provide the asset, be it money or property, to meet the financial provision the court makes in favour of the claimant. The court may order the donee of an *inter vivos* disposition to provide such money or other property as may be specified for the purposes of making financial provision for the claimant, whether or not, at the date of the order, the donee retains any interest in the property disposed of to him/her or for his/her benefit by the deceased (s 10(2)).

If the donee of the *inter vivos* disposition is dead, the court can proceed to make the appropriate orders in like manner against the personal representatives of the donee (I(PFD)A 1975, s 12(4)).

It will be seen that the provisions of I(PFD)A 1975, s 10 affect the donee, not the property given to the donee. If the donee is dead the action can be made or continued against his/her estate. The court does not, however, have power to make any orders under s 10 in respect of any property which has been distributed by the personal representatives. Furthermore, a personal representative is not liable for having distributed any such property before he/she has notice of the making of a claim under the Act in which an application is made under s 10, on the grounds that he/she ought to have taken into account the possibility that such an application would be made (s 12(4)).

I(PFD)A 1975, s 10(3) provides that where an order is made under s 10(2), as respects any disposition which consisted of the payment of money to or for the benefit of the donee, the amount of any sum of money or the value of any property ordered to be provided must not exceed the amount of the payment made by the deceased, after deducting any inheritance tax borne by the donee in respect of that payment.

Where the disposition consisted of the transfer of property (other than a sum of money) to or for the benefit of the donee, the amount of any sum of money under I(PFD)A 1975, s 10(2) must not exceed the value, at the date of the death of the deceased, of the property disposed of by him/her to or for the benefit of the donee (or if that property has been disposed of by the person to whom it was transferred by the deceased, the value at the date of disposal thereof), after deducting any inheritance tax borne by the donee in respect of the transfer of that property by the deceased (s 10(4)).

Thus, if the donee purchases property or shares with the money paid to him/her, neither the increase in the value of the property or shares, nor the income from the investment, would need to be accounted for (I(PFD)A 1975, s 10(3)). The value will be the value at the date of disposal or at the death of the deceased, after the deduction of inheritance tax. The value of the property is the capital value, and does not include income from the property which may have accrued since the disposition was made to the donee. The donee will have to provide only such sum of money or property as will meet the financial provision order made by the court in favour of the claimant.

If the donee has disposed of the asset he/she will have to provide a sum equivalent to that which satisfies the sum ordered to be made available by the court.

The court is given wide powers under I(PFD)A 1975, s 12(3) to give such consequential directions including directions requiring the making of any payment or transfer of any property, as it thinks fit for giving effect to its order or for securing a fair adjustment of the rights of the person affected.

10.2.7 Donee's right to apply

By virtue of I(PFD)A 1975, s 10(5), if an application is made for an order under s 10(2), the donee of the property in question can apply for the court to substitute, for the disposition which is the subject of the application, another disposition made to him/her by the deceased. Certain preconditions must be fulfilled. Section 10(5) provides that where an application (the 'original application') is made for an order in relation to such a disposition, then if on application under s 10(5) the court is satisfied of certain matters, the court may exercise, in relation to the person to whom or for whose benefit that other disposition was made, the powers which the court would have had under s 10(2) if the original application had been made in respect of that other disposition. The matters of which the court must be satisfied are that:

(1) less than 6 years before the date of the death of the deceased, the deceased, with the intention of defeating an application for financial provision under the Act, made a disposition other than the disposition which is the subject of the original application; and

(2) full valuable consideration for that other disposition was not given by the person to whom, or for the benefit of whom, that other disposition was made or by any other person.

Where the claim includes an application for an order under I(PFD)A 1975, s 10 it is desirable to give notice of the proceedings to the donee, so that the donee has the opportunity to apply to be joined as a party to the proceedings and to be heard before decisions are made which affect him/her and his/her rights and interests. The bona fides of the donee can be dealt with as a preliminary point in appropriate cases. This course would also be beneficial to the claimant because it would enable the claimant to seek disclosure from the donee and, if necessary, preserve the property until the determination of the claim, by obtaining an undertaking or an order prohibiting the disposal, transfer or other dealing with the property.

10.3 CONTRACTS TO LEAVE PROPERTY BY WILL

I(PFD)A 1975, s 11 gives the court jurisdiction to order any sum of money or other property bequeathed in a will by virtue of a contract to make a will, to be made available for the purposes of facilitating the making of a financial provision order, provided that the conditions in s 11 are satisfied.

10.3.1   Condition precedent for an order

Before the court can make any of the orders under I(PFD)A 1975, s 11(2) in respect of a contract to leave property by will to another, it must be satisfied that:

(1)   the deceased made a contract by which he/she agreed to leave by his/her will a sum of money or other property to any person, or by which he/she agreed that a sum of money or other property would be paid or transferred to any person, out of his/her estate;

(2)   the deceased made this contract with the intention of defeating an application for financial provision under the Act;

(3)   when the contract was made, full valuable consideration for that contract was not given or promised by the person with whom or for whose benefit the contract was made ('the donee') or by any other person; and

(4)   the exercise of the powers conferred by s 11 would facilitate the making of financial provision for the claimant under the Act.

The claimant who seeks an order under I(PFD)A 1975, s 11 must therefore prove to the satisfaction of the court that the above four conditions are met.

10.3.2   Contract

The I(PFD)A 1975 is silent on the meaning of 'contract' and therefore the assumption is that the word must be given its ordinary legal meaning. It could, however, be argued that the Act did not intend the term 'contract' to have the ordinary legal interpretation because the provisions of s 12(2) envisage a situation where 'no valuable consideration' is given. Thus, where the deceased made a promise or representation to leave property by will, and as a result the promisee or representee acted to his/her detriment, there may not be an enforceable contract, but if the evidence suggests that the doctrine of proprietary estoppel arises, there may be an enforceable claim against the estate. The same may be so if a constructive trust is implied by the agreement.

I(PFD)A 1975, s 11 extends to a contract by which the deceased agreed that his/her personal representatives would pay a sum of money or transfer other property out of his/her estate. Contracts to leave property by mutual wills (see para 7.7.2) will also fall within the provisions of s 11.

The I(PFD)A 1975 did not come into force until 1 April 1976 and therefore does not apply to contracts made before that date. Unlike the provisions of s 10, where only dispositions made less than 6 years before the date of death may be subject to an order, there are no time limits in respect of contracts to leave property by will. Time may, however, be relevant to the issue of the deceased's intention in making the contract.

Any arrangement which applies in the case of intestacy falls outside I(PFD)A 1975, s 11, because the section refers to a contract by which the deceased agreed to leave a sum of money or other property 'by will'.

10.3.3 Intention to defeat a claim

The claimant must satisfy the court that, in making the contract, the deceased had the intention of defeating a claim by the claimant for financial provision out of the estate under the I(PFD)A 1975. Certain circumstances or conduct will be presumed as indicating the required intention unless evidence proving the contrary is adduced by the donee.

I(PFD)A 1975, s 12(2) provides that, with respect to any contract made by the deceased where no valuable consideration is given or promised by any person, then it is to be presumed, unless the contrary is shown, that the deceased made the contract with the intention of defeating a claim for financial relief under the Act (cf s 10 where no such provision applies). Section 25(1) provides that 'valuable consideration' does not include marriage or a promise of marriage. It should now also exclude a civil partnership or a promise to enter into a civil partnership.

The statutory presumption is rebuttable by the donee on production of evidence to show that the deceased did not have the intention to defeat any claim for financial provision by the claimant, but that his/her motives were sincere and genuine.

The intention to defeat a claim implies a fraudulent dealing and the question then arises whether the standard of proof required to prove such intention should be that applicable where fraud is alleged; but I(PFD)A 1975, s 12(1) states that the standard to be applied is that of the 'balance of probabilities'. In some respects the donee is at a disadvantage because in most cases the motives of the deceased cannot be tested by direct evidence from the deceased, by contrast with the position in applications under Matrimonial Causes Act 1973, s 37.

As in cases under I(PFD)A 1975, s 10, the test that the court would need to apply is whether the intention of the deceased (though not necessarily his/her sole intention) in making the contract was to prevent an order for financial provision being made under the Act, or to reduce the amount of the provision which might otherwise be granted (s 12(1)). It would seem that the court, in applying the test, would be concerned with the deceased's intention subjectively; and that, in determining whether the required intention existed, the deceased would be taken to intend the natural consequences of his/her acts. All facts, statements and declarations made before, after or at the time the act occurred are relevant in determining the state of mind of the deceased.

10.3.4 Full valuable consideration

The meaning of 'full valuable consideration' is that provided in I(PFD)A 1975, s 25(1):

- it 'does not include marriage or a promise of marriage';
- it need not have been provided by the donee as long as it was provided at the time the contract was made;
- it could have been provided by any other person on the donee's behalf (s 11(2)(c)).

In view of the changes made by the CPA 2004, it should also exclude a civil partnership or a promise to enter into a civil partnership.

10.3.5 Matters to be considered by the court

The court has a discretion whether or not to make an order under I(PFD)A 1975, s 11. In determining whether or not to exercise its powers and, if so, in what manner to exercise them, the court must have regard to the following matters (s 11(4)):

(1)   the circumstances in which the contract was made;
(2)   the relationship, if any, of the donee to the deceased;
(3)   the conduct of the donee;
(4)   the financial resources of the donee; and
(5)   all the circumstances of the case.

10.3.6 Orders that can be made under I(PFD)A 1975, section 11

If the conditions outlined above are satisfied the court may make any one or more of the following orders to facilitate the making of financial provision under I(PFD)A 1975, s 2 for the claimant (s 11(2)):

(1)   if any money has been paid, or any other property has been transferred to or for the benefit of the donee in accordance with the contract, an order directing the donee to provide, for the purposes of the making of that financial provision, such sum of money or other property as may be specified in the order;

(2)   if the money or all the money has not been paid, or the property or all of the property has not been transferred, in accordance with the contract, an order directing the personal representatives not to make any further payment or transfer any property or further property, as the case may be, or directing the personal representatives to make such payment or transfer such property only as may be specified in the order.

The court may also give such consequential directions as it thinks fit (including directions requiring the making of any payments or the transfer of any property) for giving effect to the order or for securing a fair adjustment of the rights of the persons affected thereby (s 12(3)).

The orders referred to in (1) and (2) above are considered in paras 10.3.7 and 10.3.8.

10.3.7 Where money has been paid

Where the personal representatives of the deceased have made payment of money or transferred property to the donee in accordance with the contract, the court can order the donee to provide such sums of money or transfer such property as will facilitate the making of a financial provision order. The order does not attach to the specific sum of money or property as had been transferred.

10.3.8 Where money has not been paid

If the terms of the contract have not been fulfilled (whether wholly or partially) by the personal representatives, the court may forbid them from making payment and from transferring such of the money or the property as may be specified in the order. If the donee of the contract by will has died, the court can proceed to make the appropriate orders against the personal representatives of the donee (I(PFD)A 1975, s 12(4)). The court cannot, however, make any of the orders set out in s 11 in respect of any property which has been distributed by the personal representatives. Nor are the personal representatives liable for having distributed any such property before they had notice of the making of the claim which included an application for an order under s 11, on the ground that they ought to have taken into account the possibility that such an application would be made (s 12(4)).

10.3.9   Position of donee who is a trustee

The court's power to make any orders under I(PFD)A 1975, ss 10 and 11 against a trustee is limited to such sum as is, at the date of the order, in the hands of the trustee, or the value at that date of any property which represents that money. In the case of any property transferred, it is limited to so much of that property as is, at the date of the order, in the hands of the trustee and the value at that date of any property (s 13(1)).

As in the case of the personal representatives of the donee, the trustee is exempt from liability for having distributed any money or other property on the ground that he/she ought to have taken into account the possibility that such an application would be made (I(PFD)A 1975, s 13(2)).

10.3.10   Restrictions on the court's powers

The court may exercise its powers in relation to any contract made by the deceased only to the extent that the court considers that the amount of any sum of money paid or to be paid, or the value of any property transferred or to be transferred in accordance with the contract, exceeds the value of any valuable consideration given or to be given for the contract.

The property transferred or to be transferred under the contract is to be valued at the date of the hearing.

10.3.11   Rights of persons to enforce the contract

I(PFD)A 1975, s 11(5) provides that where the court makes an order under s 11(2) in relation to any contract, the contractual rights of the donee to enforce that contract or to recover damages, or to obtain other relief for the breach, is subject to any adjustment made by the court under s 12(3). The contractual relief is available to the extent only as is consistent with the court's order.

Chapter 11

Personal Representatives and Trustees

11.1 INTRODUCTION

The personal representatives of a deceased person are under a duty to collect and get in the real and personal estate of the deceased and administer it according to law. When required to so by the court, they must provide, on oath, a full inventory of the estate and, if required by the court, render an account of the administration of the estate to the court (Administration of Estates Act 1925, s 25).

The personal representatives are liable for any waste to the estate or the conversion of the real or personal estate of the deceased. Where it is apparent that a claim may be made under the I(PFD)A 1975, the personal representatives must ensure that nothing is done by them to prejudice the claim. Where a personal representative is also a beneficiary he/she and his/her legal advisers must ensure that there is no conflict of interest between his/her role as a personal representative of the estate and a beneficiary under the will and or intestacy. If there is a likelihood of a conflict it is better to err on the side of caution and step down and seek the appointment of a replacement.

The I(PFD)A 1975 provides that any claim against the estate must be begun within 6 months from the date when the grant of representation was taken out. If the personal representatives have not, on the expiry of the time limit, received any notice of a claim, they are free to distribute the estate. Again, however, to err on the side of caution, if there is any inkling of a possible claim under the Act it would be advisable to give notice of the intention to distribute the estate to the potential claimant. Where the personal representatives have notice of a claim it is their duty to ensure that no steps are taken which will have the effect of prejudicing the claim. Where distribution has taken place it is still possible for the court to direct the beneficiary/ies to meet any financial provision order it makes in favour of the claimant.

The I(PFD)A 1975 makes provisions which are aimed at providing protection to the personal representatives from liability after the end of the period of 6 months from the date when a grant has been obtained in some circumstances. These are dealt with below.

11.2 LIABILITIES UNDER THE I(PFD)A 1975

The I(PFD)A 1975 extends the categories of person to whom personal representatives owe a duty, but also provides certain protection from liability. A successful claimant is regarded in law as a person interested in the will or intestacy and is thus in the same position vis-à-vis the personal representatives as a beneficiary and has the same rights of action against them.

The personal representatives are liable to the beneficiaries and creditors for any loss of assets of the estate or breach of any trust contained in the will. Personal representatives may apply to the court for relief under Trustee Act 1925, s 61 where they have made an interim distribution of the estate without a court order. Personal representatives may be faced with the difficult situation that beneficiaries are suffering hardship because distribution has been delayed by the inheritance proceedings, while at the same time the personal representatives have a duty to the claimant to preserve property. In *Re Simson, Simson v National Provincial Bank Ltd* [1949] 2 All ER 826, Vaisey J expressed the view that it was the duty of executors faced with a claim for financial provision to make no distribution until the hearing of the claim, and to preserve the estate intact for the court to deal with. On the other hand, in *Re Ralphs, Ralphs v District Bank* [1968] 1 WLR 1522, Cross J took a different view. He advocated that executors should:

> form their own view, with the assistance of their legal advisers, as to payments which can properly be made, and if they are not prepared to make such payments on their own responsibility they should ask the parties who might conceivably be affected for their consent. If such consent was not forthcoming they could apply to the court for leave to make the payment in question. If the court finds that consent was unreasonably withheld it can penalise the party responsible in costs.

11.3 PROTECTION AFFORDED BY I(PFD)A 1975, SECTION 20

I(PFD)A 1975, s 20 makes special provision in relation to the liabilities of personal representatives in the following circumstances:

- Section 20(1) provides that personal representatives are not liable for having distributed any part of the estate of the deceased, after the end of the period of 6 months from the date on which representation with respect to the estate of the deceased is first taken out, on the ground that they ought to have taken into account the possibility:
  - that the court might permit the making of an application for an order under s 2 after the end of that period (ie extend the time for making the application); or
  - that, where an order has been made under s 2, the court might vary the order in exercise of the powers conferred on it by s 6.

  This provision, however, does not prejudice any power to recover, by reason of the making of an order under the Act, any part of the estate which has been distributed.
- Section 20(2) protects personal representatives from having made interim payments directed to be paid by an order under s 5 out of the net estate of the deceased, and thereby leaving the estate insufficient to make the payments, unless at the time of the making of the payments they have reasonable cause to believe that the estate is not sufficient.
- The postponement of the payment of money or the transfer of property out of the estate of the deceased which the deceased had agreed by contract to leave by his/her will, but which the personal representatives of the deceased have reason to believe was entered into with the intention of defeating an application for financial provision under the Act, until the expiry of 6 months from the date on which representation with respect to the estate of the deceased is first taken out or, if during that period, an application is made for an order under s 2, until the determination of that application (s 20(3)).

These provisions protect the personal representatives who distribute the assets after the period of 6 months from the grant of representation. They should, therefore, avoid any distribution which might prejudice the claim within 6 months from the grant. Where they have notice of a possible claim, they should wait until the 6 months from the grant of representation have expired, and then give notice of their intention to distribute. They are also protected if they pay any sum directed to be paid by the court by way of interim payments under I(PFD)A 1975, s 5, unless, at the time of making the payments, they had reasonable grounds for believing that the estate was insolvent.

Protection is also provided where the personal representatives make a distribution under a contract which might be caught under I(PFD)A 1975, s 11, provided they did not make any payment of money or transfer any property until after the expiry of 6 months from the date on which representation was taken out. If a claim is pending, the personal representatives must postpone any distribution until the final determination of the claim. Where they have notice of a possible claim, it would be desirable to give notice to the claimant or his/her legal advisers of the intention to distribute before doing so.

In relation to any application under I(PFD)A 1975, s 10 (see Chapter 10), if the donee of an *inter vivos* disposition is dead, the court can proceed to make the appropriate order in like manner against the personal representatives of the donee under s 10. The court does not, however, have the power to make any of the orders under s 10 in respect of any property which has been distributed by the personal representatives. Further, the personal representatives are not liable for having distributed any such property before they have notice of the making of an application under s 10 on the grounds that they ought to have taken into account the possibility that such an application would be made (s 12(4)).

Personal representatives do not have, in relation to claims under I(PFD)A 1975, protection equivalent to that provided by Trustee Act 1925, s 27. Section 27 protects personal representatives from liability to any beneficiary who does not respond in time to an advertisement notifying the personal representatives' intention to distribute the estate. If there is any doubt about whether or not the estate may be distributed, an application should be made to the court for a direction.

A personal representative who is also a beneficiary must ensure that the two capacities are kept separate. In some circumstances it may be prudent for a claimant under the I(PFD)A 1975 to apply to the court, under Administration of Justice Act 1985, s 50, to replace that personal representative.

Where, on the death of the deceased, it appears that the person appointed executor might also be a possible claimant under the I(PFD)A 1975, it may be advisable that the grant is not taken out by that person unless that person is one of a number of personal representatives appointed.

11.3.1 Responsibilities and duties after proceedings have been issued

CPR Part 57 sets out the personal representatives' duties once proceedings have been issued under the I(PFD)A 1975. These and other matters which relate to the claim are set out in Chapter 12.

11.4 TRUSTEES

I(PFD)A 1975, s 13 imposes limitations on the court's powers under ss 10 and 11. Section 13 applies where an application is made for:

(1) an order under s 10 in respect of a disposition made by the deceased to any person as a trustee;

(2) an order under s 11 in respect of any payment made or property transferred in accordance with a contract made by the deceased, to any person as a trustee.

In these cases, the powers of the court under I(PFD)A 1975, ss 10 and 11 to order the trustee to provide a sum of money or other property from which the award to the claimant is to be met, are subject to limitation. The limitation is, in the case of an application under s 10, additional to any provision regarding the deduction of inheritance tax. The limitation is that the amount of any sum of money or the value of any property ordered to be provided:

(1) in the case of an application in respect of a disposition which consisted of the payment of money, or an application in respect of the payment of money in accordance with a contract, may not exceed the aggregate of so much of that money as is at the date of the order in the hands of the trustee and the value at that date of any property which represents that money, or is derived therefrom, and is at that date in the hands of the trustee;

(2) in the case of an application in respect of a disposition which consisted of the transfer of property (other than a sum of money) or an application in respect of the transfer of property (other than a sum of money) in accordance with a contract, shall not exceed the aggregate of the value at the date of the order of so much of that property as is at that date in the hands of the trustee and the value at that date of any property which represents the first mentioned property, or is derived therefrom, and is at that date in the hands of the trustee.

Where any application is made in respect of a disposition made to any person as a trustee, or in respect or any payment made or property transferred in pursuance of a contract to any person as a trustee, the trustee is not liable for having distributed any money or other property on the ground that he/she ought to have taken into account the possibility that such an application would be made (I(PFD)A 1975, s 13(2)).

Where any such application is made in respect of a disposition made to any person as a trustee, or in respect of any payment made or property transferred in accordance with a contract to any person as a trustee, any reference in I(PFD)A 1975, s 10 or s 11 to the donee is to be construed as including a reference to the trustee or trustees for the time being in question, and any reference to a trustee is to be construed in the same way (s 13(3)).

Chapter 12

Procedure

12.1 INTRODUCTION

Before 2 December 2002, all applications under the I(PFD)A 1975 were made in the Chancery Division or the Family Division of the High Court, and were governed by Rules of the Supreme Court 1965 (SI 1965/1776), Ord 99, as amended. Order 99 was revoked by Civil Procedure (Amendment) Rules 2002 (SI 2002/2058), r 35 and Sch 10, with effect from 2 December 2002. Order 99 does not, therefore, apply to proceedings which were commenced before 2 December 2002 and still pending at that date. Order 99 has been replaced by CPR Part 57 as amended and the Practice Direction which supplements Part 57. The new rules now provide uniform practice and procedure in both the High Court and the county courts. In addition to Part 57, the CPR generally apply to claims under the I(PFD)A 1975, eg 'the overriding objective', the need to comply with the general Pre-Action Protocol and recourse to alternative dispute resolution, service and costs.

The county courts' jurisdiction to entertain a claim under the I(PFD)A 1975 was limited to estates not exceeding £30,000. This limit was removed by Courts and Legal Services Act 1990, ss 1 and 120, and the High Court and County Courts Jurisdiction Order 1991 (SI 1991/724).

12.2 PRE-ACTION PROTOCOL

The CPR impose a duty on the parties and the court to ensure that the Pre-Action Protocol is followed. CPR r 3.1(4) requires the court when giving directions to take into account whether or not a party has complied with any relevant Pre-Action Protocol and r 3.1(5) gives the court power to order a party to pay a sum of money into court if that party has, without good reason, failed to comply with a relevant protocol. The court is also required, when dealing with any application for relief from sanctions imposed for non-compliance of any rule, practice direction or order, to consider the extent to which the party in default has complied with any relevant Pre-Action Protocol. In deciding what order to make on costs, one of the factors which the court has to take into account is the conduct of the parties and this includes conduct before as well as during the proceedings, and in particular the extent to which the parties followed any relevant Pre-Action Protocol (r 44.3(5)(a)). It is, therefore, essential to follow the general Pre-Action Protocol before commencing any proceedings under the I(PFD)A 1975. It may also be useful to follow the guidance given by the Association of Contentious Trust and Probate Specialists in their ACTAPS Code (which includes claims under the I(PFD)A 1975) where appropriate (see Appendix A6).

12.3   VENUE

Proceedings may be commenced in the High Court or a county court. Proceedings in the High Court are assigned to the Chancery Division and the Family Division of the High Court (CPR r 57.15). The choice of division is a matter of discretion for the claimant. Where there have been matrimonial proceedings affecting the claimant or any of the parties to the proposed action, the court in which the matrimonial proceedings were heard would be the appropriate court in which to make a claim under the I(PFD)A 1975 if the passage of time between the previous proceedings and the proceedings under the Act is not long.

County courts have jurisdiction to hear and determine any application for an order under I(PFD)A 1975, s 2, including any application for permission to apply for such an order, and any application made in the proceedings for an order under any other provision of the Act (County Courts Act 1984, s 25). The county court in which the proceedings are commenced will be the county court for the district in which the defendants or one of the defendants live(s) or carry(ies) on business, or where the subject matter of the claim is situated.

The decision on venue is made on the basis of the nature and complexity of the case. If there is an overseas aspect to the case, or if the claim or the estate is particularly large, it would be advisable to commence the proceedings in the High Court.

Since claims under the I(PFD)A 1975 are commenced in accordance with CPR Part 8, the Masters in the Chancery Division or the district judges in the provincial Chancery District Registries, and district judges in the Family

Division have jurisdiction to hear claims under the I(PFD)A 1975 and to approve agreements reached in such claims. Pursuant to *Practice Direction: Civil Procedure Rules: Allocation of Cases: Costs,* 22 April 1999 [1999] 1 FLR 1295, para 3.2 of the *Practice Direction: Allocation of Cases to Level of Judiciary* (CPR PD 2B) applies to the Family Division district judges (including district judges of the Principal Registry), who have jurisdiction to hear and dispose of proceedings under the I(PFD)A 1975.

In proceedings in the Chancery Division, a Master or a district judge has jurisdiction to approve compromises on behalf of a person under disability where that person's interest in a fund in an application made under the I(PFD)A 1975 exceeds £100,000 (CPR PD 2B, para 5.1).

As claims under the I(PFD)A 1975 are Part 8 proceedings, a Master or district judge may also try contested or uncontested applications under the Act (CPR PD 2B, para 4.1). Where a case is likely to involve long and complex issues of fact or law, or an issue arises as to jurisdiction, it should be issued in the High Court. Where the claim is made by a widow or surviving partner or a former spouse or civil partner to whom I(PFD)A 1975, s 14 applies, it would be desirable to issue the application in the Family Division of the High Court which is accustomed to dealing with the issues which are likely to arise in such cases. Where the application involves complicated accounts partnerships and business issues, the application should be issued in the Chancery Division which is perhaps best equipped to deal with such issues, and if commenced in the county court or the Family Division an application should be made for the proceedings to be transferred.

12.4   CLAIM FORM

CPR r 8.1(2) provides that the procedure under Part 8 ('alternative procedure for claims') may be used:

(1)   where the court's decision on a question which is unlikely to involve a substantial dispute of fact is sought; or

(2)   where a rule or practice direction in relation to a specified type of proceedings requires or permits the use of Part 8 procedure and disapplies or modifies any of the rules set out in Part 8 as they apply to those proceedings.

CPR r 57.16(1) provides that a claim under I(PFD)A 1975, s 1 must be made by issuing a claim form in accordance with Part 8. Part 8 and the Practice

Directions under Part 8 therefore also apply to a claim under the I(PFD)A 1975.

Where there is more than one claimant, the claimants will usually agree to file a single claim form, but where this is not possible and separate claim forms are issued by each claimant, application should be made for the proceedings to be consolidated under CPR r 3.1(2).

12.4.1 Contents

The claim form must be entitled 'In the matter of [name] deceased' and 'In the matter of the Inheritance (Family Provision and Dependants) Act 1975'.

CPR r 8.2 requires that the claim form must state:

(1)   that Part 8 applies;

(2)   the question which the claimant wants the court to decide; or the remedy or relief which the claimant is seeking and the legal basis for the claim to that remedy or relief;

(3)   if the claim is being made under an enactment, what that enactment is;

(4)   if the claimant is claiming in a representative capacity, what that capacity is; and

(5)   if the defendant is sued in a representative capacity, what that capacity is.

Where it is intended to make any other applications for substantive orders under the I(PFD)A 1975 this must be set out in the claim form. These include the following.

12.4.2 Time limits

The claim must be issued within 6 months of the date on which representation is taken out, unless the court grants an extension of time (I(PFD)A 1975, s 4; see Chapter 3). Leave to extend the time limit must be made in the claim form. (For a draft of the order, see Appendix A1.7.)

12.4.3 Application under I(PFD)A 1975, section 9 for severance of joint tenancy

Where it is intended to make an application under I(PFD)A 1975, s 9, to treat the deceased's severable share of a joint tenancy as part of the net estate (see

Chapter 9), the application must be made within 6 months of the date on which the grant of representation with respect of the deceased's estate was first taken out. There is no power to extend this time limit (s 9(1)). An application for severance must, therefore, be made in the claim form and supported by evidence either in the claim form or in the written statement accompanying the claim form. It will be essential to identify the property which is intended to be the subject of the application and to ensure that it is indeed in the joint names of the deceased and another as joint tenants and that if jointly owned initially that the joint tenancy has not been severed (see Chapter 9).

Where the joint tenant is a third party not directly connected with the application and is not a defendant to the application for an order under I(PFD)A 1975, s 2, it will be necessary to seek direction for the person to be joined as a defendant or a respondent only to the s 9 application in order to preserve confidentiality of the claimant and the defendants who have a direct interest in the substantive application. (See, further, CPR r 19 on joinder of parties.)

12.4.4 Application under I(PFD)A 1975, sections 10 and 11 to set aside transactions made by the deceased with the intention of defeating or reducing a claim under the Act

Where it is alleged that the deceased has disposed of assets to a third party or contracted to leave property by will to a third party, with the intention of defeating or reducing a claim under the I(PFD)A 1975, it is essential that the application is made with supporting evidence filed as soon as possible and preferably when the claim form is issued, particularly where it is believed that the assets will be dissipated by the third party and there is therefore a need to preserve the asset by obtaining an injunction forbidding the disposal or transfer of the asset or any dealing with the asset or part of it where appropriate until the determination of the substantive application (see CPR Part 25) or, alternatively, to extract an undertaking from the third party in like terms.

For examples of claims which might be included in the claim form, see Appendix A1.2.

12.4.5 Claimants

The claimant must fall within the classes of person listed under I(PFD)A 1975, s 1(1) as amended (see Chapter 4). If a claim it made jointly by two or more persons, and if it later appears that there is a conflict of interests between claimants (CPR PD 57, para 17):

(1)   any claimant may choose to have separate representation or may appear in person;

(2)   if the court considers that claimants should be separately represented, it may adjourn the action until they are.

Where separate claims are issued it is open to apply for the claims to be consolidated under CPR r 3.1(2)(g).

Where a claimant is also a personal representative, provided there is another personal representative, the action may proceed with the claimant continuing as personal representative. Where, however, it appears that there may be a conflict of interests, it would be advisable for the claimant who is a personal representative to stand down.

Where a potential claimant dies before the claim is issued, the claim does not survive for the benefit of his/her estate, because the claim is personal to the claimant (see *Re Bramwell* [1988] 2 FLR 263 and *Whyte v Ticehurst* [1986] Fam 64). Similarly, where a claim is issued but the claimant dies before an order is made, the claim dies with the claimant. Where an interim order was made, for example, for the payment of periodical payments, and arrears had accumulated before the claimant's death, the right to enforce those arrears survives.

Where the claimant is a bankrupt, provided the claim is limited to maintenance for the claimant, it seems that the claim can be pursued by the claimant personally, without the leave of the trustee in bankruptcy or permission from the court. Similarly, it seems that CPR r 19.2(4) will not apply where the claimant becomes the subject of a bankruptcy order while the claim is pending and before a final order is made. It would seem that where the claim is not limited to provision for the maintenance of the claimant, but is for a capital sum or property, it could be argued that the trustee in bankruptcy should be brought in (see *Re Abrams* [1996] 2 FLR 379, where a discretionary/protective trust was created in order to avoid the benefits of the order being vested in a trustee in bankruptcy).

12.4.6 Defendants

There are no rules on who should be made a party to the claim.

Personal representatives and beneficiaries under the deceased's will or intestacy are obvious defendants. Where there are numerous beneficiaries it may be desirable first to ascertain the extent of their beneficial interests. If they are entitled to receive small legacies or devises and their interest is not likely to be affected, it should be possible to reach agreement that they should not be made defendants. In any other case it may be desirable or appropriate to apply for a representation order under CPR r 19.7, or apply for notice to be given to those who form members of a class, under r 19.8A.

Where an order under I(PFD)A 1975, s 8 (property to be treated as part of the net estate) is sought, the appropriate nominee or donee should be made a party.

Where an order under I(PFD)A 1975, s 9 is sought (property held on a joint tenancy) the person beneficially entitled to the joint tenancy should be made a party.

Where it is sought to apply to set aside, under I(PFD)A 1975, s 10, a disposition made by the deceased, the person in whose favour the disposition is made and against whom an order is sought should be made a party. The same applies where an order is sought under s 11.

Any other person who is alleged to be a constructive trustee of property belonging to the deceased or forming part of the estate should be joined in the claim.

Any other person directed by the court to be added as a defendant under the provisions of CPR r 19.7 must be so added. For example, the court may order the appointment of a person to represent an unborn person, a person who cannot be found or a person who cannot easily be identified. Where the court exercises its powers under this rule, a judgment or order of the court given in the claim, or a settlement approved by the court, is binding on all persons who are interested in or may be affected (CPR r 19.7(6) and (7)).

12.5 CLAIMANT'S WITNESS STATEMENTS/AFFIDAVIT

CPR r 8.5 provides that the claimant may rely on the matters set out in his/her claim form as evidence under the rule if the claim form is verified by a statement of truth, but see r 8.5(1), which states that if the claimant wishes to rely on written evidence, he/she should file it when his/her Part 8 claim form is issued (r 8.8(1)), unless the evidence is contained in the claim form itself. Where a claimant relies on the evidence set out in the claim form, it must be verified with a statement of truth. Information about statements of truth is contained in Part 22 and the Practice Direction which supplements it.

The written statement should contain the witness's own words so far as is practicable. The solicitor taking the statement must follow the Law Society's

Guide to the Professional Conduct of Solicitors. The person taking the statement must not try to persuade the witness of what he/she should or should not say. See, further, *Aquarius Financial Enterprises Inc v Certain Underwriters at Lloyds* (2001) 151 NLJ 694.

The form of the witness statement must comply with the requirements of CPR Part 32 and the Practice Direction which supplements it.

In addition, CPR r 57.16(3) requires that the written statement filed and served by the claimant with the claim form must have exhibited to it an official copy of the grant of probate or letters of administration in respect of the deceased's estate, and of every testamentary document in respect of which probate or letters of administration were granted.

There is no other specific requirement in the rules relating to the contents of the claimant's witness statement or affidavit, but it is suggested that the statement or affidavit should contain the following matters in addition to those set out above:

(1)   the name of the deceased, the date of his/her death and the country of his/her domicile at that date;

(2)   a certified copy of the deceased's death certificate;

(3)   the date on which representation with respect to the deceased's estate was taken out and the names and addresses of the personal representatives;

(4)   the value of the net estate (to the best of the claimant's knowledge and belief). Where possible, brief details of the property comprised in the net estate, with an approximate value and any income received therefrom, and any known liabilities, should be included;

(5)   the relationship of the claimant to the deceased, or other qualification of the claimant for making the claim (see I(PFD)A 1975, s 1 and Chapter 4). In the case of a widow, the marriage certificate should be exhibited. In the case of a judicially separated spouse, the decree of judicial separation and a copy of any orders for ancillary relief made should be exhibited. In the case of a former spouse, a copy of the decree absolute and any order for ancillary relief made in those proceedings should be exhibited. Similar evidence will need to be provided in the case of civil partners and former civil partners;

(6)   particulars of any known proceedings relevant to the claim. Such material is particularly relevant to the question whether a claim which has been commenced in a county court ought to be

transferred to the Chancery Division or the Family Division of the High Court;

(7) whether the disposition of the deceased's estate effected by his/her will or the law relating to intestacy was such as to make any provision for the claimant, and, if so, the nature of the provision;

(8) details of the persons or classes of person interested in the deceased's estate and the nature of their interests;

(9) full particulars of the claimant's present and foreseeable financial resources and financial needs, and any other information which the claimant relies on under s 3 (see Chapter 7 and *Re Smallwood, Smallwood v Martins Bank* [1951] Ch 369). The deceased's reasons, if known, for making or not making a provision should be included. In *Re Blanch, Blanch v Honhold* [1967] 1 WLR 987, Buckley J said:

> In certain cases there are likely to be respects in which the state of the deceased's mind may properly be regarded as relevant and material. For instance, the state of the deceased's mind may be very material to the weight to be attributed to any reasons which he may have given in his lifetime for failing to make provision for a dependant or making such provision as he did make for such a dependant;

(10) where appropriate, a request for the court's permission to make the claim out of time and the grounds for the delay;

(11) the nature of the provision claimed;

(12) details of any orders sought under ss 8–13.

Sample statements are set out in Appendices A1.3–A1.6.

12.6 PARTY UNDER DISABILITY

Where a party, whether a claimant or defendant, is a child or a protected person, CPR r 21 must be considered. A child is defined as a person under 18. Rule 21.1(2)(d) defines a 'protected person' as a party, or an intended party, who lacks capacity to conduct the proceedings. A 'protected beneficiary' is defined as a protected person who lacks capacity to manage and control any money recovered by him/her or on his/her behalf or for his/her benefit in the proceedings (r 21.1(2)(e)).

The Mental Capacity Act 2005 sets out a definitive test for assessing whether a person has capacity to make a specific decision at the material time. It provides for a two-stage process, namely the diagnostic stage, which is set out in Mental Capacity Act 2005 (MCA 2005), s 2(1) and a functional test which is set out in MCA 2005, s 3.

MCA 2005, s 2(1) states that:

> a person lacks capacity in relation to a matter if at the material time he is unable to make a decision in relation to the matter because of an impairment of, or disturbance in, the functioning of the mind or brain.

It does not matter whether the disturbance is permanent or temporary (s 2(2)).

The functional stage of the test is 'function specific' and it has to be demonstrated that the impairment or disturbance renders the person unable to make the decision in question for him/herself. Mental Capacity Act 2005, s 3 sets out the criteria which must be satisfied to demonstrate that a person is unable to make a decision for him/herself if he/she is unable:

(1)   to understand the information relevant to the decision;

(2)   to retain that information;

(3)   to use or weigh that information as part of the process of making the decision; or

(4)   to communicate his/her decision (whether by talking, using sign language or any other means).

MCA 2005, s 1 sets out the fundamental principles which underpin the Act and to which regard must be had in every decision made. These are:

(1)   a person must be assumed to have capacity unless it is established that he/she lacks capacity;

(2)   a person is not to be treated as unable to make a decision unless all practicable steps to help him/her to do so have been taken without success;

(3)   a person is not to be treated as unable to make a decision merely because he/she *makes* an unwise decision;

(4)   an act done, or decision made, under the I(PFD)A 1975 for or on behalf of a person who lacks capacity must be done or made, in his/her best interests;

(5)   before the act is done, or the decision is made, regard must be had to whether the purpose for which it is needed can be as effectively achieved in a way that is less restrictive of the person's rights and freedom of action.

(See, further, Nasreen Pearce, *Urgent Applications in the Court of Protection* (Jordan Publishing Ltd, 2010).)

A protected person must have a litigation friend to conduct proceedings on his/her behalf (CPR r 21.1(1)).

A child must have a litigation friend to conduct proceedings unless the court has made an order under CPR r 21.2(3) permitting the child to conduct proceedings without a litigation friend (r 21.2(2)).

Where a claim is made by or on behalf of a child or a person who lacks capacity, or against a child or a person who lacks capacity, no settlement, compromise or payment and no acceptance of money paid into court will be regarded as valid unless it has been approved by the court (CPR r 21.10(1)). Where a settlement or compromise is reached for or on behalf of a child or person who lacks capacity, or against such a person before a claim is issued, the court procedure is for a claim to be made under Part 8 seeking the court's approval for the settlement or compromise (r 21.10(2)). For this purpose it is advisable to prepare a case summary and submit a comprehensive opinion of counsel representing the child or patient setting out an analysis of the issues and the basis upon which it is suggested that the settlement is in the interest of the child or patient.

For a draft consent order setting out a compromise in favour of a claimant under disability, see Appendix A1.7.

12.7 SERVICE

The method of service set out in CPR r 6 must be followed. Service may be effected by:

(1) personal service, in accordance with r 6.4;

(2) first class post (or an alternative service which provides for delivery on the next working day);

(3) leaving a document at a place specified in r 6.5;

(4) through a document exchange in accordance with the relevant Practice Direction; or

(5) by fax or other means of electronic communication in accordance with the relevant Practice Direction.

Service by the court is the general rule and service by first class post is the most favoured unless the parties are represented, in which case service is usually effected by document exchange.

12.8   ACKNOWLEDGEMENT OF SERVICE AND DEFENDANT'S EVIDENCE

The provisions of CPR rr 8.3 and 8.5 apply to claims under the I(PFD)A 1975 (r 57.16(2)).

Defendants served within the jurisdiction must file and serve an acknowledgement of service within 21 days after service of the claim form and the supporting evidence (CPR r 57.16(4)). Any written statement in answer must also be filed within 21 days of service unless an extension of time has been agreed or granted by the court. If the claim form was served out of the jurisdiction under r 6.19, the period for filing an acknowledgement of service and any written evidence is 7 days longer than the period specified in r 6.22 or the Practice Direction which supplements Part 6 (r 57.16(4A)).

12.8.1   Position of personal representative who is a defendant

A personal representative who is a defendant and who wishes to remain neutral and abide by the decision of the court should state this in Section A of the acknowledgment of service form (CPR r 57.16(4), PD 57, para 15).

The personal representative must also file and serve a written statement which must set out the information required by CPR PD 57, para 16(1)–(4) within 21 days of service of the claim form on him/her.

The written evidence filed by a defendant who is a personal representative must state to the best of that person's ability:

(1)   full details of the value of the deceased's net estate, as defined in I(PFD)A 1975, s 25(1);

(2)   the person or classes of persons beneficially interested in the estate, and (a) the names and (unless they are parties to the claim) addresses of all living beneficiaries and (b) the value of their interests in the estate so far as they are known;

(3)   whether any living beneficiary (and if so, naming him/her) is a child or a person who lacks capacity (within the meaning of the MCA 2005); and

(4)   any facts which might affect the exercise of the court's powers under the I(PFD)A 1975.

Unlike the old provisions of the Rules of the Supreme Court, Ord 99.5(2)(d), which required a personal representative to state facts known to him/her to the best of his/her knowledge and belief, CPR r 57.16(5) and PD 57, para 16, which are both mandatory, require that the evidence filed 'must state to the best of the person's ability' the facts which might affect the court's decision. It would seem, therefore, that the rule, combined with the Practice Direction, imposes on the personal representatives a duty to make inquiries and to provide such facts as may be relevant and which may affect the exercise of the court's discretion.

12.8.2 Other defendants

It is no longer possible for defendants to a claim under the I(PFD)A 1975 to wait until the first directions hearing to file their defence or their evidence. Under CPR r 57.16(4), all defendants are required to file and serve an acknowledgement of service and any written evidence within 21 days after service of the claim form. Their statements must also comply with r 8.5 unless the court otherwise directs under r 8.6(1). It is essential to comply with the timescales in the rules (rr 8.5 and 57.16(4)). Where for some reason there may be difficulty in complying with the time limits, an application may be made for permission to file and serve the evidence out of time or for an extension of time under PD 8, para 7.4. The parties may agree in writing to extend the time for filing and serving evidence under r 8.5(3) or r 8.5(5) (PD 8, para 7.5(1)). However, an agreement extending time for a defendant to file his/her evidence under r 8.5(3) or r 8.5(5) (PD 8, para 7.5(2)):

(1) must be filed by the defendant at the same time as he/she files his/her acknowledgement of service; and

(2) must not extend by more than 14 days after the defendant files his/her acknowledgement of service.

12.8.3 Claimant's reply

The claimant may, within 14 days of service of the defendant's evidence on him/her, file and serve evidence in reply (CPR r 8.5(5) and (6)).

An agreement extending time for a claimant to file evidence in reply under CPR r 8.5(5) must not extend time to more than 28 days after service of the defendant's evidence on the claimant (PD 8, para 7.5(3)).

12.9 INTERLOCUTORY MATTERS, DIRECTIONS AND CASE MANAGEMENT

The CPR apply to claims under the I(PFD)A 1975. Where there is a risk of the assets being dissipated, particularly where it is sought to apply for an order under ss 8–11, it is important to take steps to preserve the assets. This may be done by obtaining appropriate undertakings; registering the claim as a pending land action where appropriate; applying for an injunction forbidding any dealing with the property; and, in the case of liquid funds, seeking an order freezing such assets.

At the directions hearing it will be necessary to consider matters such as disclosure; the need for an expert's report, for example a medical report; valuations; and accounts, as, for instance, in the case of a partnership or a private company.

A chronology, a summary of the facts, and a statement of issues should be provided to the court for the case management conference. It is always prudent to discuss beforehand the directions required and the reasons for them. Serious consideration should also be given to providing the court with a realistic time estimate. The availability of an interpreter, if needed, should be considered. When making a time estimate, account should be taken of the fact that the hearing takes longer when an interpreter is required or one of the parties is in person. Difficult issues, such as whether evidence by video link is necessary, where, say, a witness or a party is serving a long prison sentence or is violent, should be addressed. The question of whether the final hearing should take place in public or continue to remain private should also be considered (see below).

12.10 DISCLOSURE

The court has wide powers to order disclosure both before and during the proceedings.

Pre-trial disclosure may be applied for under CPR r 31.16 against a defendant who is likely to be a party to proposed proceedings under the I(PFD)A 1975.

Disclosure may also be ordered under CPR r 25.1(1)(g) directing a party to provide information about the location of relevant property or assets or to provide information about relevant property or assets which are or may be the subject of an application for a freezing order. This may be relevant in relation to property or assets which form part or may form part of the net estate, eg property which may be the subject of applications under I(PFD)A 1975, ss 9–11 where it may be necessary to seek orders to bring the asset within the net estate or to freeze the assets so that they are available if needed when the substantive application is heard.

Practitioners should be aware of the amendments made to CPR Part 31 and the introduction of a new PD 31B which deals with disclosure of electronic material. The new Practice Direction is introduced to regulate the approach practitioners should take when considering material relevant to a case which is stored electronically. In particular, it aims to focus the parties on the sources of electronic material and give guidance to those with less experience of dealing which such issues. This will apply to cases that are or likely to be allocated to the multi-track. The rule change supports the new Practice Direction by confirming that the questionnaire may be treated as a disclosed document. Form N150 is amended to support this change. A copy of PD 31B is set out at Appendix A4.

The Electronic Documents Questionnaire is set out in the Schedule to PD 31B.

'Electronic document' means any document held in electronic form. It includes for example emails and other electronic communication such as text messages and voice mail, word processed documents and databases, and documents stored on portable devices such as memory sticks and mobile phones. In addition, it applies to documents that are readily accessible from computer systems and other electronic devices and media. It includes documents that are stored on servers and backup systems and documents that are deleted. It also includes Metadata and other embedded data which are not typically visible on screen or a print out.

Where such documents exist or are likely to exist, it is advisable to have a joint meeting or conference to discuss how this type of disclosure should be provided so that the information is available at the case management hearing.

12.11 ATTEMPTS/OFFERS TO SETTLE

The CPR apply to claims under the I(PFD)A 1975 and therefore the court will be looking to deal with the case with the overriding objective in mind and in particular the matters set out in CPR r 1.1(2). The parties are required to help the court to further the overriding objective (r 1.3). This means encouraging the parties to make attempts to negotiate and settle the dispute between them by using alternative dispute resolution procedure. Rule 1.4 also imposes a duty on the court when managing the case to 'encourage the parties to use an alternative dispute resolution procedure if the court considers that appropriate and facilitating the use of such procedure' and to help 'the parties to settle the whole or part of the case' (r 1.4(2)(e) and (f)).

The Pre-Action Protocol requires the parties to explore the option of resolving the dispute by meetings and negotiations and to consider the use of alternative dispute resolution, which includes mediation as a more suitable process than litigation. The Pre-Action Direction now makes it clear that claims should not be issued prematurely when a settlement is being explored. If a resolution is being explored but there is concern about the s 4 time limit attempts should be made to agree that the expiry of the time limit will not be raised as an issue. Alternatively, the claim may be issued and then application made for it to be stayed for mediation to continue.

The Pre-Action Protocol should be used to obtain as much information, including information of the deceased's assets and its valuation, as possible to enable the parties to identify the issues on which the parties are agreed and those which remain in dispute. Where necessary an application should be made for pre-action disclosure. If the issues cannot be narrowed before the proceedings are issued, then when all the evidence has been filed and disclosure and valuation has taken place it is important to take stock exchange position statements and arrange a joint issue resolution meeting or round table conference to attempt to iron out the outstanding issues.

12.11.1 CPR Part 36 offer

CPR Part 36 contains a carefully structured and prescriptive set of rules which deal with the procedure for the settlement of disputes and with specific consequences in those cases where an offer is not accepted and the offer fails to do better after a trial. It prescribes in some detail the manner in which an offer should be made and the consequences which flow from accepting or failing to accept it. The offer must comply with the provisions of r 36.2(2) and the Practice Directions to the rule, and must be made not less than 21 days before the trial date.

The rules must be read in the light of the decision in *Carver v BAA* [2008] EWCA Civ 412, [2009] 1 WLR 113 and *Gibbon v Manchester City Council and Another* [2010] EWCA Civ 726, [2010] 1 WLR 2081. In *Carver v BAA*, it was held that in determining whether the judgment was more advantageous to the claimant than the Part 36 offer the court should take into account all aspects of the case including emotional distress. In *Gibbon v Manchester City Council and Another Appeal*, the Court of Appeal took the view that obtaining judgment for an amount greater than a CPR Part 36 offer is likely to outweigh all other factors. In considering the offer made a party should evaluate it by reference to an assessment of his/her case including the risk of incurring irrecoverable costs.

In *Gibbon v Manchester City Council and Another*, the Court of Appeal also held that:

- Although basic concepts of offer and acceptance clearly underpinned CPR Part 36, it should not be understood as incorporating all the rules of law governing the formation of contracts; rather it should be read and understood according to its terms without importing other rules derived from the general law, save where that was clearly intended. Moore-Bick LJ said that certainty was as much to be commended in procedural as in substantive law, especially, perhaps, in a procedural code which had to be understood and followed by ordinary citizens who wished to conduct their own litigation. Part 36 had been drafted with those considerations in mind and was to be read and understood according to its terms without importing other rules derived from the general law, save where that was clearly intended.
- The offer remains in force until it is withdrawn by service of a notice of withdrawal. Part 36 puts the onus on the maker of the offer to withdraw any existing offer if he/she does not wish it to be available for acceptance. There is no concept of implied withdrawal. If the maker of the offer wishes to withdraw the offer he/she must be do so expressly in writing. Although no particular form of notice is required, in order to avoid uncertainty the notice should include a clear reference to the date on which the offer was made and its terms. It should clearly express that the offer has been withdrawn. The offer may be accepted even though a different offer or offers has/have been made by the offeror. If the offeror varies the terms of the original offer it will continue to remain valid as from the date on which it was originally made.

12.11.2 *Calderbank* offers

A *Calderbank* offer is an offer made in a letter with a view to settling the case. The offer letter is marked 'without prejudice' save as to costs. Sometimes it is marked without prejudice but clearly stated to be subject to an express reservation of the right to refer to it on the issue of costs.

Although CPR Part 36 procedure has largely superseded the *Calderbank* offer letter, it still remains preserved and if an offer is made in such a letter, it will be taken into account when the court considers the issue of costs but the consequences set out in rr 36.10, 36.11 and 36.14 will not necessarily follow. It is thus preferable, if the decision is taken to make an offer, to use the Part 36 procedure.

12.12 HEARING

CPR PD 39A, para 1.5 also makes provision for proceedings under the I(PFD)A 1975 to be listed in private in the first instance.

CPR r 39.2 provides that in general a hearing is to be in public, but r 39.2(3) makes provision for a hearing to be conducted in private in certain circumstances, including cases which involve confidential information (including information relating to personal financial matters) and where publicity would damage that confidentiality.

12.13 ENDORSEMENT OF MEMORANDUM ON GRANT

If the court makes an order under the I(PFD)A 1975, the original grant (together with a sealed copy of the order) must be sent to the Principal Registry of the Family Division for a memorandum of the order to be endorsed on or permanently annexed to the grant in accordance with s 19(3) (CPR PD 57, para 18.2).

In the Family Division, the practice has always been for memoranda of all consent orders in proceedings under the I(PFD)A 1975 to be endorsed on the probate or letters of administration, whether or not the parties are *sui juris*. The practice in the Chancery Division was otherwise. The differences in practice between the two Divisions has been resolved by Practice Direction [1979] 1 WLR 1, which provides that every final order embodying terms of compromise made in proceedings in the Chancery Division must contain a direction that a memorandum thereof shall be endorsed on or permanently annexed to the probate or letters of administration and a copy thereof shall be sent to the Principal Registry of the Family Division with the relevant grant of probate or letters of administration for endorsement.

12.14 DRAWING UP AND SERVICE OF ORDERS

Pursuant to CPR r 57.12(2), the FPR relating to the drawing and service of orders apply to proceedings brought in the Family Division of the High Court instead of the provisions of CPR Part 40 and its Practice Direction.

12.15   Subsequent applications

Any subsequent application under the I(PFD)A 1975, for example for a variation of an order, whether made by the claimant or any other party, must be made by issuing an application notice in accordance with CPR Part 23.

The application notice must set out the order/s sought and the grounds for seeking the order/s. If the applicant intends to rely on matters set out in the notice as evidence it must be verified by a statement of truth. Where the information set out in the notice of application is inadequate and it is intended to particularise the matters relied on more fully, the notice must be supported by a written statement or affidavit. The statement or affidavit in support must set out in detail the grounds relied on for seeking the order/s applied for and any other relevant matter. Thereafter, the procedure which applies to the application is the same as for a substantive application under the I(PFD)A 1975.

12.15.1   Procedural guide

Who may apply?	The spouse of the deceased	I(PFD)A 1975, s 1(1)(a)
	The registered civil partner of the deceased	I(PFD)A 1975, s 1(1)(a); CPA 2004, s 71, Sch 4
	The former spouse of the deceased who has not remarried	I(PFD)A 1975, s 1(1)(b)
	The former civil partner of the deceased who has not formed a subsequent civil partnership	I(PFD)A 1975, s 1(1)(b); CPA 2004, s 71, Sch 4
	A cohabitant of the deceased	I(PFD)A 1975, s 1(1)(ba), s 1(1A) as amended by the Law Reform (Succession) Act 1995
	A person who lived in the same household as the deceased as his/her civil partner	I(PFD)A 1975, s 1(1)(ba), s 1(1B); CPA 2004, s 71, Sch 4
	A child of the deceased	I(PFD)A 1975, s 1(1)(c)
	Any person who was treated as a child of the family whether within a marriage or in a civil partnership	I(PFD)A 1975, s 1(1)(d)
	Any other person who immediately before the death of the deceased was being maintained by him/her	I(PFD)A 1975, s 1; CPA 2004

Which court?	High Court (Chancery or Family Division) or county court	CPR r 57.15; County Courts Act 1984, s 25
	District judges (including district judges of the Principal Registry of the Family Division) have jurisdiction to hear such applications	CPR r 57.15; I(PFD)A 1975, s 22; PD of 22 April 1999
Application	*High Court/county court* By Part 8 Claim Form which should be entitled: 'In the estate of ... deceased' and 'In the matter of I(PFD)A 1975'	CPR rr 57.16, 8.2; PD 8B
Time limit	The claim must be issued within 6 months of the date on which representation is taken out (unless extended by the court). Application to extend the time limit must be included in the claim form	I(PFD)A 1975, s 4
Documents	The applicant must file with the claim form a witness statement/ affidavit in support exhibiting an official copy of the grant of representation and of every testamentary document admitted to proof	CPR rr 57.16(3), 8.5(1), (2)
Defendants	Personal representatives Beneficiaries Other persons affected by the claim Any other person directed by the court to be added	CPR r 19.7

Service	The claim form must be served within 4 months of the date of issue	
	Extension of time must be sought under CPR r 7.6	
	Acknowledgement of service must be filed within 21 days of service of the claim form and served on the claimant and other parties if served within the jurisdiction	
	If served outside the jurisdiction extended period is permitted by CPR r 57.16(4A)	CPR rr 57.16(4), 6.19, 6.22, 8.3(1), 10.3(1)
	For service on children and patients, see CPR r 6.6	
	Otherwise, in accordance with CPR r 10.3(2)	CPR r 10.3(2)
Statement/ Affidavit in answer	Must be filed by the personal representatives within 21 days of service of the claim form (it should include the matters set out in CPR PD 57, para 16)	CPR r 57.16(4), (5); PD 57, para 16
	May be filed by other defendants within 21 days after service of the claim form	CPR r 57.16(4)
Service of answer	Every defendant who files any written evidence within 21 days in answer must serve a copy on the claimant and every other defendant who is not represented by the same solicitor	CPR r 57.16(4)
Reply	A claimant may serve a statement in reply on all other parties within 14 days of service of the defendant's evidence on him/her	CPR r 8.5(5), (6)

Directions/case management conference pretrial hearing	At the same time as issuing the claim form a directions hearing may be requested	CPR PD 8, para 4.1
	The court will in any event give directions after the defendant has filed the acknowledgement of service or after the time for filing it has expired	
	Parties must complete the listing questionnaire in Form N170 and provide an estimate of costs following which the court will consider whether to hold a pre-trial review and set a timetable and fix the date for the trial	CPR PD 8, para 4.2; r 29.6–8
Fee payable	High Court: £400	CPFO 2008, fee 1.5
	County court: £150	CPFO 2008, fee 1.5
Order	Periodical payments	I(PFD)A 1975, s 2(1)(a)
	Lump sum	I(PFD)A 1975, s 2(1)(b)
	Transfer of property	I(PFD)A 1975, s 2(1)(c)
	Settlement of property	I(PFD)A 1975, s 2(1)(d)
	Acquisition, transfer and settlement of property	I(PFD)A 1975, s 2(1)(e)
	Variation of ante-nuptial and post-nuptial settlement	I(PFD)A 1975, s 2(1)(f)
	Variation or discharge of secured periodical payments	I(PFD)A 1975, s 16
	Variation or revocation of maintenance agreements	I(PFD)A 1975, s 17
	Order setting aside disposition intended to defeat a claim under the I(PFD)A 1975	I(PFD)A 1975, ss 10, 11
	Treatment of deceased's former beneficial interest in joint property as part of his/her estate and not passing by survivorship	I(PFD)A 1975, s 9
	Interim order	I(PFD)A 1975, s 5
	Consequential orders	I(PFD)A 1975, s 2(4)

Chapter 13

Appeals

13.1 INTRODUCTION

CPR Part 52 and PD 52 apply to all appeals including those under the I(PFD)A 1975 and provide a uniform procedure for appeals in the county courts, the High Court and the Court of Appeal. The CPR are amended periodically and care should be taken to ensure that the correct rules are followed. It is important that the procedure laid down in the rules and Practice Directions are followed.

This chapter is not intended to provide a detailed commentary on the rules, Practice Directions and case studies. It sets out just the bare bones of the matters which should not be ignored.

13.2 PERMISSION TO APPEAL

Access to Justice Act 1999, s 54 provides that any right of appeal from the county court or the High Court and the Court of Appeal may be exercised only with permission.

CPR r 52.3(1) provides that permission to appeal from the decision of a judge in the county court or the High Court is required in all cases.

An application for permission to appeal should be made orally to the trial judge at the conclusion of the final hearing. If the application is refused or if the application is made subsequently, it should be made to the appeal court in the notice of appeal. If the application for permission is not made at the conclusion of the hearing the appellant should not seek to apply for leave in the lower court (CPR PD 52, paras 4.6 and 4.7). When applying for permission to appeal, a reason or explanation for seeking permission to appeal is required.

Permission to appeal will be given only where (CPR r 52.3(6)):

(1)   the court considers that the appeal would have a real prospect of success; or

(2)   there is some other compelling reason why the appeal should be heard.

'Real prospect of success' means a realistic as opposed to a fanciful prospect (see *Swain v Hillman* [2001] 1 All ER 91 and *Tanfern Limited v Cameron-MacDonald (Practice Note)* [2000] 1 WLR 131).

The respondent should not make any submissions on the merits of the application unless requested to do so. (See, further, *Jolly v Jay* [2002] EWCA Civ 277 for guidance on the role of the respondent when permission to appeal is sought.)

If permission to appeal is sought from the appeal court the application will be dealt with initially without a hearing. If the application is refused, the person seeking permission may request the decision to be reconsidered at an oral hearing (CPR r 52.3(4)) but note that where the Court of Appeal refuses permission to appeal without a hearing, it may, if it considers that the application is totally without merit, make an order that the person seeking permission may not request the decision to be reconsidered at a hearing (r 52.4(4A)).

An order giving permission to appeal may limit the issues to be heard and be made subject to conditions including the provision for security of the costs of an appeal.

13.3   ROUTE OF APPEAL

CPR PD 52, para 2A.1 sets out the court to which an appeal should be made (subject to obtaining any necessary permission) as follows:

Decision of	Appeal made to
District judge of a county court	Circuit Judge
Master or district judge of the High Court	High Court
Circuit Judge	High Court
High Court	Court of Appeal

13.4 TIME LIMITS

The appellant must file his/her notice of appeal at the Court of Appeal within 21 days of the date of the decision of the lower court, not the date on which the order was drawn up unless such period has been extended by direction of the lower court. An application for an extension of time should be made at the final hearing, to the trial judge (CPR r 52.4(2)).

13.5 STAY OF EXECUTION

Unless the appeal court or the lower court otherwise orders a stay, an appeal does not operate as a stay of any order made by the lower court. An application for a stay, if required, should be made at the conclusion of the final hearing, to the trial judge at the same time as the application for permission to appeal is made (CPR r 52.7). If an application for a stay is not made at the conclusion of the hearing, or is made but refused, a separate application for a stay, supported by evidence, may be made to the appeal court. A court will not grant a stay unless it is satisfied by cogent, full and frank evidence that there is a real risk of injustice.

13.6 GROUNDS OF APPEAL

An appeal will be allowed where the decision of the lower court was (CPR r 52.11(3)):

(1)   wrong; or
(2)   unjust because of a serious procedural or other irregularity in the proceedings in the lower court.

The effect of (1) (above) is that the appellant has to satisfy the appeal court that the decision of the lower court was:

(1)   against the weight of evidence;
(2)   wrong in law; or
(3)   an error in the exercise of the court's discretion.

Where an appeal is based on the argument that the decision of the lower court was against the weight of the evidence, the decision on appeal depends on the judge's assessment of the evidence of witnesses, their reliability and credibility; and it is only in exceptional circumstances that such an appeal will succeed.

In an appeal based on a point of law, it must be shown that the judge was plainly wrong on a point of law which was crucial to the decision. For examples, see *Moody v Stevenson* [1992] Ch 486 and *Re Besterman, Besterman v Grusin* [1984] Ch 458.

To succeed in an appeal based on an erroneous exercise of discretion, the appellant will have to show that the judge had misunderstood the facts; had taken account of irrelevant material; had failed to exercise his/her discretion; had made a decision that no reasonable judge could have made; or that there was no material before him/her to justify the decision he/she took. It has been stated that it must be shown that the decision was plainly wrong since it 'was outside the ambit within which a reasonable disagreement is possible' (see *G v G (Minors)* [1985] 1 WLR 647). See also *AEI Ltd v PPL* [1999] 1 WLR 1507, where it was stated:

> Before the court can interfere it must be shown that the judge has either erred in principle in his approach or has left out of account or has taken into account some feature that he should, or should not, have considered, or that his decision was plainly wrong because the court is forced to the conclusion that he has not balanced the various factors fairly in the scale.

In cases under the I(PFD)A 1975, where the judge has clearly gone beyond the s 3 criteria or given it an interpretation which cannot be justified and has re-written the deceased's will, it could be said that he/she has both erred in law and failed to exercise his/her discretion. (See *Barras v Harding* [2001] 1 FLR 138.)

13.7   PROCEDURE

13.7.1   Appellant's notice

Where the appellant seeks permission from the appeal court, the permission must be requested in the appellant's notice (CPR r 52.4(1)). The time allowed for filing the notice is 21 days after the date of the decision of the lower court. The filing of the notice should not be delayed until the appellant has received a copy of the transcript of the judgment under appeal. The notice should either contain the skeleton argument or be accompanied with a copy of the skeleton argument. A copy of the transcript or suitable record of the judgment (if available) should also be sent with the notice. If the skeleton argument is filed after the notice, it must be filed within 14 days of sending the notice to the court and it must be served as soon as it is filed (PD 52, paras 5.9, 5.21 and 5.32). The skeleton argument must contain the matters set out in PD 52, para 5.10. The appellant must also file with the notice of appeal the documents set out in PD 52, para 5.6(1) and an appeal bundle, which must include the documents set out in PD 52, para 5.6A(1). The bundle should be prepared in accordance with the provisions set out PD 52, paras 15.2–15.4. Where the time for filing the notice of appeal has expired, the appellant should file his notice and include in it an application for permission to appeal (if required), and for an extension of time. The appellant's notice must set out the reasons for the delay and the steps taken prior to the application being made (PD 52, para 5.2). If the notice does not include an application for permission to appeal, the respondent has the right to be heard. He must be informed of the notice of appeal, and a copy of the appeal bundle must also be sent to him. If an extension of time is granted, the appeal procedure set out in PD 52, paras 6.1–6.6 should be followed.

13.7.2 Amendment of appeal notice

An appeal may be amended only with the permission of the court. An application to amend and any opposition to it will normally be dealt with at the hearing, unless such a course would cause unnecessary expense or delay (PD 52, para 5.25). If that is likely to be the case, the court should be informed and a request made for the application for the amendment to be heard separately and before the substantive hearing.

13.7.3 Respondent's notice

The respondent may file and serve a respondent's notice. Unless the respondent wishes to cross appeal or wishes to support the lower court's decision for reasons other than those given in the lower court, he/she does not need to file a notice. A respondent who wishes to vary the order of the lower court in any way must appeal and permission will be required on the same basis as for an appellant. If he/she fails to do so, he/she will not be able to rely on any reason not relied on in the lower court unless the appeal court gives him/her permission to do. The respondent's notice must be filed within 14 days unless otherwise directed (CPR r 52.5(4) and (5)) and a copy sent to the appellant as soon as practicable and in any event within 7 days thereafter (r 52.5(6)). Where an extension of time is required, the extension must be sought in the respondent's notice and reasons given for the delay. The respondent's notice of appeal must be accompanied by his/her skeleton argument. If it is not filed with the notice, the skeleton argument must be filed and sent to the appellant within 14 days of the filing of the notice (PD 52, para 7.7(2)). If the respondent does not file a respondent's notice, the skeleton argument opposing the appellant's appeal must be filed and sent to the appellant at least 7 days before the appeal hearing (PD 52, para 7.7(2)).

The matters set out in this chapter are a brief outline of the appeal process. Practitioners and those wishing to appeal are advised to refer to CPR r 52 and the Practice Directions which supplement that rule.

13.8 PROCEDURAL TABLE

Appeal from a county court judge or High Court to the Court of Appeal

Who may appeal?	Any party to the proceedings with permission	SCA 1981, s 16 CCA 1984, s 77
Permission to appeal	Application should be made to the trial judge Application should be made to the Court of Appeal if leave is either not made or, if made, is refused	CPR r 52.3(2), (3) CPR PD 52, paras 4.6, 4.7
	Permission to appeal is applied for in the notice of appeal together with an appeal bundle skeleton argument, copy of the transcript of the judgment and the documents set out in CPR PD 52, paras 5.6 and 5.6A	CPR PD 52, paras 5.1, 5.6A
	Court considers the application without a hearing unless a hearing is requested. Respondent to the appeal is notified but does not need to attend unless requested to do so by the court	CPR PD 52, para 4.11 CPR PD 52, para 4.15
Fee payable	£200 for permission £400 if permission is not required	CPFO 2008, art 13.1
Procedure on appeal	Notice of appeal in Form N161 should be filed within 21 days of the order appealed. It must be served not later than 7 days after filing the notice of appeal. The appellant must file with the notice of appeal the documents, skeleton arguments, copy of the transcript of judgment and all relevant documents set out in CPR PD 52, paras 5.1 and 5.6	CPR r 52.4 CPR PD 52, para 5.19
Service	If permission to appeal is granted the appellant must serve on each respondent a copy of the bundle of documents within 7 days of permission being granted	CPR r 52.4(3) CPR PD 52, paras 5.2(1), 6.2

Documents to be lodged	Appellant must lodge at the Civil Appeal Registry with his notice:	CPR PD 52, para 5.6
	(a) a copy of his notice for each respondent and two further copies for the court	CPR PD 52, para 5.6A CPR PD 52, paras 5.10(3)–(5), 5.11
	(b) a copy of the skeleton argument	
	(c) a sealed copy of the order being appealed with the order giving or refusing permission to appeal together with reasons for the same	
	(d) witness statements and any sworn statements	
	(e) an appeal bundle	
	(f) any other documents	
	(g) a bundle of authorities must be filed 7 days before the hearing which must comply with the PD	
Respondent's notice	Respondent may file a notice	CPR r 52.5
	Respondent must file a notice if he/she seeks to cross appeal or seeks to oppose or uphold the decision of the lower court for different reasons within 14 days of service of the notice of appeal and serve it as soon as practicable and in any event within 7 days of filing his notice	CPR PD 52, paras 7.1–7.3
Fee on cross appeal	£200	CPFO 2008, art 13.2
Documents to be filed by the respondent	The same as that by the appellant (see above)	
Powers of the Court of Appeal	To give any judgment	CPR rr 52.10(1), (2), 52.11(2)
	To receive fresh evidence	
	To make any order which the lower court could have made	
	To order a retrial	
Further appeal	To the Supreme Court with permission of the Court of Appeal or the Supreme Court if leave is refused by the Court of Appeal	CRA 2005, s 40(2) SCR 2009, r 11(1) CPR PD 52, paras 15.19–15.21

Appeal to the Supreme Court

Permission to appeal is required to appeal from the decision of the Court of Appeal	If an appeal from the Court of Appeal from that court. If permission is refused, then from the Supreme Court	SCR 2009, r 10
Time limit	Within 28 days of the decision	SCR 2009, r 11
Documents for permission	Four copies of: (a) application for permission to appeal (b) copy of the order appealed from (c) copy of order refusing permission to appeal (d) transcript of judgment (e) any other orders and judgments given by the court (f) transcript of any unreported authorities (g) a chronology	SCR 2009, rr 11, 14 Supreme Court PD 3.2.1, PD 7
Respondent's objections	Respondent must, within 14 days of being served with the application for permission, file his notice of objection	SCR 2009, r 13 Supreme Court PD 3.1.8–3.1.10, PD 7, Form 3
Fee for application for permission	£800	SCFO 2009, fee 1.1
Fee for filing of notice of objection	£160	SCFO 2009, fee 1.2
Procedure on application for permission	Court will deal with application without a hearing and may: – grant or refuse permission – invite parties to make written submissions within 14 days – direct an oral hearing	SCR 2009, r 16 Supreme Court PD 3.3.1–3.4.8
Procedure if permission is granted	(a) the application for permission will stand as notice of appeal (b) the grounds will be those on which permission was granted and (c) within 14 days of the permission being granted the appellant must file notice of intention to proceed	SCR 2009, r 18

Fee on filing of notice of intention to proceed	£800	SCFO 2009, fee 2.1
Procedure where permission is not required	Notice of appeal must be filed within 42 days of the order appealed from with a copy of the order, order granting permission and fee of £1600	SCR 2009, r 19 Supreme Court PD 4, PD 7 SCFO 2009, fee 2.2
Respondent's cross appeal	If wishing to participate in the appeal, the respondent must within 14 days of service of notice of intention to proceed file notice in the appropriate form and pay a fee of £320 If the respondent wishes to uphold the decision on different grounds than those given by the lower court, he/she must clearly state this in the written case Permission to cross appeal is required and SCR 2009, Part 2 applies	SCR 2009, r 21 Supreme Court PD 7, Form 3 SCFO 2009, fee 2.4 SCR 2009, rr 25(2), 10–17 Supreme Court PD 8.3.1–8.3.8
Documents	Within 112 days after filing the notice of intention to proceed or notice of appeal, the appellant must lodge with the court the documents referred to in the Supreme Court PD 5.1.2–5.1.5 with the number of copies referred to and in the order mentioned. All documents must be paginated and an index of contents must be included	SCR 2009, r 22 Supreme Court PD 5.1.2–5.1.5
Fee	Payable on filing statement of relevant facts and appendix of documents: £4820	SCFO 2009, fee 2.5
Exchange of parties' cases	Appellant and respondent, every intervenor or advocate to the court must exchange and file their respective written cases	SCR 2009, r 22(4) Supreme Court PD 6.3.1–6.3.13
Core volumes	No later than 14 days after the date fixed for the hearing the appellant must file 10 core volumes and 10 volumes of authorities in the order set out in the PD	SCR 2009, rr 23, 24 Supreme Court PD 6.4.1–6.4.4, 6.5.1
Hearing	Is in open court	SCR 2009, r 27

Powers of court	All the powers of the court below. May also: – affirm, set aside or vary the order – remit any issue for determination by the court below – direct a retrial or hearing – order payment of interest – make an order for costs

Appendices

A1 PRECEDENTS

A1.1 Application for a standing search: Non-Contentious Probate Rules 1987, Schedule 1, Form 2

IN THE HIGH COURT OF JUSTICE

FAMILY DIVISION

[PRINCIPAL] [DISTRICT PROBATE] REGISTRY

In the Estate of [   ], Deceased

I apply for the entry of a standing search so that there shall be sent to me an office copy of every grant of representation in England and Wales in the estate of:

Full name of the deceased: [   ]

Full address: [   ]

Alternative or alias name: [   ]

Exact date of death: [   ]

which either has issued not more than twelve months before the entry of this application or issues within six months thereafter.

Signed: [   ]

Name in block letters: [   ]

Address: [   ]

Reference (if any): [   ]

A1.2   Example claims to be included in the Part 8 claim form

The claimant claims:

1. An order that such reasonable financial provision may be made for the claimant from the estate of [name] deceased as the court thinks just.

2. An order be made for the claimant for such periodical payments and for such term out of the estate of the deceased as may be just.

3. An order for the payment to the claimant of such lump sum[s] out of the estate of the deceased as may be just.

4. The property at [address] or such other property forming part of the estate of the deceased as the court may specify be transferred to the claimant.

5. An order for the settlement for the benefit of the claimant of such property comprised in the estate of [name] the deceased as may be specified by the court and on such terms as the court thinks just.

6. An order for the acquisition out of the property forming part of the net estate of the deceased of such property as may be specified and for the transfer of the property so acquired to the claimant or for the settlement thereof for the benefit of the claimant.

7. An order for the variation of the ante-nuptial settlement [give details of the settlement] for the benefit of the claimant [who must be the surviving spouse of the marriage to whom the settlement related] or [name] the child of the deceased and the claimant.

8. An order pursuant to section 9 of the Inheritance (Provision for Family and Dependants) Act 1975 that the severable share of [name] the deceased at the date of [his] [her] death in the property at [insert address] be treated as forming part of the net estate of the deceased.

9. An order pursuant to section 10 of the Inheritance (Provision for Family and Dependants) Act 1975 that [identify the donee of the disposition] do provide such sum or sums of money or other property for the making of reasonable financial provision for the claimant.

10. An order pursuant to section 11 of the Inheritance (Provision for Family and Dependants) Act 1975 that [name] do provide the following sums of money and property for the purposes of making an order for reasonable financial provision for the claimant:

    (a)   the sum of £[ ] contracted to be paid by the deceased to [name];

    (b)   [identify any property which was the subject of the contract].

11. An order pursuant to section 11 of the Inheritance (Provision for Family and Dependants) Act 1975 directing the personal representatives of the deceased not to [make any payment] [transfer any property under the contract] [make any further payment] [transfer any further property].

12. An order for the variation of: [set out the details of the orders under the Matrimonial Causes Act 1973 of which variation is sought; see I(PFD)A 1975, ss 16–18].

13. An order pursuant to section 5 of the Inheritance (Provision for Family and Dependants) Act 1975 for interim relief.

14. An order giving permission to issue the claim notwithstanding that more than six months have elapsed from the date on which representation with respect to the estate of the deceased was granted namely since [date] on the grounds set out in the statement of the claimant served with this claim.

15. [Set out details of any injunctive relief sought, for example, a restraining order or a freezing order.]

16. An order that the claimant's cost of this claim be paid out of the deceased's estate.

A1.3   Witness statement by the claimant (a surviving spouse)

IN THE HIGH COURT OF JUSTICE   CLAIM NO [   ]

FAMILY DIVISION

[PRINCIPAL REGISTRY] [DISTRICT REGISTRY]

In the Matter of the Estate of [   ], Deceased

And in the Matter of the Inheritance (Provision for Family and Dependants) Act 1975

BETWEEN:

[Name]   Claimant

– and –

[Name]   First Defendant

(the personal representative of the deceased)

– and –

[Name]   Second Defendant

[All interested parties should be made defendants; see Chapter 12.]

WITNESS STATEMENT OF THE CLAIMANT

I, [name] the above named claimant of [address] unemployed will say as follows:

1. I am the widow of [   ], deceased. The deceased and I were married on 10 March 1970. A copy of our marriage certificate is attached to this statement and marked '...'. We had three children, a daughter and two sons.

2. The deceased died on 21 June 2009. A certified copy of his death certificate is attached to this statement marked '...'. The deceased was domiciled in England and Wales.

3. A grant of probate with respect to the deceased's estate was taken out on 14 August 2009 by [names] his executors from the Principal Registry. An official copy of the grant with the deceased's last will dated 12 January 2009 is marked '...'.

4. To the best of my knowledge and belief the net estate is valued at approximately £ [give the value] and consists of:

[set out the details, or if a schedule has been prepared by the executors and is available, refer to the schedule and exhibit it to the statement].

5. [Set out the history of the marriage and such of the s 3 factors as may be relevant (see Chapter 5); if possible set out a schedule of income from all sources, details of capital and property and a list of expenditure. The information should also include the relevant factors which apply under Matrimonial Causes Act 1973, s 24.]

6. [If an order under ss 9–11 is sought, set out details of the reasons for seeking such an order.]

7. [Set out details of the substantive orders for financial provision sought and reasons for seeking the orders.]

STATEMENT OF TRUTH

[See CPR PD 32, para 32.20.]

I believe that the facts set out in this statement are true.

Signed: [   ]

A1.4   Witness statement of the personal representative

IN THE HIGH COURT OF JUSTICE   CLAIM NO [   ]

FAMILY DIVISION

[PRINCIPAL REGISTRY] [DISTRICT REGISTRY]

In the Matter of the Estate of [   ], Deceased

And in the Matter of the Inheritance (Provision for Family and Dependants) Act 1975

BETWEEN:

[Name]	<u>Claimant</u>
– and –	
[Name]	<u>First Defendant</u>
(the personal representative of the deceased)	
– and –	
[Name]	<u>Second Defendant</u>

[All interested parties should be made defendants; see Chapter 12.]

WITNESS STATEMENT OF THE FIRST DEFENDANT

I [name] of [address] solicitor will say as follows:

1. I am a solicitor of the Supreme Court and partner in the firm of Messrs [   ].

2. I am one of two executors of the will of the deceased. I have personal and professional knowledge of the deceased and his estate and knowledge derived from my involvement as an executor of the estate.

3. The grant of probate in relation to the deceased's estate was granted to me and [name] out of the District Registry at [   ] on 14 August 2009. A true copy of the grant is attached to my statement marked '...'.

4. The gross value of the deceased's estate was accounted for probate at £ [   ] and the net estate at £ [   ] The estate consists of:

The property at [address] valued at £ 350,000

Premium Bonds:	£ 5,000
National Savings Certificates:	£ 2,000
Cash at [ ] Bank:	£ 300
Total	£ 357,300

[Set out all identifiable assets and values, if necessary in a Schedule and the total.]

5. The deceased was entitled to receive a death benefit from his employers under the terms of his employers' pension scheme. The deceased nominated [name] his cohabitee to receive the said benefit. The death benefit amounted to £ [ ] and the said sum was paid to [name] on [date].

6. The liabilities of the deceased at the date of his death were as follows:

    [Set these out, including, for example, credit card debts, utility bills, loans, sums due under HP agreements.]

7. The funeral expenses of the deceased amounted to £ [ ].

8. The whole of the estate was liable to inheritance tax subject to exemptions. Full details of the property comprised in the estate are set out in the Schedule attached to this statement marked '...'.

9. The estate has not yet been administered.

10. [If there has been delay in making the claim and the application for an extension is opposed, set out the reasons for the objection to the application.]

11. [If an order under s 9 is sought by the claimant, set out details of the assets and any other information which may be of assistance to the court; similarly if the claim includes a claim for orders under ss 10 and 11.]

12. The persons beneficially entitled to the deceased's estate are: [set out the names and addresses of all beneficiaries, and if any of the beneficiaries is a child or under a disability, give details].

13. [If there are matters to which the court's attention needs to be drawn these should be dealt with in addition to answering any matter set out in the claimant's statement.]

A1.5   Witness statement by a cohabitant of the deceased

IN THE HIGH COURT OF JUSTICE   CLAIM NO [   ]

FAMILY DIVISION

[PRINCIPAL REGISTRY] [DISTRICT REGISTRY]

In the Matter of the Estate of [   ], Deceased

And in the Matter of the Inheritance (Provision for Family and Dependants) Act 1975

BETWEEN:

[Name]	Claimant
– and –	
[Name]	First Defendant
(the personal representative of the deceased)	
– and –	
[Name]	Second Defendant

[All interested parties should be made defendants; see Chapter 12.]

WITNESS STATEMENT OF [THE CLAIMANT]

I [name] of [address] will say:

1. The deceased was married to [name] on [date]. They had no children.

2. I met the deceased in January 2000 and shortly thereafter he left his wife [name] and came to live with me. I was then working and had lived in a flat at [address] which was owned by me. The deceased purchased the property at [address] in which I now live. I sold my flat and the net proceeds of sale were used to pay the deposit on the property. The property was purchased in the sole name of the deceased as I trusted him. The mortgage was also in his sole name. Thereafter we lived in the property as husband and wife.

3. We have two children, a son, Thomas, born on 1 January 2001 and a daughter, Samantha, born on 25 December 2003.

4. When I met the deceased I was working full time as a manager of the local supermarket store. The deceased did not like me working and when I became pregnant he asked me to give up work and be a full time carer of our child. Since then I and my children have been fully dependent on him.

5. Both children have attended public schools and the fees were paid for by the deceased. The deceased provided us with a high standard of living. We had two holidays a year with the children in Europe and sometimes further afield.

6. When the deceased began suffering from ill health I considered taking up employment to help with the finances but he assured me that there was no need for me to do so and that he would ensure that I and the children would be provided for if anything should happen to him. He also assured me that he would arrange for the property to be transferred into my name so that I would not have to worry if anything should happen to him.

7. Before the deceased could attend his solicitor to make a will he died. He was domiciled in England and Wales. A copy of his death certificate is attached to this statement marked '...'.

8. As a result of his failure to make a new will I and the children have been left without support and his widow is the main beneficiary under the will. I produce a copy of the grant taken out by his executors marked '...'.

9. Since the death of the deceased I have had to rely on state benefits. I have been unable to discharge the school fees. I have no other income. [Set out details of the claimant's earning capacity if any.]

10. I have the following outgoings: [list the outgoings or produce a schedule].

11. I am informed that the deceased's widow has insisted that the property in which I live with my children should be sold. If I have to vacate the home I and the children will become homeless. My solicitors have given to the executors and the solicitors acting for the widow all the relevant information and have been trying to negotiate a settlement. Negotiations had been progressing well. My solicitors were urged not to issue proceedings with a view to saving costs particularly as the negotiations had reached the final stages and the agreement was in the process of being drafted. Unfortunately the widow has withdrawn from the negotiations. I was obliged to apply for public funding to issue proceedings and this caused some delay. The delay, however, has been minimal. Proceedings were not issued immediately as there appeared to be a realistic hope of reaching an agreement without recourse to litigation. The estate has not yet been administered. No prejudice has been caused to any beneficiary. I therefore request that I be granted permission to pursue my claim

notwithstanding the fact that the proceedings were not issued within six months from the date when the grant was taken out.

12.   If permission to make the claim is refused I and my children will suffer extreme hardship and an injustice.

13.   [Set out in detail the orders sought and the reasons.]

14.   Statement of truth [see CPR PD 32, para 32.20].

I believe that the facts set out in this statement are true.

[This precedent should be adapted where the claimant is a same sex cohabitant].

A1.6 Witness statement of an adult person treated as a child of the family

IN THE HIGH COURT OF JUSTICE   CLAIM NO [   ]

FAMILY DIVISION

[PRINCIPAL REGISTRY] [DISTRICT REGISTRY]

In the Matter of the Estate of [   ], Deceased

And in the Matter of the Inheritance (Provision for Family and Dependants) Act 1975

BETWEEN:

[Name]	<u>Claimant</u>
– and –	
[Name]	<u>First Defendant</u>
(the personal representative of the deceased)	
– and –	
[Name]	<u>Second Defendant</u>

[All interested parties should be made defendants; see Chapter 12.]

I [name] of [address] will say as follows:

1. I am the deceased's step-son. My mother married the deceased on [date]. A copy of my mother's marriage certificate is attached to this statement marked '...' and a copy of my birth certificate is attached marked '...'.

2. I was fourteen years of age when my mother married the deceased. I lived with them and the deceased treated me as his son. My mother and the deceased had two children from their marriage. They are Solomon born on [date] and Jacob born on [date]. The deceased did not treat me any differently after the birth of my step-brothers. We all went to public schools. The deceased encouraged me to take up medicine. He paid all my college tuition fees and paid all my other expenses.

3. The deceased died domiciled in England and Wales on [date]. Copies of his death certificate and of his will and the grant of representation of the deceased's estate are attached to this statement marked '...', '...' and '...' respectively.

4. I believe that the deceased's estate is valued at £ 2.5 million. There is no provision made for me in his will although he has made provision for my step-brothers who are also adults and in full-time education.

5. My father has never seen me or maintained me. I am informed by my mother that he had a brief relationship with her when he was serving in the USA forces and was stationed here. When he discovered that she was pregnant he terminated the relationship and returned to the USA. His whereabouts are not known. I always regarded the deceased as my father.

6. [Set out the claimant's financial circumstances and any other matter of relevance under s 3.]

A1.7   Draft orders

The precedents below are intended to be a guide only. The orders made by the court vary depending on the circumstances of each individual case.

IN THE HIGH COURT OF JUSTICE   CLAIM NO[   ]

FAMILY DIVISION

[PRINCIPAL REGISTRY] [DISTRICT REGISTRY]

In the Matter of the Estate of [   ], Deceased

And in the Matter of the Inheritance (Provision for Family and Dependants) Act 1975

BETWEEN:

[Name]   Claimant

– and –

[Name]   First Defendant

(the personal representative of the deceased)

– and –

[Name]   Second Defendant

[All interested parties should be made defendants; see Chapter 12.]

UPON HEARING [counsel] [solicitor] for the Claimant and [counsel] [solicitor] for the Defendant[s] and the Third Defendant appearing in person [set out the representations or otherwise of the parties before the court]

AND UPON READING the documents in the court file and the agreed bundle of documents

AND UPON THE COURT being satisfied that the disposition of the estate of the deceased [name] effected by [his/her] [will] [intestacy] is not such as to make reasonable financial provision for the Claimant

IT IS ORDERED pursuant to section 2 of the Inheritance (Provision for Family and Dependants) Act 1975 that:

PERIODICAL PAYMENTS

There be paid out of the estate of the Deceased [name] to the Claimant [name] periodical payments to the Claimant at the rate of £ [   ] per annum payable monthly from 1 February 2010 and thereafter on the first day of each calendar month until [the claimant shall remarry] [the claimant shall cease his/her full time education etc] [if the payments relate to the income from assets, set out the rate which is equal to whole of the income] [or as the case may be] of the estate comprised by [   ].

LUMP SUM

There be paid to the Claimant the lump sum of £ [   ] out of the net estate of the Deceased within [   ] days from the date of this order; or

There be paid to the Claimant the lump sum of £ [   ] out of the estate of the Deceased in four instalments of £ [   ] payable on 31 March 20[   ], 30 June 20[   ], 30 September 20[   ] and 30 December 20[   ] [if the payments are to be made in, for example, 12 equal monthly instalments, state the same or as the case may be.]

TRANSFER OF PROPERTY

There be transferred to the Claimant from the estate of the Deceased within three months from the date of this order the property at [address].

SETTLEMENT OF PROPERTY

The property at [address] forming part of the net estate of the Deceased be settled for the benefit of the Claimant [set out the settlement ordered, eg for life] and that the form of the deed of settlement be agreed between the Claimant and the Defendants or in default of agreement be referred to conveyancing Counsel to settle.

ACQUISITION OF ASSETS

From the net estate of the Deceased there be purchased the property at [address] and that [the same be transferred into the name of the Claimant absolutely] [such property be settled for the benefit of the Claimant to the effect that [set out the terms of the settlement]] and that the form of deed of settlement be agreed and in default of agreement be referred to conveyancing Counsel to settle.

VARIATION OF ANTE-NUPTIAL/POST-NUPTIAL SETTLEMENT

The [ante-] [post-] nuptial settlement made between [name] and the Deceased, etc be varied so as to provide as follows: [set out the variation(s)].

ORDER UNDER SECTION 9

The severable share of the Deceased in the property at [address] be treated as part of the estate of the Deceased in [set out the proportions directed] for the purposes of facilitating the making of the financial provision set out in this Order.

ORDER UNDER SECTION 10 OR 11

That pursuant to section [10] [11] of the Inheritance (Provision for Family and Dependants) Act 1975 [name] is directed to provide the sum of £ [   ] to the Claimant [or transfer to the Claimant the property at [address]] [within [   ] days of the making of this order] or [within [   ] days of the receipt of this order by him/her].

ORDER UNDER SECTION 4

Pursuant to section 4 of the Inheritance (Provision for Family and Dependants) Act 1975, IT IS ORDERED THAT the period of six months prescribed by section 4 of the Inheritance (Provision for Family and Dependants) Act 1975 be extended until [   ].

DRAFT CONSENT ORDER SETTING OUT COMPROMISE OF CLAIM AND DECLARATION OF TRUST ON BEHALF OF CLAIMANT UNDER DISABILITY

UPON HEARING Counsel for the parties and reading the consents of the defendants

AND UPON READING the evidence filed and documents recorded in the court file

AND UPON THE COURT being of the opinion that the disposition of the estate of [name] the Testator effected by [his/her] will is not such as to make reasonable financial provision for the maintenance of [name] the Claimant, the Testator's son

AND UPON THE COURT being satisfied that the terms of compromise reached between the parties are for the benefit of the Claimant

THE COURT DOES APPROVE THE SAID TERMS OF COMPROMISE AND IT IT IS ORDERED THAT:

1. The First Defendant [name] as personal representative of the Testator be at liberty to and so carry the said terms of compromise into effect.

2. Pursuant to section 2(1)(d) of the Inheritance (Provision for Family and Dependants) Act 1975 that the residue of the estate of the said Testator including all accumulations of income [or otherwise identify

the property to be settled] shall be settled upon the trusts named in the will for the benefit of the Claimant in accordance with the terms set out in the Schedule hereto.

3. [Set out details of any adjustments which need to be made to any clauses in the will relating to any legacies or bequests.]

4. The costs of the Claimant and the Defendants be referred to a district judge for detailed assessment and paid out of the residuary estate of the Testator [or set out details of the agreement if any on costs].

Dated this [   ] day of [   ] 20[   ]

SCHEDULE

That the Testator's estate shall henceforth be administered as if:

1. The Testator had omitted from his Will Clause 3 and Clause 6(j) therein contained.

2. The Testator had included in his Will the following clause in substitution of Clause 2 as therein contained:

    (a) My trustees shall hold the remainder of the trust fund after payment of the foregoing legacies (hereinafter called 'the discretionary fund') upon the following trusts and with and subject to the following powers:

    (b) (i)   During the life of my son [name] (hereinafter 'my said son') my trustees shall have power in their absolute discretion to pay or apply the whole or any part or proportion of the income of the discretionary fund as they think fit to or for the maintenance care or benefit of my said son with power to pay such income to any person or persons responsible for his care without seeing to the application thereof.

         (ii) After expiration of the period of [twelve years] [or insert appropriate term] from my death my trustees shall have the further power in their absolute discretion to pay any income then arising which in their opinion is surplus to the present and future needs of my said son to the persons who would be entitled thereto if he were dead and in equal shares.

         (iii) During the period of [eighteen years] [or insert appropriate term] from my death while my said son is living my trustees shall accumulate the income of the discretionary fund which shall not be paid or applied as aforesaid as an accretion to the capital thereof but shall have power to pay or apply such accumulations to or for the maintenance, care or benefit of my said son during his life as if the same were income of the then current year.

(iv) If my said son is still living at the expiration of the said period of [eighteen years] my trustees shall thereafter during the remainder of his life pay all income then arising which shall not be paid or applied under the foregoing powers to the persons who would be entitled thereto if he were dead and in equal shares.

(c) My trustees being at least two in number or a trust corporation shall have the following powers in addition to those set out in Clause 9 of the Will and the following provisions shall apply [set out the powers, for example:]

(i) power to sell, exchange, convey, lease, mortgage, charge, agree to let, licence or otherwise conduct the management of any land of any tenure that may at any time be subject to the trusts hereof as if my trustees were the sole beneficial owners thereof;

(ii) power to change or vary any property or investments for the time being subject to the trusts hereof;

(iii) power to invest [set out details];

(iv) power to permit my son to have use and enjoyment of any chattel forming part of the discretionary fund in such manner and subject to such conditions (if any) as my trustees may consider reasonable and without being liable to account for any consequential loss;

(v) power to invest the whole or any part of the discretionary fund in the purchase or improvement of any dwelling-house or flat and to permit the same to be used as a residence for my son whether alone or jointly with another person without being required to insist upon the payment by any other person whether or not a joint occupier thereof of a market rent;

(vi) power to apply any part of the capital or income of the discretionary fund towards meeting the cost of –

A altering or adapting any residential accommodation in the ownership of any person or body for the more convenient occupation thereof by my said son as a home;

B purchasing domestic appliances or procuring domestic assistance for my said son;

C   holidays for my said son or the expenses incurred by any person with whom he resides to enable such person to accompany him on holiday or to make provision for a carer to care for him.

(d)   After the death of my said son my trustees shall stand possessed of the discretionary fund and the income thereof (or so much thereof as may not have been paid or applied under any trust or power affecting the same) in trust for the residuary beneficiaries (that is to say [name them]) in equal shares PROVIDED THAT for the avoidance of doubt should any of those persons entitled to the discretionary fund predecease my said son their share of the discretionary fund shall accrue to their estates AND PROVIDED FURTHER that (notwithstanding the aforementioned trusts) my trustees may pay out of the capital of the discretionary fund such funeral expenses in respect of my said son as they may consider appropriate and reasonable.

(e)   Any of my trustees may join in exercising any of the powers under this clause notwithstanding that he/she is one of the beneficiaries and will or may benefit from any such exercise.

(f)   Any of my trustees being a solicitor, accountant or other person engaged in any profession or business shall be entitled to be paid all usual professional or proper charges for business transacted time expended acts done by him/her or any partner of his/hers in connection with the trusts hereof including acts which a trustee not being in any profession or business could have done personally.

A2 INHERITANCE (PROVISION FOR FAMILY AND DEPENDANTS) ACT 1975

1 Application for financial provision from deceased's estate

(1) Where after the commencement of this Act a person dies domiciled in England and Wales and is survived by any of the following persons–

[(a) the spouse or civil partner of the deceased;

(b) a former spouse or former civil partner of the deceased, but not one who has formed a subsequent marriage or civil partnership;]

[(ba) any person (not being a person included in paragraph (a) or (b) above) to whom subsection (1A) [or (1B)] below applies;]

(c) a child of the deceased;

(d) any person (not being a child of the deceased) who, in the case of any marriage [or civil partnership] to which the deceased was at any time a party, was treated by the deceased as a child of the family in relation to that marriage [or civil partnership];

(e) any person (not being a person included in the foregoing paragraphs of this subsection) who immediately before the death of the deceased was being maintained, either wholly or partly, by the deceased;

that person may apply to the court for an order under section 2 of this Act on the ground that the disposition of the deceased's estate effected by his will or the law relating to intestacy, or the combination of his will and that law, is not such as to make reasonable financial provision for the applicant.

[(1A) This subsection applies to a person if the deceased died on or after 1st January 1996 and, during the whole of the period of two years ending immediately before the date when the deceased died, the person was living–

(a) in the same household as the deceased, and

(b) as the husband or wife of the deceased.]

[(1B) This subsection applies to a person if for the whole of the period of two years ending immediately before the date when the deceased died the person was living–

(a) in the same household as the deceased, and

(b) as the civil partner of the deceased.]

(2) In this Act "reasonable financial provision"–

(a) in the case of an application made by virtue of subsection (1)(a) above by the husband or wife of the deceased (except where *the marriage with the deceased was the subject of a decree of judicial separation and at the date of death the decree was in force*[, at the date of death, a separation order under the Family Law Act 1996 was in force in relation to the marriage] and the separation was continuing), means such financial provision as it would be reasonable in all the circumstances of the case for a husband or wife to receive, whether or not that provision is required for his or her maintenance;

[(aa) in the case of an application made by virtue of subsection (1)(a) above by the civil partner of the deceased (except where, at the date of death, a separation order under Chapter 2 of Part 2 of the Civil Partnership Act 2004 was in force in relation to the civil partnership and the separation was continuing), means such financial provision as it would be reasonable in all the circumstances of the case for a civil partner to receive, whether or not that provision is required for his or her maintenance;]

(b) in the case of any other application made by virtue of subsection (1) above, means such financial provision as it would be reasonable in all the circumstances of the case for the applicant to receive for his maintenance.

(3) For the purposes of subsection (1)(e) above, a person shall be treated as being maintained by the deceased, either wholly or partly, as the case may be, if the deceased, otherwise than for full valuable consideration, was making a substantial contribution in money or money's worth towards the reasonable needs of that person.

AMENDMENTS

Section 1(1)(a), (b) substituted by the Civil Partnership Act 2004, s 71, Sch 4, Pt 2, para 15(1), (2).

Section 1(1)(ba) inserted by the Law Reform (Succession) Act 1995, s 2(2).

Section 1(1)(ba): words "or (1B)" in square brackets inserted by the Civil Partnership Act 2004, s 71, Sch 4, Pt 2, para 15(1), (3).

Section 1(1)(d): words "or civil partnership" in square brackets in both places they occur inserted by the Civil Partnership Act 2004, s 71, Sch 4, Pt 2, para 15(1), (4).

Section 1(1A) inserted by the Law Reform (Succession) Act 1995, s 2(3).

Section 1(1B) inserted by the Civil Partnership Act 2004, s 71, Sch 4, Pt 2, para 15(1), (5).

Section 1(2)(a): words from "the marriage with" to "was in force" in italics repealed and subsequent words in square brackets substituted by the Family Law Act 1996, s 66(1), Sch 8, para 27(2), as from a day to be appointed; for savings see s 66(2), Sch 9, para 5 thereof.

Section 1(2)(aa) inserted by the Civil Partnership Act 2004, s 71, Sch 4, Pt 2, para 15(1), (6).

2 Powers of court to make orders

(1) Subject to the provisions of this Act, where an application is made for an order under this section, the court may, if it is satisfied that the disposition of the deceased's estate effected by his will or the law relating to intestacy, or the combination of his will and that law, is not such as to make reasonable financial provision for the applicant, make any one or more of the following orders–

(a) an order for the making to the applicant out of the net estate of the deceased of such periodical payments and for such term as may be specified in the order;

(b) an order for the payment to the applicant out of that estate of a lump sum of such amount as may be so specified;

(c) an order for the transfer to the applicant of such property comprised in that estate as may be so specified;

(d) an order for the settlement for the benefit of the applicant of such property comprised in that estate as may be so specified;

(e) an order for the acquisition out of property comprised in that estate of such property as may be so specified and for the transfer of the property so acquired to the applicant or for the settlement thereof for his benefit;

(f) an order varying any ante-nuptial or post-nuptial settlement (including such a settlement made by will) made on the parties to a marriage to which the deceased was one of the parties, the variation being for the benefit of the surviving party to that marriage, or any child of that marriage, or any person who was treated by the deceased as a child of the family in relation to that marriage;

[(g) an order varying any settlement made–

(i) during the subsistence of a civil partnership formed by the deceased, or

(ii) in anticipation of the formation of a civil partnership by the deceased,

on the civil partners (including such a settlement made by will), the variation being for the benefit of the surviving civil partner, or any child of both the civil partners, or any person who was treated by the deceased as a child of the family in relation to that civil partnership].

(2) An order under subsection (1)(a) above providing for the making out of the net estate of the deceased of periodical payments may provide for–

(a) payments of such amount as may be specified in the order,

(b) payments equal to the whole of the income of the net estate or of such portion thereof as may be so specified,

(c) payments equal to the whole of the income of such part of the net estate as the court may direct to be set aside or appropriated for the making out of the income thereof of payments under this section,

or may provide for the amount of the payments or any of them to be determined in any other way the court thinks fit.

(3) Where an order under subsection (1)(a) above provides for the making of payments of an amount specified in the order, the order may direct that such part of the net estate as may be so specified shall be set aside or appropriated for the making out of the income thereof of those payments; but no larger part of the net estate shall be so set aside or appropriated than is sufficient, at the date of the order, to produce by the income thereof the amount required for the making of those payments.

(4) An order under this section may contain such consequential and supplemental provisions as the court thinks necessary or expedient for the

purpose of giving effect to the order or for the purpose of securing that the order operates fairly as between one beneficiary of the estate of the deceased and another and may, in particular, but without prejudice to the generality of this subsection–

(a) order any person who holds any property which forms part of the net estate of the deceased to make such payment or transfer such property as may be specified in the order;

(b) varying the disposition of the deceased's estate effected by the will or the law relating to intestacy, or by both the will and the law relating to intestacy, in such manner as the court thinks fair and reasonable having regard to the provisions of the order and all the circumstances of the case;

(c) confer on the trustees of any property which is the subject of an order under this section such powers as appear to the court to be necessary or expedient.

AMENDMENTS

Section 2(1)(g) inserted by the Civil Partnership Act 2004, s 71, Sch 4, Pt 2, para 16.

3 Matters to which court is to have regard in exercising powers under s 2

(1) Where an application is made for an order under section 2 of this Act, the court shall, in determining whether the disposition of the deceased's estate effected by his will or the law relating to intestacy, or the combination of his will and that law, is such as to make reasonable financial provision for the applicant and, if the court considers that reasonable financial provision has not been made, in determining whether and in what manner it shall exercise its powers under that section, have regard to the following matters, that is to say–

(a) the financial resources and financial needs which the applicant has or is likely to have in the foreseeable future;

(b) the financial resources and financial needs which any other applicant for an order under section 2 of this Act has or is likely to have in the foreseeable future;

(c) the financial resources and financial needs which any beneficiary of the estate of the deceased has or is likely to have in the foreseeable future;

(d) any obligations and responsibilities which the deceased had towards any applicant for an order under the said section 2 or towards any beneficiary of the estate of the deceased;

(e) the size and nature of the net estate of the deceased;

(f) any physical or mental disability of any applicant for an order under the said section 2 or any beneficiary of the estate of the deceased;

(g) any other matter, including the conduct of the applicant or any other person, which in the circumstances of the case the court may consider relevant.

(2) [This subsection applies, without prejudice to the generality of paragraph (g) of subsection (1) above, where an application for an order under section 2 of this Act is made by virtue of section 1(1)(a) or (b) of this Act.]

The court shall, in addition to the matters specifically mentioned in paragraphs (a) to (f) of that subsection, have regard to–

(a) the age of the applicant and the duration of the marriage [or civil partnership];

(b) the contribution made by the applicant to the welfare of the family of the deceased, including any contribution made by looking after the home or caring for the family.

. . . In the case of an application by the wife or husband of the deceased, the court shall also, unless at the date of death a *decree of judicial separation* [separation order under the Family Law Act 1996] was in force and the separation was continuing, have regard to the provision which the applicant might reasonably have expected to receive if on the day on which the deceased died the marriage, instead of being terminated by death, had been terminated by *a decree of divorce* [a divorce order].

[In the case of an application by the civil partner of the deceased, the court shall also, unless at the date of the death a separation order under Chapter 2 of Part 2 of the Civil Partnership Act 2004 was in force and the separation was continuing, have regard to the provision which the applicant might reasonably have expected to receive if on the day on which the deceased died the civil partnership, instead of being terminated by death, had been terminated by a dissolution order.]

[(2A) Without prejudice to the generality of paragraph (g) of subsection (1) above, where an application for an order under section 2 of this Act is made by virtue of section 1(1)(ba) of this Act, the court shall, in addition to the matters specifically mentioned in paragraphs (a) to (f) of that subsection, have regard to–

(a) the age of the applicant and the length of the period during which the applicant lived as the husband or wife [or civil partner] of the deceased and in the same household as the deceased;

(b) the contribution made by the applicant to the welfare of the family of the deceased, including any contribution made by looking after the home or caring for the family.]

(3) Without prejudice to the generality of paragraph (g) of subsection (1) above, where an application for an order under section 2 of this Act is made by virtue of section 1(1)(c) or 1(1)(d) of this Act, the court shall, in addition to the matters specifically mentioned in paragraphs (a) to (f) of that subsection, have regard to the manner in which the applicant was being or in which he might expect to be educated or trained, and where the application is made by virtue of section 1(1)(d) the court shall also have regard–

(a) to whether the deceased had assumed any responsibility for the applicant's maintenance and, if so, to the extent to which and the basis upon which the deceased assumed that responsibility and to the length of time for which the deceased discharged that responsibility;

(b) to whether in assuming and discharging that responsibility the deceased did so knowing that the applicant was not his own child;

(c) to the liability of any other person to maintain the applicant.

(4) Without prejudice to the generality of paragraph (g) of subsection (1) above, where an application for an order under section 2 of this Act is made by virtue of section 1(1)(e) of this Act, the court shall, in addition to the matters specifically mentioned in paragraphs (a) to (f) of that subsection, have regard to the extent to which and the basis upon which the deceased assumed responsibility for the maintenance of the applicant, and to the length of time for which the deceased discharged that responsibility.

(5) In considering the matters to which the court is required to have regard under this section, the court shall take into account the facts as known to the court at the date of the hearing.

(6) In considering the financial resources of any person for the purposes of this section the court shall take into account his earning capacity and in

considering the financial needs of any person for the purposes of this section the court shall take into account his financial obligations and responsibilities.

AMENDMENTS

Section 3(2): words from "This subsection applies," to "of this Act." in square brackets substituted by the Civil Partnership Act 2004, s 71, Sch 4, Pt 2, para 17(1), (2).

Section 3(2)(a): words "or civil partnership" in square brackets inserted by the Civil Partnership Act 2004, s 71, Sch 4, Pt 2, para 17(1), (3).

Section 3(2): word omitted repealed by the Civil Partnership Act 2004, s 261(4), Sch 30.

Section 3(2): words "decree of judicial separation" and "a decree of divorce" in italics repealed and subsequent words in square brackets substituted by the Family Law Act 1996, s 66(1), Sch 8, para 27(3), as from a day to be appointed; for savings see s 66(2), Sch 9, para 5 thereof.

Section 3(2): words from "In the case" to "a dissolution order." in square brackets inserted by the Civil Partnership Act 2004, s 71, Sch 4, Pt 2, para 17(1), (5).

Section 3(2A) inserted by the Law Reform (Succession) Act 1995, s 2(4).

Section 3(2A)(a): words "or civil partner" in square brackets inserted by the Civil Partnership Act 2004, s 71, Sch 4, Pt 2, para 18.

4 Time-limit for applications

An application for an order under section 2 of this Act shall not, except with the permission of the court, be made after the end of the period of six months from the date on which representation with respect to the estate of the deceased is first taken out.

5 Interim orders

(1) Where on an application for an order under section 3 of this Act it appears to the court–

(a) that the applicant is in immediate need of financial assistance, but it is not yet possible to determine what order (if any) should be made under that section; and

(b) that property forming part of the net estate of the deceased is or can be made available to meet the need of the applicant;

the court may order that, subject to such conditions or restrictions, if any, as the court may impose and to any further order of the court, there shall be paid to the applicant out of the net estate of the deceased such sum or sums and (if more than one) at such intervals as the court thinks reasonable; and the court may order that, subject to the provisions of this Act, such payments are to be made until such date as the court may specify, not being later than the date on which the court either makes an order under the said section 2 or decides not to exercise its powers under that section.

(2) Subsections (2), (3) and (4) of section 2 of this Act shall apply in relation to an order under this section as they apply in relation to an order under that section.

(3) In determining what order, if any, should be made under this section the court shall, so far as the urgency of the case admits, have regard to the same matters as those to which the court is required to have regard under section 3 of this Act.

(4) An order made under section 2 of this Act may provide that any sum paid to the applicant by virtue of this section shall be treated to such an extent and in such manner as may be provided by that order as having been paid on account of any payment provided for by that order.

6 Variation, discharge, etc of orders for periodical payments

(1) Subject to the provisions of this Act, where the court has made an order under section 2(1)(a) of this Act (in this section referred to as "the original order") for the making of periodical payments to any person (in this section referred to as "the original recipient"), the court, on an application under this section, shall have power by order to vary or discharge the original order or to suspend any provision of it temporarily and to revive the operation of any provision so suspended.

(2) Without prejudice to the generality of subsection (1) above, an order made on an application for the variation of the original order may–

(a) provide for the making out of any relevant property of such periodical payments and for such term as may be specified in the order to any person who has applied, or would but for section 4 of this Act be entitled to apply, for an order under section 2 of this Act (whether or not, in the case of any application, an order was made in favour of the applicant);

(b) provide for the payment out of any relevant property of a lump sum of such amount as may be so specified to the original recipient or to any such person as is mentioned in paragraph (a) above;

(c) provide for the transfer of the relevant property, or such part thereof as may be so specified, to the original recipient or to any such person as is so mentioned.

(3) Where the original order provides that any periodical payments payable thereunder to the original recipient are to cease on the occurrence of an event specified in the order [(other than the formation of a subsequent marriage or civil partnership by a former spouse or former civil partner)] or on the expiration of a period so specified, then, if, before the end of the period of six months from the date of the occurrence of that event or of the expiration of that period, an application is made for an order under this section, the court shall have power to make any order which it would have had power to make if the application had been made before the date (whether in favour of the original recipient or any such person as is mentioned in subsection (2)(a) above and whether having effect from that date or from such later date as the court may specify).

(4) Any reference in this section to the original order shall include a reference to an order made under this section and any reference in this section to the original recipient shall include a reference to any person to whom periodical payments are required to be made by virtue of an order under this section.

(5) An application under this section may be made by any of the following persons, that is to say–

(a) any person who by virtue of section 1(1) of this Act has applied, or would but for section 4 of this Act be entitled to apply, for an order under section 2 of this Act,

(b) the personal representatives of the deceased,

(c) the trustees of any relevant property, and

(d) any beneficiary of the estate of the deceased.

(6) An order under this section may only affect–

(a) property the income of which is at the date of the order applicable wholly or in part for the making of periodical payments to any person who has applied for an order under this Act, or

(b) in the case of an application under subsection (3) above in respect of payments which have ceased to be payable on the occurrence of an event or the expiration of a period, property the income of which was so applicable immediately before the occurrence of that event or the expiration of that period, as the case may be,

and any such property as is mentioned in paragraph (a) or (b) above is in subsections (2) and (5) above referred to as "relevant property".

(7) In exercising the powers conferred by this section the court shall have regard to all circumstances of the case, including any change in any of the matters to which the court was required to have regard when making the order to which the application relates.

(8) Where the court makes an order under this section, it may give such consequential directions as it thinks necessary or expedient having regard to the provisions of the order.

(9) No such order as is mentioned in section 2(1)(d), (e) or (f), 9, 10 or 11 of this Act shall be made on an application under this section.

(10) For the avoidance of doubt it is hereby declared that, in relation to an order which provides for the making of periodical payments which are to cease on the occurrence of an event specified in the order [(other than the formation of a subsequent marriage or civil partnership by a former spouse or former civil partner)] or on the expiration of a period so specified, the power to vary an order includes power to provide for the making of periodical payments after the expiration of that period or the occurrence of that event.

AMENDMENTS

Section 6(3): words "(other than the formation of a subsequent marriage or civil partnership by a former spouse or former civil partner)" in square brackets substituted by the Civil Partnership Act 2004, s 71, Sch 4, Pt 2, para 19.

Section 6(10): words "(other than the formation of a subsequent marriage or civil partnership by a former spouse or former civil partner)" in square brackets substituted by the Civil Partnership Act 2004, s 71, Sch 4, Pt 2, para 19.

7 Payment of lump sums by instalments

(1) An order under section 2(1)(b) or 6(2)(b) of this Act for the payment of a lump sum may provide for the payment of that sum by instalments of such amount as may be specified in the order.

(2) Where an order is made by virtue of subsection (1) above, the court shall have power, on an application made by the person to whom the lump sum is payable, by the personal representatives of the deceased or by the trustees of the property out of which the lump sum is payable, to vary that order by varying the number of instalments payable, the amount of any instalment and the date on which any instalment becomes payable.

8 Property treated as part of "net estate"

(1) Where a deceased person has in accordance with the provisions of any enactment nominated any person to receive any sum of money or other property on his death and that nomination is in force at the time of his death, that sum of money, after deducting therefrom any inheritance tax payable in respect thereof, or that other property, to the extent of the value thereof at the date of the death of the deceased after deducting therefrom any inheritance tax so payable, shall be treated for the purposes of this Act as part of the net estate of the deceased; but this subsection shall not render any person liable for having paid that sum or transferred that other property to the person named in the nomination in accordance with the directions given in the nomination.

(2) Where any sum of money or other property is received by any person as a *donatio mortis causa* made by a deceased person, that sum of money, after deducting therefrom any inheritance tax payable thereon, or that other property, to the extent of the value thereof at the date of the death of the deceased after deducting therefrom any inheritance tax so payable, shall be treated for the purposes of this Act as part of the net estate of the deceased; but this subsection shall not render any person liable for having paid that sum or transferred that other property in order to give effect to that *donatio mortis causa*.

(3) The amount of inheritance tax to be deducted for the purposes of this section shall not exceed the amount of that tax which has been borne by the person nominated by the deceased or, as the case may be, the person who has received a sum of money or other property as a *donatio mortis causa*.

9 Property held on a joint tenancy

(1) Where a deceased person was immediately before his death beneficially entitled to a joint tenancy of any property, then, if, before the end of the

period of six months from the date on which representation with respect to the estate of the deceased was first taken out, an application is made for an order under section 2 of this Act, the court for the purpose of facilitating the making of financial provision for the applicant under this Act may order that the deceased's severable share of that property, at the value thereof immediately before his death, shall, to such extent as appears to the court to be just in all the circumstances of the case, be treated for the purposes of this Act as part of the net estate of the deceased.

(2) In determining the extent to which any severable share is to be treated as part of the net estate of the deceased by virtue of an order under subsection (1) above, the court shall have regard to any inheritance tax payable in respect of that severable share.

(3) Where an order is made under subsection (1) above, the provisions of this section shall not render any person liable for anything done by him before the order was made.

(4) For the avoidance of doubt it is hereby declared that for the purposes of this section there may be a joint tenancy of a chose in action.

10 Dispositions intended to defeat applications for financial provision

(1) Where an application is made to the court for an order under section 2 of this Act, the applicant may, in the proceedings on that application, apply to the court for an order under subsection (2) below.

(2) Where on an application under subsection (1) above the court is satisfied–

(a) that, less than six years before the date of the death of the deceased, the deceased with the intention of defeating an application for financial provision under this Act made a disposition, and

(b) that full valuable consideration for that disposition was not given by the person to whom or for the benefit of whom the disposition was made (in this section referred to as "the donee") or by any other person, and

(c) that the exercise of the powers conferred by this section would facilitate the making of financial provision for the applicant under this Act,

then, subject to the provisions of this section and of sections 12 and 13 of this Act, the court may order the donee (whether or not at the date of the order he holds any interest in the property disposed of to him or for his benefit by the deceased) to provide, for the purpose of the making of that financial provision, such sum of money or other property as may be specified in the order.

(3) Where an order is made under subsection (2) above as respects any disposition made by the deceased which consisted of the payment of money to or for the benefit of the donee, the amount of any sum of money or the value of any property ordered to be provided under that subsection shall not exceed the amount of the payment made by the deceased after deducting therefrom any inheritance tax borne by the donee in respect of that payment.

(4) Where an order is made under subsection (2) above as respects any disposition made by the deceased which consisted of the transfer of property (other than a sum of money) to or for the benefit of the donee, the amount of any sum of money or the value of any property ordered to be provided under that subsection shall not exceed the value at the date of the death of the deceased of the property disposed of by him to or for the benefit of the donee (or if that property has been disposed of by the person to whom it was transferred by the deceased, the value at the date of that disposal thereof) after deducting therefrom any inheritance tax borne by the donee in respect of the transfer of that property by the deceased.

(5) Where an application (in this subsection referred to as "the original application") is made for an order under subsection (2) above in relation to any disposition, then, if on an application under this subsection by the donee or by any applicant for an order under section 2 of this Act the court is satisfied–

(a) that, less than six years before the date of the death of the deceased, the deceased with the intention of defeating an application for financial provision under this Act made a disposition other than the disposition which is the subject of the original application, and

(b) that full valuable consideration for that other disposition was not given by the person to whom or for the benefit of whom that other disposition was made or by any other person,

the court may exercise in relation to the person to whom or for the benefit of whom that other disposition was made the powers which the court would have had under subsection (2) above if the original application had been made in respect of that other disposition and the court had been satisfied as to the matters set out in paragraphs (a), (b) and (c) of that subsection; and where any application is made under this subsection, any reference in this section (except in subsection (2)(b)) to the donee shall include a reference to the person to whom or for the benefit of whom that other disposition was made.

(6) In determining whether and in what manner to exercise its powers under this section, the court shall have regard to the circumstances in which any disposition was made and any valuable consideration which was given therefor, the relationship, if any, of the donee to the deceased, the conduct and financial resources of the donee and all the other circumstances of the case.

(7) In this section "disposition" does not include–

(a) any provision in a will, any such nomination as is mentioned in section 8(1) of this Act or any *donatio mortis causa*, or

(b) any appointment of property made, otherwise than by will, in the exercise of a special power of appointment,

but, subject to these exceptions, includes any payment of money (including the payment of a premium under a policy of assurance) and any conveyance, assurance, appointment or gift of property of any description, whether made by an instrument or otherwise.

(8) The provisions of this section do not apply to any disposition made before the commencement of this Act.

11 Contracts to leave property by will

(1) Where an application is made to a court for an order under section 2 of this Act, the applicant may, in the proceedings on that application, apply to the court for an order under this section.

(2) Where on an application under subsection (1) above the court is satisfied–

(a) that the deceased made a contract by which he agreed to leave by his will a sum of money or other property to any person or by which he agreed that a sum of money or other property would be paid or transferred to any person out of his estate, and

(b) that the deceased made that contract with the intention of defeating an application for financial provision under this Act, and

(c) that when the contract was made full valuable consideration for that contract was not given or promised by the person with whom or for the benefit of whom the contract was made (in this section referred to as "the donee") or by any other person, and

(d) that the exercise of the powers conferred by this section would facilitate the making of financial provision for the applicant under this Act,

then, subject to the provisions of this section and of sections 12 and 13 of this Act, the court may make any one or more of the following orders, that is to say–

(i) if any money has been paid or any other property has been transferred to or for the benefit of the donee in accordance with the contract, an order directing the donee to provide, for the purpose of the making of that financial provision, such sum of money or other property as may be specified in the order;

(ii) if the money or all the money has not been paid or the property or all the property has not been transferred in accordance with the contract, an order directing the personal representatives not to make any payment or transfer any property, or not to make any further payment or transfer any further property, as the case may be, in accordance therewith or directing the personal representatives only to make such payment or transfer such property as may be specified in the order.

(3) Notwithstanding anything in subsection (2) above, the court may exercise its powers thereunder in relation to any contract made by the deceased only to the extent that the court considers that the amount of any sum of money paid or to be paid or the value of any property transferred or to be transferred in accordance with the contract exceeds the value of any valuable consideration given or to be given for that contract, and for this purpose the court shall have regard to the value of property at the date of the hearing.

(4) In determining whether and in what manner to exercise its powers under this section, the court shall have regard to the circumstances in which the contract was made, the relationship, if any, of the donee to the deceased, the conduct and financial resources of the donee and all the other circumstances of the case.

(5) Where an order has been made under subsection (2) above in relation to any contract the rights of any person to enforce that contract or to recover damages or to obtain other relief for the breach thereof shall be subject to any adjustment made by the court under section 12(3) of this Act and shall survive to such extent only as is consistent with giving effect to the terms of that order.

(6) The provisions of this section do not apply to a contract made before the commencement of this Act.

12 Provisions supplementary to ss 10 and 11

(1) Where the exercise of any of the powers conferred by section 10 or 11 of this Act is conditional on the court being satisfied that a disposition or contract was made by a deceased person with the intention of defeating an application for financial provision under this Act, that condition shall be fulfilled if the court is of the opinion that, on a balance of probabilities, the intention of the deceased (though not necessarily his sole intention) in making the disposition or contract was to prevent an order for financial provision being made under this Act or to reduce the amount of the provision which might otherwise be granted by an order thereunder.

(2) Where an application is made under section 11 of this Act with respect to any contract made by the deceased and no valuable consideration was given or promised by any person for that contract then, notwithstanding anything in subsection (1) above, it shall be presumed, unless the contrary is shown, that the deceased made that contract with the intention of defeating an application for financial provision under this Act.

(3) Where the court makes an order under section 10 or 11 of this Act it may give such consequential directions as it thinks fit (including directions requiring the making of any payment or the transfer of any property) for giving effect to the order or for securing a fair adjustment of the rights of the persons affected thereby.

(4) Any power conferred on the court by the said section 10 or 11 to order the donee, in relation to any disposition or contract, to provide any sum of money or other property shall be exercisable in like manner in relation to the personal representative of the donee, and–

(a) any reference in section 10(4) to the disposal of property by the donee shall include a reference to disposal by the personal representative of the donee, and

(b) any reference in section 10(5) to an application by the donee under that subsection shall include a reference to an application by the personal representative of the donee;

but the court shall not have power under the said section 10 or 11 to make an order in respect of any property forming part of the estate of the donee which has been distributed by the personal representative; and the personal representative shall not be liable for having distributed any such property before he has notice of the making of an application under the said section 10 or 11 on the ground that he ought to have taken into account the possibility that such an application would be made.

13 Provisions as to trustees in relation to ss 10 and 11

(1) Where an application is made for–

(a) an order under section 10 of this Act in respect of a disposition made by the deceased to any person as a trustee, or

(b) an order under section 11 of this Act in respect of any payment made or property transferred, in accordance with a contract made by the deceased, to any person as a trustee,

the powers of the court under the said section 10 or 11 to order that trustee to provide a sum of money or other property shall be subject to the following limitation (in addition, in a case of an application under section 10, to any provision regarding the deduction of inheritance tax) namely, that the amount of any sum of money or the value of any property ordered to be provided–

(i) in the case of an application in respect of a disposition which consisted of the payment of money or an application in respect of the payment of money in accordance with a contract, shall not exceed the aggregate of so much of that money as is at the date of the order in the hands of the trustee and the value at that date of any property which represents that money or is derived therefrom and is at that date in the hands of the trustee;

(ii) in the case of an application in respect of a disposition which consisted of the transfer of property (other than a sum of money) or an application in respect of the transfer of property (other than a sum of money) in accordance with a contract, shall not exceed the aggregate of the value at the date of the order of so much of that property as is at that date in the hands of the trustee and the value at that date of any property which represents the first mentioned property or is derived therefrom and is at that date in the hands of the trustee.

(2) Where any such application is made in respect of a disposition made to any person as a trustee or in respect of any payment made or property transferred in pursuance of a contract to any person as a trustee, the trustee shall not be liable for having distributed any money or other property on the ground that he ought to have taken into account the possibility that such an application would be made.

(3) Where any such application is made in respect of a disposition made to any person as a trustee or in respect of any payment made or property transferred in accordance with a contract to any person as a trustee, any reference in the said section 10 or 11 to the donee shall be construed as

including a reference to the trustee or trustees for the time being of the trust in question and any reference in subsection (1) or (2) above to a trustee shall be construed in the same way.

14 Provision as to cases where no financial relief was granted in divorce proceedings, etc

(1) Where, within twelve months from the date on which *a decree of divorce or nullity of marriage has been made absolute or a decree of judicial separation has been granted* [a divorce order or separation order has been made under the Family Law Act 1996 in relation to a marriage or a decree of nullity of marriage has been made absolute], a party to the marriage dies and–

(a) an application for a financial provision order under *section 23* [section 22A or 23] of the Matrimonial Causes Act 1973 or a property adjustment order under *section 24* [section 23A or 24] of that Act has not been made by the other party to that marriage, or

(b) such an application has been made but the proceedings thereon have not been determined at the time of the death of the deceased,

then, if an application for an order under section 2 of this Act is made by that other party, the court shall, notwithstanding anything in section 1 or section 3 of this Act, have power, if it thinks it just to do so, to treat that party for the purposes of that application as if *the decree of divorce or nullity of marriage had not been made absolute or the decree of judicial separation had not been granted, as the case may be* [, as the case may be, the divorce order or separation order had not been made or the decree of nullity had not been made absolute].

(2) This section shall not apply in relation to a *decree of judicial separation* [separation order] unless at the date of the death of the deceased the *decree* [the order] was in force and the separation was continuing.

AMENDMENTS

Section 14(1), (2): words in italics prospectively repealed with savings and subsequent words in square brackets prospectively substituted with savings by the Family Law Act 1996, s 66(1), Sch 8, para 27(4), as from a day to be appointed; for savings see s 66(2), Sch 9, para 5 thereof.

[14A Provision as to cases where no financial relief was granted in proceedings for the dissolution etc of a civil partnership]

[(1) Subsection (2) below applies where–

(a) a dissolution order, nullity order, separation order or presumption of death order has been made under Chapter 2 of Part 2 of the Civil Partnership Act 2004 in relation to a civil partnership,

(b) one of the civil partners dies within twelve months from the date on which the order is made, and

(c) either–

(i) an application for a financial provision order under Part 1 of Schedule 5 to that Act or a property adjustment order under Part 2 of that Schedule has not been made by the other civil partner, or

(ii) such an application has been made but the proceedings on the application have not been determined at the time of the death of the deceased.

(2) If an application for an order under section 2 of this Act is made by the surviving civil partner, the court shall, notwithstanding anything in section 1 or section 3 of this Act, have power, if it thinks it just to do so, to treat the surviving civil partner as if the order mentioned in subsection (1)(a) above had not been made.

(3) This section shall not apply in relation to a separation order unless at the date of the death of the deceased the separation order was in force and the separation was continuing.]

AMENDMENTS

Inserted by the Civil Partnership Act 2004, s 71, Sch 4, Pt 2, para 20.

15 Restriction imposed in divorce proceedings, etc on application under this Act

[(1) *On the grant of a decree of divorce, a decree of nullity of marriage or a decree of judicial separation or at any time thereafter* [At any time when the court–

(a) has jurisdiction under section 23A or 24 of the Matrimonial Causes Act 1973 to make a property adjustment order in relation to a marriage; or

(b) would have such jurisdiction if either the jurisdiction had not already been exercised or an application for such an order were made with the leave of the court,]

the court, if it considers it just to do so, may, on the application of either party to the marriage, order that the other party to the marriage shall not on the death of the applicant be entitled to apply for an order under section 2 of this Act.

In this subsection "the court" means the High Court or, where a county court has jurisdiction by virtue of Part V of the Matrimonial and Family Proceedings Act 1984, a county court.]

(2) In the case of a decree of divorce or nullity of marriage an order may be made under subsection (1) above before or after the decree is made absolute, but if it is made before the decree is made absolute it shall not take effect unless the decree is made absolute.

(3) Where an order made under subsection (1) above on the grant of a decree of divorce or nullity of marriage has come into force with respect to a party to a marriage, then, on the death of the other party to that marriage, the court shall not entertain any application for an order under section 2 of this Act made by the first-mentioned party.

(4) Where an order made under subsection (1) above on the grant of a decree of judicial separation has come into force with respect to any party to a marriage, then, if the other party to that marriage dies while the decree is in force and the separation is continuing, the court shall not entertain any application for an order under section 2 of this Act made by the first-mentioned party.

[(2) An order made under subsection (1) above with respect to any party to a marriage has effect in accordance with subsection (3) below at any time–

(a) after the marriage has been dissolved;

(b) after a decree of nullity has been made absolute in relation to the marriage; and

(c) while a separation order under the Family Law Act 1996 is in force in relation to the marriage and the separation is continuing.

(3) If at any time when an order made under subsection (1) above with respect to any party to a marriage has effect the other party to the marriage dies, the court shall not entertain any application made by the surviving party to the marriage for an order under section 2 of this Act.]

AMENDMENTS

Section 15(1) substituted by the Matrimonial and Family Proceedings Act 1984, s 8; words in italics prospectively repealed with savings and subsequent words in square brackets prospectively substituted with savings by the Family Law Act 1996, s 66(1), Sch 8, para 27(5), as from a day to be appointed; for savings see s 66(2), Sch 9, para 5 thereof.

Section 15(2)–(4) prospectively substituted with savings, by subsequent sub-ss (2), (3), by the Family Law Act 1996, s 66(1), Sch 8, para 27(6), as from a day to be appointed; for savings see s 66(2), Sch 9, para 5 thereof.

[15ZA Restriction imposed in proceedings for the dissolution etc of a civil partnership on application under this Act]

[(1) On making a dissolution order, nullity order, separation order or presumption of death order under Chapter 2 of Part 2 of the Civil Partnership Act 2004, or at any time after making such an order, the court, if it considers it just to do so, may, on the application of either of the civil partners, order that the other civil partner shall not on the death of the applicant be entitled to apply for an order under section 2 of this Act.

(2) In subsection (1) above "the court" means the High Court or, where a county court has jurisdiction by virtue of Part 5 of the Matrimonial and Family Proceedings Act 1984, a county court.

(3) In the case of a dissolution order, nullity order or presumption of death order ("the main order") an order may be made under subsection (1) above before (as well as after) the main order is made final, but if made before the main order is made final it shall not take effect unless the main order is made final.

(4) Where an order under subsection (1) above made in connection with a dissolution order, nullity order or presumption of death order has come into force with respect to a civil partner, then, on the death of the other civil partner, the court shall not entertain any application for an order under section 2 of this Act made by the surviving civil partner.

(5) Where an order under subsection (1) above made in connection with a separation order has come into force with respect to a civil partner, then, if the other civil partner dies while the separation order is in force and the separation is continuing, the court shall not entertain any application for an order under section 2 of this Act made by the surviving civil partner.]

AMENDMENTS

Inserted by the Civil Partnership Act 2004, s 71, Sch 4, Pt 2, para 21.

[15A Restriction imposed in proceedings under Matrimonial and Family Proceedings Act 1984 on application under this Act]

[(1) On making an order under section 17 of the Matrimonial and Family Proceedings Act 1984 (orders for financial provision and property adjustment following overseas divorces, etc) the court, if it considers it just to do so, may, on the application of either party to the marriage, order that the other party to the marriage shall not on the death of the applicant be entitled to apply for an order under section 2 of this Act.

In this subsection "the court" means the High Court or, where a county court has jurisdiction by virtue of Part V of the Matrimonial and Family Proceedings Act 1984, a county court.

(2) Where an order under subsection (1) above has been made with respect to a party to a marriage which has been dissolved or annulled, then, on the death of the other party to that marriage, the court shall not entertain an application under section 2 of this Act made by the first-mentioned party.

(3) Where an order under subsection (1) above has been made with respect to a party to a marriage the parties to which have been legally separated, then, if the other party to the marriage dies while the legal separation is in force, the court shall not entertain an application under section 2 of this Act made by the first-mentioned party.]

AMENDMENTS

Inserted by the Matrimonial and Family Proceedings Act 1984, s 25.

[15B Restriction imposed in proceedings under Schedule 7 to the Civil Partnership Act 2004 on application under this Act]

[(1) On making an order under paragraph 9 of Schedule 7 to the Civil Partnership Act 2004 (orders for financial provision, property adjustment and pension-sharing following overseas dissolution etc of civil partnership) the court, if it considers it just to do so, may, on the application of either of the civil partners, order that the other civil partner shall not on the death of the applicant be entitled to apply for an order under section 2 of this Act.

(2) In subsection (1) above "the court" means the High Court or, where a county court has jurisdiction by virtue of Part 5 of the Matrimonial and Family Proceedings Act 1984, a county court.

(3) Where an order under subsection (1) above has been made with respect to one of the civil partners in a case where a civil partnership has been dissolved or annulled, then, on the death of the other civil partner, the court shall not entertain an application under section 2 of this Act made by the surviving civil partner.

(4) Where an order under subsection (1) above has been made with respect to one of the civil partners in a case where civil partners have been legally separated, then, if the other civil partner dies while the legal separation is in force, the court shall not entertain an application under section 2 of this Act made by the surviving civil partner.]

AMENDMENTS

Inserted by the Civil Partnership Act 2004, s 71, Sch 4, Pt 2, para 22.

16 Variation and discharge of secured periodical payments orders made under Matrimonial Causes Act 1973

(1) Where an application for an order under section 2 of this Act is made to the court by any person who was at the time of the death of the deceased entitled to payments from the deceased under a secured periodical payments order made under the Matrimonial Causes Act 1973 [or Schedule 5 to the Civil Partnership Act 2004], then, in the proceedings on that application, the court shall have power, if an application is made under this section by that person or by the personal representative of the deceased, to vary or discharge that periodical payments order or to revive the operation of any provision thereof which has been suspended under section 31 of that Act [of 1973 or Part 11 of that Schedule].

(2) In exercising the powers conferred by this section the court shall have regard to all the circumstances of the case, including any order which the court proposes to make under section 2 or section 5 of this Act and any change (whether resulting from the death of the deceased or otherwise) in any of the matters to which the court was required to have regard when making the secured periodical payments order.

(3) The powers exercisable by the court under this section in relation to an order shall be exercisable also in relation to any instrument executed in pursuance of the order.

AMENDMENTS

Section 16(1): words "or Schedule 5 to the Civil Partnership Act 2004" in square brackets inserted by the Civil Partnership Act 2004, s 71, Sch 4, Pt 2, para 23(a).

Section 16(1): words "of 1973 or Part 11 of that Schedule" in square brackets inserted by the Civil Partnership Act 2004, s 71, Sch 4, Pt 2, para 23(b).

17 Variation and revocation of maintenance agreements

(1) Where an application for an order under section 2 of this Act is made to the court by any person who was at the time of the death of the deceased entitled to payments from the deceased under a maintenance agreement which provided for the continuation of payments under the agreement after the death of the deceased, then, in the proceedings on that application, the court shall have power, if an application is made under this section by that person or by the personal representative of the deceased, to vary or revoke that agreement.

(2) In exercising the powers conferred by this section the court shall have regard to all the circumstances of the case, including any order which the court proposes to make under section 2 or section 5 of this Act and any change (whether resulting from the death of the deceased or otherwise) in any of the circumstances in the light of which the agreement was made.

(3) If a maintenance agreement is varied by the court under this section the like consequences shall ensue as if the variation had been made immediately before the death of the deceased by agreement between the parties and for valuable consideration.

(4) In this section "maintenance agreement", in relation to a deceased person, means any agreement made, whether in writing or not and whether before or after the commencement of this Act, by the deceased with any person with whom he [formed a marriage or civil partnership], being an agreement which contained provisions governing the rights and liabilities towards one another when living separately of the parties to that marriage [or of the civil partners] (whether or not the marriage [or civil partnership] has been dissolved or annulled) in respect of the making or securing of payments or the disposition or use of any property, including such rights and liabilities with respect to the maintenance or education of any child, whether or not a child of the deceased

or a person who was treated by the deceased as a child of the family in relation to that marriage [or civil partnership].

AMENDMENTS

Section 17(4): words "formed a marriage or civil partnership" in square brackets substituted by the Civil Partnership Act 2004, s 71, Sch 4, Pt 2, para 24(a).

Section 17(4): words "or of the civil partners" in square brackets inserted by the Civil Partnership Act 2004, s 71, Sch 4, Pt 2, para 24(b).

Section 17(4): words "or civil partnership" in square brackets in both places they occur inserted by the Civil Partnership Act 2004, s 71, Sch 4, Pt 2, para 24(c).

18 Availability of court's powers under this Act in applications under ss 31 and 36 of the Matrimonial Causes Act 1973

(1) Where–

(a) a person against whom a secured periodical payments order was made under the Matrimonial Causes Act 1973 has died and an application is made under section 31(6) of that Act for the variation or discharge of that order or for the revival of the operation of any provision thereof which has been suspended, or

(b) a party to a maintenance agreement within the meaning of section 34 of that Act has died, the agreement being one which provides for the continuation of payments thereunder after the death of one of the parties, and an application is made under section 36(1) of that Act for the alteration of the agreement under section 35 thereof,

the court shall have power to direct that the application made under the said section 31(6) or 36(1) shall be deemed to have been accompanied by an application for an order under section 2 of this Act.

(2) Where the court gives a direction under subsection (1) above it shall have power, in the proceedings on the application under the said section 31(6) or 36(1), to make any order which the court would have had power to make under the provisions of this Act if the application under the said section 31(6) or 36(1), as the case may be, had been made jointly with an application for an order under the said section 2; and the court shall have power to give such consequential directions as may be necessary for enabling the court to

exercise any of the powers available to the court under this Act in the case of an application for an order under section 2.

(3) Where an order made under section 15(1) of this Act is in force with respect to a party to a marriage, the court shall not give a direction under subsection (1) above with respect to any application made under the said section 31(6) or 36(1) by that party on the death of the other party.

[18A Availability of court's powers under this Act in applications under paragraphs 60 and 73 of Schedule 5 to the Civil Partnership Act 2004]

[(1) Where–

(a) a person against whom a secured periodical payments order was made under Schedule 5 to the Civil Partnership Act 2004 has died and an application is made under paragraph 60 of that Schedule for the variation or discharge of that order or for the revival of the operation of any suspended provision of the order, or

(b) a party to a maintenance agreement within the meaning of Part 13 of that Schedule has died, the agreement being one which provides for the continuation of payments under the agreement after the death of one of the parties, and an application is made under paragraph 73 of that Schedule for the alteration of the agreement under paragraph 69 of that Schedule,

the court shall have power to direct that the application made under paragraph 60 or 73 of that Schedule shall be deemed to have been accompanied by an application for an order under section 2 of this Act.

(2) Where the court gives a direction under subsection (1) above it shall have power, in the proceedings on the application under paragraph 60 or 73 of that Schedule, to make any order which the court would have had power to make under the provisions of this Act if the application under that paragraph had been made jointly with an application for an order under section 2 of this Act; and the court shall have power to give such consequential directions as may be necessary for enabling the court to exercise any of the powers available to the court under this Act in the case of an application for an order under section 2.

(3) Where an order made under section 15ZA(1) of this Act is in force with respect to a civil partner, the court shall not give a direction under subsection (1) above with respect to any application made under paragraph 60 or 73 of that Schedule by that civil partner on the death of the other civil partner.]

AMENDMENTS

Inserted by the Civil Partnership Act 2004, s 71, Sch 4, Pt 2, para 25.

19 Effect, duration and form of orders

(1) Where an order is made under section 2 of this Act then for all purposes, including the purposes of the enactments relating to inheritance tax, the will or the law relating to intestacy, or both the will and the law relating to intestacy, as the case may be, shall have effect and be deemed to have had effect as from the deceased's death subject to the provisions of the order.

(2) Any order made under section 2 or 5 of this Act in favour of–

(a) an applicant who was the [former spouse or former civil partner] of the deceased, or

(b) an applicant who was the husband or wife of the deceased in a case where *the marriage with the deceased was the subject of a decree of judicial separation and at the date of death the decree was in force*[, at the date of death, a separation order under the Family Law Act 1996 was in force in relation to the marriage with the deceased] and the separation was continuing, [or

(c) an applicant who was the civil partner of the deceased in a case where, at the date of death, a separation order under Chapter 2 of Part 2 of the Civil Partnership Act 2004 was in force in relation to their civil partnership and the separation was continuing,]

shall, in so far as it provides for the making of periodical payments, cease to have effect [on the formation by the applicant of a subsequent marriage or civil partnership, except in relation to any arrears due under the order on the date of the formation of the subsequent marriage or civil partnership].

(3) A copy of every order made under this Act [other than an order made under section 15(1) [or 15ZA(1)] of this Act] shall be sent to the principal registry of the Family Division for entry and filing, and a memorandum of the order shall be endorsed on, or permanently annexed to, the probate or letters of administration under which the estate is being administered.

AMENDMENTS

Section 19(2): in para (a) words "former spouse or former civil partner" in square brackets substituted by the Civil Partnership Act 2004, s 71, Sch 4, Pt 2, para 26(1), (2).

Section 19(2)(b): words from "the marriage with" to "was in force" in italics repealed and subsequent words in square brackets substituted by the Family Law Act 1996, s 66(1), Sch 8, para 27(7), as from a day to be appointed; for savings see s 66(2), Sch 9, para 5 thereof.

Section 19(2)(c) inserted, and word "or" immediately preceding it inserted by the Civil Partnership Act 2004, s 71, Sch 4, Pt 2, para 26(1), (3).

Section 19(2): words from "on the formation" to "or civil partnership" in square brackets substituted by the Civil Partnership Act 2004, s 71, Sch 4, Pt 2, para 26(1), (4).

Section 19(3): words from "other than an order" to "of this Act" in square brackets inserted by the Administration of Justice Act 1982, s 52.

Section 19(3): words "or 15ZA(1)" in square brackets inserted by the Civil Partnership Act 2004, s 71, Sch 4, Pt 2, para 26(1), (5).

20 Provisions as to personal representatives

(1) The provisions of this Act shall not render the personal representative of a deceased person liable for having distributed any part of the estate of the deceased, after the end of the period of six months from the date on which representation with respect to the estate of the deceased is first taken out, on the ground that he ought to have taken into account the possibility–

(a) that the court might permit the making of an application for an order under section 2 of this Act after the end of that period, or

(b) that, where an order has been made under the said section 2, the court might exercise in relation thereto the powers conferred on it by section 6 of this Act,

but this subsection shall not prejudice any power to recover, by reason of the making of an order under this Act, any part of the estate so distributed.

(2) Where the personal representative of a deceased person pays any sum directed by an order under section 5 of this Act to be paid out of the deceased's net estate, he shall not be under any liability by reason of that estate not being sufficient to make the payment, unless at the time of making the payment he has reasonable cause to believe that the estate is not sufficient.

(3) Where a deceased person entered into a contract by which he agreed to leave by his will any sum of money or other property to any person or by

which he agreed that a sum of money or other property would be paid or transferred to any person out of his estate, then, if the personal representative of the deceased has reason to believe that the deceased entered into the contract with the intention of defeating an application for financial provision under this Act, he may, notwithstanding anything in that contract, postpone the payment of that sum of money or the transfer of that property until the expiration of the period of six months from the date on which representation with respect to the estate of the deceased is first taken out or, if during that period an application is made for an order under section 2 of this Act, until the determination of the proceedings on that application.

21 . . .

AMENDMENTS

Repealed by the Civil Evidence Act 1995, s 15(2), Sch 2.

22 . . .

AMENDMENTS

Repealed by the Administration of Justice Act 1982, s 75, Sch 9, Pt I.

23 Determination of date on which representation was first taken out

In considering for the purposes of this Act when representation with respect to the estate of a deceased person was first taken out, a grant limited to settled land or to trust property shall be left out of account, and a grant limited to real estate or to personal estate shall be left out of account unless a grant limited to the remainder of the estate has previously been made or is made at the same time.

24 Effect of this Act on s 46(1)(vi) of Administration of Estates Act 1925

Section 46(1)(vi) of the Administration of Estates Act 1925, in so far as it provides for the devolution of property on the Crown, the Duchy of Lancaster or the Duke of Cornwall as bona vacantia, shall have effect subject to the provisions of this Act.

25 Interpretation

(1) In this Act–

"beneficiary", in relation to the estate of a deceased person, means–

(a) a person who under the will of the deceased or under the law relating to intestacy is beneficially interested in the estate or would be so interested if an order had not been made under this Act, and

(b) a person who has received any sum of money or other property which by virtue of section 8(1) or 8(2) of this Act is treated as part of the net estate of the deceased or would have received that sum or other property if an order had not been made under this Act;

"child" includes an illegitimate child and a child en ventre sa mere at the death of the deceased;

"the court" [unless the context otherwise requires] means the High Court, or where a county court has jurisdiction by virtue of section 22 of this Act, a county court;

["former civil partner" means a person whose civil partnership with the deceased was during the lifetime of the deceased either–

(a) dissolved or annulled by an order made under the law of any part of the British Islands, or

(b) dissolved or annulled in any country or territory outside the British Islands by a dissolution or annulment which is entitled to be recognised as valid by the law of England and Wales;]

[["former spouse"] means a person whose marriage with the deceased was during the lifetime of the deceased either–

(a) dissolved or annulled by *a decree* [an order or decree] of divorce or a decree of nullity of marriage granted under the law of any part of the British Islands, or

(b) dissolved or annulled in any country or territory outside the British Islands by a divorce or annulment which is entitled to be recognised as valid by the law of England and Wales;]

"net estate", in relation to a deceased person, means–

(a) all property of which the deceased had power to dispose by his will (otherwise than by virtue of a special power of appointment) less the amount of his funeral, testamentary and administration expenses, debts and liabilities, including any inheritance tax payable out of his estate on his death;

(b) any property in respect of which the deceased held a general power of appointment (not being a power exercisable by will) which has not been exercised;

(c) any sum of money or other property which is treated for the purposes of this Act as part of the net estate of the deceased by virtue of section 8(1) or (2) of this Act;

(d) any property which is treated for the purposes of this Act as part of the net estate of the deceased by virtue of an order made under section 9 of the Act;

(e) any sum of money or other property which is, by reason of a disposition or contract made by the deceased, ordered under section 10 or 11 of this Act to be provided for the purpose of the making of financial provision under this Act;

"property" includes any chose in action;

"reasonable financial provision" has the meaning assigned to it by section 1 of this Act;

"valuable consideration" does not include marriage or a promise of marriage;

"will" includes codicil.

(2) For the purposes of paragraph (a) of the definition of "net estate" in subsection (1) above a person who is not of full age and capacity shall be treated as having power to dispose by will of all property of which he would have had power to dispose by will if he had been of full age and capacity.

(3) Any reference in this Act to provision out of the net estate of a deceased person includes a reference to provision extending to the whole of that estate.

(4) For the purposes of this Act any reference to a [spouse,] wife or husband shall be treated as including a reference to a person who in good faith entered into a void marriage with the deceased unless either–

(a) the marriage of the deceased and that person was dissolved or annulled during the lifetime of the deceased and the dissolution or annulment is recognised by the law of England and Wales, or

(b) that person has during the lifetime of the deceased [formed a subsequent marriage or civil partnership].

[(4A) For the purposes of this Act any reference to a civil partner shall be treated as including a reference to a person who in good faith formed a void civil partnership with the deceased unless either–

(a) the civil partnership between the deceased and that person was dissolved or annulled during the lifetime of the deceased and the dissolution or annulment is recognised by the law of England and Wales, or

(b) that person has during the lifetime of the deceased formed a subsequent civil partnership or marriage.

(5) Any reference in this Act to the formation of, or to a person who has formed, a subsequent marriage or civil partnership includes (as the case may be) a reference to the formation of, or to a person who has formed, a marriage or civil partnership which is by law void or voidable.

(5A) The formation of a marriage or civil partnership shall be treated for the purposes of this Act as the formation of a subsequent marriage or civil partnership, in relation to either of the spouses or civil partners, notwithstanding that the previous marriage or civil partnership of that spouse or civil partner was void or voidable.]

(6) Any reference in this Act to an order or decree made under the Matrimonial Causes Act 1973 or under any section of that Act shall be construed as including a reference to an order or decree which is deemed to have been made under that Act or under that section thereof, as the case may be.

[(6A) Any reference in this Act to an order made under, or under any provision of, the Civil Partnership Act 2004 shall be construed as including a reference to anything which is deemed to be an order made (as the case may be) under that Act or provision.]

(7) Any reference in this Act to any enactment is a reference to that enactment as amended by or under any subsequent enactment.

AMENDMENTS

Section 25(1): in definition "the court" words "unless the context otherwise requires" in square brackets inserted by the Matrimonial and Family Proceedings Act 1984, s 8.

Section 25(1): definition "former civil partner" inserted by the Civil Partnership Act 2004, s 71, Sch 4, Pt 2, para 27(1), (3).

Section 25(1): definition "former spouse" (previously ""former wife" or "former husband"") substituted by the Matrimonial and Family Proceedings Act 1984, s 25.

Section 25(1): in definition "former spouse" (previously ""former wife" and "former husband"") words ""former spouse"" in square brackets substituted by the Civil Partnership Act 2004, s 71, Sch 4, Pt 2, para 27(1), (2).

Section 25(1): in definition "former spouse" in para (a) words "a decree" in italics repealed and subsequent words in square brackets substituted by the Family Law Act 1996, s 66(1), Sch 8, para 27(8), as from a day to be appointed; for savings see s 66(2), Sch 9, para 5 thereof.

Section 25(4): word "spouse," in square brackets inserted by the Civil Partnership Act 2004, s 71, Sch 4, Pt 2, para 27(1), (4)(a).

Section 25(4)(b): words "formed a subsequent marriage or civil partnership" in square brackets substituted by the Civil Partnership Act 2004, s 71, Sch 4, Pt 2, para 27(1), (4)(b).

Section 25(4A), (5), (5A) substituted, for sub-s (5) as originally enacted, by the Civil Partnership Act 2004, s 71, Sch 4, Pt 2, para 27(1), (5).

Section 25(6A) inserted by the Civil Partnership Act 2004, s 71, Sch 4, Pt 2, para 27(1), (6).

26 Consequential amendments, repeals and transitional provisions

(1) . . .

(2) Subject to the provisions of this section, the enactments specified in the Schedule to this Act are hereby repealed to the extent specified in the third column of the Schedule; . . .

(3) The repeal of the said enactment shall not affect their operation in relation to any application made thereunder (whether before or after the commencement of this Act) with reference to the death of any person who died before the commencement of this Act.

(4) Without prejudice to the provisions of section 38 of the Interpretation Act 1889 (which relates to the effect of repeals) nothing in any repeal made by this Act shall affect any order made or direction given under any enactment

repealed by this Act, and, subject to the provisions of this Act, every such order or direction (other than an order made under section 4A of the Inheritance (Family Provision) Act 1938 or section 28A of the Matrimonial Causes Act 1965) shall, if it is in force at the commencement of this Act or is made by virtue of subsection (2) above, continue in force as if it had been made under section 2(1)(a) of this Act, and for the purposes of section 6(7) of this Act the court in exercising its powers under that section in relation to an order continued in force by this subsection shall be required to have regard to any change in any of the circumstances to which the court would have been required to have regard when making that order if the order had been made with reference to the death of any person who died after the commencement of this Act.

AMENDMENTS

Section 26(1), (2): words omitted amend the Matrimonial Causes Act 1973, s 36, Sch 2, para 5(2).

27 Short title, commencement and extent

(1) This Act may be cited as the Inheritance (Provision for Family and Dependants) Act 1975.

(2) This Act does not extend to Scotland or Northern Ireland.

(3) This Act shall come into force on 1st April 1976.

SCHEDULE Enactments Repealed

Chapter	Short Title	Extent of Repeal
1938 c 72	The Inheritance (Family Provision) Act 1938	The whole Act.
1952 c 64	The Intestates' Estates Act 1952	Section 7 and Schedule 3.
1965 c 72	The Matrimonial Causes Act 1965	Section 26 to 28(A) and section 25(4) and (5) as applied by section 28(2).
1966 c 35	The Family Provision Act 1966	The whole Act, except section 1 and subsections (1) and (3) of section 10.

Chapter	Short Title	Extent of Repeal
1969 c 46	The Family Law Reform Act 1969	Sections 5(1) and 18.
1970 c 31	The Administration of Justice Act 1970	In Schedule 2, paragraph 16.
1970 c 33	The Law Reform (Miscellaneous Provisions) Act 1970	Section 6.
1970 c 45	The Matrimonial Proceedings and Property Act 1970	Section 36.
1971 c 23	The Courts Act 1971	Section 45(1)(a).
1973 c 18	The Matrimonial Causes Act 1973	In section 50, in subsection (1)(a) the words from "and sections 26" to the end of the paragraph, in subsection (1)(d) the words "or sections 26 to 28A of the Matrimonial Causes Act 1965" and in subsection (2)(a) the words "or under section 26 or 27 of the Matrimonial Causes Act 1965". In Schedule 2, paragraph 5(1) and in paragraph 12 the words "(a) sections 26 to 28A of the Matrimonial Causes Act 1965".
1975 c 7	The Finance Act 1975	In Schedule 12, paragraph 6.

A3 CIVIL PROCEDURE RULES
PART 8 CLAIM FORM

Claim Form
(CPR Part 8)

In the

Claim No.

Click here to clear your data after printing

Claimant

SEAL

Defendant(s)

Does your claim include any issues under the Human Rights Act 1998? ☐ Yes ☐ No

Details of claim *(see also overleaf)*

£

Defendant's name and address		
	Court fee	
	Solicitor's costs	
	Issue date	

The court office at

is open between 10 am and 4 pm Monday to Friday. When corresponding with the court, please address forms or letters to the Court Manager and quote the case number.

N208 Claim form (CPR Part 8) (10.00)   *Printed on behalf of The Court Service*

Claim No.	

Details of claim *(continued)*

Statement of Truth
*(I believe)(The Claimant believes) that the facts stated in these particulars of claim are true.
* I am duly authorised by the claimant to sign this statement

Full name _____

Name of claimant's solicitor's firm _____

signed_____ position or office held_____
*(Claimant)(Litigation friend)(Claimant's solicitor) (if signing on behalf of firm or company)
*delete as appropriate

Claimant's or claimant's solicitor's address to
which documents should be sent if different
from overleaf. If you are prepared to accept
service by DX, fax or e-mail, please add details.

A4 CIVIL PROCEDURE RULES PRACTICE DIRECTION 31B – DISCLOSURE OF ELECTRONIC DOCUMENTS
(This Practice Direction supplements CPR Part 31)

Contents of this Practice Direction

Purpose, scope and interpretation

1

Rule 31.4 contains a broad definition of 'document'. This extends to Electronic Documents.

2

The purpose of this Practice Direction is to encourage and assist the parties to reach agreement in relation to the disclosure of Electronic Documents in a proportionate and cost-effective manner.

3

Unless the court orders otherwise, this Practice Direction only applies to proceedings that are (or are likely to be) allocated to the multi-track.

4

Unless the court orders otherwise, this Practice Direction only applies to proceedings started on or after 1st October 2010. Paragraph 2A.2 to 2A.5 of Practice Direction 31A in force immediately before that date continues to apply to proceedings started before that date.

5

In this Practice Direction –

(1)   'Data Sampling' means the process of checking data by identifying and checking representative individual documents;

(2)   'Disclosure Data' means data relating to disclosed documents, including for example the type of document, the date of the document, the names of the author or sender and the recipient, and the party disclosing the document;

(3)   'Electronic Document' means any document held in electronic form. It includes, for example, e-mail and other electronic communications such as text messages and voicemail, word-processed documents and databases, and documents stored on portable devices such as memory sticks and mobile phones. In addition to documents that are readily accessible from computer systems and other electronic devices and media, it includes documents that are stored on servers and back-up systems and documents that have been deleted. It also includes Metadata and other embedded data which is not typically visible on screen or a print out;

(4)   'Electronic Image' means an electronic representation of a paper document;

(5)   'Electronic Documents Questionnaire' means the questionnaire in the Schedule to this Practice Direction;

(6)   'Keyword Search' means a software-aided search for words across the text of an Electronic Document;

(7)   'Metadata' is data about data. In the case of an Electronic Document, Metadata is typically embedded information about the document which is not readily accessible once the Native Electronic Document has been converted into an Electronic Image or paper document. It may include (for example) the date and time of creation or modification of a word-processing file, or the author and the date and time of sending an e-mail. Metadata may be created automatically by a computer system or manually by a user;

(8)   'Native Electronic Document' or 'Native Format' means an Electronic Document stored in the original form in which it was created by a computer software program; and

(9)   'Optical Character Recognition (OCR)' means the computer-facilitated recognition of printed or written text characters in an Electronic Image in which the text-based contents cannot be searched electronically.

General principles

6

When considering disclosure of Electronic Documents, the parties and their legal representatives should bear in mind the following general principles –

(1) Electronic Documents should be managed efficiently in order to minimise the cost incurred;

(2) technology should be used in order to ensure that document management activities are undertaken efficiently and effectively;

(3) disclosure should be given in a manner which gives effect to the overriding objective;

(4) Electronic Documents should generally be made available for inspection in a form which allows the party receiving the documents the same ability to access, search, review and display the documents as the party giving disclosure; and

(5) disclosure of Electronic Documents which are of no relevance to the proceedings may place an excessive burden in time and cost on the party to whom disclosure is given.

Preservation of documents

7

As soon as litigation is contemplated, the parties' legal representatives must notify their clients of the need to preserve disclosable documents. The documents to be preserved include Electronic Documents which would otherwise be deleted in accordance with a document retention policy or otherwise deleted in the ordinary course of business.

Discussions between the parties before the first Case Management Conference in relation to the use of technology and disclosure

8

The parties and their legal representatives must, before the first case management conference, discuss the use of technology in the management of Electronic Documents and the conduct of proceedings, in particular for the purpose of –

(1) creating lists of documents to be disclosed;

(2) giving disclosure by providing documents and information regarding documents in electronic format; and

(3) presenting documents and other material to the court at the trial.

9

The parties and their legal representatives must also, before the first case management conference, discuss the disclosure of Electronic Documents. In some cases (for example heavy and complex cases) it may be appropriate to begin discussions before proceedings are commenced. The discussions should include (where appropriate) the following matters –

(1)   the categories of Electronic Documents within the parties' control, the computer systems, electronic devices and media on which any relevant documents may be held, storage systems and document retention policies;

(2)   the scope of the reasonable search for Electronic Documents required by rule 31.7;

(3)   the tools and techniques (if any) which should be considered to reduce the burden and cost of disclosure of Electronic Documents, including –

    (a)   limiting disclosure of documents or certain categories of documents to particular date ranges, to particular custodians of documents, or to particular types of documents;

    (b)   the use of agreed Keyword Searches;

    (c)   the use of agreed software tools;

    (d)   the methods to be used to identify duplicate documents;

    (e)   the use of Data Sampling;

    (f)   the methods to be used to identify privileged documents and other non-disclosable documents, to redact documents (where redaction is appropriate), and for dealing with privileged or other documents which have been inadvertently disclosed; and

    (g)   the use of a staged approach to the disclosure of Electronic Documents;

(4)   the preservation of Electronic Documents, with a view to preventing loss of such documents before the trial;

(5)   the exchange of data relating to Electronic Documents in an agreed electronic format using agreed fields;

(6)   the formats in which Electronic Documents are to be provided on inspection and the methods to be used;

(7)   the basis of charging for or sharing the cost of the provision of Electronic Documents, and whether any arrangements for charging or sharing of costs are final or are subject to re-allocation in accordance with any order for costs subsequently made; and

(8)   whether it would be appropriate to use the services of a neutral electronic repository for storage of Electronic Documents.

The Electronic Documents Questionnaire
10

In some cases the parties may find it helpful to exchange the Electronic Documents Questionnaire in order to provide information to each other in relation to the scope, extent and most suitable format for disclosure of Electronic Documents in the proceedings.

11

The answers to the Electronic Documents Questionnaire must be verified by a statement of truth.

12

Answers to the Electronic Documents Questionnaire will only be available for inspection by non-parties if permission is given under rule 5.4C(2).

13

Rule 31.22 makes provision regulating the use of answers to the Electronic Documents Questionnaire.

Preparation for the first Case Management Conference

14

The documents submitted to the court in advance of the first case management conference should include a summary of the matters on which the parties agree in relation to the disclosure of Electronic Documents and a summary of the matters on which they disagree.

15

If the parties indicate that they have been unable to reach agreement in relation to the disclosure of Electronic Documents and that no agreement is likely, the court will give written directions in relation to disclosure or order a separate hearing in relation to disclosure. When doing so, the court will consider making an order that the parties must complete and exchange all or any part of the Electronic Documents Questionnaire within 14 days or such other period as the court may direct.

16

The person signing the Electronic Documents Questionnaire should attend the first case management conference, and any subsequent hearing at which disclosure is likely to be considered.

Where the parties are unable to reach an appropriate agreement in relation to the disclosure of Electronic Documents

17

If at any time it becomes apparent that the parties are unable to reach agreement in relation to the disclosure of Electronic Documents, the parties should seek directions from the court at the earliest practical date.

18

If the court considers that the parties' agreement in relation to the disclosure of Electronic Documents is inappropriate or insufficient, the court will give directions in relation to disclosure. When doing so, the court will consider making an order that the parties must complete and exchange all or any part of the Electronic Documents Questionnaire within 14 days or such other period as the court may direct.

19

If a party gives disclosure of Electronic Documents without first discussing with other parties how to plan and manage such disclosure, the court may require that party to carry out further searches for documents or to repeat other steps which that party has already carried out.

The reasonable search
20

The extent of the reasonable search required by rule 31.7 for the purposes of standard disclosure is affected by the existence of Electronic Documents. The extent of the search which must be made will depend on the circumstances of the case including, in particular, the factors referred to in rule 31.7(2). The parties should bear in mind that the overriding objective includes dealing with the case in ways which are proportionate.

21

The factors that may be relevant in deciding the reasonableness of a search for Electronic Documents include (but are not limited to) the following –

   (1)   the number of documents involved;
   (2)   the nature and complexity of the proceedings;
   (3)   the ease and expense of retrieval of any particular document. This includes:
          (a)   the accessibility of Electronic Documents including e-mail communications on computer systems, servers, back-up systems and other electronic devices or media that may contain such documents taking into account alterations or developments in hardware or software systems used by the disclosing party and/or available to enable access to such documents;
          (b)   the location of relevant Electronic Documents, data, computer systems, servers, back-up systems and other electronic devices or media that may contain such documents;
          (c)   the likelihood of locating relevant data;
          (d)   the cost of recovering any Electronic Documents;

(e)   the cost of disclosing and providing inspection of any relevant Electronic Documents; and

(f)   the likelihood that Electronic Documents will be materially altered in the course of recovery, disclosure or inspection;

(4)   the availability of documents or contents of documents from other sources; and

(5)   the significance of any document which is likely to be located during the search.

22

Depending on the circumstances, it may be reasonable to search all of the parties' electronic storage systems, or to search only some part of those systems. For example, it may be reasonable to decide not to search for documents coming into existence before a particular date, or to limit the search to documents in a particular place or places, or to documents falling into particular categories.

23

In some cases a staged approach may be appropriate, with disclosure initially being given of limited categories of documents. Those categories may subsequently be extended or limited depending on the results initially obtained.

24

The primary source of disclosure of Electronic Documents is normally reasonably accessible data. A party requesting under rule 31.12 specific disclosure of Electronic Documents which are not reasonably accessible must demonstrate that the relevance and materiality justify the cost and burden of retrieving and producing it.

Keyword and other automated searches

25

It may be reasonable to search for Electronic Documents by means of Keyword Searches or other automated methods of searching if a full review of each and every document would be unreasonable.

26

However, it will often be insufficient to use simple Keyword Searches or other automated methods of searching alone. The injudicious use of Keyword Searches and other automated search techniques –

(1)   may result in failure to find important documents which ought to be disclosed, and/or

(2)   may find excessive quantities of irrelevant documents, which if disclosed would place an excessive burden in time and cost on the party to whom disclosure is given.

27

The parties should consider supplementing Keyword Searches and other automated searches with additional techniques such as individually reviewing certain documents or categories of documents (for example important documents generated by key personnel) and taking such other steps as may be required in order to justify the selection to the court.

Disclosure of Metadata

28

Where copies of disclosed documents are provided in Native Format in accordance with paragraph 33 below, some Metadata will be disclosed with each document. A party requesting disclosure of additional Metadata or forensic image copies of disclosed documents (for example in relation to a dispute concerning authenticity) must demonstrate that the relevance and materiality of the requested Metadata justify the cost and burden of producing that Metadata.

29

Parties using document management or litigation support systems should be alert to the possibility that Metadata or other useful information relating to documents may not be stored with the documents.

Lists of Documents

30

If a party is giving disclosure of Electronic Documents, paragraph 3 of Practice Direction 31A is to be read subject to the following –

(1)   Form N265 may be amended to accommodate the sub-paragraphs which follow;

(2)   a list of documents may by agreement between the parties be an electronic file in .csv (comma-separated values) or other agreed format;

(3)   documents may be listed otherwise than in date order where a different order would be more convenient;

(4)   save where otherwise agreed or ordered, documents should be listed individually if a party already possesses data relating to the document (for example, type of document and date of creation) which make this possible (so that as far as possible each document may be given a unique reference number);

(5)   a party should be consistent in the way in which documents are listed;

(6)   consistent column headings should be repeated on each page of the list on which documents are listed, where the software used for preparing the list enables this to be carried out automatically; and

(7)   the disclosure list number used in any supplemental list of documents should be unique and should run sequentially from the last number used in the previous list.

Provision of Disclosure Data in electronic form

31

Where a party provides another party with Disclosure Data in electronic form, the following provisions will apply unless the parties agree or the court directs otherwise –

(1)   Disclosure Data should be set out in a single, continuous table or spreadsheet, each separate column containing exclusively one of the following types of Disclosure Data –

    (a)   disclosure list number (sequential)

    (b)   date

    (c)   document type

    (d)   author/sender

    (e)   recipient

    (f)   disclosure list number of any parent or covering document;

(2)   other than for disclosure list numbers, blank entries are permissible and preferred if there is no relevant Disclosure Data (that is, the field should be left blank rather than state 'Undated');

(3)   dates should be set out in the alphanumeric form '01 Jan 2010'; and

(4)   Disclosure Data should be set out in a consistent manner.

Provision of electronic copies of disclosed documents

32

The parties should co-operate at an early stage about the format in which Electronic Documents are to be provided on inspection. In the case of difficulty or disagreement, the matter should be referred to the court for directions at the earliest practical date, if possible at the first case management conference.

33

Save where otherwise agreed or ordered, electronic copies of disclosed documents should be provided in their Native Format, in a manner which preserves Metadata relating to the date of creation of each document.

34

A party should provide any available searchable OCR versions of Electronic Documents with the original. A party may however choose not to provide OCR versions of documents which have been redacted. If OCR versions are provided, they are provided on an 'as is' basis, with no assurance to the other party that the OCR versions are complete or accurate.

35

(1)   Subject to sub-paragraph (2) below, if a party is providing in electronic form copies of disclosed documents and wishes to redact or otherwise make alterations to a document or documents, then –

    (a)   the party redacting or altering the document must inform the other party in accordance with rule 31.19 that redacted or altered versions are being supplied; and

    (b)   the party redacting or altering the document must ensure that the original unredacted and unaltered version is preserved, so that it remains available to be inspected if required.

(2)   Sub-paragraph (1) above does not apply where the only alteration made to the document is an alteration to the Metadata as a result of the ordinary process of copying and/or accessing the document. Sub-paragraph (1) does apply to the alteration or suppression of Metadata in other situations.

Specialised technology

36

If Electronic Documents are best accessed using technology which is not readily available to the party entitled to disclosure, and that party reasonably requires additional inspection facilities, the party making disclosure shall co-operate in making available to the other party such reasonable additional inspection facilities as may be appropriate in order to afford inspection in accordance with rule 31.3.

SCHEDULE

Electronic Documents Questionnaire

Part 1 – Your disclosure

Extent of a reasonable search

Date range and custodians
1.
What date range do you consider that your searches for Electronic Documents should cover ('the date range')?

2.
Identify the custodians or creators of your Electronic Documents whose repositories of documents you consider should be searched[1].

Communications
3.
Which forms of electronic communication were in use during the date range (so far as is relevant to these proceedings)?

A	B	C	D	E
Communication	In use during the date range? (yes/no)	Are you searching for relevant documents in this category? (yes/no)	Where and on what type of software/ equipment/ media is this communication stored[2]?	(a) Are back-ups or archives of this communication available, and (b) if so, are you searching the back-ups or archives?
i) E-mail[3]				
ii) Other (provide details for each type[4])				

Electronic Documents
4.
Apart from attachments to e-mails, which forms of Electronic Documents were created or stored by you during the date range?

A	B	C	D	E
Document Type	In use during the date range? (yes/no)	Are you searching for relevant documents in this category? (yes/no)	Where and on what type of software/equipment/ media are these documents[5]?	(a) Are back-ups or archives of these documents available, and (b) if so, are you searching the back-ups or archives?
i) Word (or equivalent – state which)				
ii) Excel (or equivalent – state which)				
iii) Electronic Images[6]				
iv) Other[7] (state which)				

Databases of Electronic Documents
5.

In the following table identify database systems, including document management systems, used by you during the date range and which may contain disclosable Electronic Documents.

A	B	C	D	E
Name	Brief description	Nature of data held	Are you disclosing documents held in this database? (yes/no)	Proposals for provision of relevant documents to or access by other parties to this litigation
1.				
2. (etc)				

Method of search

Key words
6.

Do you consider that Keyword Searches should be used as part of the process of determining which Electronic Documents you should disclose?

If yes, provide details of –

(1)   the keywords used or to be used (by reference, if applicable, to individual custodians, creators, repositories, file types and/or date ranges)[8]; and

(2)   the extent to which the Keyword Searches have been or will be supplemented by a review of individual documents.

Other types of automated searches

7.

Do you consider that automated searches or automated techniques other than Keyword Searches (for example, concept searches or clustering) should be used as part of the process of determining which Electronic Documents you should disclose? If yes, provide details of –

(1)   the process(es) used or to be used (by reference, if applicable, to individual custodians, creators, repositories, file types and/or date ranges);

(2)   the extent to which the processes have been or will be supplemented by a review of individual documents; and

(3)   how the methodology of automated searches will be made available for consideration by other parties.

8.

If the answer to Question 6 or 7 is yes, state whether attachments to (a) e-mails (b) compressed files (c) embedded files and (d) imaged text will respond to your Keyword Searches or other automated search.

9.

Are you using or intending to use computer software for other purposes in relation to disclosure? If so, provide details of the software, processes and methods to be used.

Potential problems with the extent of search and accessibility of Electronic Documents

10.

Do any of the sources and/or documents identified in this Electronic Documents Questionnaire raise questions about the reasonableness of the search which ought to be taken into account[9]? If so, give details.

11.

Are any documents which may be disclosable encrypted, password-protected or for other reasons difficult to access, or do you have any reason to believe that they may be[10]? If so, state which of the categories identified at Questions 3, 4 and 5 above are affected, and your proposals for making them accessible.

12.

Are you aware of any other points in relation to disclosure of your Electronic Documents which require discussion between the parties? If so, give details.

Preservation of Electronic Documents
13.

Do you have a document retention policy?

14.

Have you given an instruction to preserve Electronic Documents, and if so, when?

Inspection
15.

Subject to re-consideration after receiving the responses of other parties to this Electronic Documents Questionnaire, (a) in what format and (b) on what media do you intend to provide to other parties copies of disclosed documents which are or will be available in electronic form?

16.

Subject to re-consideration after receiving the responses of other parties to this Electronic Documents Questionnaire, do you intend to provide other parties with Disclosure Data electronically, and if so, (a) in what format and (b) on what media?

17.

Insofar as you have available or will have available searchable OCR versions of Electronic Documents, do you intend to provide the searchable OCR version to other parties[11]? If not, why not?

Part 2 – The disclosure of other parties

The extent and content of their search
18.

Do you at this stage have any proposals about the date ranges which should be searched by other parties to the proceedings? If so, provide details.

19.

Do you at this stage have any proposals about the custodians or creators whose repositories of documents should be searched for disclosable documents by other parties to the proceedings? If so, provide details[12].

20.

Do you consider that the other party(ies) should disclose all available Metadata[13] attaching to any documents? If yes, provide details of the documents or categories of documents.

Proposals for the method to be adopted for their searches

21.

Do you at this stage have any proposals about the Keyword Searches, or other automated searches, which should be applied by other parties to their document sets? If so, provide details.

Inspection

22.

Subject to re-consideration after receiving the responses of other parties to this Electronic Documents Questionnaire, (a) in what format and (b) on what media do you wish to receive copies of disclosed documents which are or will be available in electronic form?

23.

Subject to re-consideration after receiving the responses of other parties to this Electronic Documents Questionnaire, do you wish to receive Disclosure Data electronically, and if so, (a) in what format and (b) on what media?

STATEMENT OF TRUTH

*[I believe][The [claimant][defendant] believes] that the facts stated in the answers to this Electronic Documents Questionnaire are true.
*I am duly authorised by the [claimant][defendant] to sign this statement.

Full name
....
Name of legal representative's firm
....
Signed
....
Position or office held (if signing on behalf of firm or company)
....
Date
....
* *delete as appropriate*

WARNING: Unless the court makes some other order, the answers given in this document may only be used for the purposes of the proceedings in which the document is produced unless it has been read to or by the court or referred to at a hearing which has been held in public or the Court gives permission or the party who has completed this questionnaire agrees.

Guidance Notes:

1.

Technical expressions are defined in Practice Direction 31B.

2.

The questions in the Electronic Documents Questionnaire are not intended to give rise to any implication about how disclosure should or should not be carried out. They are intended only to provide information to other parties and to the court.

3.

Further facts and matters may come to parties' attention over the course of the proceedings which affect the answers to the Electronic Documents Questionnaire. Where detailed information is not yet available at the time the Electronic Documents Questionnaire is first answered, parties should give such information as they can, and supplement or amend their answers when further information is available. Answers should be updated by notifying other parties and the court without undue delay, and in any event before each case management conference at which disclosure is likely to be considered.

4.

Some of the questions in the Electronic Documents Questionnaire require only a brief answer which may need to be elaborated after Electronic Documents Questionnaires have been exchanged. The purpose of such questions is to assist the parties in identifying the points which may require elaboration in order for meaningful discussions to take place between them.

5.

Questions which refer to sources of Electronic Documents that are not considered to be relevant may be answered with a statement to that effect.

6.

Questions about 'your' documents and about software, hardware or systems used by 'you' are directed, in the case of solicitors, to the solicitor's lay client's documents or to documents prepared on the lay client's behalf.

Footnotes

[1] Include names of all those who may have or have had custody of disclosable documents, including secretaries, personal assistants, former employees and/or former participants. It may be helpful to identify different dates for particular custodians.

[2] State the geographical location (if known). Consider (at least) servers, desktop PCs, laptops, notebooks, handheld devices, PDA devices, off-site storage, removable storage media (for example, CD-ROMs, DVDs, USB drives, memory sticks) and databases.

[3] Consider all types of e-mail system (for example, Outlook, Lotus Notes, web-based accounts), whether stored on personal computers, portable devices or in web-based accounts (for example, Yahoo, Hotmail, Gmail).

[4] For example, instant messaging, voicemail, VOIP (Voice Over Internet Protocol), recorded telephone lines, text messaging, audio files, video files.

[5] State the geographical location (if known). Consider (at least) servers, desktops and laptops.

[6] For example, .pdf, .tif, .jpg.

[7] For example, Powerpoint or equivalent, specialist documents (such as CAD Drawings).

[8] Where Keyword Searches are used in order to identify irrelevant documents which are to be excluded from disclosure (for example a confidential name of a client or customer), a general description of the type of search may be given.

[9] See Practice Direction 31B, which refers to the following matters which may be relevant: (a) the number of documents involved; (b) the nature and complexity of the proceedings; (c) the ease and expense of retrieval of any particular document; (d) the availability of documents or contents of documents from other sources; and (e) the significance of any document which is likely to be located during the search.

[10] For example, back-ups, archives, off-site or outsourced document storage, documents created by former employees, documents stored in other jurisdictions, documents in foreign languages.

[11] There is no requirement that you should obtain OCR versions of documents, and this question is directed only to OCR versions which you have available or expect to have available to you. If you do provide OCR versions to another party, they will be provided by you on an 'as is' basis, with no assurance to the other party that the OCR versions are complete or accurate. You may wish to exclude provision of OCR versions of documents which have been redacted.

[12] Include names of all those who may have or have had custody of disclosable documents, including secretaries, personal assistants, former employees and/or former participants. It may be helpful to identify different dates for particular custodians.

[13] 'Metadata' is information about the document or file which is recorded in the computer, such as the date and time of creation or modification of a word-processing file, or the author and the date and time of sending of an e-mail. The question is directed to the more extensive Metadata which may be relevant where for example authenticity is disputed.

A5 CIVIL PROCEDURE RULES
PART 57
PROBATE AND INHERITANCE

Contents of this Part

Scope of this Part and definitions
57.1

(1) This Part contains rules about –
    (a) probate claims;
    (b) claims for the rectification of wills;
    (c) claims and applications to –
        (i) substitute another person for a personal representative; or
        (ii) remove a personal representative; and
    (d) claims under the Inheritance (Provision for Family Dependants) Act 1975.

(2) In this Part:

(a)   'probate claim' means a claim for –
     (i)   the grant of probate of the will, or letters of administration of the estate, of a deceased person;
     (ii)   the revocation of such a grant; or
     (iii) a decree pronouncing for or against the validity of an alleged will;

not being a claim which is non-contentious (or common form) probate business;

(Section 128 of the Supreme Court Act 1981 defines non-contentious (or common form) probate business.)

(b)   'relevant office' means –
     (i)   in the case of High Court proceedings in a Chancery district registry, that registry;
     (ii)   in the case of any other High Court proceedings, Chancery Chambers at the Royal Courts of Justice, Strand, London, WC2A 2LL; and
     (iii) in the case of county court proceedings, the office of the county court in question;

(c)   'testamentary document' means a will, a draft of a will, written instructions for a will made by or at the request of, or under the instructions of, the testator, and any document purporting to be evidence of the contents, or to be a copy, of a will which is alleged to have been lost or destroyed;

(d)   'will' includes a codicil.

I PROBATE CLAIMS
General
57.2

(1)   This Section contains rules about probate claims.

(2)   Probate claims in the High Court are assigned to the Chancery Division.

(3)   Probate claims in the county court must only be brought in –
     (a)   a county court where there is also a Chancery district registry; or
     (b)   the Central London County Court.

(4)   All probate claims are allocated to the multi-track.

How to start a probate claim
57.3

A probate claim must be commenced –
     (a)   in the relevant office; and
     (b)   using the procedure in Part 7.

Acknowledgment of Service and Defence
57.4

(1) A defendant who is served with a claim form must file an acknowledgment of service.

(2) Subject to paragraph (3), the period for filing an acknowledgment of service is –

 (a) if the defendant is served with a claim form which states that particulars of claim are to follow, 28 days after service of the particulars of claim; and

 (b) in any other case, 28 days after service of the claim form.

(3) If the claim form is served out of the jurisdiction under rule 6.32 or 6.33, the period for filing an acknowledgment of service is 14 days longer than the relevant period specified in rule 6.35 or Practice Direction 6B.

(4) Rule 15(4) (which provides the period for filing a defence) applies as if the words 'under Part 10' were omitted from rule 15.4(1)(b).

Lodging of testamentary documents and filing of evidence about testamentary documents
57.5

(1) Any testamentary document of the deceased person in the possession or control of any party must be lodged with the court.

(2) Unless the court directs otherwise, the testamentary documents must be lodged in the relevant office –

 (a) by the claimant when the claim form is issued; and

 (b) by a defendant when he acknowledges service.

(3) The claimant and every defendant who acknowledges service of the claim form must in written evidence –

 (a) describe any testamentary document of the deceased of which he has any knowledge or, if he does not know of any such testamentary document, state that fact, and

 (b) if any testamentary document of which he has knowledge is not in his possession or under his control, give the name and address of the person in whose possession or under whose control it is or, if he does not know the name or address of that person, state that fact.

(A specimen form for the written evidence about testamentary documents is annexed to Practice Direction 57.)

(4) Unless the court directs otherwise, the written evidence required by paragraph (3) must be filed in the relevant office –

 (a) by the claimant, when the claim form is issued; and

 (b) by a defendant when he acknowledges service.

(5)   Except with the permission of the court, a party shall not be allowed to inspect the testamentary documents or written evidence lodged or filed by any other party until he himself has lodged his testamentary documents and filed his evidence.

(6)   The provisions of paragraphs (2) and (4) may be modified by a practice direction under this Part.

Revocation of existing grant
57.6

(1)   In a probate claim which seeks the revocation of a grant of probate or letters of administration every person who is entitled, or claims to be entitled, to administer the estate under that grant must be made a party to the claim.

(2)   If the claimant is the person to whom the grant was made, he must lodge the probate or letters of administration in the relevant office when the claim form is issued.

(3)   If a defendant has the probate or letters of administration under his control, he must lodge it in the relevant office when he acknowledges service.

(4)   Paragraphs (2) and (3) do not apply where the grant has already been lodged at the court, which in this paragraph includes the Principal Registry of the Family Division or a district probate registry.

Contents of statements of case
57.7

(1)   The claim form must contain a statement of the nature of the interest of the claimant and of each defendant in the estate.

(2)   If a party disputes another party's interest in the estate he must state this in his statement of case and set out his reasons.

(3)   Any party who contends that at the time when a will was executed the testator did not know of and approve its contents must give particulars of the facts and matters relied on.

(4)   Any party who wishes to contend that –
    (a)   a will was not duly executed;
    (b)   at the time of the execution of a will the testator lacked testamentary capacity; or
    (c)   the execution of a will was obtained by undue influence or fraud,
    must set out the contention specifically and give particulars of the facts and matters relied on.

(5)

    (a)   A defendant may give notice in his defence that he does not raise any positive case, but insists on the will being proved in solemn form and, for that purpose, will cross-examine the witnesses who attested the will.

    (b)   If a defendant gives such a notice, the court will not make an order for costs against him unless it considers that there was no reasonable ground for opposing the will.

Counterclaim
57.8

    (1)   A defendant who contends that he has any claim or is entitled to any remedy relating to the grant of probate of the will, or letters of administration of the estate, of the deceased person must serve a counterclaim making that contention.

    (2)   If the claimant fails to serve particulars of claim within the time allowed, the defendant may, with the permission of the court, serve a counterclaim and the probate claim shall then proceed as if the counterclaim were the particulars of claim.

Probate counterclaim in other proceedings
57.9

    (1)   In this rule 'probate counterclaim' means a counterclaim in any claim other than a probate claim by which the defendant claims any such remedy as is mentioned in rule 57.1(2)(a).

    (2)   Subject to the following paragraphs of this rule, this Part shall apply with the necessary modifications to a probate counterclaim as it applies to a probate claim.

    (3)   A probate counterclaim must contain a statement of the nature of the interest of each of the parties in the estate of the deceased to which the probate counterclaim relates.

    (4)   Unless an application notice is issued within 7 days after the service of a probate counterclaim for an order under rule 3.1(2)(e) or 3.4 for the probate counterclaim to be dealt with in separate proceedings or to be struck out, and the application is granted, the court shall order the transfer of the proceedings to either –

        (a)   the Chancery Division (if it is not already assigned to that Division) and to either the Royal Courts of Justice or a Chancery district registry (if it is not already proceeding in one of those places); or

        (b)   if the county court has jurisdiction, to a county court where there is also a Chancery district registry or the Central London County Court.

(5)   If an order is made that a probate counterclaim be dealt with in separate proceedings, the order shall order the transfer of the probate counterclaim as required under paragraph (4).

Failure to acknowledge service or to file a defence
57.10

(1)   A default judgment cannot be obtained in a probate claim and rule 10.2 and Part 12 do not apply.

(2)   If any of several defendants fails to acknowledge service the claimant may –

(a)   after the time for acknowledging service has expired; and

(b)   upon filing written evidence of service of the claim form and (if no particulars of claim were contained in or served with the claim form) the particulars of claim on that defendant;

proceed with the probate claim as if that defendant had acknowledged service.

(3)   If no defendant acknowledges service or files a defence then, unless on the application of the claimant the court orders the claim to be discontinued, the claimant may, after the time for acknowledging service or for filing a defence (as the case may be) has expired, apply to the court for an order that the claim is to proceed to trial.

(4)   When making an application under paragraph (3) the claimant must file written evidence of service of the claim form and (if no particulars of claim were contained in or served with the claim form) the particulars of claim on each of the defendants.

(5)   Where the court makes an order under paragraph (3), it may direct that the claim be tried on written evidence.

Discontinuance and dismissal
57.11

(1)   Part 38 does not apply to probate claims.

(2)   At any stage of a probate claim the court, on the application of the claimant or of any defendant who has acknowledged service, may order that –

(a)   the claim be discontinued or dismissed on such terms as to costs or otherwise as it thinks just; and

(b)   a grant of probate of the will, or letters of administration of the estate, of the deceased person be made to the person entitled to the grant.

II RECTIFICATION OF WILLS
Rectification of Wills
57.12

(1)   This Section contains rules about claims for the rectification of a will.
(Section 20 of the Administration of Justice Act 1982 provides for rectification of a will. Additional provisions are contained in rule 55 of the Non-Contentious Probate Rules 1987.)

(2)   Every personal representative of the estate shall be joined as a party.

(3)   Practice Direction 57 makes provision for lodging the grant of probate or letters of administration with the will annexed in a claim under this Section.

III SUBSTITUTION AND REMOVAL OF PERSONAL REPRESENTATIVES
Substitution and Removal of Personal Representatives
57.13

(1)   This Section contains rules about claims and applications for substitution or removal of a personal representative.

(2)   Claims under this Section must be brought in the High Court and are assigned to the Chancery Division.
(Section 50 of the Administration of Justice Act 1985 gives the High Court power to appoint a substitute for, or to remove, a personal representative.)

(3)   Every personal representative of the estate shall be joined as a party.

(4)   Practice Direction 57 makes provision for lodging the grant of probate or letters of administration in a claim under this Section.

(5)   If substitution or removal of a personal representative is sought by application in existing proceedings, this rule shall apply with references to claims being read as if they referred to applications.

IV CLAIMS UNDER THE INHERITANCE (PROVISION FOR FAMILY AND DEPENDANTS) ACT 1975
Scope of this section
57.14

This Section contains rules about claims under the Inheritance (Provision for Family and Dependants) Act 1975 ('the Act').

Proceedings in the High Court

57.15

    (1)   Proceedings in the High Court under the Act shall be issued in either –

        (a)   the Chancery Division; or

        (b)   the Family Division.

    (2)   The Civil Procedure Rules apply to proceedings under the Act which are brought in the Family Division, except that the provisions of the Family Proceedings Rules 1991 relating to the drawing up and service of orders apply instead of the provisions in Part 40 and Practice Direction 40B.

Procedure for claims under section 1 of the Act

57.16

    (1)   A claim under section 1 of the Act must be made by issuing a claim form in accordance with Part 8.

    (2)   Rule 8.3 (acknowledgment of service) and rule 8.5 (filing and serving written evidence) apply as modified by paragraphs (3) to (5) of this rule.

    (3)   The written evidence filed and served by the claimant with the claim form must have exhibited to it an official copy of –

        (a)   the grant of probate or letters of administration in respect of the deceased's estate; and

        (b)   every testamentary document in respect of which probate or letters of administration were granted.

    (4)   Subject to paragraph (4A), the time within which a defendant must file and serve –

        (a)   an acknowledgment of service; and

        (b)   any written evidence,

    is not more than 21 days after service of the claim form on him.

    (4A)   If the claim form is served out of the jurisdiction under rule 6.32 or 6.33, the period for filing an acknowledgment of service and any written evidence is 7 days longer than the relevant period specified in rule 6.35 or Practice Direction 6B.

    (5)   A defendant who is a personal representative of the deceased must file and serve written evidence, which must include the information required by Practice Direction 57.

A6 CIVIL PROCEDURE RULES
PRACTICE DIRECTION 57 – PROBATE
(This Practice Direction supplements CPR Part 57)

Contents of this Practice Direction

I PROBATE CLAIMS
General
1.1
This Section of this practice direction applies to contentious probate claims.

1.2

The rules and procedure relating to non-contentious probate proceedings (also known as 'common form') are the Non-Contentious Probate Rules 1987 as amended.

How to start a probate claim

2.1

A claim form and all subsequent court documents relating to a probate claim must be marked at the top 'In the estate of [*name*] deceased (Probate)'.

2.2

The claim form must be issued out of –

    (1)   Chancery Chambers at the Royal Courts of Justice; or
    (2)   one of the Chancery district registries; or
    (3)   if the claim is suitable to be heard in the county court –
        (a)   a county court in a place where there is also a Chancery district registry; or
        (b)   the Central London County Court.

There are Chancery district registries at Birmingham, Bristol, Caernarfon, Cardiff, Leeds, Liverpool, Manchester, Mold, Newcastle upon Tyne and Preston.

(Section 32 of the County Courts Act 1984 identifies which probate claims may be heard in a county court.)

2.3

When the claim form is issued, the relevant office will send a notice to Leeds District Probate Registry, Coronet House, Queen Street, Leeds, LS1 2BA, DX 26451 Leeds (Park Square), telephone 0113 243 1505, requesting that all testamentary documents, grants of representation and other relevant documents currently held at any probate registry are sent to the relevant office.

2.4

The commencement of a probate claim will, unless a court otherwise directs, prevent any grant of probate or letters of administration being made until the probate claim has been disposed of.

(Rule 45 of the Non-Contentious Probate Rules 1987 makes provision for notice of the probate claim to be given, and section 117 of the Senior Courts Act 1981 for the grant of letters of administration pending the determination of a probate claim. Paragraph 8 of this practice direction makes provision about an application for such a grant.)

Testamentary documents and evidence about testamentary documents
3.1
Unless the court orders otherwise, if a testamentary document is held by the court (whether it was lodged by a party or it was previously held at a probate registry) when the claim has been disposed of the court will send it to the Leeds District Probate Registry.

3.2
The written evidence about testamentary documents required by this Part –

(1)   should be in the form annexed to this practice direction; and

(2)   must be signed by the party personally and not by his solicitor or other representative (except that if the party is a child or protected party the written evidence must be signed by his litigation friend).

3.3
In a case in which there is urgent need to commence a probate claim (for example, in order to be able to apply immediately for the appointment of an administrator pending the determination of the claim) and it is not possible for the claimant to lodge the testamentary documents or to file the evidence about testamentary documents in the relevant office at the same time as the claim form is to be issued, the court may direct that the claimant shall be allowed to issue the claim form upon his giving an undertaking to the court to lodge the documents and file the evidence within such time as the court shall specify.

Case management
4
In giving case management directions in a probate claim the court will give consideration to the questions –

(1)   whether any person who may be affected by the claim and who is not joined as a party should be joined as a party or given notice of the claim, whether under rule 19.8A or otherwise; and

(2)   whether to make a representation order under rule 19.6 or rule 19.7.

Summary judgment
5.1
If an order pronouncing for a will in solemn form is sought on an application for summary judgment, the evidence in support of the application must include written evidence proving due execution of the will.

5.2
If a defendant has given notice in his defence under rule 57.7(5) that he raises no positive case but –

> (1)   he insists that the will be proved in solemn form; and
> (2)   for that purpose he will cross-examine the witnesses who attested the will;

any application by the claimant for summary judgment is subject to the right of that defendant to require those witnesses to attend court for cross-examination.

Settlement of a probate claim
6.1
If at any time the parties agree to settle a probate claim, the court may –

> (1)   order the trial of the claim on written evidence, which will lead to a grant in solemn form;
> (2)   order that the claim be discontinued or dismissed under rule 57.11, which will lead to a grant in common form; or
> (3)   pronounce for or against the validity of one or more wills under section 49 of the Administration of Justice Act 1985.

(For a form of order which is also applicable to discontinuance and which may be adapted as appropriate, see Practice Form No. CH38.)

(Section 49 of the Administration of Justice Act 1985 permits a probate claim to be compromised without a trial if every 'relevant beneficiary', as defined in that section, has consented to the proposed order. It is only available in the High Court.)

6.2
Applications under section 49 of the Administration of Justice Act 1985 may be heard by a master or district judge and must be supported by written evidence identifying the relevant beneficiaries and exhibiting the written consent of each of them. The written evidence of testamentary documents required by rule 57.5 will still be necessary.

Application for an order to bring in a will, etc.
7.1
Any party applying for an order under section 122 of the Senior Courts Act 1981 ('the 1981 Act') must serve the application notice on the person against whom the order is sought.

(Section 122 of the 1981 Act empowers the court to order a person to attend court for examination, and to answer questions and bring in documents, if there are reasonable grounds for believing that such person has knowledge of a testamentary document. Rule 50(1) of the Non-Contentious Probate Rules 1987 makes similar provision where a probate claim has not been commenced.)

7.2
An application for the issue of a witness summons under section 123 of the 1981 Act –

(1)   may be made without notice; and
(2)   must be supported by written evidence setting out the grounds of the application.

(Section 123 of the 1981 Act empowers the court, where it appears that any person has in his possession, custody or power a testamentary document, to issue a witness summons ordering such person to bring in that document. Rule 50(2) of the Non-Contentious Probate Rules makes similar provision where a probate claim has not been commenced.)

7.3
An application under section 122 or 123 of the 1981 Act should be made to a master or district judge.

7.4
A person against whom a witness summons is issued under section 123 of the 1981 Act who denies that the testamentary document referred to in the witness summons is in his possession or under his control may file written evidence to that effect.

Administration pending the determination of a probate claim
8.1
An application under section 117 of the Senior Courts Act 1981 for an order for the grant of administration pending the determination of a probate claim should be made by application notice in the probate claim.

8.2

If an order for a grant of administration is made under section 117 of the 1981 Act –

   (1)   Rules 69.4 to 69.7 shall apply as if the administrator were a receiver appointed by the court;

   (2)   if the court allows the administrator remuneration under rule 69.7, it may make an order under section 117(3) of the 1981 Act assigning the remuneration out of the estate of the deceased; and

   (3)   every application relating to the conduct of the administration shall be made by application notice in the probate claim.

8.3

An order under section 117 may be made by a master or district judge.

8.4

If an order is made under section 117 an application for the grant of letters of administration should be made to the Principal Registry of the Family Division, First Avenue House, 42–49 High Holborn, London WC1V 6NP.

8.5

The appointment of an administrator to whom letters of administration are granted following an order under section 117 will cease automatically when a final order in the probate claim is made but will continue pending any appeal.

II RECTIFICATION OF WILLS
Scope of this Section
9

This Section of this practice direction applies to claims for the rectification of a will.

Lodging the grant
10.1

If the claimant is the person to whom the grant was made in respect of the will of which rectification is sought, he must, unless the court orders otherwise, lodge the probate or letters of administration with the will annexed with the court when the claim form is issued.

10.2

If a defendant has the probate or letters of administration in his possession or under his control, he must, unless the court orders otherwise, lodge it in the relevant office within 14 days after the service of the claim form on him.

Orders

11

A copy of every order made for the rectification of a will shall be sent to the Principal Registry of the Family Division for filing, and a memorandum of the order shall be endorsed on, or permanently annexed to, the grant under which the estate is administered.

III SUBSTITUTION AND REMOVAL OF PERSONAL REPRESENTATIVES

Scope of this Section

12

This Section of this practice direction applies to claims and applications for substitution or removal of a personal representative. If substitution or removal of a personal representative is sought by application in existing proceedings, this Section shall apply with references to the claim, claim form and claimant being read as if they referred to the application, application notice and applicant respectively.

Starting the claim

13.1

The claim form must be accompanied by –

    (1)   either –

        (a)   a sealed or certified copy of the grant of probate or letters of administration, or

        (b)   where the claim is to substitute or remove an executor and is made before a grant of probate has been issued, the original or, if the original is not available, a copy of the will; and

    (2)   written evidence containing the grounds of the claim and the following information so far as it is known to the claimant –

        (a)   brief details of the property comprised in the estate, with an approximate estimate of its capital value and any income that is received from it;

        (b)   brief details of the liabilities of the estate;

        (c)   the names and addresses of the persons who are in possession of the documents relating to the estate;

        (d)   the names of the beneficiaries and their respective interests in the estate; and

        (e)   the name, address and occupation of any proposed substituted personal representative.

13.2

If the claim is for the appointment of a substituted personal representative, the claim form must be accompanied by –

    (1)   a signed or (in the case of the Public Trustee or a corporation) sealed consent to act; and

    (2)   written evidence as to the fitness of the proposed substituted personal representative, if an individual, to act.

Production of the grant

14.1

On the hearing of the claim the personal representative must produce to the Court the grant of representation to the deceased's estate.

14.2

If an order is made substituting or removing the personal representative, the grant (together with a sealed copy of the order) must be sent to and remain in the custody of the Principal Registry of the Family Division until a memorandum of the order has been endorsed on or permanently annexed to the grant.

14.3

Where the claim is to substitute or remove an executor and the claim is made before a grant of probate has been issued, paragraphs 14.1 and 14.2 do not apply. Where in such a case an order is made substituting or removing an executor a sealed copy of the order must be sent to the Principal Registry of the Family Division where it will be recorded and retained pending any application for a grant. An order sent to the Principal Registry in accordance with this paragraph must be accompanied by a note of the full name and date of death of the deceased, if it is not apparent on the face of the order.

IV   CLAIMS UNDER THE INHERITANCE (PROVISION FOR FAMILY AND DEPENDANTS) ACT 1975

Acknowledgment of service by personal representative – rule 57.16(4)

15

Where a defendant who is a personal representative wishes to remain neutral in relation to the claim, and agrees to abide by any decision which the court may make, he should state this in Section A of the acknowledgment of service form.

Written evidence of personal representative – rule 57.16(5)

16

The written evidence filed by a defendant who is a personal representative must state to the best of that person's ability –

(1)   full details of the value of the deceased's net estate, as defined in section 25(1) of the Act;
(2)   the person or classes of persons beneficially interested in the estate, and –
   (a)   the names and (unless they are parties to the claim) addresses of all living beneficiaries; and
   (b)   the value of their interests in the estate so far as they are known.
(3)   whether any living beneficiary (and if so, naming him) is a child or a person who lacks capacity (within the meaning of the Mental Capacity Act 2005); and
(4)   any facts which might affect the exercise of the court's powers under the Act.

Separate representation of claimants
17
If a claim is made jointly by two or more claimants, and it later appears that any of the claimants have a conflict of interests –

(1)   any claimant may choose to be represented at any hearing by separate solicitors or counsel, or may appear in person; and
(2)   if the court considers that claimants who are represented by the same solicitors or counsel ought to be separately represented, it may adjourn the application until they are.

Production of the grant
18.1
On the hearing of a claim the personal representative must produce to the court the original grant of representation to the deceased's estate.

18.2
If the court makes an order under the Act, the original grant (together with a sealed copy of the order) must be sent to the Principal Registry of the Family Division for a memorandum of the order to be endorsed on or permanently annexed to the grant in accordance with section 19(3) of the Act.

18.3
Every final order embodying terms of compromise made in proceedings under the Act, whether made with or without a hearing, must contain a direction that a memorandum of the order shall be endorsed on or permanently annexed to the probate or letters of administration and a copy of the order shall be sent to the Principal Registry of the Family Division with the relevant grant of probate or letters of administration for endorsement.

ANNEX
A form of witness statement or affidavit about testamentary documents (CPR rule 57.5)
(*Title of the claim*)
I [*name and address*] the claimant/defendant in this claim state [on oath] that I have no knowledge of any document –

   (i)   being or purported to be or having the form or effect of a will or codicil of [*name of deceased*] whose estate is the subject of this claim;

   (ii)   being or purporting to be a draft or written instructions for any such will or codicil made by or at the request of or under the instructions of the deceased;

   (iii) being or purporting to be evidence of the contents or a copy of any such will or codicil which is alleged to have been lost or destroyed,

except ... [*describe any testamentary document of the deceased, and if any such document is not in your control, give the name and address of the person who you believe has possession or control of it, or state that you do not know the name and address of that person*] ...

[I believe that the facts stated in this witness statement are true] [*or jurat for affidavit*]

(*NOTE: 'testamentary document' is defined in CPR rule 57.1*)

A7 ACTAPS PRACTICE GUIDANCE FOR THE RESOLUTION OF PROBATE AND TRUST DISPUTES (ACTAPS CODE)[1]

Paragraph 4 of the Practice Direction on Protocols has been substantially amended. It states that 'in cases not covered by any protocol, the court will expect the parties to act reasonably in exchanging information and documents relevant to their claim and in trying to avoid the necessity for the start of proceedings'.

Moreover, with effect from 1 April 2003, the 30th update to the CPR imposes on all parties to a dispute (whatever its nature) an obligation to comply with specified procedures designed to avoid litigation commencing.

Practitioners will no doubt remember the dicta of the Court of Appeal in *Carlson v Townsend* [2001] 3 All ER 663 where it stated the use of the protocol was not limited to fast track cases. The spirit if not the letter of the protocol was equally appropriate to some higher value claims. In accordance with the aims of the civil justice reforms, the courts expected to see the spirit of reasonable pre-action behaviour applied in all cases regardless of the existence of a specific protocol.

The Association of Contentious Trust & Probate Specialists 'ACTAPS' and the Trust Law Committee have, as many practitioners will be aware, given much thought to the possibility that a special Pre-Action Protocol ought to be developed for disputes within their area of expertise. Indeed a draft has for some time been on the ACTAPS website (www.actaps.com) and has since been the subject of extensive discussions with representatives of the judiciary concerned.

It is now clear that no special protocol will be adopted, despite a recognition that the draft contains useful elements. It will be seen that it deals in particular with the following matters:

(a)   appointment of a representative to act on behalf of beneficiaries who cannot be ascertained or traced;

(b)   requirement for a letter of claim setting out the basis of claim;

(c)   early disclosure of documents;

(d)   use of joint experts where possible;

---

[1]   The ACTAPS Code is reproduced by kind permission of the Association of Contentious Trust and Probate Specialists (Henry Frydenson, Frydenson & Co, Chair ACTAPS, Central Court, 25 Southampton Buildings, London, WC2A 1AL).

(e)   a joint letter of request for medical records;
(f)   a joint *Larke v Nugus* letter; and
(g)   a joint letter requesting details of deceased's capacity.

In these circumstances the committee of ACTAPS has concluded that it would be useful to encourage members to have regard to The ACTAPS Code as a means of developing best practices in areas where special problems may arise, for example the need to have representatives for persons who cannot speak for themselves in a context where others may feel that mediation would be desirable.

It is understood that the judges who have considered The ACTAPS Code have expressed no concerns that it is out of line with the CPR objectives or that to follow its principles would give rise to unnecessary problems in practice. In particular it is thought that CPR Rule 19.7(3)(b) gives the necessary scope for securing the appointment of representatives of those who are absent, unborn, or members of a large class, as well before as after the commencement of proceedings.

It is also hoped that in the context of probate issues the common difficulty of medical practitioners considering that they may as a matter of professional confidence be restricted in releasing records can be overcome by joint application (and following discussions between ACTAPS and the BMA the latter has confirmed that its future guidance will facilitate disclosure in accordance with The ACTAPS Code). The ACTAPS Code contains an outline for such a letter.

In these circumstances it is suggested that practitioners in the areas of trust and probate law should seek to follow the approaches indicated in The ACTAPS Code, approved by the Trust Law Committee and ACTAPS, on the basis that it may serve to amplify the basic principles of the general protocols and indicate considered methods of carrying the objectives of the general protocols into effect in areas which may be found to give rise to special difficulties with which the general protocols do not grapple. In putting forward this suggestion the committee of ACTAPS believes that it has the support of all who have been concerned to consider the draft protocol; the rejection of the proposal that it be adopted as a special protocol owes nothing (so far as is known) to any perception of defects and merely reflects the belief that the public interest is best served by seeking, where possible, to avoid specific protocols and to develop best practices in areas where general protocols have to be supplemented to meet the needs of special situations.

With that in mind the committee of ACTAPS encourages members and other users to help move the search for best practices forward by commenting on any defects, inadequacies or other difficulties which may be found to arise in carrying the terms of The ACTAPS Code into effect. Please make any such comments to the ACTAPS Chairman's or the ACTAPS Secretary's e-mail address.

Practitioners will wish to bear in mind the need for trustees and executors to consider the adequacy of their powers to enter into any particular course of conduct and the possibility that they may need eg Beddoes type directions if they propose a course of conduct to which their beneficiaries might wish to raise objection (as for example where the trustees wish voluntarily to disclose confidential documents to third parties) or which may involve material burdens of costs (as for example the institution of a lengthy mediation). But of course in circumstances where the aim is to explore ways of reaching agreement or otherwise saving costs any necessary order might be expected to be forthcoming (within the appropriate limits) without difficulty on the basis that the Court would be being asked to facilitate a course of action essentially in accordance with the overriding objective.

1. Introduction

The Scope of The Code

1.1   This Code is intended to apply to disputes about:

- the devolution and administration of estates of deceased persons
- the devolution and administration of trust funds ('probate and trust disputes'). It is not intended to displace other protocols if in the circumstances of the case they can be seen to be more appropriate.

The main types of disputes within the ambit of this Code can be expected to be:

- challenges to the validity of a will, for example on grounds of want of capacity or knowledge and approval, undue influence or forgery
- claims under the Inheritance (Provision for Family and Dependants) Act 1975 ('the Inheritance Act')
- actions for the removal of an administrator or executor or trustee or the appointment of a judicial trustee
- actions for the rectification of a will or other document
- disputes as to the meanings of provisions in a will or a trust
- administration actions
- allegations of breach of trust.

The ACTAPS Code may also apply to certain types of dispute where the provisions of a trust or the devolution of an estate are of the essence, for example where a claimant seeks in the alternative to set aside or overturn a trust or to take advantage of rights under a trust.

The Code has two aims; to encourage the resolution of disputes without hostile litigation; and even where litigation may be necessary to ensure that it is simplified as far as possible by maximizing the scope for the exchange of relevant information before the litigation process has commenced.

The Code is in general terms unlikely to be appropriate for disputes which involve:

- disputes as to the rights appertaining under rules of forced heirships under the law of some foreign jurisdiction
- the need for emergency injunctions
- (except in so far as concerns pre-action exchange of information) the need for a binding precedent or a declaration by the Court as to the true construction of some trust instrument or testamentary disposition.

The Code is formed in general terms to cover the broad range of trust and probate disputes; but it is recognised that the appropriate investigations and exchange of information will vary according to the circumstances of the dispute. However one of its primary purposes is to provide for a special feature of disputes in this area, namely that there may be beneficiaries who cannot speak for themselves but whose interests must be protected.

1.2   In cases where the express terms of The Code is not appropriate parties will be expected to follow the spirit of The Code and seek to achieve its aims so far as practicable in the particular case.

1.3   It is also to be borne in mind that there are certain cases in which a trust or probate dispute seeks to fulfil some non-contentious purpose, as for example where a question of difficulty is identified to which the parties are agreed that the best solution lies in inviting the Court to approve constructive proposals by way of compromise or where the objective is simply to find the cheapest way of protecting trustees or personal representatives against the risks involved in the existence of some theoretical doubt. In such cases The Code is unlikely to have any role to play.

1.4   One of the principal features of trust and probate disputes is that they may affect the interests of persons not of full capacity, as yet unborn or unascertained, or interested as members of a large class of persons who have similar beneficial interests. The Code is thus designed to make express provision for the need to find mechanisms that assist despite the absence of such persons (providing in particular an expedited process for Court approval of agreements reached in mediation). It is thus wrong in principle to regard a dispute as not amenable to the use of The Code just because there are persons concerned who cannot speak for themselves.

2. Principal guidelines

Parties

2.1 The parties to the probate or trust dispute will usually be trustees (or personal representatives or persons claiming to be entitled as such) and beneficiaries of the trust or estate who are of full capacity, though The Code is designed also to be capable of being used in exterior/third party disputes where appropriate.

2.2 In the case where interests of unascertained persons, minors, unborns, mentally incapacitated persons or members of a large class (such that it is not appropriate for all members of the class to be made parties to the dispute) will be affected, the procedure to be adopted will be an application to the Court (see Annex A) whether or not a claim has yet been instituted before the Court.

Status of Letters of Claim and Response

2.3 A letter of claim or of response is not intended to have the same status as pleadings. Matters may come to light as a result of investigation after the letter of claim has been sent or after the defendant has responded. These investigations could result in the pleaded case of a party differing in some respects from the case outlined in that party's letter of claim or response. It would not be consistent with the spirit of The Code for a party to complain about this difference provided that there was no indication of any intention to mislead.

Disclosure of Documents

2.4 The aim of the early disclosure of documents by the defendant is not to encourage 'fishing expeditions' by the claimant, but to promote an early exchange of relevant information to help in clarifying or resolving issues in dispute. The claimant's solicitors can assist by identifying in the letter of claim or in a subsequent letter the particular documents or categories of documents which they consider are relevant, and by providing copies of these where appropriate.

2.5   All documents are disclosed on the basis that they are not to be disclosed to third parties (other than legal advisers) or used for any purpose other than the resolution of the dispute, unless otherwise agreed in writing or permitted by the court.

Experts

2.6   Expert evidence appropriate to probate and trust disputes may include in particular medical evidence, handwriting evidence, valuation evidence, tax-related or actuarial evidence.

2.7   The Code encourages joint selection of, and access to, experts. However, it maintains the flexibility for each party to obtain their own expert's report. It is for the court to decide whether the costs of more than one expert's report should be recoverable.

Costs

2.8   Where The Code provides for the initial cost of obtaining information or reports to be borne by one party, it shall not restrict the court's discretion in relation to ultimate liability for such costs.

Negotiations/Mediation

2.9   Parties and their legal representatives are encouraged to enter into discussions and/or negotiations prior to starting proceedings. The parties should bear in mind that the courts increasingly take the view that litigation should be a last resort, and that claims should not be issued prematurely when a settlement is in reasonable prospect. Mediation of probate and trust disputes may assist in achieving a compromise, particularly in relation to disputes between family members. The form of the mediation will be set out in the mediation agreement between the mediator and the parties.

2.10   Mediation can be used to try to achieve a compromise whenever negotiation is appropriate and can be used at any stage in a trust dispute. Typically mediation may be considered:

   (i)   before proceedings have commenced but once the issues are fairly well defined and the parties affected by them are known;
   (ii)   even after proceedings have commenced and the statements of case have been served so that the parties have a better appreciation of the issues;

(iii)   at any critical stage in the litigation such as after disclosure of documents, exchange of experts' reports, exchange of witness statements and in the lead up to the trial.

The parties should seek to conclude a mediation within 42 days of the appointment of the mediator.

2.11   Since mediation negotiations are treated by the Courts as without prejudice, points disclosed during an attempt to reach a settlement will be confidential between the parties and cannot be used as evidence in subsequent Court proceedings unless expressly agreed by the party who made the disclosure. The mediator will not divulge information without consent. Also he will not pass on such information to outside parties or act for either party to the dispute in subsequent proceedings.

2.12   A settlement reached pursuant to a mediation should be recorded in writing and signed by the parties or their authorised representative. In probate and trust disputes, if and insofar as the subject matter of the dispute requires the sanction and approval of the Court, any agreement achieved as a result of the mediation should be expressed to be subject to the approval of the Court.

2.13   In a probate or trust dispute where the position of the Inland Revenue may have some bearing on any compromise solution which may be reached, any agreement may be made conditional upon indications of the Inland Revenue's position or adjourned to enable clarification of its position to be sought.

3. The Code

Letters of Claim

3.1   The Claimant shall send a letter of claim to each of the deceased's personal representatives or to the trustees, as the case may be and, unless it is impractical (e.g. because there is a large class of beneficiaries or the beneficiaries are minors) to each beneficiary or potential beneficiary of the estate or trust fund likely to be adversely affected by the claim (referred to as 'the proposed Defendants'), as soon as sufficient information is available to substantiate a realistic claim which the Claimant has decided he is prepared to pursue.

3.2   The letter shall contain a clear summary of the claim and the facts upon which it is based and state the remedy sought by the claimant.

3.3 Solicitors are recommended to use a standard format for the claim letter. A sample letter is set out at Annex B; this can be amended to suit the particular case.

3.4 In claims under the Inheritance Act the claimant should give details to the best of his ability of the matters set out in Section 3 of the Inheritance Act as relevant to the exercise of the Court's discretion (see Annex B).

3.5 Copies of documents in the claimant's possession which he wishes to rely upon or which any other party is likely to wish to rely upon should be enclosed with the letter of claim. Examples of documents likely to be relevant in different types of dispute are set out at Annex C. These lists are not exhaustive. The letter of claim may specify classes of document considered relevant for early disclosure by the proposed defendants.

Letter of Response

3.6 Each of the proposed defendants should respond to the letter of claim within 21 days stating whether he admits or denies the claim, responding in outline to the matters of fact relied upon by the claimant and setting out any particular matters of fact upon which he relies. If a proposed defendant intends to make an answering claim on his own behalf, the letter of response should contain the same information and documents as a letter of claim in relation to the Part 20 claim. If a proposed defendant is unable to respond within the time limit on any particular matter, the letter of response should give the reasons for the absence of a full response and state when it will be available.

3.7 In claims under the Inheritance Act each proposed defendant should give details to the best of his ability of the matters set out in Section 3 of the Inheritance Act as relevant to the exercise of the Court's discretion (and set out in Annex B).

3.8 Copies of documents in the proposed defendant's possession which he wishes to rely upon or which any other party is likely to wish to rely upon should be enclosed with the letter of response. Examples of relevant documents in relation to different categories of disputes are set out at Annex C. These lists are not exhaustive.

Documents

3.9 In relation to the documents in Annex C, the personal representatives of the deceased (including executors named in the last alleged will of the deceased) or trustees as appropriate should provide copies of such documents (if available) to a party requesting a copy within 14 days of the date of a letter of request (or such other reasonable time as may be agreed between the parties) or, if a copy is only available from a third party with the consent of the personal representatives or trustees, provide to the party making the request written authority to the third party to provide a copy of the document to that party.

3.10   Trustees or personal representatives should not be inhibited from making full disclosure by the absence of litigation.

Applications for documents or information in control of third parties

3.11   In a probate dispute the release of medical notes may cast much light on the likely outcome and it should be assumed for the purposes of The Code that they ought to be disclosed at the outset absent special reason.

3.12   If so requested in writing by any party all parties shall (in the absence of good reason to withhold the relevant items) within 14 days of any such request (or such longer period as shall reasonably be agreed):

(1)   Sign and return to the party making the request, a joint application for the provision of copies of the deceased's medical notes or social worker's reports to all parties. The notes and/or reports should be sent separately and directly to each party. A specimen joint application is at Annex D.

(2)   Sign, and return to the party making the request, a joint application for a statement by the solicitor who prepared the will of the deceased setting out all the circumstances leading up to the preparation and making of the will. A specimen joint application is at Annex E.

3.13   The party making the request for a joint application for information or documents from a third party shall:

(1)   Submit it to the third party within 7 days of receipt of the joint application completed by the other parties.

(2)   on receipt of the information or documents from the third party check that they have been received by all other parties and, if not, provide them with copies within 7 days of receipt.

3.14   In cases where the mental capacity of a deceased at the date of a testamentary instrument is in issue, the party seeking to uphold the testamentary instrument should obtain a report as to the deceased's mental capacity from his GP as soon as possible after the issue is identified and send it to all other parties within 7 days of receipt. A specimen letter of request is at Annex F.

Experts

3.15   Parties should consider the use of jointly instructed experts so far as possible. Accordingly before any prospective party (the first party) instructs an expert he should (unless of the opinion that another party will want to instruct his own expert) give the other (second) party a list of the name(s) of one or more experts in the relevant discipline whom he considers are suitable to instruct.

3.16   Within 14 days the second party may indicate an objection to one or more of such experts and suggest alternatives. The first party should then instruct a mutually acceptable expert.

3.17   If an expert to be jointly instructed is not agreed, the parties may then instruct experts of their own choice. It would be for the court to decide subsequently, if proceedings are issued, whether either party had acted unreasonably. No party shall be entitled to instruct an expert proposed in a list of experts for joint instructions until it is clear that joint instructions cannot be agreed and thereafter the party who submitted the list of experts shall be entitled to nominate one of the experts on this list as his own chosen expert and no other party shall instruct any expert named on the list until such nomination has taken place.

3.18   If the second party does not object to an expert nominated, he shall not be entitled to rely on his own expert evidence within that particular discipline unless:

(1)   the court so directs, or
(2)   the first party's expert report has been amended and the first party is not prepared to disclose the original report.

3.19   Either party may send to the expert written questions on the report, relevant to the issues, via the first party's solicitors. The expert should send answers to the question separately and directly to each party.

3.20   The cost of the report from an agreed expert will usually be paid by the party first proposing that a joint expert be instructed. The costs of the expert replying to questions will usually be borne by the party asking the questions. The ultimate liability for costs will be determined by the Court.

ANNEX A

REPRESENTATION IN ESTATE OR TRUST DISPUTES OF INTERESTED PERSONS WHO CANNOT BE ASCERTAINED ETC.

(1) In any estate or trust dispute concerning:-

(a) property comprised in an estate or subject to a trust or alleged to be subject to a trust; or

(b) the construction of a written instrument; or

(c) a situation where the interests of beneficiaries may require separate representation

the Court, if satisfied that it is expedient to do so, and that one or more of the conditions specified in paragraph (2) are satisfied, may appoint one or more persons to represent any person (including a person under a disability, a minor or an unborn person) or class who is or may be interested (whether presently or for any future, contingent or unascertained interest) in or affected by the dispute.

(2) The conditions for the exercise of the power conferred by paragraph (1) are as follows:-

(a) that the person, the class or some member of the class cannot be ascertained or cannot be readily ascertained, or is not of full capacity; or

(b) that the person, the class or some member of the class, though ascertained, cannot be found; or

(c) that, though the person or the class and members thereof can be ascertained and found, it appears to the Court expedient (regard being had to all the circumstances, including the amount at stake and the degree of difficulty of the point to be determined) to exercise the power for the purposes of saving expense or for any other reason.

(3) Where, in any case to which paragraph 1 applies, the Court exercises the power conferred by that paragraph, a judgment or order of the Court given or made when the person or persons appointed in exercise of that power are before the Court shall be binding on the person or class represented by the person or persons so appointed.

(4) Where, in any such case, a compromise is proposed and some of the persons who are interested in, or who may be affected by the compromise have not been consulted (including persons under a disability, minors or unborn or unascertained persons) but

(a)   there is some other person in the same interest before the Court who assents to the compromise or on whose behalf the Court sanctions the compromise; or

(b)   the absent persons are represented by a person appointed under paragraph (1) who so assents, the Court, if satisfied that the compromise will be for the benefit of the absent persons and that it is expedient to exercise this power, may approve the compromise and order that it shall be binding on absent persons, and they shall be bound accordingly except where the order has been obtained by fraud or non-disclosure of material facts.

ANNEX B

To
Defendant

Dear

Re:

The estate of [name of deceased]
The Settlement made by [Settlor] on [date]

We are instructed on behalf of [claimant] [give details of relief sought eg to seek reasonable provision out of the estate of the above-named deceased; to set aside probate of the will of the above-named deceased dated [date]; to seek a declaration that upon a proper construction of the above settlement our client is entitled to ...]

The basis of our clients claim is: [brief outline]

The facts upon which our client relies are as follows:- [set out material facts with sufficient clarity and detail for the proposed defendants to make a preliminary assessment of the claim]

The details of matters to which the Court would have regard under Section 3 of the Inheritance (Provision for Family and Dependants) Act 1975 insofar as they are known to our client are:-

(a)   Financial resources and needs of claimant;

(b)   Financial resources and needs of any other claimant;

(c)   Financial resources and needs of beneficiaries;

(d)   Obligations and responsibilities of deceased towards claimants and beneficiaries;

(e)   Size and nature of estate;

(f)   Disabilities of claimants and beneficiaries;

(g)   Any other matter; and if claimant spouse or co-habitee,

(h)   age of claimant, length of marriage/co-habitation and contribution to family welfare.

We enclose the following documents which are relevant to the claim:- [list documents]

In accordance with The ACTAPS Code for probate and trust disputes, we look forward to receiving a letter of response, enclosing the documents in your possession and relevant to the claim within [21] days. We believe that the

following documents relevant to the claim are likely to be in your possession:-
(list documents)

Pursuant to The ACTAPS Code as [personal representatives of the deceased/trustees of the settlement] we invite you to furnish us within 14 days of the date of this letter with copies of the following documents or written authority, in the form enclosed, to obtain copies of such document(s):- [list asterisked documents required]

We have also sent a letter of claim to (name and address) and a copy of that letter is enclosed.

Yours faithfully

ANNEX C

All documents upon which you rely or upon which the other party is likely to wish to rely including but not limited to the following categories:

1. In disputes in which the assets of an estate/trust fund or the financial resources of an individual are relevant; eg claims under the Inheritance Act, breach of trust claims:

    – The Inland Revenue Account and any Corrective Account;

    – A schedule of the capital assets (with values, estimated where appropriate) and income of the estate, trust fund or individual as appropriate;

    – Trust or Estate Accounts.

2. In disputes in which the mental capacity or medical condition of an individual is relevant, eg challenges to testamentary capacity, Inheritance Act claims where disability is alleged:

    – A copy of the medical records of the individual or, if appropriate, the written authority of the personal representatives of a deceased to obtain his medical records together with an office copy of the grant of probate or letters of administration or other proof of their status.

3. In disputes as to the validity, construction or rectification of a will or other testamentary instrument of the deceased:

    – A statement setting out details of any testamentary script (now in CPR called testamentary document) within the knowledge of the claimant or proposed defendant and details of the name and address of the person who, to the best of his knowledge, has possession or control of such script.

Nb1: The provision of the statement in 3 above is of vital importance to all parties in a dispute since it ensures that the correct testamentary documents are being considered. This will prevent the problem of a dispute over a later testamentary document being allowed to overshadow the existence of an intermediate testamentary document which would be upheld if the later testamentary document fails.

Also it helps identify the correct parties to the existing disputes.

Nb2: Following from Nb1 above, it is most important that the fullest and most exhaustive search for all testamentary documents is made. Accordingly while the following list is not exhaustive it is incumbent upon all parties to check:-

(i)   with all known solicitors of the deceased as to the existence of a testamentary document;

(ii)   with all attesting witnesses to testamentary documents as to the existence of testamentary documents;

(iii) with all named executors of testamentary documents as to the existence of testamentary documents;

(iv)   with immediate family members (brothers, sisters, parents and children of the deceased) as to the existence of testamentary documents.

Nb3: Definition of Testamentary Script (now in CPR called Testamentary document)

A will, a draft of a will, written instructions for a will made by or at the request of, or under the instructions of, the testator, and any document purporting to be evidence of the contents, or to be a copy, of a will which is alleged to have been lost or destroyed. The word 'will' includes a codicil.

ANNEX D

JOINT APPLICATION FOR MEDICAL NOTES OR SOCIAL WORKER'S REPORTS

To: The medical records officer/social services

Dear Sir

Re: (Name) Deceased of (address), (date of birth)

We the undersigned Messrs (firm's name) (ref) of (firm's address), Solicitors for (the Executors named in the Will of the late (deceased's name) of (deceased's address) who died on (date of death) and we, the undersigned Messrs (firm's name) of (firm's address), Solicitors for parties interested in his/her estate, hereby authorise you to forward [a full set of copies of the deceased's Medical Records] [all social workers reports and notes relating to the deceased] to each of the aforementioned firms.

We confirm that we will be responsible for your reasonable photocopying charges and your invoice in this regard should be sent to (firm's name) and marked for the attention of (ref.).

Dated [   ] 20[   ]

Signed
[   ]

Signed
[   ]

ANNEX E

JOINT APPLICATION LETTER TO SOLICITORS WHO PREPARED WILL REQUESTING LARKE v NUGUS STATEMENT

Dear Sirs

[Name of Deceased] deceased

We, the undersigned Messrs (firm's name)(ref:) of (firm's address), solicitors for the Executors named in the Will of (deceased's name) of (deceased's address) and we, the undersigned Messrs (firm's name)(ref:) of (firm's address), solicitors for parties interested in his/her estate regret to inform you that (deceased's name) died on (date of death).

We understand that you drafted the deceased's last will dated [ ].

You may be aware that in 1959 the Law Society recommended that in circumstances such as this the testator's solicitor should make available a statement of his or her evidence regarding instructions for the preparation and execution of the will and surrounding circumstances. This recommendation was endorsed by the Court of Appeal on 21st February 1979 in *Larke v Nugus*.

The practice is also recommended at paragraph 24.02 of the Law Society's *Guide to the Professional Conduct of Solicitors*, 7th edition (page 387).

Accordingly, we hereby request and authorise you to forward to each of the aforementioned firms statements from all appropriate members of your firm on the following points:

- How long had you known the deceased?

- Who introduced you to the deceased?

- On what date did you receive instructions from the deceased?

- Did you receive instructions by letter? If so, please provide copies of any correspondence.

- If instructions were taken at a meeting, please provide copies of your contemporaneous notes of the meeting including an indication of where the meeting took place and who else was present at the meeting.

- How were the instructions expressed?

- What indication did the deceased give to you that he knew he was making a will?

- Were you informed or otherwise aware of any medical history of the deceased that might bear upon the issue of his capacity?

- Did the deceased exhibit any signs of confusion or loss of memory? If so, please give details.

- To what extent were earlier wills discussed and what attempts were made to discuss departures from his earlier will-making pattern? What reasons, if any, did the testator give for making any such departures?

- When the will had been drafted, how were the provisions of the will explained to the deceased?

- Who, apart from the attesting witnesses, was present at the execution of the will? Where, when and how did this take place?

- Please provide copies of any other documents relating to your instructions for the preparation and execution of the will and surrounding circumstances or confirm that you have no objection to us inspecting your relevant file(s) on reasonable notice.

We confirm that we will be responsible for your reasonable photocopying charges in this connection and your invoice in this regard should be sent to (each firm's name etc) and marked for the attention of (each firm's ref.).

Dated this [   ] day of [   ] 20[   ]

Signed
[   ]

Signed
[   ]

ANNEX F

LETTER TO DECEASED'S GP REQUESTING REPORT AS TO MENTAL CAPACITY

To: Deceased's GP

Dear Dr [ ]

Re: (Name) Deceased of (address), (date of birth)

We the undersigned Messrs (firm's name) (ref) of (firm's address) are Solicitors for (the Executors named in the Will of the late (deceased's name) of (deceased's address) who died on (date of death)) and we, the undersigned Messrs (firm's name) of (firm's address), are Solicitors for parties interested in his/her estate.

We enclose a photocopy of the deceased's last Will. The clauses in the Will which cause particular concern are (clause numbers).

The question of the deceased's mental capacity at the time of the making of his/her last Will dated has now been raised.

The test of testamentary capacity remains that established in the case of *Banks -v- Goodfellow* where it was said:-

> 'It is essential that a testator (1) shall understand the nature of the act and its effects; (2) shall understand the extent of the property of which he is disposing; and (3) shall be able to comprehend and appreciate the claims to which he ought to give effect, and; with a view to the latter object, (4) that no disorder of mind shall poison his affections, pervert his sense of right or pervert the exercise of his natural faculties; (5) that no insane delusions shall influence his mind in disposing of his property and bring about a disposal of it which if his mind had been sound, would not have been made.' (We have added numbers for convenience).

(Set out the nature of the Estate if complex).

We would therefore be grateful if you would kindly provide us with a report setting out:-

1. Your medical qualifications and your experience in assessing mental states and capacity.

2. For how long you were the deceased's GP, how well you knew the deceased and a summary of his/her medical condition, insofar as it may have bearing upon the deceased's mental capacity.

3. Your findings as to the deceased's mental capacity at and around the time of the date of his/her last will.

4. Please also deal with any mental disorder from which the deceased may have been suffering at the relevant time, and any medication which could have affected his/her capacity as detailed above.

5. Please also consider any issues of vulnerability or suggestibility at or around the date of the deceased's last Will.

We confirm that we will be responsible for your reasonable fees in the preparation of your report which we look forward to receiving as soon as possible.

Dated this [   ] day of [   ] 20[   ]

Signed
[   ] (ref:)

Signed
[   ] (ref:)

Index

References are to page numbers